William W. Scott

The Teetotaler's Hand Book in Four Parts

Being a Compilation of Valuable Information for the Use of all Classes

William W. Scott

The Teetotaler's Hand Book in Four Parts
Being a Compilation of Valuable Information for the Use of all Classes

ISBN/EAN: 9783337077198

Printed in Europe, USA, Canada, Australia, Japan

Cover: Foto ©Paul-Georg Meister /pixelio.de

More available books at **www.hansebooks.com**

THE

TEETOTALER'S HAND-BOOK,

IN FOUR PARTS,

BEING

A COMPILATION OF VALUABLE INFORMATION FOR THE
USE OF ALL CLASSES,

WITH

AN INTRODUCTION AND APPENDIX,

BY THE

REVEREND WILLIAM SCOTT,

Editor of the Canada Temperance Advocate
from 1851 to 1858.

———•—•—•———

TORONTO:
PUBLISHED BY ALFRED DREDGE,
88 YONGE STREET.

"I have seen a print after Corregio, in which three female figures are ministering to a man, who sits fast bound to the root of a tree. Sensuality is soothing him, Evil Habit is nailing him to a branch, and Repugnance at the same instant of time is applying a snake to his side. In his face is feeble delight, the recollection of the past, rather than perception of present pleasures, languid enjoyment of evil with utter imbecility to good, a sybaritic effeminancy, a submission to bondage, the springs of the will give down like a broken clock, the sin and the suffering so instantaneous, or the latter forerunning the former, remose preceding action; all this represented in one point of time! When I saw this, I admired the wonderful skill of the painter. But when I went away, I wept, because I thought of my own condition."

CHARLES LAMB'S ELIA.

INTRODUCTION.

The Publisher has thought proper in the title page to refer to my connection with the "Canada Temperance Advocate" for a number of years. It is not offensive to me that he should do so, for on the review of those years of literary labour I do not find any ground for regret, except that my convictions of the nature and importance of the temperance movement were often very inadequately expressed. Such however being my public relations to the cause, it was perhaps not incongruous that I should be invited to introduce this volume to the friends of temperance, and especially to those who are not ashamed to be called "TEETOTALERS."

This Hand-book makes no pretension to anything above a compilation of various and important intelligence for general circulation. On examination of the table of the contents it will be observed that while there is no attempt at historical detail or argumentative reasoning, there is nevertheless a considerable amount of that information which it is desirable should be in the hands of the temperance people of Canada. Passing over the history of the great temperance reformation contained in the first part of the book, the thoughtful advocate of the cause will be gratified that so much has been accomplished in many places towards the attainment of the entire prohibition of the traffic. In Canada, we are yet far behind many States of the neighbouring Union, and have scarcely gained as much ground as the friends of Prohibition in England. Yet even here, from the record of Canadian action, it will be seen that temperance men have stood firm to the principle, and the republication of their proposed enactments, will afford food for contemplation and may be considered standards for future action.

INTRODUCTION.

The large amount of poetic selections, will be found adapted to various tastes and capacities and may be exceedingly useful in enlivening public meetings and social gatherings of those who by anniversaries and soirees seek to promote the good of community. Facts and anecdotes are always interesting, and of these sufficient will be found in this volume to gratify the desires of most, for that kind of instructive amusement.

The time has not come when the temperance people of Canada can honourably relax their exertions. The traffic has too strong a hold in the land for that. It is a subject of deep regret, that both in high and low places, the fiend of intemperance still grasps his victims, and paralyzes human hopes. Every where there exist abundant reasons for exertion, but it is in vain to trust in any schemes of reformation but those which are founded on the unchangeable word of the Eternal God. This book may, it is believed, in some measure, contribute to the mitigation or abolition of our great national iniquity, and therefore its publication should be followed by a circulation commensurate with the expenses incurred, and with the demands of our great moral enterprise.

The community professing temperance principles have often been charged with parsimony when called upon to contribute anything toward the attainment of the public good by means of the press. For my own part I will not reiterate the complaint, but rather express my gratitude for what has been done. Wherever an advertisement of this book may come I entertain the hope that not only will there be a desire to possess it, but that the friends of the cause will use their best endeavours to promote its circulation. Read and think about the evils of using strong drinks and the terrible effects of the traffic, and you will the more heartily enter into every public scheme for the overthrow of the most gigantic evil of our times.

W. S.

THE TEETOTALER'S HAND-BOOK.

CONTENTS OF PART FIRST.

HISTORY OF THE TEMPERANCE CAUSE.

American Organization in 1804,	16	London Temperance League,	38
" Temperance Union,	17	Lycurgus of Sparta,	14
Am. Tem. Anniversary in 1859,	18	Massachusetts in 1811,	16
Agents of Montreal Society,	25	Mathew, Rev. Theobold,	27
Ancient Societies,	14	Modern Temperance Societies,	16
Bands of Hope,	56	National Tem. Society, England,	36
Bible Evidence,	9	Origin of Certain Societies,	38
Cadets,	50	Parliamentary Committee, Eng.,	36
Canada pioneers,	21	Plato, his approval,	14
Canada Temperance Advocate,	23	Rechabites of Scripture,	11
Centuries. fifteenth and following,	14	Romans, Temperance of the,	13
Chinese, Temperance of the,	13	Rechabite Societies,	38
Convention in Montreal, 1834,	22	Russian Distilleries, &c.	20
" " 1859,	26	Sons of Temperance,	42-48
Cold Water Army,	41	Spaniards, Temperance of the,	14
Constitution of Bands of Hope,	57-61	Scriptures in favor of Abstinence,	10
Dashaways, The	61	Scotland, Tem. Soc. 100 yrs. ago,	15
Daughters of Temperance,	50	" first Tem. Society in,	30
England, the Tem. Cause in,	33	Scottish Tem. League,	32
Egyptians, Temperance of the,	13	Temple of Honor, The	49
Forbes, Dr., his views of Ireland,	30	U. Canada, first Total Abst. Soc'ty,	22
General Remarks,	38	Wadsworth's, Mr. Tem. Tour,	23
Good Templars, I. O. of	51-56	Wales, Temperance in,	38
Indians, Temperance among The,	62	Washingtonians, The	40
Ireland, Tem. movements in,	27	Wolfe, Rev. Joseph, in Asia,	39
Juvenile Sisters of Temperance,	50		

CONTENTS OF PART SECOND.

THE PROHIBITORY MOVEMENT.

Act, submitted in 1860, 160-188	Maine Law, origin and history, 117
Appeal to people of Canada, 203-8	" " from Heaven, 131
Bibles in place of dissipation, 144	Memorial to Councils, U. Canada, 156
Bill of J. J. E. Linton, 188-193	Moral right to drink considered 70-72
Brougham, Lord, his views, 201	New Brunswick anti-Liquor Law, 73
Canada, first Parliamentary Com, 80	On we go, 145
" New. Municipal Law, 114	Parliamentary Action, 72
Canadian action, 1859-60, 155-8	Prohibition in Pitcairn Island, 74
Constitutionality of Prohibition, 63	" " Madagascar, 76
Economy of Maine Law, 139-141	" " Liberia 75, Hawaia, 77
Evil of the Traffic, 66	" " England, 77
Evidence given before Parliamentary Temperance Committee, 80— J. Beatty, A. Farewell, Hon. Neal Dow's letter to Hon. M. Cameron, G. L. Allen, Governor of Toronto Jail, J. Carling, M. P. P., George Duggan, Esq., Recorder of Toronto, Rowland Burr, Esq, Toronto; George Gooderham, Esq., Rev. H. Mulkins; Customs Department, &c. 82-103	" " South Seas, 77
	" Results of, in Connecticut 125
	" " " Maine, 126
	" " " Massachu. 146
	" " " Michigan, 149
	" " " Rhode Isl'd, 150
	" " " Vermont, 153
	Permissive Bill of U. K. A., 195
	Society's right to protect itself, 63
	Testimonies in favour of Prohibition,—Chesterfield 77—Bishop of Salesbury 77—Bishop of Oxford, 78— Stephen Hales 78 —Northwick 78—John Milton 79—John Wesley 79.
Forbes Mackenzie Act, Scotland, 110	
" " Canada, 111-119	
Governor Morrell of Maine, 127	
Great Britain, Maine Law, 194-8	
Landowners, Prohibition, 199	Traffic, Prohibited, 72
Leeds Mercury, opinion of, 196	United Kingdom Alliance, 195
License to sell rum, Mr. Doty's 68	Yale College, 134
Lumbermen, Maine Law among, 145	

CONTENTS OF PART THIRD.

POETRY, SONGS AND HYMNS.

Abstainer's Rock,	230	Bucket, which hung &c., The,	269
All's well,	228	Caution,	286
Anniversaries, Hymn for,	287	Cold Water,	308
Anniversary,	299	Closing Ode,	280
Annual Meeting,	300	Cold Water Army, The,	275
Auld Lang Syne,	227	Come and sign,	228
Away the Bowl,	259	Come, Young Abstainers,	221
Bible Teetotalers,	284	Confession of a Drunkard,	215
Blessing implored,	300	Convivial Banquets,	209
Bowl, The,	284	Come all ye Children,	240

CONTENTS.

Title	Page	Title	Page
Cold water for me,	261	Prayer,	302
Come, Brothers, Come,	265	Prayer to God,	298
Cup of Death, The,	278	Pure water for me,	271
Dash it down,	309	Reformer's Song,	271
Desert the sparkling Wine,	226	Rejoice, rejoice,	242
Dismission,	301	Searching questions,	256
Drinker turn and leave your bowl,	239	Samaritan's appeal, The good,	260
Drunkard's Boy, The,	249	Sailor's Song,	281
Drunkard's Song, The,	250	Singing, The voice of,	261
Drunkard's Wife, The,	220–299	Sing, Sisters, sing,	264
Drunkard's Home, The,	219	Sons of Temperance, The,	238
Drunkard's Children, The,	289	Ship of the Sons, The,	251
Drunkard's Hope, The,	301	Slave to the Bottle, A,	223
Dying Drunkard, The,	298	Sobriety's praise,	230
Example,	297	Social glass, The,	233
Family Pledge,	294	Sparkling and bright,	235
Females invited,	290	Star of Temperance, The,	269
Fireman, The Temperance,	236	Soldier's Appeal, The,	277
Freemen, We're a band of	238	Supplication,	295
Funeral, The,	307	Sympathy for the Drunkard,	286
Go not back,	292	Selfpunished,	285
Go, go thou that enslav'st me,	267	Sparkling bowl, The,	288
Good time coming, The,	243	Standard, The,	303
Gough's, J. B., lament,	272	Stop and think,	303
Happy Home,	253	Temperance Trumpet,	304
Hark, o'er hill and dale,	286	Tempter, The,	306
Help Lord,	302	Temperance National Anthem,	296
I love a little sup,	232	Thanksgiving,	296
I'm not to blame,	233	Teetotal forever,	252
Intemperance,	211–216	Three Topers, The,	247
Inebriate, I am a poor,	297	Temperance Band,	242
I've thrown the bowl aside,	270	Temperance Anthem,	231
Joyful day,	241	There's nae luck about the house,	229
Ladies Song,	263	Temperance Champion,	226
Lasses, To the,	222	Trumpet, The Temperance,	225
Look not upon the Wine,	246	Try, John,	217
Maine Law, The,	235	Temperate drinking,	215
Might with the Right, The,	224	Temperance,	214
Mischiefs of drinking, The,	268	Temperance Star,	282
Never forget,	277	Triumph of Sobriety,	285
No quarter to Alcohol,	266	Turn, O, turn,	291
Ode to Rum,.	212	There is a happy time,	264
Oh, Temperance is a noble plan,	223	Voice from Heaven,	306
Only this once,	281	Water, O water for me,	273
Old dirty Bottle, The,	250	We Temperance Chiefs,	222
Oh, pledge not with Wine,	257	When is the time to sign,	221
Ode,	203	Water King, The,	274
Our Flag,	237	Water the drink for me,	276
Paradise, The drink of,	261	We will praise Thee,	295

CONTENTS.

Will you come to the Bower,	244	Widow's appeal, The,	305
Will you sign the pledge,	245	Wife's appeal, The,	311
We will be free,	246	Young Wife's last appeal, The,	310
Warning, The Drunkard's,	254	Youth of Canada,	283
We'll never drink again,	258		

CONTENTS OF PART FOURTH.

FACTS AND ANECDOTES.

Ancient Pledge,	388	Legal suppression, 50 years ago,	329
Adulteration of liquors,	313–317	Low position defined,	387
Alexander, Death of,	325	Liquor seller's excuse,	399
Anacreon's plea and ladies retort,	376	Methodist Conference in Mass.,	318
Asylum for inebriates,	328	Missionaries, Opinions of	318
Beer houses,	32–36	Minister and the demijohn,	395
Can't give up my besetting sin,	379–80	Noble boy, A,	392
Cost of Intemperance,	388	Physicians of Canada, Testimony,	385
Confession of a Drunkard,	333	Parsonage, How to adorn a,	402
Decanter, Song of the,	382	Prayer, The value of,	393
Dashaway, A,	378	Ross, Capt., his practice,	322
Excitants and temperature,	403	Rumseller's Dream,	394
Expensive,	338	Sad testimony,	337
Father Matthew's conversion,	324	Sabbath, The,	337
Female Intemperance,	330	Seamen's wages,	399
Grocer's Wife, The,	396	Shingling a house,	400
How to rise in life,	327	Teetotalism favorable to religion,	334
History of a Distillery,	329	Teetotal spoons,	381
Homer and Pope,	347	Tree of Dissipation,	383
Heroic woman, The,	377	True use of the Vine,	401
Immense waste,	332	Various interesting facts &c,	339–346
Indian, The, and Distiller,	390	Valuable Testimonies,	384
Incontrovertible facts,	336	Washwoman, The Scotch,	390
Interesting facts, warnings,	351–376	Wesley on the Traffic,	351
Jay, Rev. Wm. of Bath, his views,	385	Wesleyans, To,	350
Jack and Harry,	392	Young man on fire,	386
Keeping Tavern,	398		

APPENDIX.

The Prince of Wales' Visit to British America,	405	bodies of Upper Canada,	406
		Reply to Address,	407
Address from the Temperance		Concluding remarks,	408

PART FIRST.

THE TEETOTALER'S HAND-BOOK.

CHAPTER I.

HISTORY OF THE TEMPERANCE CAUSE.

BIBLE EVIDENCE—SCRIPTURE IN FAVOR OF ABSTINENCE.

The inspired writers employ a number of different terms to denote various kinds of drink, and speak of these in great diversity of tone and language. We leave out of account here, *tirosh*, the name of *vine fruit*, as this, though uniformly rendered wine in our version, has been proved not to signify a liquor at all. The other terms occur in Scripture, altogether *two hundred and twenty-three* times. The drink denoted by one of these (*shechar*) is invariably disapproved by God, and its use, as a common beverage, denounced in terms of loudest warning and woe. The drink denoted by another of them (*yain*) is sometimes represented as a possible good, but in the vast majority of cases, it is branded as a mighty evil to man. The articles denoted by the other words are spoken of with diversity of expression, as it seems, according to the presence or absence from them, of the intoxicating principle. Altogether, there are about *a hundred and thirty* warnings and admonitions in Scripture against intoxicating drinks, while there are not over *twenty* instances of distinct approval of wine, under all its names, in the whole Bible. And these passages, as far as their evidence is explicit, show the wine commended, to be of an unintoxicating quality. All the other cases in which the word wine occurs, are doubtful or neutral in the Temperance question, since they contain no proof, either on the one side, or on the other.

Are not these most important and significant facts? Who can fail to perceive they have a voice and a meaning? How can any one stand in doubt, as to the conclusion to which they point?

SCRIPTURE IN FAVOR OF ABSTINENCE.—The Bible not only discountenances the evil, but it encourages the good. We have seen how it withholds its sanction from intoxicating liquor. We proceed to show how it approves of entire abstinence from it, and of approach, to the use of it. It does this by *living examples*. It is remarkable how many of the great men, and distinguished communities, of the Bible, were abstainers, encouraged in this, too, by God's approbation and blessing. We point then in illustration, to the whole nation of Israel, during their forty years' journey through the wilderness. God could as easily have given them wine, as He rained down manna on them from heaven, and caused water to flow to them from the smitten rock. But he did not so. Through all these years, we are told, they "drank neither wine nor strong drink." The Lord was ever kind to them, He fed them with angels' food, He cherished them with Divine care, but they were a nation of abstainers, trained to be so, all this time, by the only wise God. Again we point to Samson. His mother, when promised a son, was thus commanded—"Now therefore beware, I pray thee, and drink not wine nor strong drink, and eat not any unclean thing. For lo! thou shalt conceive, and bear a son, and no razor shall come on his head, for the child shall be a Nazarite unto God from the womb, and he shall begin to deliver Israel out of the hand of the Philistines."

> O madness to think use of strongest wines,
> And strongest drinks our chief support of health,
> When God, with these forbidden, made choice to rear
> His mighty champion, strong above compare,
> Whose drink was only from the limpid brook.

Further, we point to Samuel. His pious mother received him, in answer to her prayer, and she pledged herself in this, to devote him as a *Nazarite* all the days of his life. Notice here, also, the issue, in the consecration and character of his noble career. In early years he was chosen of God to the prophetic office. He acted as judge of his nation through a long period of its history. He was honoured as its reformer till he descended to the grave in a good old age, beloved and lamented by his weeping country. Moreover, we point to Daniel and his three friends. In the Court of Babylon, 'the King appointed them a daily provision of the wine which he drank,' 'but Daniel purposed in his heart not to defile himself with it,' and behold the result in his health and vigour. He and his companions preferred this request, 'Give us pulse to eat, and water to drink;' 'and at the end of ten days their countenances appeared fairer and fatter in flesh, than all the children who did eat the portion of the king's meat.' Yet again we point to John the Baptist. In announcing his birth to Zacharias, the angel Gabriel thus foretold his abstinence, 'He shall drink neither wine nor strong drink.' And note here, also, what follows in the description of his character, 'He shall be filled with the Holy Ghost, even from his mother's womb;' and Christ, whom he was chosen to herald, declared, 'Among those born of women, there has not arisen a greater than John.'

Once more we point to the Rechabites. They were a community especially devoted to God. They were remarkable for their strict piety, they were bound to drink no wine, but to give themselves to a contemplative life, and avoid all occasions of luxury and avarice. 'They were,' observes Dr. Chalmers, 'a Temperance Society,' united, it has been added, by a family pledge, to which they adhered with intelligent fidelity, and for doing so they are commended by God.' Then observe here the striking connection and consequence of the laws of this sacred fraternity. 'Jonadab,' say they, 'the son of Rechab, our father, commanded us, saying— Ye shall drink no wine, ye, nor your sons for ever, that ye may *live long in the land wherein you are strangers.*' In a word, we point to the Nazarites. 'One part of the special sanctity of a Nazarite consisted in a total abstinence from wine or anything that intoxicates, that he might the better attend to the study of the law, and other exercises of religion, which justifies in part what Maimonedes says, that Nazarites were advanced to the dignity of priests, who were not allowed to drink wine in the time of their ministration.' And mark the design of this Divine appointment. It was intended of God, to preserve a people for Himself, eminent for a life of sanctity and devotion. 'There will be found,' says Dr. Haweis, 'some more eminent for their graces than others—the Nazarites, among their brethren, not to taste wine, that they might show themselves patterns of sobriety, and be ever fit for the service of God. They who have a deep concern about their soul, will have a noble neglect of the body."

God commands total abstinence from it, while the priests minister in the sanctuary; and that no appearance of the evil might exist, he permits no wine of any kind whatever to be used by the priests, while discharging their sacred functions, throughout all their generations. "And the Lord spake to Aaron, saying, Do not drink wine, nor strong drink, thou, nor thy sons with thee, when ye go into the tabernacle of the congregation, lest ye die; it shall be a statute for ever throughout your generations; and that ye may teach the children of Israel all the statutes which the Lord hath spoken unto them, by the hand of Moses.' 'This is a strong reason,' says Dr. Adam Clarke, 'why they should drink no inebriating liquor; that their understandings being clear, and their judgments correct, they might be always able to discern between the clean and unclean, and ever pronounce righteous judgments.' As a remedy for intemperance, does not the Bible thus exhibit abstinence as the plan of God himself, and prove it to be in accordance with His eternal wisdom?

Romans xiv. 21—" It is good neither to eat flesh, nor to drink wine, nor anything whereby thy brother stumbleth, or is offended, or is made weak."

CHAPTER II.

ANCIENT TEETOTALISM.

Temperance of the Chinese—Turks—Egyptians—Romans—Grecians—Spaniards—Ancient Societies, 1517—One Hundred Years Ago.

TEMPERANCE OF THE CHINESE.—About eleven hundred years before Christ, a Chinese emperor, at a solemn assembly of the states, *forbade the use of wine*, as what proves the cause of almost all the evils which happen on the earth.

TEMPERANCE OF THE TURKS.—Warnerus says,—' The more devout Pagan Arabs *totally abstained from wine* long before the birth of Mohamed.'

Busbequius says,—' His prohibition of wine hindered many of the prophet's contemporaries from embracing his religion. Yet several of the most respectable of the Pagan Arabs, *like certain of the Jews and early Christians*, abstained totally from wine, *from a feeling of its injurious effects upon morals, and, in their climate, upon health.*'

TEMPERANCE OF THE EGYPTIANS.—*They were early accustomed to sobriety*, by not being permitted to eat of viands prepared by too refined a cookery.

' Psametichus, in the year of the flood, 2339, *was the first of the Egyptian kings who drank wine*, yet was it more than 2000 years since Noah had planted the vine."

" With respect to wine, some of them *did not drink it at all*, and others drank very little of it, *on account of its being injurious to the nerves, oppressive to the head, an impediment to invention, and* AN INCENTIVE TO LUST."

TEMPERANCE OF THE ROMANS.—" *In early times* no female at Rome enjoyed the privilege, and it was *unlawful* for women, or indeed for young men below the age of thirty, *to drink wine*, except at sacrifices."

PLATO approves "the *Carthaginian* law, that *no sort of wine be drunk in the camp, nor anything save water:* and that every judge and magistrate *abstain from wine during the year of his magistracy.*"

"*Athenian laws of* SOLON. An Archon, who was the chief magistrate, if seen drunk in public, was punished with death."

"LYCURGUS, *of Sparta.* A Lacedæmonian knew not what it was to drink for pleasure. Drunkenness was infamous. Slaves were made drunk, *and exhibited in this condition to the youth,* in order to inspire them with abhorrence of this filthy vice."

TEMPERANCE OF THE SPANIARDS.—" In war their sustenance was coarse and simple; *their common drink water,* seldom wine. The lightness and activity of their bodies were wonderful."

FIFTEENTH AND THREE FOLLOWING CENTURIES.—" On the revival of literature, after the dark ages, intemperance in drinking was exceedingly prevalent; but, as men became more enlightened, they had recourse to measures calculated to prevent it. And it is a curious fact, that in the fifteenth and sixteenth centuries, *temperance societies* were formed by the most intelligent and influential men, for the purpose of stopping intemperance in drinking. One was called the Society of St. Christopher, others were called temperance societies, and the members of one took the appropriate name of the Golden Band."

ANCIENT SOCIETIES, 1517—" The first association of this kind of which we have any account, was instituted by Sigismond de Sietrichstein, under the auspices of Dt. Christopher, A.D. 1517. Maurice, Landgrave of Hesse, formed, A.D. 1600, a similar association, under the name of ' The Order of Temperance.' Several of the reigning princes, and many of the principal noblemen of Germany, ranked among its supporters. The first law of this association was as follows:—' Be it ordained, that every member of this society pledges himself, from its institution, which dates December 25th, 1600, never to become intoxicated.' The other rules of this association, however, strangely contrast with its professed object, as specified in its first regulation. Each member was limited to fourteen glasses of wine daily. A knight, for example, was allowed at each meal (twice a-day) seven *bacaux*, or glasses of wine, which were to be drunk in not less than three draughts. The size of the cups is not specified. A society, for instance, established about the sixteenth century, for the promotion of temperance, had its fundamental law constituted on the principle, that none of its members should drink more than fourteen glasses of wine daily. A certain general, in one of his regulations, ordered, that no officer who dined at his table should exceed two bottles of wine."

A TEMPERANCE SOCIETY IN SCOTLAND ONE HUNDRED YEARS AGO.—" We, the inhabitants of Leadhills, having taken into our most serious consideration the former direful effects of the malt distilleries, and being justly apprehensive of the like fatal consequences in time coming, as we hear that these devouring machines are again to be let loose, unanimously come to the following resolutions:—

" 1st. That the malt distilleries have been the principal cause of the immoderate use of spirituous liquors, which has been found, by experience, highly detrimental, not only to the health, but also to the morals of mankind, especially to the labouring part thereof; it being productive of all kinds of debaucheries, drunkenness, indolence, and, in fine, the very enemy of social happiness.

" 2dly. They have, ever since they came to any height, been a principal cause of the famine, while such immense quantities of the best food, designed by the bountiful hand of Providence for the subsistence of His creatures, have been, by them, converted into a stupifying kind of poison, calculated for the sure, though slow, destruction of the human race: and therefore,

" 3dly. We are firmly resolved, in order to prevent their baneful influence, to discourage, to the utmost of our power, by all public methods, that pernicious practice, being determined to drink no spirits so distilled; neither frequent, nor drink any liquor in, any tavern or ale-house that we know sells or retails the same. And as we have no other means left to combat these enemies of plenty, we have chosen this public way of intimating our sentiments to the world, craving the concurrence of all our brethren in like circumstances in town and country, tradesmen, mechanics, and labouring people of all denominations."

CHAPTER III.

MODERN TEMPERANCE SOCIETIES.
America—Canada—Ireland—Scotland—England—Wales.

AMERICA.—"In America, this movement began in 1804, by the inquiries instituted by Dr. Rush into the effects of ardent spirits upon the body and mind. These he published, and they were made the foundation of all subsequent experiments. In 1805, the Rev. Dr. Ebenezer Porter preached a sermon on the effects of ardent spirits, and a society was organized at Allentown, New Jersey, called the Sober Society, numbering 58 members at the start. In 1808, a society was organized by Dr. B. J. Clarke, at Moreau, Saratoga County, New York; the pledge was total abstinence from all kinds of distilled liquors, unless required by medical authority, and also retrenchment of wine, with some exceptions.

"On the 26th of June, 1811, the General Association of Massachusetts appointed Rev. Samuel Worcester, D.D., Rev. Jedediah Morse, D.D., Rev. Abiel Abbot, Rev. Benjamin Wadsworth, Reuben D. Mussey, M.D., William Thurston, Esq., Joseph Torrey, M.D., and Jeremiah Evarts, Esq., a committee to co-operate with committees of the General Assembly of the Presbyterian church, and the General Association of Connecticut, in devising measures which may have an influence in preventing some of the numerous and threatening mischiefs that are experienced throughout our country, from the excessive and intemperate use of spirituous liquors. This committee met at different times for consultation, corresponded on the subject, and, finally, determined to make an effort for the formation of a State Society for the Suppression of Intemperance. A sub-committee, consisting of Dr. Worcester, Dr. Torrey, and Mr. Wadsworth, was appointed to prepare a Constitution. After being presented to the whole committee, and adopted, it was presented, by them, to a more general meeting, in Boston, on the 4th of February, 1813. At another meeting, at the State House, on the 5th, the Constitution was adopted, and a Society formed, called 'The Massachusetts Society for the Suppression of Intemperance.' The object, as expressed in the second article of the Constitution, was, ' *To discountenance and suppress the too free use of ardent spirit, and its kindred vices, profaneness and gaming, and to encourage and promote temperance and general morality.*"

In 1813, the Rev. Dr. Memphrey published a series of publications on the causes, effects, and remedies of intemperance. The Massachusetts Society for the Suppression of Intemperance was then formed at Boston; and various ministers of religion were holding up the matter in their various circles as a subject of inquiry. The next step was organization, in 1826. The American society was formed, having for its object abstinence from distilled spirits. At this time, Dr. Beecher's celebrated sermons, the substance of which had been preached at Boston, were published. His mind had been training, and he came out at a critical moment. Many complained we were going on too fast; but on we went, and in 1833, we called a Convention; 440 delegates attended, and the question to be decided was, that the traffic in ardent spirits was morally wrong, and ought to be abandoned. It was again said, we were going too fast. However, we adopted the principle. Then we found that men were getting drunk on wine and beer, and were compelled to take up the new position of total abstinence from all intoxicating liquor. In 1835, a year remarkable as being the year when a prosecution was commenced against Mr. Delavan, damages laid at 300,000 dollars, for publishing in the papers that the water they used for making porter was obtained from a stagnant pool filled with the carcases of dead animals, and into which the drainings of the burial-ground ran,—just about such stuff as is used by the London brewers to make their brown stout. In 1840, the action was decided against them; and the costs were put on the brewers.

The Anniversary of the American Temperance Union, was celebrated in the great Hall of the Cooper Institute, on the 11th of May, 1859. The Hon. George N. Briggs in the chair. Dr. Marsh, Corresponding Secretary, read the following abstract of the Annual Report:—

"At our Twenty-third Anniversary, and the Thirty-third of the Temperance Reformation, your Committee are able to speak of four victories which have been obtained over the alcoholic foe:— a victory in the individual man; a victory in the family; a victory in the Church; and a victory in the State.

"1. Individual man is delivered from the delusion which was a tyranny of the worst description, perilling everything of value for time and eternity, that intoxicating liquor was both needful and useful in health and in sickness, in summer and winter, in seed-time and harvest, at home and abroad, and that he only did justice to his system who bowed to its demands, and consented to be enslaved by its customs; and many millions are now profiting by it.

"2. The family is exempted from that curse which once brought thousands, even of Christian households, down, amid wounds, and woes, and strifes, to death; and the family may now be born, be reared, be reputable, be useful; discharging all its duties in the house, the school, the workshop, the field, at the marriage and the funeral, and yet touch not, taste not, handle not, the accursed thing.

"3. The Church, which was once in league with this remorseless enemy of God and man, sustaining it by her wealth, and pouring out upon its altars the best blood of her ministers and sons, now, in many of her branches, holds it in utter abhorrence, and stamps it in the dust. To the Bible, with few exceptions, she no longer appeals as supporting its claims. Her children she no longer lays upon its altars; and in her daily prayer, 'Thy kingdom come,' she earnestly prays that this terrific foe, blasting revivals, hindering Christian missions, retarding the millenium, and dragging souls without number to the pit, may be subdued to rise no more.

"4. One State after another which legalized this traffic, which once protected the drunkard-maker in his employment, derived revenue from his spoils, and submitted peacefully to the work of death, if it was but done according to law, have pronounced it a nuisance and an outlaw, expelled it from their borders, created a forfeiture of all its claims, and followed with fine and imprisonment every guilty abettor. The people, suffering beyond what they could bear, have demanded the protection. Legislators have granted it; judges and juries have confirmed it; and while distillers and venders have cried, unconstitutionality, oppression, human rights; drunkards and the friends of drunkards have rejoiced in their downfall, and cried in their turn, Alleluia! true and righteous is the judgment.

"Leaving others to speak of discouragements, your Committee will here notice only some of the prominent cheering incidents of the year.

"1. The extension of the Band of Hope movement, by which temperance principles and practices are to be handed down to the generations which come after us, which have been great, both with us, in the Canadas, and in Great Britain.

"2. The reception in love of our great principles by some thousands of young men, who, under the power of the Spirit of God, have become hopefully pious, and have united with Christian churches. This, together with an unusual activity in Christian laymen in breaking up the strongholds of wickedness in our great cities, has given a severe blow to intemperance.

"3. The restoration of the prohibitory law in Maine, after a two years' license law, under which the State was flooded with intoxicating drinks, and once more abandoned to all its evils. By a vote in the Legislature, the question was submitted to the people at the ballot-box, when 28,864 votes for the restoration, and only 5,912 for the continuance of license. The law went into operation on the 15th of July last, with perfect quietness. At that time 500 grog-shops were open in Portland, the chief city, doing all their work of death, whereas there are few or none visible now. Drunkenness, and arrests for drunkenness, have diminished more than one-half, and pauperism a third; and Maine has once more become the true and blessed asylum for the unfortunate inebriate.

"4. The decision of Chief Justice Shaw, of Massachusetts, that, under the law which declares all intoxicating liquors kept illegally for sale, and the implements and vessels actually used and buildings employed, common nuisances, they are to be treated as such, and every person may destroy them. And though a full Bench have decided that the nuisance must be personal, otherwise it can be proceeded against only by indictment, yet it is a decision which gives the community protection against all illegal sale before unknown, and presents this once honoured and protected traffic in its true light, to be shunned and abhorred by all good citizens.

"Such have been some of the encouraging events in the past year in our land.

"In Russia, where 647 distilleries are annually yielding 271 million gallons of spirits, a great revolt from all drinking customs has arisen, through an increased taxation upon brandy, and thousands in the central provinces are pledging themselves to drink no more. In Australia, the cause of temperance is prosperous, under the patronage of Chief Justice a Becket; and, in the Sandwich Islands, the large mission churches hold fast their temperance integrity. But time would fail your Committee to tell of Africa and India, of Sweden and Norway, of California and Oregon, where temperance and prohibition are slowly but efficiently working; and of our own seamen too, on the wide ocean, proving the benefit of total abstinence, and who, were it not for the land sharks, licensed by our Christian and civilized governments, might be as proverbial for their temperance as they are for their generosity and bravery. More than thirty thousand have, in a course of years, united with the New York Mariner's Society; and of nine hundred who have been at the Seamen's Home since January last, but twenty-five have been marked as intemperate men. For all those things we thank God and take courage. To men who say our cause is dead, we reply—It is not so. God never suffers a good thing to perish. Our institution is mighty in the earth. Its course is onward. Like the sun in the heavens, it encircles and blesses the globe."

CANADA.—Foremost in the rank of pioneers in the Temperance cause in Canada, may be justly placed Revs. Joseph S. Christmas, G. W. Perkins, W. Taylor, and T. Osgood; Messrs. Cooper, J. B. Sutherland, Hoisington, Greig, DeWitt, Fraser, Hedge, W. Lyman, B. Workman, D. P. Janes, J. E. Mills, Greene, Brewster, Moore, Christie, Orr, Court, and Dougall.

Early and persevering interest was also taken in the cause by Messrs. Workman and Bowman, proprietors of the *Canadian Courant*, who, in the midst of ridicule and opposition, contended for temperance principles, and kept the columns of their journal open for reports and extracts upon the subject.

There has been some dispute as to which society was first organized in Canada, and it is believed the Montreal Society carries off the palm. Dr. Schofield of Bastard said that he organized the first society, June 10, 1828; but the following authentic report settles the point:—

"According to intimation, given in the public papers, a considerable number of persons convened in St. Andrew's Church, St. Peter's Street, on the evening of June 9, 1828.—After some statements on the subject of intemperance, by the Rev. J. S. Christmas, the following preamble was submitted, and signed on the spot by 29 persons of different religious denominations."

The organization of societies went forward rapidly in 1830, '31, '32. At this period, there were about 150 societies in Canada, and a membership of 10,000 persons,—mostly enjoying the public patronage, and being in a flourishing condition,—while twelve newspapers lent their aid to the advance of temperance principles.

The first Provincial Temperance Convention for Lower Canada as held in the Baptist Chapel, Montreal, February 26, 1834. Present—22 ministers, 28 doctors, and 40 other gentlemen. Twenty-seven societies reported 4250 members.

On the 15th day of June, 1835, the first Total Abstinence Society in Canada was formed at St. Catharine's, in the Gore District, when upwards of 40 signatures were obtained. On the 22d day of October following, the Montreal Society for the promotion of Temperance, adopted the teetotal principle, conjointly with the moderate system. The able assistance of the Rev. Dr. Edwards, and E. C. Delevan, Esq., was secured on this occasion, rendering the meeting one of unusual interest—the Rev. W. Lord presided.

A Convention was held at Montreal, 23d of February, 1836. The following abstract from the report of its proceedings, will show the state of the cause at this period:—Number of societies reported, 30; Ordinary Members, 4751; Total Abstinence do., 764; Expelled, 205; Withdrawn or Removed, 272; Taverns, 358; Stores Selling Liquor, 207; Temperance Inns or Stores, 34; Distilleries or Breweries at Date of Formation, 43; Ditto now, 21.

This is a condensed review of the various reports made to the Committee, showing in round numbers about 5500 members of the Temperance Society in the Districts from which reports have been received. A number of the Societies state that they have not adopted the total abstinence pledge yet, though many of their members act upon that principle.

The first Temperance Soiree was held on the evening of St. Andrew's Day, 1837. Messrs. William Addy and A. Stevenson had abandoned the sale of intoxicating drinks. Mr. Elliott was the first agent employed. Active measures were in contemplation for the wider spread of light on the subject.

MODERN TEMPERANCE SOCIETIES.

The next Convention was held at Montreal, July 5, 1837, when a constitution for the Lower Canada Total Abstinence Society was adopted; 27 societies were represented, having a membership equal to 4859.

The first extensive mercantile houses which abandoned the traffic in intoxicating liquors, were those of Messrs. J. & J. Dougall, Amherstburgh, and J. G. Parker, of Kingston. This year the *Canada Temperance Advocate* became exclusively devoted to the advocacy of *Total Abstinence*.

The month of August was rendered remarkable by the arrival of a temperance ship in the port of Montreal, whose commander, Captain Henry Hudson, a teetotaler, had been instrumental in adding no fewer than 226 to the Society. He was presented with a beautiful silver medal " in grateful acknowledgment of his exertions."

In the spring of 1839, the friends of the cause began again to lift up their heads and consider new plans of usefulness—and in this they were much cheered and encouraged by reports of the astonishing success of Father Mathew's efforts in Ireland. In imitation of whom, the Rev. P. Phelan, of this city, and the Rev. C. Chiniquy, of Beauport, followed by others, established temperance societies amongst the Irish and French Canadian population in this province, which soon enrolled many thousands, and exerted an extraordinary influence in rendering drinking usages unpopular, and diminishing intemperance amongst the masses; whilst the celebrated Mr. Buckingham, in his travels through this country, endeavoured to enlighten the higher classes upon the same subject.

Mr. Wadsworth, the travelling Agent, writes:—

" My second temperance tour through the Eastern Townships has been completed with considerable satisfaction to myself, and in some instances given an impetus to the good cause, which it is hoped will be followed up by energetic plans and efforts on the part of the officers of societies. Returned after an absence of 20 days, having travelled 330 miles, visited 23 places, held 21 public meetings, delivered 27 addresses and lectures, obtained 433 names to the teetotal pledge, originated 11 societies, procured 11 subscribers to the *Advocate*, and circulated a large quantity of temperance tracts and *Advocates*. I found it extremely hard to induce *moderationists* to give up their *brandied* wines, home-brewed beer, and cider. Many persons in the townships are making drunkards without license. This outrage upon the laws must not be allowed. Where in former days, in the County of Stanstead, were 27 distilleries and breweries, there is now but *one*, and that conducted by a *Christian!* In another place, a member of a church keeps a tavern."

"I have now completed my tour through the Prince Edward District, during which I have held 24 meetings, seen 275 persons sign the pledge of total abstinence, and obtained 26 new subscribers to the *Advocate*, exclusive of some who sent through the Post Office, and others who will soon send. It is now just two years since societies were first formed in this District on total abstinence principles. At present the old ground of abstinence from distilled spirits only, is almost totally abandoned; there is not, I believe, one organized society on this principle, and but about 150 scattered members."

In 1842, he says:—"At no former period in the history of teetotalism in Canada, could it be said, 'We are a hundred and twenty thousand strong'; yet this may safely be affirmed now. The influence of so large a body, pledged to entire abstinence from alcoholic drinks, is sensibly felt and palpably plain; else why, I ask, do those who refuse to join us—instead of denouncing us as ultraists, or pretending pity for our insane attempts at the final overthrow of the *demon's reign*—offer a variety of flimsy excuses, objections which have been a thousand times refuted, and then close by saying, 'It is a good cause, I wish it well, but my mind is not yet made up to join.' Yes, well may our conquering hosts exult, whether retrospectively or prospectively, contemplating the work to be accomplished or already done."

In a communication of later date (1845) he writes:—" Well may it be inquired, 'Watchman, what of the night?' In answering this significant question, permit me to offer some general remarks, and make a few strictures. It will be conceded that from my extensive tours, and favourable opportunities of procuring information, I may arrive at safe conjectures concerning our present position. I suppose we are 150,000 strong, organized in 600 societies; of this number, 60,000 are male adults, 52,000 female adults, and 38,000 juveniles, say from five to sixteen years of age. The Pledge adopted by three-fourths of these societies, is the 'Universal Pledge,' or the one published in the *Advocate.*" * * * * * * * *

The Rev. Richard Saul, P. Roblin, and J. M'Donald, Esq., were employed by the Montreal Society, and laboured with very great success.

One of these Agents writes:—" In the order of a kind Providence, I arrived home on the 5th March, from a tour of four months through the Newcastle District, as agent in the temperance cause; during which time I had many very interesting meetings, and was ably assisted by many valuable and able advocates on the platform, and succeeded in obtaining 932 names to the pledge, and collected £15, 15s. for the *Advocate.* I could have wished for better success; but when we see an under-current at work, and that current set in motion by individuals from whom we would expect better things, we are thankful to the giver of all good for the success that has attended the labours of the temperance friends in that district."

Of late years, the success of Teetotalism must be traced through the Reports of the numerous existing organizations, and the marked advances in Legislation by which the sale of Intoxicating Drinks is forbidden on Public Works, during Election Days, and from Saturday evening till Monday morning, as well as the extensive power given to Municipalities for regulating or entirely preventing the retail of such liquors.

Temperance Convention.—The Convention called by the Committee of the Montreal Temperance Society, assembled in that city on Friday, 30th September, 1859. The Business Committee reported five resolutions which received the unanimous assent of the Convention. These resolutions are plain and emphatic, and quite in keeping with the present state of the cause in Canada.

"*Resolved,*—I. That this Convention, while urging on all Temperance Organizations, such as the Rechabites, Sons of Temperance, and Good Templars, the necessity of renewed exertions for the advancement of the Temperance cause, strongly recommends the propriety of organizing Societies on the plan of the original Total Abstinence Society, to act in harmony with them; so that the entire community may be embraced, and the public mind thoroughly leavened with Temperance principles.

"II. That this Convention, feeling the importance of imbuing the minds of the rising generation with Temperance principles, would urge the formation of Bands of Hope, or other juvenile associations.

"III. That this Convention, in order more effectually to counteract the influences hostile to the Temperance cause, and to secure its triumph, would seek to impress on its friends the necessity of circulating Temperance Tracts, and sustaining Periodicals devoted to the cause, as well as by holding public meetings.

"IV. That this Convention, while attaching the greatest importance to the moral suasion aspect of the Temperance movement, yet believe that the object at which we aim cannot be fully attained without the enactment of a Prohibitory Liquor Law, recommend the formation of an Anti-Liquor-Law League, to embrace all classes, without reference to political or religious opinions, or personal abstinence.

"V. That in view of the importance of Prohibitory Legislation, this Convention recommend united effort on the part of all Temperance Organizations, in the employment of suitable Lecturers, that a more general public sentiment in favor of Temperance may be created; and Petitions praying for Prohibition be prepared, and numerously signed, and forwarded to Parliament during the early part of its next session.

IRELAND.—In the summer of 1829, Dr. Edgar of Belfast set on foot the Irish temperance movement, assisted by Rev. George Carr; and it is believed that the first European temperance society was established by the latter, at New Ross, about June or July, 1829.

In June, 1835, Mr. John Finch aided in forming the first Teetotal Society in Ireland at Strabane. The next person who made an effort to promote teetotalism in Ireland was R. G. White, Esq., of Dublin. Mr. Thomas Swindlehurst, of Preston (partner of Mr. Finch), also made an effort to promote the cause in Ireland; he held a large meeting at Waterford; he also spoke of its beneficial effects at various places with good success. Mr. Robert M'Curdy, from Halifax, in Yorkshire, also visited Ireland, and his labours were attended with considerable advantages. The societies that were formed by these gentlemen and others, received a wonderful stimulus from the visit of Mr. J. Hocking, the Birmingham blacksmith, and Mr. M'Kenna, of Liverpool. Thus it was that total abstinence may be considered to have first taken root in Ireland. And, to assist in forwarding the temperance reformation, the friends of teetotalism, in Ireland, combined together and established the National Temperance Society, on the principle of abstinence from all intoxicating liquors; the Irish Temperance Union was also designed for the same purpose.

To complete the success of the temperance reformation in the sister kingdom, the Rev. Theobald Mathew, of Cork, a Catholic clergyman, and a friar of the order of Capuchins, long distinguished for his devoted and disinterested zeal in every cause connected with the welfare of the poor, about eight years ago, prevailed upon a few members of his congregation to form themselves into a Temperance Society. This society rapidly increased in numbers. In January, 1839, it comprehended six thousand persons of both sexes. The work proceeded so quietly, that many wondered how it happened that so few drunken men appeared in the streets of Cork. The Rev. N. E. Duncombe, an active member of the Established Church, then formed a parochial society, and acted as president; from it various branches were formed: William Martin, a member of the Society of Friends, established a society. Richd. Dowden also organized a society. These and other societies had been working prosperously for some years, when Mr. Mathew came forward, at the earnest request of Mr. Martin, and interested himself in their behalf. He put himself at the head of the Cork Temperance Society on the 10th of April, 1838. For a year and a-half, Father Mathew held his temperance meetings in the Horse Bazaar, Cork, twice a-week. Many early prophesied failure and defeat; but the work of enrolment still went on, and the society swelled in numbers. Hundreds of the most abandoned drunkards were reclaimed; and towards the end of the year 1838, it was stated that Cork was fast taking the lead in the temperance movement, and that the people there, and from all the country round, were joining the ranks of Father Mathew in hundreds and thousands. We have no space to describe the interesting scenes which were perpetually presented; suffice it to say, that at the close of the year 1838, the numbers registered in his books amounted to 150,000. In the following year, Father Mathew adopted the plan of travelling through the country, so that, in the course of five years, almost every part of Ireland has participated in the blessings of his mighty mission. On the 2d of December, 1839, he visited Limerick, which presented one of the most extraordinary appearances on record. The Cork entrance to the city was filled with a dark and dense crowd for above two miles; the streets were all but impassable; every house, and room, and cellar, was literally filled; and yet, after all, more than 5000 persons were without a bed on that cold December night! The scene was one of the most remarkable ever witnessed. With the military to keep perfect regularity, 20,000 persons were seen at once kneeling in Mallow Street, and retiring in order as soon as the pledge was administered. The terms of the pledge, which it may be interesting to know, were these,—" I promise, so long as I shall continue a member of the Teetotal Temperance Society, to abstain from all intoxicating liquors, unless recommended for medical purposes, and to discourage, by all means in my power, the practice of intoxication in others;' Mr. Mathew adding, 'May God bless you, and enable you to keep your promise.' On the following day, the work went on, at the close of which 150,000 persons had been enrolled or pledged. On the 10th, 11th, and 12th of December, he visited Waterford, and administered the pledge to upwards of 60,000 in that district. He seemed perfectly unconscious of the excitement he had produced, and spoke and acted as if he regarded himself as the least remarkable man of the age.

Improvement was not confined to a diminution of brawls, fights, and crimes; the people had become better clothed, better fed, and possessed of greater domestic comforts. Money was also saved; capital began to accumulate, instead of being for ever dispersed on vicious indulgences. The depositors in the Savings Bank Association of Dublin increased from 7264 in 1838, to 9585 in 1841. In July, August, and September, 1840, £31,057, 18s. 3d. was lodged in the bank; and in July, August, and September, 1841, £39,596, 14s. 6d.; being an increase of £8,538, 16s. 3d. As many as 237 public-houses were closed in Dublin during the year 1840. Up till November, 1844, he had registered in Ireland 5,640,000 adherents of total abstinence principles. Of these it is computed that there are one million children. It is ascertained that not more than one in five hundred, on an average, has violated the pledge; and of this number the majority avail themselves of the first opportunity to be once more admitted as members.

O. H. Fitzgerald, late Mayor of Limerick, says:—" A moral reformation has taken place among the people of this city, which is really most astonishing, and truly gratifying to every philanthropic mind. Our police reports are much lessened, petty sessions business considerably reduced, and even summonses in the Court of Conscience have fallen off one-third."

Dr. Forbes, Physician to Her Majesty's Household, says:—

"My memorandums clearly establish the fact, that the great banded army of pledged abstainers from intoxicating drinks has been broken in pieces, and the numbering of the host has come down from millions to thousands, and from thousands to hundreds. They show, however, at the same time, that though the organization is gone, the influence of the movement for good has survived its formal existence. It has left Ireland, comparatively speaking, a temperate nation; and the seeds scattered by it throughout the land in its days of triumph, are now, after lying dormant for a season, springing up everywhere with a broader root and a firmer stem. The encouragers and directors of the new arrangements, discarding the dangerous aid of enthusiasm, now strive to base them on the safer ground of reason and experience; and although they advise and accept pledges, as useful auxiliaries, more especially in the commencement, they depend for permanent success much more on a man's convictions of what is for his own good, than on his word of promise. I have strong hope, founded on my own limited observation and inquiries—as recorded in these volumes —that Ireland, within a period of not many years, will once more exhibit the gratifying spectacle of a whole people—not indeed repudiating altogether the use of strong drinks, yet consuming them in an amount so small, as may be called marvellous."

SCOTLAND.—The first Temperance Society was organized Sept., 1829, at Greenock, by John Dunlop, Esq.,—our friend and co-labourer, J. J. E. Linton, Esq. (Stratford, C. W.), being secretary of the meeting. In the early part of October, 1829, a lady, a member of the Society of Friends, named Miss Allen, formed a society at Mary Hill, near Glasgow. Then followed the formation of the Glasgow Society, on the 12th of November. Mr. Wm. Collins, Mr. Cruickshank, and others, organised many other societies in Scotland: during the first year of their labours, half a million of tracts were circulated, 100 societies established, and 15,000 members obtained. In the city of Glasgow, in the year 1831, parties in connection with the moderation society met together to partake of tea and coffee, and were addressed by different friends of the cause, without the presence of any intoxicating liquors.

From the outset of the movement, the principle first started with, if principle it could be called, was found defective. Although a few contended from the very first for abstinence from all alcoholic liquors, yet the general voice of the friends of the cause prevailed, and the most of the societies formed simply enjoined upon their members abstinence from distilled liquors. It required, however, but a brief experience to discover that the temperance ship was leaky. It was remarked that in certain districts, where the consumption of distilled liquors was decreased through the influence of the temperance society, the consumption of fermented liquors was proportionately increased; that many of those who were apparently reformed, either got themselves drunk upon ale and porter, or by means of these relapsed into their former intemperate habits; and that all the reformed, who actually stood, practised abstinence from all liquors capable of intoxicating. It was also argued that the pledge of such societies was very accommodating to ladies and gentlemen, but very uncompromising with the mechanics and carters, cotton-spinners and weavers, and that they could well afford to give up whisky, who could buy wine.

The first attempt known of to improve upon the old temperance principle was made at Dunfermline, in September, 1830. Upon the motion of Mr. John Davie, a society was formed " for the promotion of temperance, by the relinquishment of all intoxicating liquors." In January, 1832, Mr. James M'Nair, Dr. Richmond, and a few others, formed, in a school-room situated in Oxford Street, Glasgow, the " Tradeston Total Abstinence Society."

In September, 1836, Mr. John Finch introduced Long Pledge tee-totalism into Scotland, by forming a good Tee-total Society at Annon, since which, by the able assistance of Mr. E. Morris, the Rev. Gray Mason, John Dunlop, Esq., and other able advocates, societies have been established at Glasgow, Edinburgh, and most of the large towns, and many of the villages; and it has progressed with amazing success. The zeal and energy of Messrs. J. Livesey, J. Teare, and T. Swindlehurst, of Preston, caused them to visit Scotland, for the purpose of aiding the cause; their efforts proved very beneficial, and the places which they visited received a powerful stimulus.

To assist in the more general diffusion of tee-totalism, the Scottish Temperance Union was formed, at a meeting of delegates, held on the 5th and 6th of August, 1838, in Spreul's Court Chapel, Glasgow; and by the united efforts of Scotland's best friends, at the close of 1838, there were registered 70,000 pledged tee-totallers. At a meeting of delegates, held in the Freemasons' Hall, Edinburgh, on Tuesday, June 4th, 1839, the Scottish Union was divided into two district associations, to be called the Eastern and Western, Edinburgh being the centre of the former, and Glasgow the centre of the latter, each having its monthly periodical.

Large and extensive shipping concerns have sent the whole of their ships to sea on the tee-total principle, and the plan (as in America and England) has been found to work well: and tee-totalism in Scotland has emerged from the obscurity which enshrouded its origin, and it now rears its head as high, and with claims as important, as any of the political, moral, benevolent, or religious enterprises which have been commenced to rescue man from the service of sin.

The Scottish Temperance League was formed at Falkirk on the 5th November, 1844, and consists of those abstainers who neither give nor take intoxicating liquors, and who contribute 2s. 6d., or upwards, annually, to its funds. It employs several able advocates, issues the *Scottish Review*, *Abstainer's Journal*, and the *Adviser*, and also publishes a great variety of able tracts on the various aspects of the temperance question. No previous association in Scotland has taken the same position among benevolent institutions, or contributed so powerfully to advance the cause.

There are also in Scotland several hundred local societies, comprising hundreds of thousands of members. Many of them are in a state of most efficient operation, and are succeeding in creating a public sentiment upon the subject of drinking which bids fair to render it ere long disreputable.

ENGLAND.—The movement was carried into England from Scotland by Henry Forbes, Esq., a merchant of Bradford, who had attended a public meeting of the Glasgow association. By his influence, a temperance society was formed in Bradford in the spring of 1830. Similar associations were soon after established in Leeds and other large towns in the north of England. Mr. William Collins, of Glasgow, being in London about this time, put forth great and successful exertions towards the formation of a society in the metropolis. The first public meeting of the London, since distinguished as the British and Foreign Temperance Society, was held on the 29th of June, 1830.

Two years thereafter, in July, 1832, many of the visitors and speakers began to abstain entirely from all kinds of intoxicating liquor. Messrs. Livesey Swindlehurst, and a few others, soon afterwards began to preach up the entire abstinence doctrine at the meetings, which not only led to greater exertion, but created much discussion on the subject, amongst those who took an interest in the success of the Society. On Thursday, August 23rd, 1832, Messrs. John King and Joseph Livesey signed a total abstinence pledge in Mr. Livesey's shop, Church-street. On Saturday, September 1st, 1832, some of the leaders of the society called a meeting to be held at the Temperance Hall, and at this meeting, John King, Joseph Livesey, John Gratrix, Edward Dickinson, John Broadbelt, John Smith, and David Anderton, signed the following pledge, viz.—" We agree to abstain from all liquors of an intoxicating quality, whether ale, porter, wine, or ardent spirits, except as medicine;" whilst Joseph Dearden, Thomas Lang, George Gratrix, and some others, expressed themselves unwilling to advance beyond the moderation pledge. The effects of the abstinence doctrine were very soon perceived; the principles began to be more constantly and earnestly advocated, and the greater part of the Committee soon became abstainers. The Preston

D

Temperance Hotel, on entire abstinence principles, was opened on the 24th of December, 1832, which was kept, in the first instance, by Mr. Henry Bailey.

To prevent young persons of both sexes from going to public houses and beer shops, tea parties were encouraged. The first tea party on a large scale held at Preston, was on Wednesday, July 11th, 1832, at which 550 sat down at one time; and at another held on Christmas day, 950 sat down, when the visitors were highly delighted. To such an extent had drunkenness prevailed, that it had very frequently been noticed even at funerals; to prevent which, a hand bill, headed "Funeral admonitions," was printed and distributed at funerals where intoxicating liquors were used. A change, however, took place, and coffee, tea, buns, and biscuits, were adopted as substitutes for liquor. In one case the corpse had to be taken to Poulton, (being that of Mr. G. Gratrix) a distance of 20 miles, yet the same strict rule was observed even at the public house at which the attendants had to stop, and at the destination, water was the only beverage used. And to prove to the world that barley might be used for other purposes than converting into intoxicating liquor, the tee-total women of Preston began to make puddings of barley, instead of using rice.

In March, 1833, the committee of the Preston Temperance Society agreed to propose the incorporation of the new pledge with the existing one; and at a large general meeting of the society on the 26th of the same month, it was proposed accordingly, and carried by a large majority. Thirty-four persons attached their signatures to the new pledge on the night it was publicly sanctioned. Assisted by an earnest band of reformers, including several reclaimed drunkards, the principles spread throughout the district with great rapidity. It was at a meeting of this society, that a simple, eccentric, but honest and consistent reclaimed drunkard of the name of Dickie Turner, said, in allusion to the old system—"I'll have nou't to do wi' this moderation, botheration pledge. I'll be right down tee-tee-total for ever." "Well done!" exclaimed the audience. "Well done, Dickie!" said

Mr. Livesey, the originator of the new society, "that shall be the name of our new pledge." It may be mentioned that the prefix "tee" is sometimes used in Lancashire to express emphasis. Thus, a thing irrecoverably lost, is said to be "tee-totally" lost; or a piece of work completed, is said to be "tee-totally" finished. This phrase, then, became the popular designation of the new pledge, and is now known over the world as such.

Before the close of the year 1833, nearly 600 persons, including many drunkards, subscribed the temperance pledge at Preston, and the friends were cheered on by the improved appearances and ameliorated circumstances of many of the members and their families. The drinking habits received a check, and crime diminished in such a degree, as to call forth the special notice of the chaplain of the jail in his annual reports, and the commendation of Baron Alderson when presiding over the assizes in Lancaster. The men of Preston extended their gratuitous efforts to the surrounding villages, and five of their leaders set a week apart for missionary labours in the principal towns of Lancashire. Lectures, and the free circulation of tracts, awakened attention, and excited controversy. This resulted in the accession of many converts, and the formation of numerous and flourishing societies.

From Preston, as a centre, the principles of entire abstinence radiated to other quarters, and in 1834, were introduced into the metropolis by Mr. Livesey with considerable success; and from the metropolis, they were introduced into many of the towns of the south—publicity being advanced by various small periodicals which had already been established in different places. From 1834 to 1838, it may be said that nearly the whole of the original societies throughout England extended their principles on the new and broader declaration, and with no little enthusiasm, without which it would be impossible for any cause of this nature to prosper. The success of these fresh operations having been made known in the United States, the temperance societies there, which had fallen into a languishing condition, adopted the same formula of doctrine, and with like advantage.

Parliamentary Committee.—On the 3rd of June, 1834, on the motion of J. S. Buckingham, Esq., a select committee was appointed by the British House of Commons, "to inquire into the extent, causes, and consequences, of the prevailing vice of intoxication, among the labouring classes of the United Kingdom, in order to ascertain whether any legislative measures could be devised to prevent the further spread of so great an evil." This committee was composed of thirty-eight members, and included Lord Althorp, then Chancellor of the Exchequer and leader of the House of Commons; Sir Robert Peel, the late Prime Minister of England; Admiral Fleming, of the Royal Navy; Colonel Williams, of the King's Army; Mr. Alexander Baring, the most eminent of British merchants; and representatives of the agricultural, manufacturing, and maritime counties of England, Scotland, and Ireland; so that every interest in the empire was represented in its composition. It extended its daily sittings from the 9th of June to the 28th of July, 1834; in the course of which, no less than fifty-eight witnesses were examined at great length, and these included physicians and surgeons of the greatest eminence, magistrates and officers of justice, ministers of religion and education, officers of the navy, the army, and the mercantile marine, large landed proprietors, opulent merchants, extensive manufacturers, chemists, distillers, keepers of hotels and taverns, and labouring men in several departments of industry. Never, perhaps, in the annals of Parliament, was a committee composed of more eminent or impartial members—never was there a greater variety of witnesses from all classes of society, and all professions in life, carefully examined—and never was there greater unanimity than in the conclusions to which the committee came in the report which they ultimately founded on this evidence, and which was adopted and printed by order of the House of Commons, as well as the large body of evidence itself, forming a folio volume of several hundred pages.

The National Temperance Society continued up to 1850 its metropolitan mission on a smaller scale, and with particular relation to seamen and Sunday schools; maintained a lecturing agency 1847-50; petitioned Parliament and various public bodies; widely circulated copies of two valuable certificates, both originating with John Dunlop, Esq., the first bearing nearly 2000 signatures, comprising those of the chief members of the medical profession, and the second subscribed by 1600 employers, in opposition to compulsory drinking usages; published a prize essay on the best means of advancing the cause; and aided the temperance cause throughout the world.

In July, 1851, the London Temperance League, which has co-operated with the metropolitan societies, instituted a successful series of annual demonstrations and fetes, and procured from the United States the services of Mr. F. W. Kellogg, in 1851-52, and of Mr. J. B. Gough in 1853, whose transcendent capabilities as a temperance advocate began to be developed in America nine years before.

On the 1st of June, 1853, a society was formed at Manchester, called the "United Kingdom Alliance, to procure the total and immediate legislative suppression of the traffic in all intoxicating liquors, as beverages." Letters of adhesion intsantly came pouring in from all quarters, and there was soon a general council of 200, since augmented to above 400 names of leading persons among different denominations of Christians and philanthropists, and including such names as the Earl of Harrington, Sir W. C. Trevelyan, Bart., Sir William A'Becket, Chief Justice of Victoria, Sir W. Lawson, Bart., Lawrence Heyworth, M.P., Rev. Dr. Burns, Rev. Newman Hall, Rev. W. W. Robinson, M.A., Dr. F. R. Lees, Father Eathew, and many other clergymen, dissenting ministers, justices of the peace, aldermen, &c., &c.

The first aggregate meeting of this General Council, for the public inauguration of this Alliance, was held in Manchester, on Wednesday, October 26th, 1853. About 100 members of the council, from various parts of England, Scotland, Ireland, and Wales, assembled. Upwards of 200 members of the Alliance and friends were also present as visitors.

D*

The second aggregate meeting of the General Council was held in Manchester, October 25th, 1854.

WALES.—In Wales, the number of societies and members have increased wonderfully, and much has been accomplished. There are, it is stated, more than two millions teetotallers in the principality; and her churches are rewarded for the decided part they have taken in the glorious work, in the increased number and piety of their members.

GENERAL REMARKS.—In 1836, the Temperance enterprise found its way into Sweden, Prussia, India, New South Wales, and the West Indies. In 1837, into the Sandwich Islands, South Africa, Turkey, New Zealand, and Brazil. In 1838, into Russia, Central Asia, Ceylon, and Australia. The movement was so rapid and simultaneous, that it has been found extremely difficult to chronicle by regular date the numerous societies, all actuated by one grand self-denying principle, and aiming at the same goal— the overthrow of the drinking usages, the reformation of the fallen, and the preservation of future generations from the terrible woes denounced by Holy Writ in the books of Proverbs, Isaiah, and Habbakuk.

CHAPTER IV.

ORIGIN, ETC., OF CERTAIN SOCIETIES.

RECHABITES.—It is difficult to determine the precise period when this Ancient Order was first established; but memorable mention is made of their obedience and fidelity so early as the year of the world 3397, or 607 B. C., on which occasion, that gracious promise was made, "Because ye have obeyed the commandment of Jonadab your father, and kept all his precepts, and done according unto all that he hath commanded you. Therefore thus saith the Lord of Hosts, the God of Israel; Jonadab the son of Rechab shall not want a man to stand before me for ever." Hence you perceive total abstinence is not a modern invention, for here is the fact of a Total Abstinence Society existing at a period of time two thousand five hundred years prior to the organization of modern Temperance Societies, and what is no less strange, the same order with its ancient practice and principles now exists, and which the following extract will substantiate:—

The Rev. Joseph Wolf says:—" On my arrival at Mesopotamia, some Jews that I saw there, pointed me to one of the Ancient Rechabites. He stood before me, wild like an Arab, holding the bridle of his horse in his hand. I shewed him the Bible in Hebrew and Arabic, which he was much rejoiced to see, as he could read both languages, but had no knowledge of the New Testament. After having proclaimed to him the glad tidings of salvation, and made him a present of the Hebrew and Arabic Bibles and Testaments, I asked him 'whose descendant are you'"? 'Mousa,' said he boisterously, 'is my name, and I will show you who are my ancestors;' on which he immediately began to read from the 5th to the 11th verse of Jeremiah xxxv. 'Where do you reside?' said I. Turning to Genesis x. 27, he replied, 'At Hadoram, now called Simiar by the Arabs; at Uzal, now called Sanan by the Arabs;' and again referring to the same chapter, verse 30th, he continued, 'At Mesha, now called Mecca, in the deserts, around those places. We drink no wine, and plant no vineyard, and sow no seed, and live in tents, as Jonadab our father commanded us; Hobab was our father too. Come to us, and you will find us 60,000 in number, and you see thus the prophecy has been fulfilled, ' Therefore, thus saith the Lord of Hosts, the God of Israel, Jonadab, the son of Rechab, shall not want a man to stand before me forever;" and saying this, Mousa, the Rechabite, mounted his horse and fled away, and left behind a host of evidence in favour of sacred writ."

At the commencement of the temperance reformation in the Old Country, attention was given to every thing bearing upon it: hence the discovery that the *drinking usages* were the prolific source of the wide-spread evil under which the land mourned. To supersede associations having a very laudable object in view, but which, from the drinking connected with them, were productive of immense evil, and in numerous instances defeated their own ends, a new Society was projected called the Independent Order of Rechabites. It was in 1835, at Salford, near Manchester, England, that the first modern Rechabite Society was formed. At a subsequent period, namely, August 2, 1842, the American Order was established, and at a still later period, May 27, 1844, the first Tent was opened in Canada in the City of Montreal.

Tent meetings afford frequent opportunities for fraternal intercourse, which are happily adapted to the peculiar circumstances of those who are making laudable efforts to conquer a dangerous habit and a depraved appetite. Here the intellectual and social powers are improved, and the spirit of true friendship is cherished and practised.

As there are equal payments, equal benefits, and equal risks,—the "strong bear, that strength may be given to the weak"—mutual interest strengthens mutual friendship, while the common bond includes all, irrespective of any difference in religion, nation, or politics. No title or degrees are admitted, but all enjoy equal immunities. Money can never place one brother above another in the scale of respectability; and if there be any distinction whatever, it arises from good conduct and gentlemanly deportment alone.—*Address by R. D. Wadsworth, P.C.R.*

EXTRAORDINARY TEMPERANCE REFORMATION OF DRUNKARDS CALLED WASHINGTONIANISM.—This work, the wonder of the age, and almost miraculous in its character, commenced in the city Baltimore, April 5, 1840, with six intemperate men, who were carousing at a tavern. One of their number, Mr. William K. Mitchell, suddenly resolved he would drink no more; went out and wrote the following pledge, which he signed, and which he induced the others to sign :—

"We, whose names are annexed, desirous of forming a society for our mutual benefit, and to guard against a pernicious practice, which is injurious to our health, standing, and families, do pledge ourselves, as gentlemen, that we will not drink any spirituous or malt liquors, wine or cider."

Here was laid the foundation of an institution, the Washington Temperance Society, which was to fill the nation with blessed triumphs. In the early stage of the temperance reformation, between 1826 and 1833, more than 12,000 drunkards reformed—but they only signed the ardent spirit pledge; and, continuing to drink cider, and beer, and wine, great numbers of them went back to drunkenness. The Baltimore reformers commenced with total abstinence from all intoxicating liquors. This they saw to be the only true principle of reform. They invited many of their old bottle companions to join them. Each man made it a business to bring a man to their weekly meetings. They soon increased in number—many hopeless drunkards became suddenly sober men. In their meetings they related their experience; told their awful history; the horrors of drunkenness, and their happy exchange. Their meetings attracted attention. Sure as a drunkard came to listen—he was a convert—signed the pledge, and became an active and efficient member. And in less than one year, there were in Baltimore city more than 1000 reformed drunkards.

COLD WATER ARMY.—As early as 1841, the attention of the zealous friends of Temperance was turned to the dangers of the youth, and the desirableness of organizing them into juvenile associations. The popular name of "Cold Water Army" was adopted in the State of Massachusetts—40,000 were enrolled. In Connecticut and New Jersey they spread through the agency of Rev. C. J. Warren and T. B. Segur. In Sunday schools all over the States, they became generally introduced.

The first in Canada at Montreal was established August 1842, by Mr. Wadsworth; five years afterwards it numbered 5000; after spreading throughout the Province and into adjoining sections, the interest declined, and they have given place to other better organized and more efficient societies.

SONS OF TEMPERANCE.—On Thursday evening, the 29th of September, 1842, a meeting was convened in Teetotaler's Hall, 71 Division Street, New York, consisting of sixteen persons (all Washingtonians), to whom was submitted a Constitution: Daniel H. Sands was chairman, and John W. Oliver, secretary. The following was unanimously adopted:—

"*Resolved*, That we now form a Society, to be called New York Division, No. 1, Sons of Temperance."

At the second meeting, Oct. 7, the following were elected officers:

Daniel H. Sands, *Patriarch.*
Ephraim L. Snow, *Associate.*
John W. Oliver, *Recording Scribe.*
James Bale, *Financial Scribe.*
George M'Kibben, *Treasurer.*
Thomas Edgerley, *Conductor.*
Thomas Swenerton, *Sentinel.*

At this meeting, sixteen persons were proposed. The Infant Order had no A. R. S., A. C., or O. S. The titular prefix of "Worthy" was applied by consent for the sake of euphony, and subsequently adopted. At the next meeting, the Committee on Initiation reported in favor of a form, and submitted an outline which was unanimously approved. Under this form, one of the brothers was first initiated, who, in turn, initiated the remainder. This was the origin of the B. B. or Blue Book—the book of ceremonies. Regalia were adopted very similar to the present; a decision made not to receive any other organized body into this association; and it was resolved to afford mutual assistance in case of sickness.

The first Grand Division of the Order was organized in New York, December 10, 1842. The first Grand Officers were:—

Daniel H. Sands, *G. W. P.*
E. L. Snow, *G. W. A.*
John W. Oliver, *G. W. S.*
James Bale, *G. W. T.*
Evan Griffith, *G. Chaplain.*
Thomas Edgerley, *G. W. C.*
F. E. Wolfe, *G. Sentinel.*

June 17, 1844—in this session the Order assumed the name of "The National Division of Sons of Temperance of the United States"; and on May 15, 1849, at the suggestion of M. W. P. Carey, "to meet its extension in the British Provinces of North America," a change of style was unanimously agreed to, and the National Body became the "National Division of Sons of Temperance of North America."

There were now 35 Grand Divisions, 4398 Subordinate Divisions, and 221,000 members. The organization was now perfected to Grand Divisions in every State of the Union, and four of the British Provinces. Of late years, the success of the Order has varied—*its principles never.* It takes high ground on the abstinence principle, as relates to individual *use* and the *Traffic.*

Officers of the National Division:—

M. W. P., B. D. Townsend, Bennettsville, S. Carolina.
M. W. A., E. W. Jackson, Gorham, Maine.
M. W. S., Frederick A. Fickardt, Bethlehem, Penn.
M. W. T., Robert M. Foust, Philadelphia, Penn.
M. W. Con., John Moffat, Hamilton, Canada West.
M. W. Chap., John Leach, Thorntown, Indiana.
M. W. Sen., S. A. Duke, Keokuk, Iowa.

Order of Sons of Temperance in Canada, East and West.— Lower Canada.—In 1846, Philip S. White visited Montreal, and during his stay a Division of the Sons of Temperance was formed, called Montreal Division, which continued working for a short time. Mr. White again visited Montreal in the fall of 1849, when the subject of instituting a Division of the Sons of Temperance was once more mooted, and in consequence a Division was successfully formed in March, 1850, under the title of Howard Division, No. 1, which is still in successful operation. Brother J. C. Becket was at this time named D. M. W. P. for Canada East, with power to grant charters, &c. Shortly after the formation of Howard Division, Gough Division, Quebec, was instituted, receiving its charter through D. W. M. P. Becket.

Then followed St. Andrew's Division, St. Andrews; Victoria Division, Lachute; Lancaster Division, Lancaster; Jonadab Division, Montreal; and Lochaber Division, Lochaber.

In the fall of 1851, it having been considered of the highest importance to the consolidation and spread of the Order, that a Grand Division should be formed for Canada East, an application was made to the National Division for a charter. A charter was accordingly granted, dated 17th November, 1851, and a Grand Division for Canada East was organised on 7th January, 1852. Several Divisions located in C. E., but deriving their charters from Grand Divisions in C. W., as well as several located in C. W., but lying contiguous to C. E., having expressed a desire of joining, and being placed under the jurisdiction of, the G. D. of C. E., an application was made to the G. D. of C. W., for its consent to those Divisions separating themselves from the jurisdiction of said G. D., and joining that of Canada East, which was granted in so far as regarded Divisions located in C. E., but refused as to those located in C. W. By this means seven additional Divisions were added to the jurisdiction of Canada East.

The following is a list of G. W. P.'s and G. S.'s from the formation of the Grand Division to the present time:—

Jan. to Oct. 1852,	John C. Becket, G.W.P.		C. P. Watson, H. Rose, G.S.	
Oct. 1852–3,	Robert Kneeshaw,	,,	Henry Rose,	,,
1853 4,	Archd. M'Eachem,	,,	John S. Hall,	,,
1854–5,	George Matheson,	,,	Henry Rose,	,,
1855–6,	Joseph B. Cleff,	,,	,,	,,
1856–7,	John S. Hall,	,,	,,	,,
1857–8,	A. Smeaton,	,,	,,	,,
1858–9,	T. C. Haynes,	,,	,,	,,
1859–60,	Henry Rose,	,,	John S. Hall,	,,

Present Statistics :—In the last Annual Report, the G. W. P. says :—" Let us be encouraged : vast changes have taken place in social, political, and civil economy within the past half century, and we may as safely predict, if not as great improvements in the progress and triumph of inventive genius and research, at least a greater advancement of the moral condition of mankind. The next half century will be an age of reform and revolution in the moral and intellectual relations of the mind of the people. And a Temperance Millenium will be one of the blessings of the times. That it may not be always an expectation, but a reality is most devoutly to be wished, and most zealously to be labored for."

The Grand Secretary says:—" I am glad to be able to state, that the Order throughout our jurisdiction is in as good a position as it ever has been, and its prospects for the future of a far more cheering and encouraging kind than any in my experience. In the Eastern Townships, where only a year or two ago, we had not a single Division, there are now six or seven, and within the last week, one Charter has been issued and another Division formed, and the prospect before us is, that before another annual session, your Grand Scribe will have to report the existence of as many more. The following is a synopsis of returns for quarter ending June 30, from 20 Divisions:—Members Admitted, 206; Total Number of Members, 793; Temperance meetings held, 32; Number Withdrawn, 35; Representatives to Grand Division, 52. Cash Received, $304.99; Paid for Benefits, $31.50; Cash on Hand, including money invested, $1595.26; Total Expenses for the Quarter, exclusive of benefits, $255.42; Per Capita Tax to Grand Division, $54.97."

Upper Canada.—On the 21st day of June, 1848, the banner of the Order of Sons of Temperance was first unfurled in Canada West by George Boyd, D. M. W. P., in the Town of Brockville, upon which was inscribed in golden letters, " Love, Purity, and Fidelity." The little band only numbered 18, but it continued to receive recruits, until on the 19th of January, 1850, the whole number in the Order was nearly 2000.

The application for charter to open a Grand Division, 12th April, 1849, was signed by the following W. P.'s, and P. W. P.'s: Wm. Dick, C. Leggo, W. H. Ellerbeck, R. Dick, Wm. Boyle,

E

J. P. Sutton, T. O. Butler, J. Creighton, A. B. Pardee, J. M. Haskins, H. Williams, A. Parish, R. Coleman, J. Coleman, and J. L. Macdonald, representing Brockville, Frontenac, North Augusta, Farmersville, Coleman's Corners, and Gananoque Divisions. The brother who instituted was P. S. White, Esq.

The Pioneer D. G. W. P.'s were R. Dick, A. B. Pardee, T. O. Butler, E. Stacey, R. Boyd, J. R. Wright, John Kilborn, F. G. Callender, G. V. N. Rollyea, Wm. Smart, John F. Wilson, W. S. Burnham, R. D. Wadsworth, John Williams, John Andrews, H. Whitney, J. A. Spencer, &c., &c.

The following Table will show the growing state of the Order, and keep in remembrance those Brothers who have been honored with filling the two most important offices. Wm. Boyle was the first G. W. P., and W. H. Ellerbeck the first G. W. S. Six Subordinate Divisions—268 members :—

AN. SESS.	G. W. P.'s	G. SCRIBES.	PLACE.	S. D.	MEM.	F. V.
Oct. 10, '49.	John L. Macdonald.	W. H. Ellerbeck.	Brockville.	24	1,032	
24, '50.	Wm. S. Burnham.	"	"	176	12,000	
22, '51.	A. B. Pardee.	H. W. Jackson.	"	330	15,353	
27, '52.	W. H. Ellerbeck.	"	Oshawa.	385	17,827	
26, '53.	Rev. J. E. Ryerson.	Edwd. Stacey.	Kingston.	315	12,000	
25, '54.	J. A. R. O'Reilly.	"	Bytown.	353	11,260	
24, '55.	John Beatty, M.D.,	"	Toronto.	353	10,270	
22, '56.	Rev. T. Short, D.D.	"	Whitby.	359	10,065	
Dec. 2, '57.	John Beatty, M.D.	"	Port Hope.	331	10,864	2,862
1, '58.	A. Farewell.	"	London.	339	8,839	3,616
7, '59.	John Wilson.	"	N'market.	314	9,416	3,556

The late Annual Report of this body is very encouraging: from the G. W. P. we learn :—

"There are in connection with the National Division, as last reported, 41 Grand Divisions, numbering 1985 Subordinates. Average number to each Grand Division, 41. Canada West stands first on the list, and has 335.

"The number of members admitted to all the Subordinate Divisions during the last year, is 37,987; average to each Grand Division, 926. Canada West stands second on the list, and admitted 4018 new members. Total number of contributing members connected with the National Division, 76,422; average to each Grand Division, 1864. Canada stands first on the list, and numbers 10,479. Total number of Females connected with the Order, 23,988; average to each Grand Division, 588. Canada West stands second on the list, and numbers 3468.

"In the number of Temperance Meetings held, and Tracts distributed, Canada West is far ahead of any other Grand Division. Of the former, you number 879; of the latter, 12,676. These data are sufficient to show the important position you occupy in the National Councils of this, the great philanthropic movement of the 19th century.

"I can also congratulate you upon the present state and future prospects of the Order within the jurisdiction of this Grand Division. Though our numbers have not materially increased since the Semi-Annual Session, yet the peace and tranquillity pervading the brotherhood, the activity and energy of very many Subordinate Divisions, and the healthy tone of public opinion upon the question of Prohibition, are cheering indications that seed has been sown in good ground, and that, ere long, we may look for a bountiful harvest.

"During the past Summer and Autumn, numerous public Temperance Demonstrations have taken place, attended in nearly every instance with gratifying success. A considerable number of Deputies refer, in their communications, to those Soirees with much satisfaction. In many places loud calls are made for Lecturers during the approaching Winter. Not a few Divisions desire again to petition the Legislature in favour of Prohibition, and many Deputies bear testimony to the great good attending the admission to the Division of Lady Visitors."

From the Report of the G. S., we have the statistics:—

"The following is an abstract of the Quarterly Returns received from 249 Divisions, for the Quarter ending June 1859:—Number of Subordinate Divisions made returns, 249; admitted New Members, 837; by Card, 40; Female Visitors, 3658; Withdrawn, 231; Deaths, 8; Contributing Members, computed from 249 Divisions which made returns, 9719; Public Meetings held, 170; Temperance Tracts distributed, 330; Representatives to Grand Division, 596; Representatives to National Division, 11. Cash received by Subordinate Divisions, £744, 14s. 6d.; Paid for Benefits, £33, 2s. 9d.; Cash on Hand, including money invested in Subordinate Divisions, £4757, 2s. 8d.; Total Expenses, exclusive of benefits, £574, 8s. 5d.; Per Capita Tax to Grand Division, £75, 0s. 4d.

"The above statistics are collected from actual Returns received from 249 Divisions, and if compared with the preceding March Quarter, as reported last Session, will be found to show a gain both in numbers of contributing members and female visitors.

"During the past year, thirty-three Divisions have been added to the list, and it must be gratifying to know that those Divisions have already made rapid progress in our truly benevolent and philanthropic enterprize.

"Twenty-six sections of Cadets of Temperance have been organized since the Annual Session, and the progress of this Juvenile Order, although not rapid, is advancing favourably, and wil receive fresh impetus when the amendments contemplated by your Committee are perfected."

The following are the Officers of the Grand Division Sons of Temperance in Canada West for the current 1859-60 :—

John Wilson, Grafton, *G. W. P.*
J. Breakenridge, Brockville, *G. W. A.*
E. Stacey, Kingston, *G. S.*
S. W. Sherrard, Brougham, *G. T.*
Rev. J. M'Killican, Martintown, *G. Chaplain*
S. Roadhouse, Newmarket, *G. C.*
E. Carswell, Oshawa, *G. S.*
A. Farewell, Oshawa, *P. G. W. P.*

Female Visitors were first admitted to Divisions, June 1854—at the age of 16—do not vote—but take part in various ways, and may be invited to speak, read essays, or otherwise contribute to the improvement and elevation of the members. The number of Lady Visitors is rapidly increasing; and this concession on the part of the National Division has done much to check the retrogression of our cause in sundry places. United we stand, divided we fall.

THE TEMPLE OF HONOR.—The Temple of Honor was brought into existence by prominent Sons of Temperance, and designed by them for a branch of their own Order;—the object being to strengthen the fraternal relations of the brotherhood; to afford additional benefits, without uniting with other organizations where total abstinence was not regarded as a fundamental principle; and to render the beneficial system progressive in moral and intellectual improvement.

The first Temple was organized in New York city, Dec. 5, 1845—the first Grand Temple, (that of New York) Feb. 21, 1846. On the 6th of November, 1846, a National Temple was organized.

Not very long after, the separation of the two bodies took place, and after suffering from various causes, so strong was the attachment of the brethren to the Temple of Honor, that they patiently endured all. A new Ritual was prepared, new life was infused into the Order, suspended Temples were revived, the membership increased, so that in 1854, there were 13 Grand Temples, 292 Temples, and 9234 members, officers, &c.

Officers of the Supreme Council :—

M. W. T., Rev. J. Boynton, Hastings, Barry Co., Mich.
M. W. V. T., B. C. Hyatt, Monticello, Drew Co., Ark.
M. W. R., J. Wadsworth, Cincinnati, Ohio.
M. W. Treas., Alex. Van Hamm, Cincinnati, Ohio.
M. W. Chap., James Davison, Covington, Kentucky.
M. W. U., George F. Turner, Philadelphia, Pa.
M. W. G., S. P. Ohr, Carrolton, Green Co., Illinois.

E*

DAUGHTERS OF TEMPERANCE.—The Order of the Sons of Temperance had been established for some months, and its good effects observed by certain ladies in the city of New York. The idea suggested itself, that possibly, similar results might follow were the females interested in a like association. Accordingly, on 21st October, 1843, with the assistance of several of the *Sons*, a number of ladies were organized into a *Union* of the Daughters of Temperance, dedicating it to the work of promoting and diffusing among the female portion of the community, the sentiments of virtue, love, and temperance. The features of their constitution and by-laws are very much the same as those of the Sons of Temperance. Their pledge is total abstinence—they admit no one who has not a good moral character—the benefit scheme is added. They have only a password which is necessary to be kept secret.

This Order was introduced into Canada, and worked efficiently for many years, but is now almost entirely superseded by the Good Templars, a large majority of the Daughters having joined that Order.

JUVENILE SISTERS OF TEMPERANCE.—Answering to the Cadets, this Order is designed to complete the chain of Temperance Organizations. As yet, it does not boast of many *Assemblies*, as the several little societies are denominated. The effects of the institution on the minds of the young girls who are members, is salutary. The regalia worn is a blue girdle. Their motto is, "Truth, Virtue, Honor." They declare that they believe Intemperance to be an injury to mankind, and a wickedness in the sight of God; that they regard a good example as often powerful to save and bless; and that they are desirous of shielding brothers, parents, sisters, and themselves, from the terrible evils of intemperance.

CADETS.—As early as 1850, this organization was set on foot, and for some years conducted prosperously, but from various causes declined, till it almost ceased to exist in Canada. It has, however, been revived again (June, 1859), and is now in full operation. The statistics we are not prepared to give.

RISE OF THE INDEPENDANT ORDER OF GOOD TEMPLARS.

The Independant Order of Good Templars originated in Central New York in the year 1851. L. E. Coon, Esq., was the first G. W. C. T. In August, 1852, Nathaniel Curtis, Esq., was placed at the head of the Order as G. W. C. T. By the month of December following, at the Annual Meeting, the number of representatives was quite respectable, and the Order began to present an imposing front. At Ithaca, N. Y., in Dec. 1853, the Order took the name of the Grand Lodge of North America— D. W. Bristol, G. W. C. T., and H. P. Barnes, G. S. In 1854, the Grand Lodges of Pennsylvania, Canada West, Iowa, and Ohio, were organized. At the close of the year, there were about 800 Subordinate Lodges, 5 Grand Lodges, and over 25,000 members. At Corning, in December of this year, N. W. Davis was elected, and the R. W. G. L. of N. A. was organized partially, but more fully at Cleveland, Ohio, May 16th, 1855. The officers were as follows:—

    James W. Moore, R. W. G. T., Louisville, Ky.
    Dr. W. J. A. Case, R. W. G. C., Hamilton, Canada.
    O. W. Strong, R. W. V. T., Chicago, Ill.
    S. Steele, R. W. G. T., Marshall, Mich.
    M. C. Ruckman, R. W. G. S., Mansfield, Pa.
    G. Taylor, R. W. G. Chap., Romeo, Mich.
    B. H. Mills, R. W. G. M., St. Louis, Mo.
    A. Stone, R. W. G. D. M., Winchester, Ind.
    H. Hoover, R. W. G. I. G, Alliance, O.
    W G. Fearis, R. W. G. O. S., Washington, Ia.
    N. W. Davis, R. W. P. G. T., Oswego, N. Y.

Other Temperance Orders discriminate as to age and sex in making up their membership; but none manifests greater liberality than this. Into this Order both sexes are admitted as early as 14 years of age. The ladies have a vote, and are eligible to office; their ever-refining and elevating influence is felt with decided advantage. As the basis of the Order is laid in the great moral principles inculcated by our Heavenly Father in his Holy Word, it was thought advisable to unfold their bearings by "degrees," so as to give the greatest possible impressiveness to the instruction which they are designed to impart. Tests also have been adopted for protection against imposition. The rapid spread of this noble institution, is evident from the fact, that the number of Grand Lodges has steadily increased:—1856, 11; 1857, 14; 1858, 15; 1859, 18, with a membership of 70,000.

Officers of the R. W. Grand Temple:—

R. G. C. T., Simeon B. Chase, Great Bend, Pennsylvania.
R. G. C., Julius A. Spencer, Cleveland, Ohio.
R. G. V. T., Amanda M. Way, Winchester, Indiana.
R. G. S., W. A. Ferguson, Hamilton, Canada West.
R. G. T., Jonathan H. Orne, Marblehead, Massachusetts.
R. G. Chaplain, Rev. J. W. Pender, Holley Springs, Miss.
R. G. M., J. N. Stoddard, Joliet, Illinois.
R. G. I. G., A. G. Skipwith, Nashville, Tennessee.
R. G. A. M., George W. McCrary, Keokuk, Iowa.
R. G. O. G., John Evans, Bellevue, Michigan.

Independant Order of Good Templars in Canada.—In Canada, the I. O. G. T. was organized 28th Oct., 1853, at Merrickville, by Nathaniel Curtis, D. G. W. C. T.—named Harmony, No. 1. The Grand Lodge (now styled Grand Temple) was instituted at Hamilton, on Nov. 21st, 1854, by H. P. Barnes, R. W. G. S.; at this date there were 54 Sub-Lodges, and 1500 members.

The progress of this Order in Canada West is very encouraging, as the following statistics will show:—

An. Sess.	S. L.	Members.	Grand Officers.
Niagara, Oct. 16, '55.	97	4,668 { 3162 / 1506 }	Dr. W. J. A. Case, G.W.C.T., and J. W. Stone, G.W.S.
Hamilton, Oct. 15, '56.	138	6,183 { 4084 / 2099 }	Dr. J. M. VanNorman, do., and J. W. Stone, do.
Brockville, Nov. 25, '57.	148	10,470 { 6780 / 3690 }	Dr. J. M. VanNorman, do., and W. A. Ferguson, do.
London, Oct. 6, '58.	242	13,877 { 8999 / 4878 }	David Abel, Esq., do., and W. A. Ferguson, do.
Peterboro, Oct. 4, '59.	350	18,672 { 12,149 / 6,523 }	Dr. J. W. Ferguson, and W. A. Ferguson, do.

The following is the "Platform" adopted by the Grand Lodge of Canada, embodying their views on Prohibition:—

"1st. Total abstinence from all intoxicating liquors as a beverage.

"2nd. No license in any form, or under any circumstances, for the sale of such liquors to be used as a beverage.

"3rd. The *absolute prohibition* of the manufacture, importation, and sale of intoxicating liquors for such purposes—prohibition by the will of the people expressed in due form of law, with the penalties deserved for a crime of such enormity.

"4th. The creation of a healthy public opinion upon the subject, by the active dissemination of truth in all the modes known an enlightened philanthropy.

"5th. The election of good, honest men, to administer the laws.

"6th. Persistence in efforts to save individuals and communities from so direful a scourge, against all forms of opposition and difficulty, until our success is complete and universal."

The peculiar advantages of this Order we give from a Circular lately issued—(we believe the remarks which follow will generally apply to the "Sons" also):—

"The Grand Lodge of Canada is composed of P. W. C. T.'s, W. C. T.'s, and ladies who have served as W. V. T. one full term or more, who are contributing members of Lodges subordinate to this Grand Lodge, and who have been admitted constitutionally.

"Every Subordinate Lodge is entitled to one Representative for 50 members or less, (to be styled Regular Representative,) and one for every additional 50, to be elected for one year, (in the month of August.) And every Subordinate Lodge has the right to elect a Proxy Representative for the same term. Their expenses to be borne by each Subordinate Lodge. These Representatives, with the Grand Officers, make our laws, and are responsible for all decisions of Grand Lodge; hence the importance of every Subordinate Lodge sending a Representative to Grand Lodge Sessions, and that Representative faithfully attending to the business which may pass before him.

"In Subordinate Lodges, all the Offices are open to every member who possesses the necessary qualification, without exception.

"Thus it may be easily seen that the ordinary Member of the remotest Subordinate Lodge may rise to the highest post of honor in the R. W. G. T. All who have filled, or that will ever fill, the Chair of R. W. G. T., must once have occupied the lowest position among the members of this truly Independent and Honorable Order.

"The Revenue of the R. W. G. T. is derived from G. L. Charter Fees; dues from G. L. at the rate of $30 per annum for each Representative, (consequently our Grand Lodge dues are $90); proceeds of sale of Books, Cards, Diplomas, Odes, and Certificates. The Disbursements are for salary of R. W. G. S., travelling expenses of Representatives, Printing Proceedings, Rituals, &c. If it be asked what pecuniary advantages do we derive from our connection with the R. W. G. T., it may be answered: 1. We get our books, &c., for half the price it would cost to print sufficient number for our use. 2. We have actually drawn from its funds $36 more for expenses of Representatives than the amount of our tax; since organization, our tax only being one half-cent per member.

"The Revenue of our own Grand Lodge is derived from Subordinate Lodge Charter fees, sale of Rituals, Odes, Cards and Blanks and Assessment, said Assessment being fixed at the Annual Session by the Finance Committee. The $9 charged for Charter Fee, &c., is applied as follows: $4 to Deputy, and remaining $5 for Charter, 3 Rituals, 3 Degree Books, 22 Odes, 3 Officers' Cards, Treasurer's Bonds and Return Sheets. It will be perceived at once that the charges are reasonable. The Disbursements are expenses of the Grand Officers attending Session of Grand Lodge, salary of G. W. S., dues to R. W. G. L., Printing Proceedings, Charges, Cards, &c., and incidental expenses, such as Postage, Express Charges, &c.

"Each Subordinate Lodge having a place and vote in the Grand Lodge by its regular Representatives, or proxy, can always guard its own rights: and so also the Grand Lodge of Canada, through its three Representatives in the R. W. G. T., watches over the general interests of our whole Order in this Province. We cannot suppose, therefore, that there is the slightest ground for suspicion or want of confidence in the financial disposition of the affairs of this extensive organization; but, on the contrary, the most satisfactory evidence is afforded to call forth the hearty co-operation of Subordinate Lodges to uphold the Grand Lodge, and the G. L. in its turn to sustain the R. W. G. T. At the last Annual Meeting of R. W. G. T., we had 12,000 members, being 2000 over any other Grand Lodge, and only paid the same amount of tax as Ohio Grand Lodge, with 6000 membership.

"In such matters, it would be easy to show that the I. O. of G. T. in Canada will compare favourably with other bodies similarly constituted.

"The advantage to members travelling ought not to be overlooked. This Order has not less than 15 Grand Lodges, and Subordinate Lodges dotting North America from Canada to Mississippi, and from New York to California. Wherever our members go, a ready home greets them, and ready blessings attend them."

The present Officers of the Grand Temple of Canada are as follows:—

Dr. J. W. Ferguson, Woodstock, G. W. C. T.
Mrs. Ellen Michell, Pickering, G. W. C.
J. W. Gifford, Orono, G. W. V. T.
W. A. Ferguson, Hamilton, G. W. S.
R. D. Wadsworth, Hamilton, G. W. T.
James Adams, Embro, G. W. Chaplain.
H. H. Stovel, Mount Forest, G. W. M.
Mrs. M. A. Heather, Peterboro', G. W. D. M.
W. Johnston, Peterboro', G. W. I. G.
H. C. Crain, Augusta, G. W. O. G.

State of the Order in Canada.—" In presenting to you my Report, as Secretary, permit me to congratulate you on the prosperity of our noble Order. A prosperity under the peculiar difficulties in which we were placed nearly a year ago, beyond our most sanguine expectations, and to me, clearly demonstrates that our principles are just, and must triumph. There has been 110 Temples organized during the year. Total number of Temples, 350, 26 of which made no returns since February, but no doubt will do so very soon. You will perceive that our increase has been gradual. We number: males, 12,149; females, 6526; initiated during the year, 7100; violated pledge, 600; restored, 200; expelled for violation, 400; expelled for non-payment of dues, 1600; withdrawn by card, 480; admitted by card, 213; withdrawn from the Order, 480. Total number of members, 18,672.—Peterboro', C. W., Oct. 4, 1859."

BANDS OF HOPE.—Bands of Hope are simply juvenile temperance societies, formed for the purpose of promoting the early training of the young in the practice of total abstinence from all intoxicating drinks, tobacco, and profanity. Now perhaps some will ask why they are called Bands of Hope? I will tell you. A few years ago, Mrs. Carlisle, a warm-hearted and benevolent Irish lady, who had visited prisons much with the celebrated Elizabeth Fry, and who saw that intemperance sent a large proportion of the inmates to prison, asked if something could not be done to prevent the young from becoming intemperate? She said, " Let us form the boys and girls into juvenile temperance societies." "What name shall we give these societies?" inquired a friend. " Why, as our hope is in the young, and we wish to band them together, suppose we call them Bands of Hope?" replied Mrs. Carlisle.

I will give you a brief account of the formation of the first one ever formed. One Monday night, about a dozen years ago, seven little Sunday School scholars were assembled around their teacher in a small room in one of the ancient cities of England. The teacher had witnessed the sorrows caused in many families through intoxicating liquors. He had heard of Mrs. Carlisle's suggestion, and felt desirous that scholars should not only be trained up in the practice of total abstinence, but that they should also be induced to sympathize with and seek to reclaim the poor drunkards who abounded in that city.

The object of the meeting was one upon which the teacher felt God's blessing could be solicited, and therefore, after reading a portion of Scripture, the little group knelt down, and prayer was offered that He who seeth in secret, and rewardeth openly, would graciously smile upon this feeble effort to do good. Several temperance songs were then sung, after which the teacher endeavored to bring before his youthful audience, the evils of intemperance, that the prisons are crowded with those who are sent there from the results of liquor, and that drunkenness is the most fertile source of crime. After addressing them a short time, and reading several short and interesting pieces upon temperance, they closed the meeting with singing.

The seven members soon increased to 21, and the 21 to 100. Several warm-hearted Sunday School teachers readily came forward to lend their aid to the hopeful movement.

Band of Hope Constitution.—Art. 1. This Association shall be called the "Band of Hope."

Art. 2. The object of the Association is to encourage the young to abstain from Intoxicating Liquors, Tobacco, and Profanity, and those who sign the Constitution agree thus to abstain.

Art. 3. The officers shall consist of a President, three Vice-Presidents, a Secretary, and Treasurer, who shall hold office for three months. The officers may be either males or females.

Art. 4. Any one may join this Band of Hope, by signing the Constitution and Pledge, and paying ——— cents into the treasury.

F

Art. 5. Adults may become honorary members by paying not less than 25 cents into the treasury, if proposed by a member of the Band.

Art. 6. The meetings shall be held at such time and place as the Officers shall direct, and shall be opened with the reading of Scripture or prayer.

Art. 7. The general management of this Band of Hope shall be under the control of a Superintendent.

Art. 8. The following Pledge shall be used, and the members shall repeat it in concert at each meeting:—

PLEDGE.

I hereby solemnly pledge myself to abstain from the use of all Intoxicating Liquors as a beverage, from the use of Tobacco, and from all Profanity.

Art. 9. This Constitution may be altered at any regular meeting, by a vote of two-thirds of the members present.

I. O. G. T. Constitution of Bands of Hope.—1. This Association shall be called the ——————— Band of Hope.

2. The object of this Band of Hope is to aid and encourage the young of both sexes to abstain from the use of Intoxicating Liquors, Tobacco, Profane and Obscene Language; and those who sign this Constitution, pledge themselves thus to abstain.

3. Any person may become a member of this Band of Hope who is not over fourteen years of age, on being proposed by a member, and duly elected by a show of hands, and by paying the sum of Ten Cents into the treasury.

4. The regular dues of this Band of Hope shall be Two Cents per month. If, however, it is found that the current expenses of the Band do not require so much, the dues may, at any regular meeting, be lowered or entirely abolished.

5. The Officers of this Band shall consist of not less than two Superintendents, chosen from the Temple, and a President, Vice-President, Secretary, Treasurer, and Door Keeper, who shall be elected once in three months. If thought proper, the Band may at the same time elect Monitors.

6. The duty of the Superintendents is to see that the meeting is opened and closed at the regular hours; to commence the meeting with reading of the Scriptures and Prayer; and to maintain order during the proceedings.

The duty of the President is to preside over the meetings; put all motions and declare the result; see that all the Officers attend to their duties; give the casting vote in case of a tie; and maintain order and decorum.

The duty of the Vice-President is to act in the absence of the President.

The duties of the Secretary are to keep a proper minute of the proceedings of each meeting; receive all money and pay it over to the Treasurer; and perform all other offices generally devolving upon Secretaries.

The Treasurer shall receive all money from the Secretary, to whom he shall give receipts for the same, and pay them over as he may be directed by vote of the Band.

The duty of the Door Keeper is to see that no children are admitted who are not members or about to become such, and also to prevent any improper running in and out of the members during the meeting.

When Monitors are appointed, it shall be their duty to take charge each of one bench or seat, and see that those seated thereon pay proper attention and act with propriety.

7. Any of the Officers may be either a Boy or Girl.

8. The meeting shall be held at such time and place, and as often, as the Superintendents, or a vote of the Temple, may direct. The meetings should never be later than six o'clock P.M. in winter, and seven P.M. in summer, and whenever practicable a still earlier hour should be chosen.

9. The following pledge shall be used, and the members shall repeat it aloud in concert at each meeting:—"I hereby solemnly pledge myself to abstain from the use of all Intoxicating Liquors, from the use of Tobacco, and from Profane and Obscene Language."

10. If any member is accused of violating his or her pledge, the case shall be heard before the whole Band; and if the accused is found guilty, he or she shall be reprimanded by the Superintendents for the first or second offence, while for the third the offender shall be expelled.

11. In all cases when practicable, a portion of the time of each meeting—which shall not exceed one hour and a half—shall be devoted to the recitation of Temperance pieces, dialogues, or to extempore speeches by the members. The members to discharge these duties shall be nominated the preceding meeting. Singing Temperance melodies at intervals during the service, shall be in order.

12. Each member shall be furnished with a copy of this Constitution on the evening of his or her election. If this copy should be lost, or another one required, it may be purchased for one cent. of the Secretary.

13. Adults may become members of this Band of Hope by a vote of the meeting, on the payment of 25 cents.

14. Any member of this Band of Hope, who is fourteen years of age, and has been a member for one year, may be admitted to the Temple, the Band paying the usual entrance fee.

15. A roll containing the pledge, with the members' names and ages, shall be kept by the Secretary, and if requisite, it shall be mounted on a roller, in order to be properly preserved.

16. This Constitution can only be altered or amended by the Grand Temple of Canada, at its Annual or Semi-Annual Session.

What is Wanted to be Done.—Teach them to sing abstinence melodies—to recite abstinence pieces—to read abstinence books—to take abstinence papers—to tell abstinence stories—to study what the Bible says in favor of abstinence, and against drinking and drunkards—to pray for abstinence—to pray for the drunkard and his poor suffering children. Tell them what drink has done, is doing, and will do. Warn them—oh! warn them—not to enter a liquor shop: create in them a hatred of drink and everything connected with it, and continue to do so, and in due season you will reap, if you faint not.

Provide innocent recreation at home—let the Band of Hope provide innocent recreation abroad, and train the young in it so that holidays may be appropriately spent, and leisure hours healthfully, joyfully employed.

Let there be a weekly meeting of the children, under the superintendence of some adult male or female who sympathizes with children, at an early hour on a week-day afternoon, to last an hour. Begin by singing, then prayer. Even children can open such meetings by repeating the Lord's prayer. Then let the exercises be diversified by a passage of Scripture in favor of abstinence, and one against drink or drunkenness, repeated in concert. Pieces spoken, and hymns or melodies sung, alternately—no piece to exceed three or five minutes. Let there be ten minutes for an address by an adult friend; and when the hour has been thus employed, close by the doxology. Then take the names of the new members; and so proceed week after week.

The children make the best agents for bringing in their companions to meeting—for instructing them in their meetings—for retaining them in attendance on their meetings—for getting them to sign and keep the pledge. Engage the children in the work: you will find them the most numerous, most zealous, most permanent, most successful, labourers in the cause.

THE DASHAWAYS.—A new Temperance Order has been established in California, which promises to be very successful. The members are designated "Dashaways," because they dash the liquor away. Their pledge, however, is to abstain only for six or twelve months, as may be agreed upon; but the probationary period will no doubt with multitudes be the forerunner of the life pledge. The inspiration of this new Order has already crossed the Rocky Mountains, and been received with favour in Missouri, there having been a "Dashaway Club" formed in St. Louis. In

California, the Society commenced with five firemen, and it has spread with great rapidity. The members in San Francisco now number over 1400; they opened a "Home for Inebriates," hired a superintendent, nurse, and physician, and then gathered in many of the most notorious drunkards in the city, in the hope of saving them.—1859.

TEMPERANCE SOCIETY AMONG THE INDIANS.—Some of the Indians on Lake Superior have formed a Temperance Society. The occasion of this was as follows:—A large number of them had collected a considerable amount of money in small sums, which they entrusted to the keeping of a chief in whom they had implicit confidence. This dignitary was not infallible, and one day went on a spree and spent it all. The red man had an indignation meeting over it, and after a most emphatic series of grunts, formed a self-protective association, based on fundamental principles—that is to say, the first Indian who got drunk was to be tied to a stump and whipped with twenty-five lashes.—*Montreal Paper, Nov.* 1859.

PART SECOND.

THE TEETOTALER'S HAND-BOOK.

CHAPTER I.

PROHIBITION.

The Constitutionality of a Prohibitory Law—The evil of Selling Intoxicating Drinks—Mr. Doty's License to Sell Rum!—The Moral Right to Drink and Sell Spirituous Liquors.

THE CONSTITUTIONALITY OF A PROHIBITORY LAW: SOCIETY HAS A RIGHT TO PROTECT ITSELF.—As this principle is interpreted by society, it extends to everything which would affect good order, its safety, its prosperity, its existence:—a protection of society extended *in behalf* of all that would promote its welfare; a protection against all that would injure, endanger, or destroy it. It is a protection extended to the peaceful pursuits of industry; to the person and reputation of individuals; to all that contributes to good morals and order; to the rights of conscience; to life, liberty, and the pursuit of happiness. It is a protection of the community against all that would invade it by force and arms; against all that would corrupt and weaken it; against all that would undermine the public morals; against all vices, as Blackstone specifies, which are of a public nature, and which tend by example to be of pernicious effects in society.

On these principles of self-protection, society legislates against lotteries, against gaming, against counterfeiting the public coin, against drunkenness, against profaneness, against poisonous and corrupted drugs, against any employment that in its nature tends to endanger the public health, peace, or morals. No man, on this principle, is allowed to set up and prosecute a public business, however lucrative it may be, which will have either of these effects—for the public good is of more consequence than any private gain could be. If, for instance, a man should set up a *bakery* in this city, in which, by the infusion of a deleterious drug into his bread, he would endanger the public health, society would not hesitate a moment in regarding this as a proper subject of legislation, and would never dream of tolerating it, or taxing it, or regulating it, or licensing it. If, from the bakeries of this city, bread of such a character should go forth for a single morning, and there was a general concert and understanding among the bakers to continue this practice as a regular line of their business—if there was not law enough in the community to put a stop to it, there would not be *patience* and *forbearance* enough to prevent a storm of public indignation that would in a day lay every such bakery in ruins.—There are, I presume, not as many bakeries in this city as there are houses for selling intoxicating liquors.

Another principle in regard to legislation, is equally clear and equally important. It is, that society should not undertake to regulate evil by law. Its business is to *remove* it; not to *regulate* it. This principle, also, would seem to be plain enough on its very announcement, but it bears so directly on the point before us, that it is proper to dwell on it a moment longer. What would a government be that should undertake to regulate murder, arson, adultery, burglary, or theft? What would laws be that should "license" such crimes in any circumstances, and under any restrictions?

The object of law is not to *regulate*, but to *remove* evil. This principle has been applied to lotteries, to horse-racing, and to gaming. It has been applied to the crimes of arson, theft, murder, treason, duelling, adultery, and polygamy. It has been applied to the barbarous sports of the amphitheatre, to bull-baiting, and to open and disgraceful contests between man and man. But it has not been applied to all things. There is one great evil that still lingers among us, where the principle is adopted and acted on that it is to be regulated and not removed; that it is to be placed under suitable restraints, and made subservient to the purposes of government by raising a revenue. This stands by itself, perhaps almost the solitary instance of this kind of legislation in civilized lands.

Nuisances or evils that individuals or society have a right to protect themselves against, are such things, as defined in the law books, as the following:—A man's building his house so near to mine that his roof overhangs my roof; erecting a house or other building so near to mine that it obstructs my ancient lights and windows; keeping noisome animals so near to the house of another that the stench of them incommodes him, and makes the air unwholesome; a setting up and exercising an offensive trade—as a tanner's or a tallow-chandler's; erecting a smelting-house for lead so near to the land of another that the vapour and smoke kills his corn and grass, and damages his cattle. And so to stop or divert water that uses to run to another's meadow or mill, or to corrupt or poison a water-course, by erecting a dye-house or lime-pit for the use of trade in the upper part of the stream, is a nuisance which society has a right to abate.—3 Blackstone, 217, 218. " So clearly," says the great author of the Commentaries on the laws of England, " does the law of England enforce that excellent rule of gospel morality, of doing to others as we would they should do unto ourselves." And so the same great writer in another place says, " all disorderly inns, or ale-houses, bawdy-houses, gaming-houses, stage-plays, unlicensed booths and stages for rope-dancers, mountebanks, and the like, are public nuisances."— 4 Blackstone, 167.

Another principle in regard to legislation is, that society has a right to prevent or remove an evil, by destroying private property, or rendering it valueless, if necessary. Yet there is no property that so certainly and so uniformly works evil in a community as that which is employed in the manufacture and sale of intoxicating drinks; and all the capital on the face of the earth invested in damaged hides, and corrupted drugs, and tainted butcher's meat, and counterfeiter's tools, is not doing an appreciable quantity of the mischief that is done by the property that is invested in this business.

These principles seem plain, and are such as are ac'ed on in the ordinary course of legislation. Society could not exist if they, all of them, or any one of them, were denied; and, in ordinary matters, we all feel that in a case covered by these principles, we have a right to appeal to the interposition of the legislative power.

The Evil of Selling Intoxicating Drinks.

There was a time when the owners did not know the dangerous and destructive qualities of this article—when the facts had not been developed and published, nor the minds of men turned to the subject; when they did not know that it caused such a vast portion of the vice and wretchedness of the community, and such wide-spreading desolation to the temporal and eternal interests of men; and although it then destroyed thousands, for both worlds, the guilt of the men who sold it was comparatively small. But now they sin against light, pouring down upon them with unutterable brightness; and if they know what they do, and in full view of its consequences continue that work of death—not only let the poison go out, but furnish it, and send it out to all who are disposed to purchase,—it had been better for them, and better for many others, if they had never been born. For,

1. It is the selling of that, without the use of which, nearly all the business of this world was conducted, till within less than 300 years; and which, of course, is not *needful*.

2. It is the selling of that, which was not generally used by the people of this country, for more than a hundred years after the country was settled; and which, by hundreds of thousands, and some in all kinds of lawful business, is not used now. Once they did use it, and thought it needful, or useful. But by experiment, the best evidence in the world, they have found that they were mistaken, and that they are in all respects better without it. And

the cases are so numerous as to make it *certain*, that should the experiment be fairly made, this would be the case with all. Of course, it is not *useful*.

3. It is the selling of that which is a real, a subtle, and very destructive *poison;* a poison which, by men in health, cannot be taken without deranging healthy action, and inducing more or less disease, both of body and mind; which is, when taken in any quantity, positively *hurtful;* and which is, of course, forbidden by the Word of God.

4. It is the selling of that, which tends to form an unnatural and a very dangerous and destructive appetite; which, by gratification, like the desire of sinning in the man who sins, tends continually to increase; and which thus exposes all who form it, to come to a *premature grave*.

5. It is the selling of that, which causes a great portion of all the pauperism in our land; and thus for the benefit of a few, (those who sell) brings an enormous tax on the whole community. Is this fair? Is it just? Is it not exposing our children and youth to become drunkards? And is it not inflicting great evils on society?

6. It is the selling of that, which excites to a great portion of all the crimes that are committed; and which is thus shown to be in its effects hostile to the moral government of God, and to the social, civil, and religious interests of men; at war with their highest good, both for this life and the life to come.

7. It is the selling of that, the sale and use of which, if conti nued, will form intemperate appetites, which if formed will be gratified; and thus will perpetuate intemperance, and all its abominations, to the end of the world.

8. It is the selling of that which makes wives widows, and children orphans; which leads husbands often to murder their wives, and wives to murder their husbands; parents to murder their children, and children to murder their parents; and which prepares multitudes for the prison, for the gallows, and for hell.

9. It is the selling of that which greatly increases the amount and severity of sickness; which in many cases destroys reason; which causes a great portion of all the sudden deaths; and brings down multitudes, who were never intoxicated, and never condemned to suffer the penalty of the civil law, to an untimely grave.

10. It is the selling of that which tends to lessen the health, the reason, and the usefulness, to diminish the comfort and shorten the lives, of all who habitually use it.

11. It is the selling of that which darkens the understanding, sears the conscience, pollutes the affections, and debases all the powers of man.

12. It is the selling of that which weakens the power of motives to do right, and increases the power of motives to do wrong; and is thus shown to be in its effects hostile to the moral government of God, as well as to the temporal and eternal interests of men; which excites men to rebel against him, and to injure and destroy one another. And no man can sell it without exerting an influence which tends to hinder the reign of the Lord Jesus Christ over the minds and hearts of men, and to lead them to persevere in iniquity, till, notwithstanding all the kindness of Jehovah, their case shall become hopeless.

Mr. Doty's License to Sell Rum!

"Mr. Doty,

"Sir:

"You have always been a true friend to my cause on earth, for which I respect you, and feel disposed to assist you in your present embarrassment. I was present yesterday at the meeting of the board, and as soon as they refused to grant you license, I hastened back to the infernal regions, entered the council chamber of hell, called around me warriors, princes, and potentates, and laid before them your case: whereupon it was unanimously resolved that you have license to do the following things, namely:—

"You are hereby authorized to create an appetite for strong drink in all the virtuous, intelligent, and enterprising young men that you can draw under your influence; to instruct them in gambling, to make them profane and Sabbath-breakers. You need have no misgivings if you discover that they are becoming thieves, liars, and murderers, for this is your master's good pleasure. If any of them marry, do what you can to alienate their affections from their wives, and to neglect and abuse them; and if, in three years' time, you succeed in separating them, you need have no scruples of conscience. Draw around you as many of the middle-aged as you can, especially of such as have families. Induce them to whip their wives; and if they kill them, no matter. Take from them all their earnings, that their children may suffer for bread and fuel, and grow up without education; that they may become thieves, liars, robbers, burglars, and midnight assassins. By a unanimous vote of the citizens of Pandemonium, you are authorized to make paupers of as many of your customers as you can. Send their families to the poor-house, and make temperance men support them. Make criminals of as many of them as possible. Send them to jail, to prison, or the gallows, and charge the expense of trying and executing them to your opponents.

"All this you are licensed to do, and are hereby commanded to be faithful, as you ever have been, and hold out to the end; and you shall have your reward. Hearken not to them who would dissuade you from your work. If they quote from the Bible, 'Woe unto him that puttest thy bottle to thy neighbor's mouth, and makes him drunken,' heed them not. Tell them it is a false translation, or the Bible is not true.

"*Signed under my Hand and Seal*,

"DIABOLUS,

"*Chief of Fallen Angels*,
and
King of the Bottomless Pit."

The Moral Right to Drink and Sell Spirituous Liquors.

No man has a moral right to do any action, or pursue any course, the influence of which is certainly and inevitably hurtful to his neighbor-man. I have a legal right to do many things which would be hurtful to myself,—such as the consumption of opium, or even the taking of arsenic,—but I have no moral right to commit this self-destruction.

I have a legal right to attend the theatre occasionally or regularly. There is no civil law to forbid my entering that ensnaring place of entertainment. No policeman stands guard to repel me —no officer of justice dares to eject me while my conduct is orderly and quiet. But, as a minister of God's word, I have *no moral* right to go there, not merely because I may see and hear there what shall pollute my memory for days and years, but because that whole garnished and glittering establishment, with its bewildering attractions, is to many a young man a chandeliered and crimsoned hell, the very yawning maelstrom of moral death. The dollar which I gave at my entrance is my contribution towards sustaining an establishment whose dark foundations rest on the murdered souls of thousands of my fellow-men. Their blood stains its walls, and from the seats of that "pit" they have gone down mayhap to a lower pit where no sounds of mirth ever come. And now, I ask you, what right have I to enter a place where the tragedies that are played off before me by painted men and women, are as nothing to the fearful tragedies of ruined souls that are enacted in all parts of that house every night? What right have I to give the sanction of my example to such haunts of folly and vice, and, by walking into the theatre myself, aid to decoy others there likewise.

Now, on the same principles, not of *self*-preservation, (for of that I am not now speaking,) but on the principle of avoiding what is hurtful to others, what right have I to sustain those magazines of death, where poisonous drinks are sold? What right have I, as a lover of God and man, to petition for them, or to sustain that traffic in any shape or manner? If a glass of wine on my table will entrap some young man, or some one whose inclination is very susceptible to alcoholic stimulant, into dissipation, what right have I to set that trap for his life? What right have I to throw over that drinking practice the sanction of my usages and influence, so that he shall go away and acknowledge me as his tempter, and quote me as his authority for sinning? If the contents of that sparkling glass make my brother to stumble, he stumbles over me. I am an accomplice in the wrong. If he goes away from my table, and commits some outrage under the effects of that stimulant, I am, to a certain degree, guilty of that outrage. The blow he struck was mine; the oaths he uttered in his debauch were, to a certain degree, my blasphemies. I have a partnership right in them. But for me, he might not have uttered them, and by giving him the incentive I prompted him to them. The man who (in the language of Scripture) "puts the bottle to his neighbor's lips," is accountable for what comes from those lips under the influence of the exciting draught, and is accountable, too, for what the maddened and bewildered man may do during his temporary insanity.

But, in the next place, if it be wrong for good men to set before others an example of drinking alcoholic drinks, how much more is it wrong to offer them directly as a matter of merchandize and traffic? Here, too, I wish to present the moral argument. That the sale of alcohol is legalized in many of our States, I do not deny. I see that, and know it, and weep over it. Under the existing regulations of the commonwealth in which I reside, the traffic in intoxicating drinks is made legal, and for certain specified sums men have "license"—as it is technically termed—to dispose of alcoholic drinks in certain quantities, to be drank as a beverage. They have license—a legal permission. But, in spite of the ridicule that has lately been levelled at the doctrine, I submit whether there be not in existence a *higher law* than the enactments of this commonwealth?—I submit whether the infinite Jehovah of Hosts be not a mightier Potentate than the governor of any state, or the council of any city? And in the primal statute-book of the universe I read this anathema—whose thunderbolt no human hand can stay—" Woe unto him who putteth the bottle to his neighbor!" This is the Divine declaration, however men may sophisticate themselves or delude each other.

The full import and power of a license to "put the bottle" to a neighbor's lips, is greatly misunderstood and over-rated. Will a "license" free a man's conscience from the legitimate effects of that which he is doing? Will that make reparation to a man for the loss of his money, time, character, health, and soul? Will that make reparation to families robbed of protection, and the community robbed of its real wealth, the name and strength of its sons? Will that license soothe the widow, whose outward badges of mourning are but faint emblems of the darkness that hangs like night upon her broken spirits? Is there any trafficker in strong drink who means to take his license up to the Judgment bar? If so, I entreat him to look well, and see whose "image and superscription it bears." He may then find that fatal document countersigned in blood, and registered with the tears of the lost in God's book of remembrance.—*Temperance Messenger*, U. S.

CHAPTER II.

PARLIAMENTARY ACTION.

The Traffic Prohibited in Various Countries—Testimonies—First Parliamentary Committee in Canada—Forbes M'Kenzie Act of Scotland—Ditto for Canada—Canadian New Municipal Law.

THE TRAFFIC PROHIBITED IN VARIOUS COUNTRIES.

PROHIBITED IN AFRICA.—The following proclamation, on the subject of ardent spirits, appears in the *Graham's Town* (Cape of Good Hope) *Journal* of 22d March, 1838. It has been printed in the Dutch, Bichuana, and English languages, and extensively circulated in the country north of the Orange river :—

"*Thaba 'nohu, Bichuana Land—A Law Prohibiting the Traffic in Ardent Spirits.*

"Whereas, the introduction of ardent spirits into this country has, in a great measure, been subversive of the good effects, both of religious and civil government, in every part where it has been allowed, and immediately caused disorder, immorality, and vice, and more remarkably, poverty and distress, demoralization and destruction of life, by incessant depredations upon the property rights of the weaker tribes of these parts:

"Be it hereby known, that the traffic in ardent spirits in every part of the country under my government, shall, from the date hereof, be illegal; and any person or persons found transgressing this my law, shall be subject to the confiscation of all the spirits thus illegally offered for sale, with all other property of every kind belonging to the person or persons thus found transgressing, that may be on the spot at the time of seizure, and in any way connected with the same.

"Given at *Thaba 'nohu*, this eighteenth day of October, in the year of our Lord one thousand eight hundred and thirty-seven.

"The mark X of MOROKA,
Chief of the Borolongs."

Lieut. Forbes, a recent African traveller, states in his journal that "drunkenness is not allowed in Dahomey. As a public example, the king kept a drunkard and fed him on rum, and exhibited him at the customs (the annual festival), that his emaciated and disgusting appearance might shame his people from making beasts of themselves."

ANTI-LIQUOR LAW OF NEW BRUNSWICK.—Petitions in great numbers preceded its introduction into the Local Assembly, where it was carried—then it passed the Legislative Council—and was signed by the Lieut.-Governor April the 7th, 1852. It was then sent to England for ratification, which it finally obtained by the signature of her Majesty. The preamble is,—" Whereas, experience has proved that the use of intoxicating liquors as a beverage is the cause of a very large proportion of the ills that affect communities, in producing crime, poverty, disease, and demoralization: And, whereas it is the duty of all governments to legislate for the happiness, comfort, and prosperity of the people." The number of clauses in the Act is 17; the 15th of which repeals all laws inconsistent with this, and the 17th fixes the 1st of June, 1853, as the period when the Act shall come into force. The *scope* of the law is to suppress the manufacture and sale of all alcoholic liquors *except beer, ale, porter, and cider* —i. e., fermented liquors are to be allowed as heretofore, but all spirituous liquors are prohibited, and the manufacture of them placed in the category of illegalities along with the coining of base money.

PROHIBITED IN PITCAIRN ISLAND.—About sixty years ago, a number of English merchants interested in the prosperity of the West India possessions, fitted out an expedition with the view of introducing the bread fruit tree into the islands of those seas. The ship Bounty, ladened with the plants, and under the command of Lieutenant Bligh, was on her way from Otaheiti. Exasperated by the overbearing conduct of the commander, Fletcher Christian, the mate, assisted by several of the inferior officers and men, seized the commander, and forcing him, along with nineteen others, into a small boat, set them adrift upon the wide ocean. Fletcher Christian, the leader of the mutiny, took the Bounty to Otaheiti, where a great part of the crew left her; part of whom were afterwards apprehended, while he and eight others, who each took wives, and six natives, shortly afterwards proceeded to Pitcairn's Island, ran the ship ashore, and broke her up.

In consequence of the gross oppression to which the mutineers subjected the Otaheitans, revolt succeeded revolt, until the sole survivors consisted of a man named Smith, and eight or nine women and several children. This man subsequently assumed the name of John Adams, and became patriarch of the colony. The dwellers on this lone islet in the drear expanse of the South Pacific, now number eighty-six females and eighty-eight males, or nearly two hundred in all. They still speak the language and profess the faith of the English nation.

But the fact remains to be stated to which the extraordinary character of this people is doubtless in no small degree traceable. M'Koy, one of the mutineers, had formerly been employed in a Scotch distillery, and being an intemperate man, set about making experiments, and unfortunately succeeded in producing an intoxicating liquor. This success induced a companion, named Quintal, to turn his kettle into a still. The consequence was that both were habitually drunk, and M'Koy, one day, in a fit of delirium, threw himself from a cliff and was killed on the spot. His companion's conduct was so horribly savage, that John Adams, along with another, considered it necessary for the preservation of the general safety, to put him to death by felling him with a hatchet. The conduct of M'Koy and Quintal so shocked the rest of the community, that they resolved never again to touch intoxicating liquors, and to this day they have kept their resolution. The only spirituous liquors allowed to be landed on their shores, are a few bottles of wine and brandy for the medicine chest of the doctor. Were these simple islanders not wise in joining in a confederacy of entire and perpetual abstinence? The visitor of their secluded ocean home will search in vain amid its deep ravines, and towering mountains, and lofty trees, for an hospital a workhouse, or a barred and grated jail.

PROHIBITION IN LIBERIA.—In Liberia is a prison which deserves more the designation of a Model Prison than ours. *It has no inmates*, and is scarcely ever entered except to " clear it of the insects, and keep it clean." In answer to inquiries, I learned that in Monrovia, the capital, there were only three places of public entertainment; and that there was so high a tax upon spirits, that they were but little used. I asked, if public-houses were multiplied, and taxes reduced, how would it be with the prison? "It would soon be tenanted," was the reply. This simple people have not attained to the *wisdom* of older and greater states.

PROHIBITION IN THE SOUTH SEAS.—The evil had become so alarming that the missionaries felt that something must be attempted, and therefore determined to set the people an example, by abstaining entirely from the use of ardent spirits, and by forming temperance societies. These worked exceedingly well, especially at Parpara, the station occupied by our venerable and indefatigable brother, Mr. Davis. In one place Mr. Williams remarks,—"I am truly thankful—and in this feeling every friend of missions will participate—that the people, with their chief, have been brought to see their folly, and abandon the use of that which was unfitting them for earth and heaven, by rendering them poor, profligate, and miserable." "In this very critical period, we are further informed, the Parliament met, and before the members proceeded to business, they sent a message to the Queen, to know upon what principles they were to act. She returned a copy of the New Testament, saying, 'Let the principles contained in that book be the foundation of all your proceedings;" and, immediately, they enacted a law to prohibit trading with any vessel which brought ardent spirits for sale; and now, there is but one island in the group, Porapora, where these are allowed."

PROHIBITION IN MADAGASCAR.—Madagascar contains four million inhabitants; all total abstainers from intoxicating drinks. In this island, the Maine Law is ingrafted on the constitution. When the Rev. David Griffiths was on the point of administering the solemn rite of the sacrament, for the first time, an edict came direct from the throne, ordaining—not for the first time—that no intoxicating wine was to be used, it being a breach of their laws. In obedience to that law, he made use of the pure pressed juice of the grape.

PROHIBITION IN HAWAII.—The king of the Hawaiin Islands enacted a law, in October, 1840, prohibiting the manufacture and use of intoxicating liquors within his domains.

PROHIBITION IN ENGLAND.—It is a curious and important fact, that during the period when the distilleries were stopped, in 1796 and 1797, although bread and every necessary of life was considerably higher than during the preceding year, the poor, in that quarter of the town where the chief part resides were apparently more comfortable, paid their rents more regularly, and were better fed, than at any period for some years before, even although they had not the benefit of the extensive charities which were distributed in 1795.

TESTIMONIES IN BEHALF OF PROHIBITION.
SENTIMENTS EXPRESSED CENTURIES AGO.

LORD CHESTERFIELD, in the course of the debates on the Gin Act, in 1743, when the distillers flooded London with their poison, drunkards lay in heaps on the streets, and government was defied by the mob—addressed the House of Lords in the following terms:—" Luxury, my lords, is to be taxed, but vice *prohibited*, let the difficulty in the law be what it will. It appears to me, my lords, that really, if so formidable a body are confederate against the virtue or the lives of their fellow-citizens, it is time to put an end to the havoc, and to interpose, whilst it is yet in our power, to stop the destruction. If their liquors are so delicious that the people are tempted to their own destruction, let us, at least, my lords, *secure* them from their fatal draught, by bursting the vials that contain them. Let us crush at once these artists in human slaughter, who have reconciled their countrymen to sickness and ruin, and spread over the pitfalls of debauchery such a bait as cannot be resisted!"

THE LORD BISHOP OF SALISBURY said, in the course of the same debate:—" If this bill be passed into a law, I hope some of your lordships will rise up and move for a repeal of the riot act;

for I should think it very hard to entice poor people to become riotous by provoking them to drink gin, and then to murder them because they are riotous."

THE BISHOP OF OXFORD said in the same debate:—" Poisons, my lords, of all kinds, ought to be confined to the apothecary's shop, where the master's character, and even his bread, depends upon his not administering too great a dose to any person whatever, and where the price is generally too high for any poor man to commit a debauch. Will you, then, commit the care of dispensing this poison to every ale-house-keeper in the kingdom, I may say to every man in the kingdom who is willing to pay half-a-crown to the justices, and twenty shillings a-year to the government for a license? Will you enable them to dispense this poison at so cheap a rate that a poor thoughtless creature may get drunk for threepence, and may purchase immediate death for a shilling? A cordial may be necessary in some distempers, and may be of service to the patient when moderately and skilfully administered; but no climate, no temperature of the air, can make a dram of spirituous liquors necessary to a person in full health and vigour."

STEPHEN HALES, D.D., Clerk of the Closet to H.R H. Prince of Wales, who published a tract, in 1754, entitled, " Friendly Admonitions to the Drinkers of Gin, Brandy, &c. With an humble representation of the necessities of restraining a vice so destructive of the Industry, Morals, Health, and Lives of the People,' says,—" Now, since it is found by long experience, extremely difficult for the unhappy habitual dram-drinkers to extricate themselves from this prevailing vice; so much the more it becomes the duty of the governors of the nations to withhold from them so irresistible a temptation."

NORTHWICK, in his " History of London," referring to the doings of Parliament in 1552, remarks:—" The increase of taverns and wine-vaults now engaged their attention, and it was enacted, that the number of taverns or retailers of wine in London should not exceed forty, nor those of Westminster exceed three. If the increase of the revenue was not thought of more national consequence than the morals of the people, some restriction would yet be observed in the discretionary powers of granting license to public-houses. There are villages in remote country places, which can date the commencement of their poor-rate from the introduction of a public-house; the rulers of the land complain of the licentiousness of the populace to little purpose, while other views cause them to tempt the people from sobriety."

JOHN MILTON said,—" What more foul common sin among us than drunkenness? And who can be ignorant, that if the *importation of wine* and the use of all strong drinks were *forbid*, it would both *clean rid the possibility* of committing that odious vice, and men might afterwards live *happily and healthfully without the use of intoxicating liquors?*"

REV. JOHN WESLEY, in a letter which he addressed to the Right Hon. William Pitt, says,—" Bath, Sept. 6, 1784.—Servants of distillers inform me that their masters do not pay for a fortieth part of what they distil; and this, only last year, (if I am rightly informed), amounted only to £20,000. But have not the spirits distilled this year cost 20,000 lives of his Majesty's liege subjects? Is not, then, the blood of these men vilely bartered for £20,000 —not to say anything of the enormous wickedness which has been occasioned thereby, and not to suppose that these poor wretches have souls? But, to consider money alone, is the king a gainer, or an immense loser? To say nothing of many millions of *quarters of corn* destroyed, which, if exported, would add more than £20,000 to the revenue, be it considered, *dead men pay no taxes;* so that, by the death of 20,000 persons yearly (and this computation is far under the mark,) the revenue loses far more than it gains. But how can the price of wheat and barley be reduced? By prohibiting FOR EVER—by making a full end of that bane of health, that destroyer of life and virtue —DISTILLING."

First Parliamentary Committee in Canada.

On the 24th day of Feb., 1859, the following were named a Select Committee to receive all Petitions in favor of a Prohibitory Liquor Law, examine their contents, and Report with all convenient speed—viz.: Mr. Simpson, Hon. Mr. Cameron, Mr. Playfair, Mr. McDougall, Mr. Walker Powell, Mr. McKellar, Mr. Cook, Hon. Mr. Mowat, Mr. Hartman, and Mr. A. P. McDonald. On the 30th of March, they made the following Report:—

"REPORT.

"There have been referred to your Committee, up to the date hereof, 240 petitions, signed by 108,894 individuals, 22 petitions from Municipalities, 3 petitions from temperance organizations, and 1 petition from the Canada Christian Conference, praying for the enactment of a stringent Prohibitory Liquor Law; 2 petitions from Municipalities, praying that the use of liquors may be prohibited, except for medicinal and mechanical purposes; and 3 petitions, signed by 328 individuals, praying that the sale of liquor may be restrained.

"Your Committee have had before them several gentlemen who have long taken a deep and active interest in the extension of the cause of temperance—viz.: Messrs. Beatty, (of Cobourg,) Farewell, (of Oshawa,) and Burr, (of Toronto,) whose evidence and observations accompany this Report.

"Your Committee were anxious to obtain, and, through one of their number, invited, the attendance of the Honorable Neal Dow, as they considered his thorough practical acquaintance with the subject referred to them would be of signal value. Mr. Dow, however, was unable to leave his official duties for the length of time requisite for a journey to Toronto, but kindly favored your Committee with a very interesting communication on the history and working of the prohibitory system in the State of Maine, which also accompanies this Report.

"Your Committee invited the attendance of the Police Magistrate and Recorder of Toronto, the Governor of the Toronto Gaol, and the Episcopal Chaplain of the Provincial Penitentiary. The evidence and remarks of these able and experienced officers also accompany this Report.

"And among the evidence will be found the statements and views of two gentlemen, one of whom is largely engaged in brewing, the other in distilling. And your Committee append returns showing the quantity of whiskey and beer manufactured in Upper Canada during the year 1858; and also the quantity of wines, liquors, and beer imported into the Province during the same year.

"Your Committee forwarded a series of questions bearing upon the subjects referred to them, to the Sheriffs and Wardens of Counties; the Mayors, Recorders, and Police Magistrates of Towns and Villages in Upper Canada; copies of which appear in the Appendix to this Report.

"Returns have been received from the Sheriffs of 38 of the 42 counties of Upper Canada, from which it appears that in the gaols under their control, 15,975 persons were imprisoned during the three years ending with 1858; and as from the united testimony of these gentlemen more than three-fourths of the prisoners were committed for drunkenness, or for offences perpetrated while under the influence of liquor, it follows that 12,000 for the three years, or 4000 per annum, of the entire commitments, are directly traceable to the use of liquor. By the same returns, it is shewn that in 24 of the counties intemperance is on the increase, while in 14 no increase has been observed.

"From the evidence appended to this report, from the returns received by your Committee from all parts of the country—from villages, towns, and cities, as well as from the rural municipalities—and from their own personal observation, your Committee are thoroughly convinced—

"1. That indulgence in the use of intoxicating liquors is the cause of most of the suffering and sorrow, the poverty and crime, which afflict Upper Canada; and,

"2. That it is the duty of Parliament to mitigate, diminish, and, if possible, extirpate the cause of these evils.

"Your Committee therefore recommend that an Act be passed authorizing and establishing the prohibitory system in all the Municipalities in Upper Canada, wherein, in the month of July next, at a meeting of persons authorized to vote for school trustees, held for the express purpose of considering the matter, the majority of persons present at such meeting shall not vote against its taking effect within the limits of said Municipality."

We take the evidence of the different parties in the order in which we find it in the Report:—

JOHN BEATTY, Esquire, of Cobourg, was in attendance, and was examined as follows:—

1. What do you consider the state of the public morals in reference to the use of intoxicating liquors?—My convictions are, that the prevalent use of intoxicating liquors has a most deplorable effect upon public morals, and is a principal cause of the very great majority of the crimes which so seriously affect all classes of the community. These convictions are based upon—1st. Personal observation forced upon me in pursuit of my profession. 2. Personal experience as Surgeon to a County Gaol for several years (at different intervals.) 3. Upon the discharge of duties for many years as a Magistrate, wherein a very large majority of the cases coming before me are directly caused by intemperance; and I think I would not be overstating the matter by saying that 19-20 of these cases may be traced directly or indirectly to this cause. 4. The privations and suffering affecting so large a proportion of the lower classes in cities and towns, are, without doubt, in my mind, vastly augmented, if not directly caused, by the more than wasteful expenditure of limited means, and by the thriftlessness which the habit of intemperance begets. 5. Statistics of crimes published by Police authorities, records of all descriptions of Criminal Courts, testimony of public officers, presentments of Grand Juries, and the history of public executions, will all confirm the truth of the convictions above expressed.

2. What remedy would you suggest for the evils now existing? The remedy must be in some degree commensurate with the evil, and the only one which appears to present any such feature, is a stringent prohibitory law, directed against the common traffic in liquors of every form. Personally I would use every effort and influence to enforce any restrictive measure, but it would still be with the conviction that a temporary palliation was being applied to the evil, not an effectual remedy. In surgery, it would be unhesitatingly condemned as malpractice, to apply an emollient poultice or soothing sedative to a gangrenous limb, where nothing but excision could save the life of the patient; what estimate should be formed of similar Legislative practice, for a moral and social gangrene of the most formidable character, judge ye!

3. Do you think the public generally are prepared to sustain a Prohibitory Liquor Law?—I think that the public in cities and towns, judging from the increase of intemperance therein, is not favorable to such a law; nevertheless I am certain that the appaling magnitude of the evil is forcing very many to look anxiously for a remedy, who were formerly adverse to anything like restrictive legislation on this subject. The rural communities, I believe, are prepared to sustain such a law, and it would, in my opinion, be enforced as well as all laws of that class are. The Synods, Conferences, &c., of almost every religious denomination of the Province, have pronounced in favor of, and petitioned for a prohibitory law. I believe, if time be allowed, that public opinion will be expressed by the number of petitions which will be presented to Parliament, in a manner that would be deemed very significant on any other subject, whatever opinion may be entertained thereupon in reference to this.

4. What has been the effect in other countries with which you are acquainted of the passage of the Maine Law, or other laws of a restraining or prohibitory nature?—License or restraining laws have entirely failed everywhere to afford a remedy for the evils of intemperance; indeed, such laws may be said to have nourished,

quite as much as to have restrained, the ends referred to. Prohibitory laws, even where partially enforced, have been essentially and largely beneficial and remedial. As I am informed that the Hon. Neal Dow is expected to appear before the Committee, it is quite unnecessary to enlarge on this point.

5. In what manner has the power vested in the Municipalities for prohibition and restraint been exercised, and with what effect?—This power has been exercised in but a few instances, and the attempt to do so has been almost, if not quite, abandoned. This has arisen from two causes: First, from the conviction of the very great difficulty which must be met with in the attempt to enforce such a measure in one municipality when surrounded by those pursuing a contrary course. Secondly, from adverse decisions given in the Superior Courts upon cases of appeal.

The decisions convinced the friends of such measures that it would be almost impossible to frame a by-law that could not be set aside. In the decision of Chief Justice Robinson, in the case of Barclay *versus* the Township of Darlington, it appeared to be set forth that the Municipal Councils cannot by by-law prohibit the sale of liquors in taverns. Other decisions of a similar character are to be found in the records of our Law Courts. On this point I would refer the Committee to a lengthy and instructive note by Mr. Harrison, upon section 245 of the last Municipal Act, to be found in the last edition of the Municipal Manual. Circumstances like those referred to, led to the conviction that local measures of a prohibitory character could only lead to vexation and expensive issues, and that a general law affords the only ground for hope of ultimate success.

A. FAREWELL, Esq., of Oshawa, gave the following:—

1. What do you consider the state of public morals in reference to the use of intoxicating liquors?—I understand your first question to have reference to the effects produced upon public morals by the use of intoxicating liquors. The public is an aggregation

of individuals, and as you find individual morals generally, so you may expect to find those of the public. I am clearly of opinion that the liquor traffic, from beginning to end, produces a debasing and corrupting influence upon the minds of those connected with that traffic. Consider first the effect upon the manufacturer and vendor of spirits. It is asserted with confidence by those who ought to know, that the most of the liquors consumed in this country are adulterated—some to a greater extent, and some to a less degree; and proof is not required that persons engaged in this work of adulteration, are either hardened sinners, or in a fair way to become such.

A large dealer in spirits in Albany said that the process of adulteration is carried on to so vast an extent in Europe that it was doubtful whether one gallon in one hundred imported into America was pure; and it is alleged that upon this Continent, like manufacturers may be found! but those who have the means of knowing, allege that the great proportion of liquors of all kinds are adulterated, and that the most deleterious drugs and poisons are freely used in the compounding operations—surely the direct tendency of such an avocation cannot be otherwise than corrupting to the mind. Take the first case of the honest manufacturer or vendor; can he reflect with satisfaction upon the business in which he is engaged? Does he in times like the present, that all our available grain is required for human food, does he consider that for the large sums of money which he receives from the labouring classes he gives them in return what benefits them not—nay, what does them a great deal of harm? Can he dare to lift his eyes and voice to heaven, and implore a blessing upon the work in which he is engaged? If not, his avocation produces in his own mind a moral apathy, and tends to destroy spiritual life. Consider, secondly, the effect upon those who drink to excess. Both science and observation teach that the animal passions and propensities of man become inflamed and excited under the operation of spirits; that drinking disturbs the equilibrium of the intellect, and lays a ruthless hand upon the whole moral and spiritual nature of man; that it confuses and deadens the mind, and lets the passions loose without guidance or restraint. It lights the torch of the incendiary, guides the dagger of the assassin, and steels the heart to the commission of all crime; it deadens all the healthy sensibilities, and produces coarseness and stupefaction, thus putting an end to all culture, and shutting up the source of the pure and lofty pleasures of reading and meditation—spiritual growth entirely ceases, and moral life becomes extinct. Morally, the traffic bites like a serpent, and stings like an adder. The statistics of crime, the records of criminal courts, work-houses, jails, and penitentiaries, throughout Christendom, fully confirm the above statements. About three-fourths of all the criminal cases in all communities where spirits are freely used as a common beverage, are directly attributable to the agency of those drinks. So apparent has this become in our own country, that for some time past it has claimed the special attention of all parties connected with the administration of justice. In this city, it would be a matter of surprise if a Grand Jury were to make a presentment without special reference to intemperance as the frightful source of the most of the crimes committed. But a short time since, an intelligent Grand Jury of this city stated that, in common with all past Grand Juries, the members of the present one cannot but reiterate their conviction, from painful experience, that the large proportion of crime and misery found in this city and everywhere throughout the country, must be traced to the facilities furnished by the municipal authorities for the sale of strong drinks. And his Honor Chief Justice Draper, C.B., in answering that Jury, said:—" You rightfully point out as one of the most frightful sources of crime, the multiplication of places in which liquors are sold, and in which drunkenness prevails ?

2. What remedy would you suggest for the evils now existing ? —My answer to your second question is—Prohibition, entire prohibition from dealing in intoxicating drinks, except for medicine and to be used in the arts. The history of the traffic proves that you cannot abolish the free use of liquors, and the evils resulting

therefrom, by the license system; and all persons conversant with the working of Prohibitory Liquor Laws agree that the more stringent the measure the more easily and effectually it can be enforced.

3. How do you think the public generally are prepared to sustain a Prohibitory Liquor Law?—I have no hesitancy in answering your third question. The most of the rural districts in Canada West are ready to sustain and enforce a Prohibitory Liquor Law. The villages, towns, and cities are not. Why this difference? Some say a higher moral tone of feeling exists in the rural than in the more populous parts of a country. Whether this opinion be correct or not, certain it is that in the villages, towns, and cities of Canada, a much larger interest is invested in the liquor business than in the country parts, and the difference in feeling upon the Prohibitory question may be fairly attributable to this interest. Propose any sanitary or moral reform, and as far as you propose to affect our pocket interest, without an adequate return to pocket, so far, generally speaking, you create enemies to the measure. All men are selfish in one sense of the term, some much more so than others. 'Tis Heaven's first law that man should take care of No. 1; but we are not to regard our own without reference to the welfare of others, and men generally do not. But we have seen that the traffic in liquors reasonably and naturally produces an effect upon the minds of those engaged therein calculated to weaken those strong sympathies and good wishes which God designed man should have for the welfare of his fellow man. All Prohibitory Laws have been, and will continue to be, violated, and the more directly such laws cross the path of interest, the more determined the violation. The grasping avariciousness of some, and the cold selfishness of others, no doubt, will lead to frequent violations of a Prohibitory Liquor Law in this country. But are the best interests of the many to be forever sacrificed to the selfishness of the few? I think not, and am of opinion that a large majority of the people of this country think not. A stringent Prohibitory Law would at once be enforced in very many parts of the country, and

gradually and by degrees their influence would produce so irresistible an effect upon the villages, towns, and cities, as to compel them to yield obedience also.

4. Do you think the public mind prepared for a Prohibitory Liquor Law?—In answering your fourth question, I would remark, that apparently much difference of opinion exists with reference to the successful working of Prohibitory Liquor Laws in those countries where they have been in operation.

The character of this difference of opinion is worthy of consideration. The difference is between two classes. The friends of prohibition generally agree that when the law has had a fair opportunity and a fair trial, it works well; some of the enemies state the contrary. Having been commissioned in 1855, by the Prohibitory Liquor Law League of Canada, to visit, in company with G. P. Ure, of this city, the Eastern States, in order to ascertain from personal observation the workings of prohibition; and having travelled on that occasion through most of the towns and cities in New England, and having the opportunity of personal intercourse with very many of the leading men in those States, I unhesitatingly answer that prohibition was working well wherever it was getting a fair trial. Governors of States, Senators, Legislators, Judges, Sheriffs, Jailors, Police Magistrates, Justices of the Peace, Keepers of Almshouses, and Merchants, Manufacturers, and Tradesmen, all agreed that the law was working well, and doing more good than its friends had anticipated. I cannot refrain from giving you the testimony of several of these persons as it fell from their lips in our presence. Before doing so, however, I would remark that many of the disadvantages under which the friends of prohibition in the United States labour, could not be encountered in Canada.

All their laws require to be so drafted as not to conflict with their own written constitution nor that of the United States, while in Canada the public weal is the constitution, and the people have only to will prohibition, and the constitution yields to their inclinations.

PARLIAMENTARY ACTION.

Testimony of *John W. Bull*, Hartford, Connecticut.—I have been engaged in the importation and sale of earthenware here for the last 25 years. I was opposed to the Maine Law when it passed, and when the select-men called a meeting for the purpose of appointing agents for selling liquor under the law, I and my friends opposed the appointment of agents, thinking thereby to render the law obnoxious to the people, so as to cause them to demand its repeal. But the agents were appointed, and we determined to give the law a trial. From that time to the present it has been growing in public favor. Those friends who acted with me in resisting the law at first, are now all decidedly in its favor, and property holders take a deep interest in maintaining the law.

Professor *Silliman*, Yale College.—My impression is that the law has worked very favorably. My wife has been in the habit of visiting the poor, and where she used to find misery and vice, she now finds happiness and comfort.

Governor *Dutton*, Connecticut.—The law has completely swept the pernicious traffic, as a business, from the State. The longer the beneficial effects of the law are seen and felt, the more firmly it becomes established.

Governor *Morrill*, Augusta, Maine.—In all our cities and towns where the authorities have been favorable to the law, it has worked admirably. It is too much to suppose that you can extinguish intemperance at once; but the traffic has been wonderfully circumscribed, and will finally be driven out. The people demand that the law shall be made more stringent; but where the present one has been enforced, it has done much good. I can give you a list of towns where rumselling has been absolutely extinguished.

Calvin Record, Councillor and Attorney, Maine.—In the practice of my profession, previous to and since the passing of the law, I have had an opportunity of witnessing the change, which has been very marked indeed. In Danville, where I reside, it was thought the law could not be enforced. It was at first difficult to convict the accused, but the enforcement of the law in other places produced a favorable impression upon us, and now, when the law requires it, conviction is easily obtained. The people require the law to be made more stringent.

W. H. McElrith.—The firm with which I am connected employed 700 men in the lumbering business last winter. We supplied no liquor to the camp, nor was any used by the men, and both employers and employed were delighted with the workings of the law. The men endure fatigue, perform more work, and do it better, than in former years.

J. L. Adams, County Clerk, Burlington, Vermont.—The Grand Jury, in their last report, say, " We would also express our gratification at finding the Jail destitute of inmates; a circumstance attributable, in a very great measure, we believe, to the suppression of the sale of intoxicating liquors."

" The Maine Law Illustrated," from which I have copied the above extract, gives the evidence of hundreds of persons, chiefly of the better class of society, nearly all to the same effect.

This pamphlet of 94 pages was published by the Anti-Liquor-Law League in this city, and I think Mr. G. P. Ure, of this city, may have a few copies in his possession.

5. Your fifth question, regarding the action of the Municipalities in passing and enforcing prohibitory laws, can be answered briefly.

Up to the passing of the present Municipal Law, the action of the courts has been against the Municipalities, which, with the difficulty necessarily attending the enforcement of a law of this nature, so local in its operations, has prevented many of the Municipalities from availing themselves of this provision of the Statute.

Many of the friends of general Prohibition oppose the passing of these local measures, saying they cannot be enforced so easily as a general measure, and the strong desire of the country appears to be, to have an opportunity of trying the effects of such a measure.

[Circular No. 1.]

Sir,—The Select Committee to which was referred the subject of a Prohibitory Liquor Law, beg to submit the following questions, and hope you will return the same, with answers, as soon as possible:—1. How many prisoners have been confined in your Gaol during the years 1856, 1857, and 1858? 2. How many of these were committed for drunkenness? 3. How many for offences committed while under the influence of drunkenness? 4. Is intemperance on the increase in your County or not? 5. Has the number of places for the sale of intoxicating liquors, in your County, increased or diminished during the last three years? 6. Are the regular Taverns as productive of injury to the community as the Saloons, Recesses, and other Groggeries? 7. Is the public mind, in your judgment, prepared to receive and carry out a Prohibitory Liquor Law? 8. Or would you think it advisable, in order to prepare the public mind gradually for such a result, to suppress all mere Groggeries, by Legislative enactment, and to restrict the number of Taverns in proportion to the number of resident inhabitants, and the probable proportion of travellers to be accommodated? 9. Would it, in your judgment, be more acceptable to the public generally, with a view that no interest should suffer, that the diminution should be made as existing licenses drop through any cause, or that the work of suppression should be at once commenced?

JOHN NOTMAN,
Clerk to Committee.

[Circular No. 2.]

Sir,—The Select Committee to which was referred the subject of a Prohibitory Liquor Law, beg to submit the following questions, and hope you will return the same, with answers, as soon as possible:--1. What was the number of convictions before your Court in 1858? 2. How many of those were attributable to the use of intoxicating liquors? 3. Can you suggest any beneficial amendments to existing laws relative to the use of intoxicating liquors? 4. Do you think the public mind prepared for a Prohibitory Liquor Law?

JOHN NOTMAN,
Clerk to Committee.

The Chairman read the following letter received from the Hon. Neal Dow by Hon. M. Cameron, dated Portland, Maine, March 8, 1859 :—

DEAR SIR,—On my return from Augusta—our State Capital—for a day or two, where I am for the winter, being a member of the Government for this year, I found your note of the 4th, inviting me to visit Toronto, to give any information in my possession in relation to the Maine Law in this State, and its operation and effects.

It will be very difficult for me to spare so much time, just now, as a visit to you would require, but I would be very glad to give you any aid in my power in the work you have in hand.

In this State, as everywhere else in the civilized world, the system of licensing shops and taverns for the sale of alcoholic liquors to be used as a drink, continued until 1846. In that year the entire licensing policy was abandoned in Maine, the question of its evils and impolicy having been discussed freely amongst us for many years. An attempt was made in 1847 to repeal the law of prohibition, but the Bill introduced for that purpose was refused even a consideration.

But the law of 1846, while it prohibited the sale of all alcoholic drinks, did not provide adequate penalties and summary processes for the enforcement of its provisions. The traffic, however, was very greatly diminished by it, chiefly for the reason, that, being outlawed and rendered infamous by the statute, the traffic was immediately abandoned by all respectable citizens, and by all who wished to maintain even a decent position in society.

This was a very great point gained, because the public opinion came very soon to regard the liquor traffic as on a level with the keeping a gambling house or house of ill-fame, or any other infamous occupation inconsistent with the general welfare.

The agitation of the question of prohibition continued until, in 1851, it culminated in the enactment of the Maine Law, so called now, and known by that name, over all the world. But I may remark here, that among the many thousand of petitioners for the law, there were a great many of our best men who lent us their names from sympathy with our general objects, but who frankly told us they did not believe we could accomplish them in the way we proposed. They gave us their influence that we might have an opportunity to try the experiment of stringent prohibition, though they were sure the experiment must fail. There were others, in large numbers, persons of influence and respectability, who declined to lend us their names, not from disapproval of the object we had in view, but from the conviction that the measure we proposed was unwise, and would aggravate the evil which they deplored as much as we did.

Immediately upon the enactment of that law in 1851, the liquor traffic throughout the State received a severe check, everywhere it was greatly diminished in amount. In considerable sections of the country it ceased entirely; the wholesale trade was utterly destroyed without a single prosecution, and where any remnant of the traffic remained, it fled for shelter to secret places and dark retired corners, so that everywhere in the State the law seemed to have a perfect execution, because the liquor traffic was nowhere to be seen among our various occupations.

Under the operation of the law, pauperism and crime diminished wonderfully. In some of our towns pauperism ceased entirely, and in all, the falling off in that department was very great. In some of our counties the jails were literally tenantless, and in all of them the number of prisoners were greatly diminished. In a word, the effects of the law were more immediately favorable than its most sanguine friends had even hoped that they could be. I am sure it is not too much to say that the quantity of alcoholic drinks consumed in Maine under that law, were not one-fiftieth part so great as it was before its enactment.

But, from various causes which would not interest you, which are not pertinent to this enquiry, and which it would require large space to explain, another party came into power in 1856, and the Maine Law was repealed. The leaders of this party, however, had pledged themselves to the people, that they would not repeal the Maine Law, except for the purpose of substituting for it a more suitable prohibitory law. Instead of keeping faith with the people, however, they restored the license system.

The effects of this return to the old system were everywhere visible, and that immediately, in increased intemperance, poverty, pauperism, and crime. Grog-shops everywhere sprung up all over the State, like toad-stools, in a single night, and the traffic was carried on as freely, openly, and extensively, as before the enactment of the law of 1851.

Many friends of temperance despaired of success, and gave up all for lost; but I never for a moment doubted the triumph of the cause of prohibition, because I knew it to be right and philosophically sound, and had faith in the virtue and intelligence of our people. This new law (the license system) was enacted in April, 1857, and was in operation only five months, when, at the election in September of the same year, the license party was swept out of power amid the scorn and execrations of the people. Only one person of the entire Legislature, who voted for the repeal of the Maine Law, was re-elected! No party ever before had so crushing a defeat in Maine; and now, prohibition is the law and the fixed policy of the State. It is conceded on all hands, that no license law will be re-enacted here.

The present law is not executed so thoroughly as the original enactment was. This may be accounted for by the fact that for about seven years the public mind has been greatly excited on this subject, and agitated by alternate success and apparent defeat. Now, again, prohibition is in the ascendant, and the excitement of the contest has passed away with the last victory, and there is quiet amongst the people. At least for a year past there has been comparative quiet, but now the people are beginning to arouse themselves to a new effort to complete the work, so auspiciously commenced, with a resolution and energy which we have never yet seen equalled.

Under the operation of the law, the liquor traffic is greatly crippled and curtailed. In this city, for example, there are no open liquor shops at all; but at the time of the enactment of the law, in July, 1858, there were more than five hundred, many of them wholesale shops. At least one-half of these shops ceased the traffic entirely and immediately, without any prosecution, by the moral force of the law, while all the remainder that continue to sell, do so with very great caution, and only in secret places. The wholesale traffic is entirely destroyed.

The favorable effect of the law upon intemperance, pauperism, and crime, is again very apparent. Pauperism in this city has fallen off thirty-seven per cent., and drunkenness more than one-half, and the same results are observed throughout the State. And I am very glad to be able to say that great numbers of the persons of character, and influence, of whom I spoke as doubting the expediency and wisdom of our movement, or as opposed to it entirely as certain to work mischievous results, have changed their views, and co-operate with us now in favor of entire and absolute prohibition, as not only the best, but the only, mode by which intemperance, with its long and frightful array of evils, can be eradicated from society.

I earnestly hope that the Canadian Parliament will also adopt this policy. It would certainly promote, not only the happiness of the people, but the material prosperity of the Canadas, more than any other measure that could possibly be devised. The liquor traffic drains away to entire waste more of the wealth of the people than all other causes of loss combined. The money that is spent in it is not only a dead loss to the people and the country, but the traffic entails a more fearful mischief upon the people, by under-mining their habits of industry and thrift, and by inducing directly and inevitably a vast amount of ignorance, poverty, pauperism, suffering, and crime. As the liquor traffic is the greatest curse by which your people can possibly be afflicted, so its suppression by law would be the greatest benefit and blessing which the Government can bestow upon them. I hope most earnestly that the happy results of this policy may very soon be experienced among you.

GEORGE L. ALLEN, Esq., Governor of Toronto Gaol, attended the Committee in obedience to a summons, and stated that the queries addressed to the Sheriff had been sent to him for reply, and which read as follows:—

DEAR SIR,—I beg leave herewith to transmit you a tabular statement containing the answers to the two first queries of the circular addressed to you by a Committee of the Legislative Assembly. In reference to the third query in the circular, I can afford no positive information, not being myself personally aware of the circumstances connected with the primary arrest of the offenders, nor of the circumstances under which the crimes were committed; but, from my experience in such matters, having been now going on fourteen years dealing with them, I unhesitatingly assert, that were the criminals not actually committed for drunkenness analyzed, it would be found that three-fourths of them committed the offences with which they were charged, through the agency, directly or indirectly, of intoxicating drinks.

No. 4. My opinion is that intemperance has increased in a far greater proportion than the increase of our population would fairly warrant.

No. 5. The number of places for the sale of intoxicating liquors has increased, and very largely increased, in your country, within the last *three years*,—more particularly has that increase been visible in the City of Toronto, for, while its population cannot be said to have doubled its numbers within that period, the number of places for the sale of ardent spirits, licensed and unlicensed, has increased more than three-fold within the past four years.

No. 6. I feel quite satisfied that the regular taverns are not productive of anything like the amount of injury to the community that is produced through the agency of saloons, recesses, and other groggeries. Regularly-kept hotels and taverns are generally closed at an early hour of the night, and are frequented by a different class of persons from those usually found in saloons, and it must be perfectly evident to every one, that it is, and will continue to be, impossible to maintain first-class hotels and taverns in the community, so long as almost the only profitable portion of the trade is permitted to be nearly entirely absorbed by small or large recesses or saloons, which are thus doubly injurious. To show that I am not exaggerating on this point, you must be aware that nearly every one of our first class hotel-keepers have become insolvent within the last two years. It is a notorious fact that many of these saloons, recesses, and other groggeries, are kept open all night for the accommodation of the very worst class of society, both male and female. In these places all sorts of crimes are hatched, and their perpetration determined on, at hours when all decent members of society are at rest.

While I am free to admit that a very large proportion of the public is fully prepared to carry out a prohibitory liquor law, and another portion of the public would be willing to give it a fair trial, although not placing much faith in its efficacy—I think that a stringent license law, by which houses of entertainment should be rigidly regulated, and their numbers curtailed according to a fixed scale hereafter to be devised, according to population; high rates and grades of license or otherwise, as the case may be, would afford the most general satisfaction to the entire community.

No. 8. This is a very difficult question to dispose of, and indeed I do not almost see how it is to be met. Most certainly it would be advisable to suppress mere groggeries at any time, but I do not think that would be the best course to adopt to prepare the public mind gradually for the enactment of a prohibitory law. It would, I think, create agitation, and irritate the public mind, and probably cause a hostile public feeling against such a law being enacted.

Another reason why this question is difficult of solution, is, that some saloons are absolutely required in cities, where those gentlemen who are living outside their limits, but whose daily avocations oblige them to resort to the city, should be able to procure necessary refreshments at mid-day; but there can be no doubt that three-fourths of those places now in existence in Toronto, might be suppressed with great advantage to the public, and any recesses or saloons licensed ought only to be allowed in connection with large taverns or hotels, in order that such establishments may be maintained in the community efficiently.

No. 9. In my humble opinion, the work of this suppression of these new groggeries cannot begin too soon. But, in order to gradually steal on the public mind, as it were, and prevent a popular *furor* being raised against it, I think it would be more advisable, "that no interest might suffer," and the cause of temperance be advanced, that the diminution should be made as existing licenses drop through.

But, beyond all question, the licensing power should be invested in some body not dependent upon popular election.

Statement exhibiting the whole Number of Prisoners committed to Gaol in the United Counties of York and Peel, for the Years 1856, 1857, *and* 1858, *and also shewing those who were committed especially for Drunkenness :—*

1856,	....	Number	of Commitments,	....	1979
"	....	"	for Drunkenness,	....	1511
1857,	....	"	of Commitments,	....	1906
"	....	"	for Drunkenness,	....	1530
1858,	....	"	of Commitments,	....	1941
"	....	"	for Drunkenness,	....	1482

JOHN CARLING, Esq., M.P.P., was then examined as follows :—

What is your name and business ?—John Carling; my business is that of a Brewer.

What number of barrels do you make annually ?—About 6000; average value, $8 each.

What number of bushels do you consume?—20,000 bushels of barley, and grown in my own neighbourhood; about 8 tons of hops, grown also in Canada. Hops $15 per hundred weight.

What amount of capital invested?—$40,000.

What amount in buildings?—$25,000, and employ 15 or 16 hands.

What would you lose if your business was prohibited?—About $12,000 in the buildings and the fixtures.

Do you employ deleterious drugs to any extent in the manufacture of beer?—Not any, and I am not aware that such drugs are used.

What is your opinion of the policy of a law prohibiting the manufacture of intoxicating liquors?—I don't think it could be carried out.

The Committee then adjourned.

GEORGE DUGGAN, Recorder, Toronto, submitted answers to the four following questions:—

1. What was the number of convictions before your Court in 1858?—I say the number convicted in the year 1858, before my Court, was fifty-eight.

2. How many of those were attributable to intoxicating liquors?—That twenty of these were attributable to the use of intoxicating liquors.

3. Can you suggest any beneficial amendments to existing laws relative to the sale of intoxicating liquors?—The answer to this is embraced in the answer to number four.

4. Do you think the public mind prepared for a Prohibitory Liquor Law?—I consider the public mind strongly imbued with a deep sense of the enormous amount of immorality, pauperism, violence, crime, and misery of every kind, of which intoxicating liquors are the fruitful source. I also think that the public at large is impressed with the belief that existing laws afford no adequate protection against the great evil complained of, and that

they would accept, and carry out with results highly beneficial, any measure largely and in earnest facilitating restraint upon the use of intoxicating liquors, and reserving to the communities to be affected thereby ample privileges in relation to its application to themselves. Then I would respectfully suggest that, in amendment to existing laws, a law should be passed, to come into force at a future day, say January 1860 or 1861, prohibiting everywhere throughout Upper Canada the sale or purchase, directly or indirectly, by retail, of intoxicating or fermented liquors, except for medicine for the sick and under medical direction, to be given in writing with the signature of the practitioner, with power from time to time, however, to any County (which shall include the Town and Village therein), and to any City, to authorize the sale by retail of spirituous liquors within the same for a period of two years at a time, upon the passage or adoption, by the Municipal Council of such County or City, of a resolution declaring that, in the opinion of such Council, it would be truly beneficial to the inhabitants of the Municipalities to authorize the sale by retail of spirituous liquors therein, and upon such resolution being approved by a majority of the ratepayers; the time of the year for the above proceedings to be fixed by statute. It would be desirable that the party to grant individual licenses should not be subject to those influences which are generally pressed on persons seeking periodical elections in the community in which he is to act, and the resolution above suggested should also state the maximum number of licenses to be at any time existing during each of the two years. Drunkenness to be declared a misdemeanor. Also, when any person is found drunk in any inn, place of public entertainment, or other house or place where intoxicating or malt liquors are sold, the proprietor, keeper, agent, or other person in charge or exercising control thereat for the time being, to be deemed the cause of drunkenness and guilty of a misdemeanor, unless such party proves that the person so found drunk had been received at such inn, &c., for protection and care, and had not during his continuance there partaken of any spirituous or fermented liquors. It should also be made unlawful for any person on Sunday (persons belonging to the house, boarders, and travellers, excepted), to be at or within any inn or other place where spirituous or malt liquors are retailed, or to be thereat between the hours of 8 p.m. and 8 a.m. on week days, unless having other business than that of occupying the place as an inn, &c.. This provision, I think, would check idling and tippling, and the desertion of the family circle and domestic hearth by both young and old, rich and poor, so deeply interesting to society at large. I would recommend that the buyer and seller be competent witnesses where either is concerned, providing that no one be convicted on evidence given by himself as a witness in any such case. I would advise moderate penalties, summary authority for the trial of offences against this law, with power on third, or other subsequent conviction, to sentence to hard labour to the extent of three months, and that all Peace officers should be authorized to enter inns, &c., in the day time, and at any time at night whilst some of the guests or inmates are still unretired for the night, to see that this law is observed.

Rowland Burr, Esquire, of Toronto, then submitted the following:—

1st. I believe the morals of the public are greatly injured by the use of intoxicating liquors. My experience as a Justice of the Peace and Jail Commissioner for nearly twenty years, shews that 9 out of 10 of the male prisoners, and 19 out of 20 of the female prisoners, have been brought there by intoxicating liquor. I have visited the Jails from Quebec to Sandwich, through the length and breadth of Canada, and I have personally examined nearly 2000 prisoners in the Jails, of whom two-thirds were males and one-third females: they nearly all signed a petition that I presented to them for a Maine Liquor Law, many of them stating that it was their only hope of being saved from utter ruin, unless they could go where intoxicating liquors were not sold.

I examined the Jailors' books, wherein they all kept a record of the number of persons, their age, country, and occupations, and their crime, also whether they were brought there by the use of intoxicating liquors. In four years there were 25,000 prisoners in the Jails, and it appeared from the records that 22,000 of that number had been brought there by intoxicating liquors, and I believe, from the 2000 whom I examined, that 24,000 out of the 25,000 would never have been there had it not been for Liquor Trade and License Law. I have the record now before me, kept by myself, of the Liquor Dealers of Yonge Street, for 54 years past, 100 in number, and I will mention the abstract of the record, viz.:—

Number of Ruined Drunkards in the 100 Families,	214
Loss of Property once owned in Real Estate,	£58,700
Number of Widows left,	46
,, Orphans ,,	235
Sudden Deaths,	44
Suicides publicly known,	13
Number of Premature Deaths by Drunkenness,	203
Murders,	4
Executions,	3
Number of Years of Human Life Lost by Drunkenness,	1,915

I have been acquainted with these 100 families, and I have kept written records of them, for the purpose of printing them, leaving out the names.

2nd. The remedy, and the only remedy, in human power, is a Prohibitory Law.

In this opinion I am supported by the Report of the Committee of 39 of the most illustrious members of the British House of Commons, recommending such a law, after sitting in Committee during three months, and taking evidence from Judges, Sheriffs, Mayors, Jailors, Magistrates, Naval and Military Officers, from all parts of England. The Report of the Committee occupies nearly 600 pages, mostly of evidence of such a black character as I never saw before.

I am also supported by the testimony of thousands of persons wishing in their sober moments to refrain, but when the liquor is within their reach, the sight, taste, or smell of it overcomes all good desires, and they are ruined.

3rd. I believe the people of Canada are prepared to sustain a Prohibitory Liquor Law. In the towns and cities there would be difficulty and labor at first; but in the city of Toronto there is a sufficient number of Prohibitory Law men to fairly support such a law if we had it; but it must be a strong one. If the law is mistified, and not clear so that all could understand it, it would then fail. But give us a clear, strong, sensible Law, and I have no fear but that in 20 years the Government would be out of debt most assuredly, and not one pauper or prisoner to where there are now ten. Some years ago, when there was a Bill before the House for a Maine Liquor Law, there were 180,000 persons petitioned for it, and I have no doubt that two-thirds of the householders are in favor of it now.

4th. The effect it had on the State of Maine worked well for some time, but its friends relaxed their energy, and the opponents got new men in power, who repealed the law; and the liquor-dealers sprang up like mushrooms. Crime and misery returned to such a fearful extent, that, in about five months, the people of the State became aroused like a lion bereaved of her young, and at one sweep sent all the Members out of the House who voted for the repeal, save one, and re-enacted the law stronger than ever; and it is now a blessing to the people of the State.

I have travelled through six States which now have the Maine Law—they are all doing well: the State of Minnesota has embodied it in the constitution on becoming a State. It is not entirely carried out in any of the States, but is increasing, and the people are generally satisfied with it; there is no class of people so much benefitted by the law as the liquor dealers themselves. It has been ascertained to a demonstration that three-fourths of the dealers themselves were ruined by the traffic, and often their fami lies. I visited their jails: some were without a prisoner, some had one or two; and Judges, Juries, Magistrates, Lawyers, and Jailors, had little to do.

5th. As to the power of the Municipalities of restraining the sale of it, I reply, in answer, that the Township of York exercised its full power, and would not grant licenses. The Supreme Court of Law quashed their By-Law, and every man got a license that asked for it, and made the matter worse than ever. Chinguacuosy, in their council, discussed the matter, and decided that, the way the law stood, they had not the power to refuse any man a license that had a certificate of certain qualifications, whatever might be their situation or standing in society. So all got licenses that asked and had the qualification. The Township of Lobo carried it out until the decision of the Judges in the York Township case; then they threw open the flood gates. Sarnia and Darlington were similar cases.

Amount of Wine and other Intoxicating Liquors Consumed in the Province:—

The importation in the year 1855, ... £250,672 1 4
    Do.   do.   1856, ... 360,252 4 11
    Do.   do.   1857, ... 122,380 4 11

Amount of Duty
For 1855, ... £ 85,498 7 4
 „ 1856, ... 133,117 4 11
 „ 1857, ...   55,436 19 7

Amount of Spirits Distilled in the Province:—

Year	Lower Canada.	Year	Upper Canada.
1855,	6 stills, 668,694 gallons.	1855,	112 stills, 2,011,882 gals.
1856,	6 „ 618,766 „	1856,	107 „ 2,346,057 „
1857,	14 „ 936,824 „	1857,	94 „ 2,218,732 „

Amount of Duty on Stills and Liquors:—

	Lower Canada.		Upper Canada.
Year 1854, ...	£2,836 4 6	Year 1854, ...	£9,133 15 6
„ 1855, ...	3,192 3 4	„ 1855, ...	9,472 16 10
„ 1856, ...	3,658 18 8	„ 1856, ...	13,620 1 3
„ 1857, ...	9,555 2 11	„ 1857, ...	14,807 1 6

Total Amount of Duty in the Year 1857, £24,362, 4s. 5d.

The annual average amount of gallons is 3,000,000. This is more than doubled by drugs and water, and costs the consumer at least half a dollar a-gallon, equal to $3,000,000.

Imported Spirits and Wine amount to £1,000,000, and that will cost the consumer double the foreign cost.

I may safely say that Liquor costs Canada *Five Millions* per annum, or *Fifty Millions* in the last ten years.

The average income to the Government on the Duties and Licenses on Wines and Intoxicating Liquors, is as follows:—

Average Duties on Imports,	$400,000
Cost of Collecting do.	200,000
Net proceeds,	$200,000
Duties on Stills and Liquors,	100,000
Tavern and Shop License in every way,	200,000
Annual amount,	$500,000

The Government derives, in ten years, 5 millions; it costs the people 50 millions; leaving a loss of 45 millions of dollars in 10 years to the whole Province.

The number of bushels of grain annually used in the Distilleries, chiefly wheat, is one million, equal to 10 millions in the last 10 years.

The amount of barley used in brewing, for the last 10 years, amounts to ten million bushels, and costs the Province ten million dollars, amounting to 55 million loss in ten years.

Then the cost of Criminal Justice is annually $100,000, of which can fairly be set down to liquor one half, which amounts in ten years to $500,000—making a fair average loss of $55,500,000 in 10 years, deducting the revenue derived from the business.

According to the table which I have kept of 100 liquor dealers for 50 years, the loss of human labour by drunkenness in 10 years would amount to 30,000 years, which labour, at $200 per annum, would amount to six millions of dollars, which should be added,

There are many other ways in which the Province has suffered great loss in dollars and cents, of which I have not the statistics, and cannot compute.

But I have answered the 5 questions which you put to me, to the best of my ability.

GEORGE GOODERHAM, Esquire, in obedience to summons from Committee, submitted the following :—

1. What is your name and business ?—George Gooderham.

2. How long has your firm been engaged in the distillery business ?—Upwards of twenty-five years.

3. What amount of capital have you now invested ?—In distilling, between eighty and one hundred thousand dollars.

4. How many bushels of grain do you distil annually ?—About one hundred thousand.

5. How many gallons do you make annually ?—About half a million of gallons at 35 per cent. under proof.

6. What is the wholesale price of whiskey per gallon ?—Just now, twenty-seven cents.

7. Is your whiskey consumed in this Province, or do you send any abroad ?—Our trade extends to Belleville, north to Collingwood, and west to London; this extent of country consumes all we make now.

8. If a law were passed prohibiting the manufacture of distilled liquor for use as a beverage, confining the sale to foreign purchasers and for domestic use in the arts, how would your business be affected ?—It would nearly destroy our home trade, and oblige us to have recourse to exportation, which is at all times critical, and could not be prosecuted to advantage, only at particular times, and during the season of navigation.

The Rev. HANNIBAL MULKINS, Chaplain to the Provincial Penitentiary, was summoned before the Committee, and submitted the following :—

17th March, 1859.

To the Chairman of the Select Committee on the Prohibitory Liquor Law.

Sir,—I beg to submit to you the following answers to the several questions preferred by the Committee, as far as it is in my power to do so, and as far as they relate to the Provincial Penitentiary.

1. I cannot say as to the Gaol; but the number of prisoners confined in the Provincial Penitentiary for the years mentioned, are as follows:—'55, 707; '56, 836; '57, 907; '58, 1036.

2. Cannot say.

3. In the Provincial Penitentiary, the number of convicts of the different Protestant denominations in the several years above mentioned, and the official returns concerning them on the subject of intoxicating drinks, are as follows:—

Total Number Protestant Convicts in 1855, ... 408
Total Abstainers, 10; Moderate Drinkers, ... 60
Intemperate, 169; Habitual Drunkards, ... 82
Under the Influence of Liquor at the time of the Commission of the Crime, ... 141

In 1857, of the Protestant Convicts then in Prison, 146 were in the habit, before conviction, of using liquor to excess; 73 used intoxicating liquors in moderation; 186 had been drinking at the time the crime was committed.

The returns for 1856 and 1858 are not at hand.

4. I think it is.

5. I am of opinion that the number of places for the sale of intoxicating liquors has largely increased during the last three years.

6. I do not think the regular and well-kept taverns as productive of injury to the community as the saloons, recesses, and various places where liquors are to be had. Yet, notwithstanding, the regular taverns, and especially in the country, are very injurious to public morality.

7. The public mind, in my opinion, is much divided on the subject on this question. I believe that in the old settlements of the country, and in the Townships generally, a judicious Prohibitory Law would be well received and carried out. In these places I think the population are prepared for it. In the Cities and Towns there is not the same preparation in the public mind, as, in these places, greater interest will be affected by it, and a more compact organization to resist it is in existence.

8. In answer to this question, no doubt much might be done to prepare the public mind for final and total prohibition, if an act were passed to suppress all places where liquors are sold for the purposes of drink, and leaving it with the Municipalities to decide whether any Taverns should be licensed or not; that no Municipality should issue a license unless the people in the said Municipality, called to vote for that purpose, should cast a majority of votes in favor of issuing licenses; and that the statute should fix the number in proportion to population, beyond which no Municipality could go.

9. I do not think it would be more satisfactory to the public generally. It would leave the question open, and become a source of constant irritation and contention.

In regard to the second list of questions, being four in number, submitted by the Committee, the 3rd and 4th are the only ones to which it is necessary for me to reply.

3. I think many suggestions might be made for the amendment of existing laws on the traffic in liquors, especially that their importation should bear a high duty, that the duty on the manufacture should be increased, and that the adulterations of liquor offered for sale should be deemed a very grave offence, if not made penal.

4. The liquor traffic is unquestionably the source of great evils, of numerous vices, immoralities, and crimes, which infest and corrupt society. Any measure which will diminish these evils will be a boon to the country; and, moreover, a Prohibitory

Liquor Law would have a most beneficial and salutary effect in promoting the general morality of society, and is called for upon the same principle as any other law which is intended to suppress the causes of other vices and immoralities.

In the Provincial Penitentiary, a large proportion of the convicts have, in my opinion, been addicted to the use of intoxicating liquors, and a large number have admitted that it was directly the cause of their criminal acts; while others, and not a few, have stated that it had indirectly led them on from vice to vice, until—with property lost, and character blighted, and hopes destroyed—it had ultimately plunged them into crime.

The degree of mortality among the convicts is usually small. I do not think that any convict has suffered much sickness, much less death, in consequence of his sudden abandonment of liquor, or separation from his evil habits, in consequence of his imprisonment. During the visitation of the cholera, a few years ago, about fourteen convicts died. I am of opinion that these persons had generally been addicted to the use of intoxicating drinks before their incarceration, and that therefore they fell more easily victims to that terrible disease.

Yours, very truly,

HANNIBAL MULKINS.

Mr. Chairman then read the following statement from the Customs Department:—

Statement of the Number of Gallons of Proof Spirits Distilled in Canada West in the Year 1858:—

Number of Stills,.................................. 110
Gallons Manufactured,.......................... 2,543,701

Return of the Number of Gallons of Malt Liquors Brewed in Upper Canada, with the Number of Licenses Issued from 8th August to 31st December, 1858:—

Number of Licenses Issued,.................... 101
    „   Gallons Brewed,........................ 850,375

Brandy and Other Liquors:—
General Statement of Imports, 1857.

	Gallons.	Value.
Brandy,	25,591	$ 52,531.33
Cordials,	3,238	7,191.71
Gin,	99,976	56,862.13
Rum,	21,725	14,640.08
Whisky,	313,551	138,291.75
Wine,	222,547	222,007.96
Ale and Beer,	366,361	102,074.98

Gallons,...1,052,989   Value,...$593,599.94

The Committee then adjourned.

Forbes M'Kenzie Act of Scotland.

Forbes Mackenzie's Bill, enacted in 1853, provides and enacts—

"That no grocer shall be allowed to sell spirits, or give gratuitously, a glass of wine or spirits, to be consumed on the premises, in any town in Scotland.

"No confectioner, or dealer in provisions or eatables of any kind, shall receive a license to sell wines and spirits, to be consumed on the premises.

"Every inn or hotel, having four sleeping apartments or upwards, shall be prohibited from supplying any party, excepting lodgers and travellers, with wines and spirits, before eight in the morning, or after eleven o'clock at night; and no such house shall be allowed to supply either a public or private supper party, or ball, with wines or spirits, later than eleven P.M.

"No such inn or public-house shall be allowed to supply a townsman with wines or spirits during any part of Sunday, nor shall a lodger be permitted to invite a friend to any meal where wines or spirits are required, during any part of that day."

Mr. Duncan M'Laren, when Lord Provost of the City of Edinburgh, said:—

"It is hardly correct to describe this Act as a new law, embodying a principle not formerly recognized in the legislation of this country, although this has been confidently asserted; for it is merely a restoration of the ancient Sabbath law of Scotland, embodied in five Acts of the Parliament of Scotland, passed from 1661 to 1701, which made it a crime to sell *anything* on the Sabbath except for the accommodation of *bona fide* travellers. In an act passed in 1828, commonly called Mr. Home Drummond's Act, a clause was embodied in one of the schedules, intended to repress with greater strictness, and to punish in a more summary manner than was competent under the Scotch Acts, the trade of selling spirits on Sunday, which had then crept into use in some places; but, by a decision of the Court of Justiciary on 25th February, 1833, in a case in which the Magistrates of Edinburgh were parties, it was found that the clause had been so framed as by implication to sanction the sale of spirits on Thursday, except during the hours of Divine worship. From the date of that decision the sellers of spirits became a privileged class in Scotland, being allowed to carry on their trade on Sunday, while all other traders were restricted by the ancient Sabbath law. The effect of Mr. Forbes Mackenzie's Act has therefore been, not to introduce a new principle, but merely to abolish this peculiar privilege which the spirit-dealers had inadvertently acquired, and to put them on the same footing as the traders in Bibles, for example, or other commodities, all of which it is unlawful to sell on the Sabbath-day."

Forbes M'Kenzie Act of Canada.

We give below a certified copy of the above Act, from the Official *Gazette*, of the 9th April, and which is now the law of the land. The assent of the Governor General was given on the 26th March, 1659.

We hail this measure as a first instalment of a more general and extended Act for the whole province and for every day in the year; we regard this measure as a very important step in the right direction, not only on account of the good that is likely to flow from it, but also from the fact, that the Legislature has now admitted their right and duty to legislate in this direction, on this subject. Remember that it is not merely a By-Law of any one municipality, but a Statute of the country, passed by the Legislature, and having received the assent of his Excellency the Governor General, may not be violated or evaded with impunity.

The Law, 22 Vic., 6 cap., 1859.

"*Whereas* it is expedient to restrain the sale of intoxicating liquors during certain periods: Therefore Her Majesty, by and with the advice and consent of the Legislative Council and Assembly of Canada, enacts as follows:—

" 1. In all places where, by the laws of that part of this Province called Upper Canada, intoxicating liquors are or may be allowed to be sold by wholesale or retail, no sale or other disposal of the said liquors shall take place therein, or on the premises thereof, or out of or from the same, to any person or persons whomsoever, from or after the hour of seven of the clock on Saturday night till the hour of eight of the clock on Monday morning thereafter, or during any further time on the said days, and any hours on other days, during which, by any By-Law of the Municipality wherein such place or places may be situated, the same, or the bar-room or bar-rooms thereof, ought to be kept closed, save and except to travellers lodging at, or ordinary boarders lodging at, the place or places where such liquor is sold, and save and except in cases where a requisition, for medicinal purposes, signed by a licensed medical practitioner, or by a justice of the peace, is produced by the vendee or his agent, nor shall any such liquors be permitted or allowed to be drunk in any such places, except as aforesaid, during the time prohibited by this Act for the sale of the same.

" 2. A penalty for the first offence of not less than twenty do'lars, with costs, in case of conviction, shall be recoverable from, and leviable against the goods and chattels of, the person or persons who are the proprietors in occupancy, or tenants or agents in occupancy, of said place or places, who shall be found by himself or herself, or themselves, or his, her, or their servants or agents, to have contravened the enactment in the first section hereof, or any part thereof,—for the second offence, a penalty against all such of not less than forty dollars, with costs,—for a third offence, a penalty against all such of not less than one hundred dollars, with costs,— and for a fourth or any after offence, a penalty against all such of not less than three months' imprisonment, with hard labour, in the common gaol of the County wherein such place and places may be,—the number of said offences to be ascertained by the production of a certificate from the convicting Justice, or by other satisfactory evidence to the Justice before whom the information or complaint may be made; and it is hereby enacted that convictions for several offences may be made under this Act, although such offences may have been committed in the same day: Provided always, that the increased penalties hereinbefore imposed, shall only be recoverable in the case of offences committed on different days.

"3. Any person or persons may be the informant or informants, complainant or complainants, in prosecuting under this Act; all proceedings shall be begun within twenty days from the date of the offence; all informations, complaints, or other necessary proceedings, may be brought and heard before any one or more Justices of the Peace of the County where the offence or offences were committed or done; and the mode of procedure in, and the forms appended to, the Act sixteenth Victoria, chapter one hundred and seventy-eight, for summary proceedings, may be followed as regards the cases and proceedings under this Act.

"4. The said penalties in money, or any portion of them which may be recovered, shall be paid to the convicting Justice or other acting Justice in the case, and by him paid equally, one half to the informant or complainant, and the other half to the Treasurer of the Municipality where the place or places referred to are situated.

"5. The word "Liquors" shall be understood to mean and comprehend all spirituous and malt liquors, and all combinations of liquors or drinks which are intoxicating.

"6. This Act shall apply to Upper Canada only."

The New Municipal Law,
Sec. 245 of 22d Vic., cap. 99, A. D. 1858.

As the Municipal Act of last session differs very materially in many essential points from former Acts governing Municipal affairs, we deem it advisable to give a short synopsis of so much of it as will be of immediate use to our readers, without reference to former Acts or parts of Acts.

The qualification for a Councillor in Townships is Freehold to four hundred or Leasehold to eight hundred dollars. In Incorporated Villages, Freehold to forty and Leasehold to eighty dollars per annum. In Towns, Freehold eighty dollars per annum. In every case, the property, whether leasehold or freehold, must have been assessed against them, in their own names, on the last revised assessment roll of the township, village, or town. The term "lease-hold" means tenancy by the year, but not for a shorter period. They must be British subjects of the full age of 21 years.

Those disqualified are the Judges, Jailers, Officers of any Municipality, Bailiffs, Sheriff's Officers, Inn, Tavern, or Saloon keepers, persons receiving pay from Corporations (except as Mayor, Warden, Reeve, Deputy Reeve, or Councillor), persons or their partners, or those whose partners have any contract with or on behalf of Corporations.

Of those who are exempt we shall make no remarks, because if such claim the exemption, well and good—if not, they cannot be disturbed.

Those having a right to vote at election for Councillors, are the Male Freeholders of every Municipality, and such of the household thereof as have resided in the Municipality one month prior to the election, and who were severally rated on the last revised assessment rolls for such property, held in their own right or that of their wives, as proprietors or tenants. They must be subjects of Her Majesty, and of the full age of 21 years.

In Towns and Incorporated Villages, the property, whether freehold or leasehold, which entitles a person to vote, must have been rated, in Town at twenty dollars, and in Villages at twelve dollars, annual value.

When Municipalities are divided into Wards, no Elector is entitled to vote in more than one Ward.

When landlord and tenant are both assessed for the same property, both are entitled to vote.

Joint owners or occupants of real property, when such property is assessed at an amount sufficient, if equally divided between them, to qualify each to vote, shall each have a vote; but if insufficient to qualify each, when divided, then none of such joint owners or occupiers can vote.

Elections, for the future, cannot be held in Taverns, or houses wherein spirituous liquors are sold.

Municipal Councils are empowered by By-Law to fix the place or places for holding the next ensuing elections, otherwise the election may be held at the place or places where last held.

The election of Councillors shall take place on the first Monday in January in each year, and when there is no division of the Municipality into Wards, the election shall be by a general vote, otherwise, in each Ward.

Returning Officers, for every Municipality or Ward, shall be appointed yearly by By-Law. In case of the death or absence of the Returning Officer on the day and at the place of election, the electors shall, after the expiration of one hour from the time the election should have commenced, choose from among themselves a person who shall be Returning Officer for such Ward or Municipality.

Returning Officers are required to give ten days' notice, by posting up, in four public places in his Municipality or Ward, notices of the election to be held by him.

Township Clerks are required to furnish to Returning Officers a correct copy of so much of the then last revised assessment roll as contains the names of the householders and freeholders in each Ward or Municipality, which copy or copies shall be verified by the Clerk to be true and correct.

Returning Officers to furnish poll books, and to commence the elections at ten o'clock in the forenoon. He may close the election in one hour, if no more candidates are proposed than by his writ he is bound to return. If, however, there are more than one candidate proposed, and a poll is demanded, he must keep the poll open until four o'clock in the afternoon of the first day, and then adjourn until ten o'clock next morning, and continue until four o'clock of that day, unless he is satisfied that all the electors have had a fair opportunity to vote, and if one hour at one time elapses without any qualified elector giving or tendering his vote, the Returning Officer may close the election.

The oaths which can be required of voters are—that he is 21 years of age; that he is a subject by birth or naturalization; that he is the person named in the last revised assessment roll, and that he is, and has been for one month, a resident householder in the Municipality; that he has not before voted at that election; and that he has not received, nor does he expect to receive, any gift or reward for his vote. Returning officers to administer such oath or oaths to any person tendering his vote, at the request of any candidate or elector.

The Returning Officer shall publicly declare the candidate having the greatest number of votes at the close of the election, duly elected.

CHAPTER III.

PROHIBITORY ACTION IN UNITED STATES.

Maine Law Movement—Its Origin—and Results: what it has done for the United States, and would do for Canada.

MAINE LAW MOVEMENT IN UNITED STATES.

ITS ORIGIN.

In the State of Maine, some of the promoters of the temperance reformation had so far forgotten their principles as to compromise with wine-drinkers, and form with them a consolidated body called the "Maine Temperance Union." A school of sound temperance men (among whom was Neal Dow) arose from the ruins of the old organization, and their first appearance in the Legislature of the State was in 1837, when a memorial, drawn up by General James Appleton, of Portland, was presented, demanding, not only an abrogation of all license laws, "as the support and life of the traffic," but also "an entire prohibition of all sale, except for medicine and the arts," for the same reason that the State makes laws to "prevent the sale of unwholesome meats, or for the removal of anything which endangers the health and life of the citizen, or which threatens to subvert our civil rights or overthrow the government."

Much credit is due to General Appleton for this truly gallant achievement; for, however brave he may have been in the exercise of his profession, we cannot suppose that he remembers any action on the battle-field with anything approaching the satisfaction with which he may reasonably regard this "first attack" on the greatest enemy of every civilized community, a "legalized liquor traffic."

In 1837, however, the country did not seem prepared for so decided a step as that proposed by General Appleton.

I

Many took the strong position, that "if the rum traffic could not be outlawed, no permanent ground could be gained; and that while moral suasion was to be used with the inebriate, the man who effected the ruin must not only no longer be licensed in his horrid work, but must be rooted out and driven from his business by the strong arm of civil power, for it could be done in no other manner." To this one object did Neal Dow devote his life from this time forward, sparing neither labor nor money to arouse in the people of Maine that righteous indignation at the atrocious liquor traffic which resulted in the enactment, in 1851, of the first Prohibitory Liquor Law in the United States.

The labours by which this great victory was achieved are worthy of a permanent record. Neal Dow first advocated the principle of prohibition in 1839, before the Board of Aldermen. He then succeeded in inducing the Board of Aldermen to refer the question of license or no license to the direct vote of the citizens of Portland. In a vote of 1163 he was defeated only by a majority of 35. The fact, however, that in a population of about 15,000, 564 of the adult male citizens had voted against granting licenses for the sale of liquor, was regarded by Neal Dow as a cheering indication of ultimate success.

Neal Dow's next aim was to secure a municipal regulation which should render the whole traffic in intoxicating liquors illegal. Unwilling to assume this responsibility, the authorities referred this question to a vote of the people. The progress made in public sentiment in about three years, chiefly through the exertions of Neal Dow, was indicated by the result of this ballot. From a minority of 35 on the simple question of withholding licenses in 1838, we find him, in less than four years, carrying the still more important point—prohibition of the liquor traffic, by a majority of 440.

In 1843, Neal Dow printed and circulated, at his own expense, petitions to the Legislature, praying for a stringent law, and "that the traffic in intoxicating drinks might be held and adjudged as an infamous crime." The petitions were received, and in Feb.

1844 he appeared before a committee in the Representatives' Hall in the Capitol, which was crowded with an intelligent audience, and there, with his own convincing arguments and earnest eloquence, he advocated the claims of the petitioners. The committee reported a bill favorable to his views, which passed the House, but was unsuccessful in the Senate.

In the fall of 1844, Neal Dow again printed and circulated petitions, again addressed a committee in the Hall of Representatives, in the Capitol at Augusta, but with no better success than before. From this time the friends of temperance began to bestir themselves generally. They determined to appeal to the "sovereign people." Meetings were held through 1844, '45, and '46, in every part of the State. Neal Dow was pressed to attend them, and zealously did he pursue the work. The winter's cold, the summer's heat, snow, rain, exposure, and expense, were all disregarded when his duty to this important mission needed his attendance, and "many," says one of his companions in travelling, "are the school districts, those hiding-places of power, which can testify to the force of his reasoning, the aptness of his illustrations, and the severity of his animadversions on the traffic and the traffickers." In every speech his great object was to show rumselling to be an infamous crime, and the ballot-box its antidote. The faith of an apostle seemed to inspire him. He worked like one who knows his mission, and he never doubted his ultimate success, but knew well that it could only be secured by his own unceasing diligence. In the spring of 1846 he travelled over four thousand miles, within two months, in the counties of York, Oxford, and Cumberland, and at numerous meetings he came in contact with many thousands of citizens, creating a deep-rooted and wide-spread enthusiasm among the people which the experience of years has fully justified. The conviction which he impressed upon the citizens was, that talking and working for temperance would do little good without voting for it as well; and there can be no better proof of the lasting character of the conviction he produced than the fact that the Legislature became at every election more and more composed of

Maine Liquor Law men, until this became a test of universal application and an issue at all elections.

In July, 1846, Neal Dow appeared again before a committee of the Legislature, and presented one petition from Rutland, fifty-nine feet in length, with three thousand eight hundred names, most of which had been obtained by his own personal efforts. That it might be seen to advantage, it was suspended from the book-cases on either side of the speaker's chair. This was followed by other petitions, and the aggregate names signed in favor of prohibition at this session was forty thousand. This heavy pressure from without could no longer be resisted with impunity, and a bill abolishing the license system, and leaving all sale forbidden, was passed by a vote of eighty-one to forty-two in the House, and twenty-three to five in the Senate.

Neal Dow, in communicating this cheering intelligence to the Secretary of the American Temperance Union, said, "This is the first instance, I believe, in which the government of a civilized Christian State has declared by statute that there shall not be within its borders any traffic in intoxicating liquors to be used as a drink; and that if any such liquors shall be sold for such purpose, under any circumstances, it shall be against law and equity and a good conscience. It was enacted in answer to petitions of more than forty thousand of the good people of the State, and constitutes the *first blow* only which the friends of temperance here propose striking at the traffic in strong drinks."

It will be seen, therefore, that Neal Dow, although a great enthusiast, conducted the work with the coolness and judgment of a philosopher and the foresight of a statesman. If he could not secure all he desired, he would accept whatever the Legislature would grant, and patiently labor till the next session, again to renew his exertions for more perfect legislation.

The act of 1846 for a time produced a good effect; but as the penalties for its violation were small and the profits large, the law was evaded by a variety of subterfuges.

The liquor-dealers, although in many cases still continuing their accustomed calling, found themselves subjected to so many inconveniences, that in 1847 they roused themselves, got up a petition signed by seven thousand citizens, covertly gained, for a repeal of the law. This was confronted by a loud remonstrance from the friends of the law. Both parties were heard in the Hall of Representatives before a committee of the Legislature and a numerous audience, including a majority of both Houses. On this occasion Neal Dow made a speech which has been described as one of "burning irony, withering rebuke, and caustic satire." The committee, having a tavern-keeper for its chairman, reported a bill repealing the law of 1846; but it was refused a second reading in the House, and never reached the Senate.

The result of these exertions was manifest in the passage by both Houses of a bill in 1849, which, though not entirely satisfactory, was a great improvement upon the former bill. This bill, however, was vetoed by Governor Dana, which proved to him an act of political suicide.

Still persevering, Neal Dow again appeared in the Hall of Representatives in August, 1850, with a bill of his own drafting, subsequently known as the "Maine Law." He there made another of his clear, logical speeches, and pressed the adoption of the bill. It was reported in the House and adopted without alteration, but it was lost in the Senate by a tie vote. This indication of a coming victory inspired the friends of temperance with a new hope throughout the State, and, in the succeeding elections in the fall, many a zealous advocate of the temperance cause was elected for the express purpose of carrying through the new bill.

For several years had Neal Dow devoted himself to this particular work: the bringing up public opinion—the popular feeling of the State—to a point where a stringent prohibitive law would be sustained. Politicians of all parties found that they could no longer calculate upon the results of elections, and were no longer sure of the offices for themselves and their friends. They no longer dared bring a barrel of rum to the hustings—the potent instrument wherein they formerly carried elections—for the rum would now *drive away* the respectable, though it might draw the depraved. The people were thus drawn away more and more from their old party attachments to the new movement against the grog-shops, and he was hated more and more, and opposed more and more, by all the seekers after office, and by all who lusted after the spoils of political victories.

It was under these circumstances that he was proposed for mayor of his native city in April, 1851; but his nomination was violently resisted by the mere politicians of all parties, who were unable, however, to prevent the masses of the people from making the nomination.

While Neal Dow suddenly became installed into an office involving all the important interests connected with such a growing city, and while he performed all the duties of that office with a diligence, punctuality, and promptness which a mere politically chosen magistrate seldom dreams of, his official position caused him in no degree to relax his ardor in the cause of prohibition.

Hitherto Neal Dow had labored as a private citizen and philanthropist, striving for the achievement of a moral reform, but from this time he appeared as endowed with the additional authority of official position. As mayor of the principal city of the State, he again appeared in the House of Representatives at Augusta. It was on the 25th of May, 1851, the sixth time of his addressing the Legislature on this subject. The representatives of the people had obtained their instructions from their constituents. The subject had been discussed throughout the State, and had been the issue on which the election had turned. The action of the government was all that remained to give the people's voice the authority of the law. Hon. Neal Dow spoke for an hour and a half in his usual style of acute reasoning, strong sense, and impassioned eloquence. He presented a bill, which was received and soon after acted upon by the Legislature.

While the bill was under consideration, Neal Dow was assailed by his opponents in the most violent manner, and bitter indeed were the invectives cast upon him. "Why," said Senator Carey, the only leading man in the Senate who spoke in opposition to the bill, "should the lord-mayor of Portland come down here with his rum-bill, all cut and dried, for this legislature to enact into a law? If this bill passes, he expects to be the greatest toad in the puddle." * * "This mandate, this ukase, was cut and dried for the adoption of the legislature by the mayor of Portland, who was before the License Committee, pricking them up to report in its favor, and is he to be allowed to dictate to a democratic legislature what enactment it shall pass, or what policy it shall pursue, on this question?"

Notwithstanding the force of opposition arrayed against it in the House, the bill speedily passed that body by a vote of eighty-six to forty. The Senate was no less prompt and decided in its action, as it immediately passed the bill without alteration or amendment, as it had been prepared by its originator, by a vote of eighteen to ten. The Governor signed the bill on the 2d of June. So prompt and decided was the action of the legislative and executive departments of government on this measure, that from the time it was taken up to its becoming the law of the State, three days only had elapsed. As this may be regarded as too rapid for judicious legislation, it must be borne in mind that the question had been under the consideration of the people and of the legislature for about ten years, and consequently further debate was unnecessary when it became known that a large majority were in favor of its immediate passage.

The next step was the enforcement of the law. With the confidence of a man who has right on his side, and the support of the moral part of the community, he issued his proclamation, stating his determination to enforce the law to the letter at the end of two months from the period of its approval by the Governor. This step showed that he tempered his enthusiasm with discretion, justice, and right policy, giving ample time for rum-sellers to dispose of their stock before it became subject to confiscation or seizure.

During this period of two months, the law being operative as soon as approved, the rum-shops rapidly diminished; and when the period of probation had expired, the mayor, ever true to his word, issued search-warrants for such places as were believed to continue the traffic. The first seizure was directed by the mayor in person. He was at the post of danger, if danger there was, to show that he did not fear the threats which had been thrown out, of personal violence, etc. About two thousand dollars' worth (at market prices) of liquor was seized and openly destroyed. This proceeding was witnessed in respectful silence by a large concourse of persons. Where were "the brave defenders of the rights of the citizens and their firesides?" Where were the men who had declared death to the executors of the law? One courageous man and a few policemen put the law into execution, and no attempt even was made to carry the threats of those political demagogues into execution. From this time the most vigorous enforcement of the law excited no more attention than the enforcement of any other statute for the preservation of the public peace, and the personal attendance of the mayor no longer became necessary. The results of the first three months of Maine Law operations were published in an address to the citizens of Portland in September, 1851, declaring that at that time there were no places where liquors were openly sold, and only a few where they were sold with great caution and secrecy.

Neal Dow's example was immediately followed by the mayors and municipal authorities of other cities and towns in the State, and thus the act was established as *a fait accompli*.

On the 15th of January, 1852, the mayor of Portland presented a statement to the Board of Aldermen, indicating the results of the first six months' experience of the Maine Law, from which it appeared that the law had been rigidly enforced, and cheerfully and quietly submitted to by the people. That the wholesale dealers promptly abandoned the business, and all retailers who had self-respect pursued the same course. The results to as reclamation from intemperance, public health, peace, etc., were reported, together with the returns from the almshouse, house of correction, etc., which deserve special attention, as indicating the practical advantages resulting from the proper enforcement of the law.

During 1852-4, Neal Dow had closely and carefully observed the workings of the Maine Law: its evasions and its successful enforcement in various parts of the State. It had been also adopted, in principle at least, in Connecticut, Massachusetts, Michigan, Rhode Island, and Vermont, with varied success. It had passed through the ordeal of courts, where judges and counsel used their best tact and talent to prove its inefficiency or its inconsistency with the constitutions of the several States. From the experience thus acquired, he determined upon certain improvements in order to render the Maine Law more stringent, so as to meet the requirements of the case. He well knew that the people and their representatives at the State capitol would readily adopt any measure he might deem necessary to the complete extirpation of the rum traffic. He therefore prepared a draft of a new bill embodying these improvements, and making the law more stringent than ever. This bill passed the Legislature, and was signed by the Governor on the 16th of March, 1855, to take effect on the 1st of May following.

RESULTS.
WHAT IT HAS DONE FOR THE UNITED STATES, AND WOULD DO FOR CANADA.
CONNECTICUT.

TESTIMONY OF GOVERNOR DUTTON AND OTHERS.—*The Best Prohibitory Law.*—As a witness to the merits and utility of a prohibitory law, I am able to speak. I think it is not too much to claim for the Connecticut law, that it is the best prohibitory law ever framed, because it was framed after long deliberation, and with a special regard to its being consistent with other existing laws.

Period of Enforcement.—The Maine Liquor Law was first enforced on the first of August, 1854, and its operation has been decidedly successful.

The Traffic Suspended.—Not a grog-shop, so called, is to be found in the State of Connecticut since the law came into force. No matter what the local balance of interest in any town, city, or spot in the State, the law was so framed that it should operate in all and each. I do not mean that there are not a few dark spots where, by falsehood and secrecy, evasion may be managed; but, in a word, the traffic is suspended.

No Drunkards in the Streets.—The effects are all that could be wished. I have not seen a drunkard in the streets since the 1st of August. I had not been in New York ten minutes before I saw a man drunk. Such is the contrast between a State with and one without a Maine Law.

Crime.—The statistics of crime have been materially diminished; the crimes which directly result from rum have fallen away fully half.

Families Supplied with Comforts.—There are hundreds—I have no doubt thousands—of families who are in this inclement weather well supplied with comforts, who, but for our law, would be destitute.

Public Peace and Security.—The general effect is a sober, calm, quiet air of security pervading the whole community, which is delightful to behold and enjoy.

Domestic Security.—There is one idea that a prohibitory law will invade personal and domestic security; the father of lies never invented a greater. You feel more secure when rowdyism fills the streets? Do you suppose that under the law your firesides would not be secure, and that they could be invaded under the pretext of ascertaining if you sold liquor? No such thing.

Opposition to the Law.—The opposition predicted to the enforcement of the law is not realized; I have never known it opposed; its enemies can not get up a combination against it, because it commends itself to all men's judgments, and is better liked the longer it is known. Another reason is, the incentive to violence is taken away; riot is always preceded by rum. Take away the rum, and you can't have the riot; and this is the great advantage of a prohibitory law.

Direct Action of the Maine Liquor Law.—Its beauty is its simplicity. When you see a nuisance, you at once remove it; that is our principle; we take the "abominable thing" and put it away in some safe place. So, when we see an individual unable to take care of himself, we simply take him (no matter who he may be) and put him where he cannot hurt himself or others.

Legal Suasion versus Moral Suasion.—We have found by practice that legal suasion is better than moral suasion. The latter is quite useless, except with moral men. When men are governed merely by appetite or love of gain, moral suasion has no effect; legal suasion saves breath and labor, and accomplishes the object in the simplest manner possible.

The Ladies Unanimous.—The ladies are all on the side of temperance, and surely gentlemen will not be so ungallant as not to take places by the side of the ladies.

No Drunken Brawls.—In our cities and manufacturing villages, streets that were previously constantly disturbed by drunken brawls, are now as quiet as any other. The change is so palpable that many who have been strongly opposed to such a law have become forced to acknowledge the efficiency of this.

The State Fair.—At the late State Agricultural Fair it was estimated that on one day from 26 to 30,000 persons of every condition of life were assembled, and not a solitary drunkard was seen, and not the slightest disturbance was made. The effect was so manifest that the law has been regarded with more favor since than it was before.

Prisons becoming Tenantless.—The statistics of our courts and prisons prove that criminal prosecutions are rapidly diminishing in number. Some jails are almost tenantless.

Two to One.—In one instance where a hotel-keeper fenced up his well, the good people of E. H. went forthwith and dug two others in the street close by, which are much more convenient than the former. That is the way. These men will find two to one, all over the State, before they get through.

Effects of the Maine Liquor Law on the Domestic and Religious Habits of the People.—The effects of our law consist not simply in closing rum-shops, preventing disorder and crime, and emptying prisons and alms-houses; they are already felt, we believe, in many a family that has long been cursed with the evils of intemperance. Many a miserable abode has been converted into a pleasant, happy home; many a heart-broken wife gladdened by the reformation of her intemperate husband; many a group of suffering children provided with the comforts of life. Indeed, wherever the influences of the liquor traffic have been felt in years that are past, there the influences of this most excellent law are felt *now;* and the tendency is to prevent, and in a measure to undo, the countless evils which flow from the traffic in ardent spirits. These thoughts have been suggested by a particular case which we have had occasion recently to notice: A man who for several years has not even entered the sanctuary or attended any religious meeting whatever, has been repeatedly of late in the house of God on the Sabbath. For a long time neither himself nor his family were provided with clothing suitable to enable them to attend public worship. The money that should have been used in purchasing clothing and other articles necessary to their comfort, was expended for rum. But they are all well-dressed now, and we shall be greatly disappointed if they are not, in future, habitual attendants upon the sanctuary. They are provided, too, with the comforts of life, and prepared for the approaching winter far better, probably, than they ever were before. Who can witness one such case without lifting his heart to God and thanking him for this Prohibitory Law? Who can think of hundreds like it scattered all over the State, and not feel himself called upon to do all in his power to enforce and perpetuate this law?

LOUNGING AND IDLENESS.—Not half the time is spent in lounging and idleness, within my observation, that there was before.

TRADE AND INDUSTY.—I expect, as a natural result of these improvements, that the legitimate home trade and industry have proportionably increased.

NO DANGER TO THE POOR MAN'S CASTLE.—The opposition to it is chiefly based on the assumption that it interferes with the natural rights of the citizens, and the danger of the poor man's castle being invaded. But not a single case of hardship from the right of search has ever been heard of; in fact, search can not be made in a private dwelling unless there are very good grounds for the authorities to entertain the belief that the owner has invaded the *sacredness* of his own house with the rum bottle, and turned it into a dram-shop.

PROPERTY IMPROVED.—The law is decidedly beneficial, and property-holders everywhere are becoming more and more in favor of its strict enforcement.

PUBLIC OPINION.—So strong is its hold upon the community already, that no political or other combination, in my opinion, could be entered into to repeal the law. Any change will be to make it more stringent, in order to its more thorough enforcement. Public opinion is bearing in strongly in favor of the law, and I have no doubt that in a few years it will be as easily and as thoroughly enforced as the laws against theft, licentiousness, and gambling.

RECLAIMED FROM INTEMPERANCE.—I could give a long list of names of men formerly idle and drinking, who are now sober and industrious. So it is in Hartford County.

JAILS AND ALMS-HOUSES.—Their jails and alms-houses are almost empty. These are samples of the effects of the law.

ATTENDANCE AT CHURCH.—The attendance at places of worship has improved as an invariable result of increased sobriety.

SALE OF LIQUOR NOT RESPECTABLE.—No respectable man is now engaged in the liquor traffic in this town.

PUBLIC HEALTH.—Physicians complain of having nothing to do.

TRADE.—The increase in legitimate home trade is very great. One grocer told me that his business had increased one third. Another said he had twelve men with plenty of cash on Saturday evenings, at his store, who had always before been represented by little girls with a few cents.

DRINKING DIMINISHED.—I have been police justice here for the last twenty years, and I know a very great difference since this law went into operation. I think that when the people become tired of selling in violation of the law, my occupation will be pretty nearly gone. If you stop drinking, you stop the cause of all the quarrels and fights. It is perfect nonsense—it is a perfect falsehood—to say that the law has increased drunkenness. That drinking is totally stopped, nobody claims; but it is stopped at least three fourths. I have known some of our constables here have as high as $90 in a quarter for fines for breaches of the peace; if they reach $25 now, it is the head. The parties brought before the police court will average eight out of ten Irish. The Irish are our only foreign population, with a few Germans.

DRUNKARDS DECREASED TEN TO ONE.—I have been a policeman here since the 1st of May, 1854. I have seen ten men drunk on the streets before this law passed for one that I have seen since. These men, although they would have been liable for prosecution under the new law, were not taken up under the old law. It was only when a drunken man was making some assault that he was taken up formerly. On one Sunday, before the law was passed, I arrested seven men for breaches of the peace while in drink. Since the 1st of August I have only arrested two men on Sunday for being drunk. There are eight night-watchmen, and seldom a night passed without some man being taken up by them for beating his wife or children while in a state of intoxication. Now it is a rare thing to take up one. This law has taken at least $6 a-month right out of my pocket, for we have no fines now. It would be almost impossible to make any one believe the difference in the quiet of our city.

THE MAINE LIQUOR LAW FROM HEAVEN.—I have been in the field as city missionary for three years and a half. I have a Mission Sabbath School, planned after the Five Points School of New York. Since the 1st of August it has increased more than one third in numbers. Before that time there was hardly a Sabbath but there was some one there the worse for liquor. Since the 1st of August there has been but one instance that even the smell of liquor was in the school. Before the law passed, I could many a day have gathered up a wagon-load of intemperate men —almost, indeed, any day; since the 1st of August I have seldom met with an instance. I have many times seen, in passing my rounds, wives and mothers, and even young women, the worse for liquor; but all that has changed, and in my conversations with the poor people many of them say that the law must have come from Heaven—it is too good to have been framed by man. The little children that used to run and hide from their fathers when they came home drunk, are now well dressed and run out to meet them.

OPPONENTS BECOMING FRIENDS.—Many of the opponents of the prohibitory enactment have become its friends.

A TREE IS KNOWN BY ITS FRUIT.—In a word, the law works admirably! The fruit of it is good, and only good. While it infringes upon the just and lawful rights of no one, it protects the rights of those who have long been a prey to the rum-seller.

PUBLIC HEALTH.—The *delirium tremens*, which I regard as the worst kind of insanity, was formerly prevalent, the cases being frequent, but now there are no such cases.

Ex-Rumsellers becoming Industrious.—We have near us a little hamlet where there were a number of groggeries; and though there was no need of a single public house in that vicinity, the proprietors of these places lived comfortably by selling the poison to the neighbors and the hands of two furnaces near by. The law cut off their profits and set them to looking out for some other way to get their bread. One of them, who was formerly a mason, but had not done a day's work in some years, was glad to solicit a job in stone-laying, and the others are most of them now getting their living honestly, and the character and condition of the neighborhood is so changed that it does not appear the same. The change is noticed and spoken of by all who are acquainted with the place.

Improvement in Dress, etc.—In dress and general appearance some who were intemperate have decidedly improved.

A Woman's Blessing for the Maine Liquor Law.— "*Mr. Editor:* I want—I must tell you my thoughts. My heart is running over with happiness, and my soul goeth forth in praise toward Him who hath blessed me and all the State with me. Blessed be God for the Maine Law. My husband—be still, my heart, while I tell the glad tidings—he who so often returned to me with—in place of his own kind heart—the rum fiend, and has been so harsh, so cruel, *is himself!* And now he's kind and affectionate; we have all we desire, and happiness, full, complete, is all our own. Again let me say, blessings on the Maine Law, the true friend of the poor. If all who have suffered from rum in this State might speak, what a shout of joy and thanksgiving would go up to the glad blue sky! a cry right from the heart, of thanks for the blessing of God. You may think that this is strong language, but

> ' Go feel what I have felt,
> Go bear what I have borne,'

and see whether your feelings are not altered.—Rachel."

MATERNAL THANKFULNESS.—An aged widow, who has a son who was addicted to intemperance, said to me last week, "I cannot be thankful enough for the Maine Liquor Law." Such is the language of the reformed inebriate's relatives everywhere.

BLOATED FACES.—A decided improvement has taken place here in many bloated faces.

"THE MOST BLESSED THING."—An excellent lady, who for many years had suffered almost to death from a drunken husband, said to me, from experience, "Is not the Maine Liquor Law the most blessed thing that ever took place?"

THIRTY DOLLARS SAVED IN ONE MONTH.—One formerly very intemperate man remarked one month after the Maine Liquor Law went into operation, that he had thirty dollars in cash, and that had it not been for the law, he should not have had a cent.

PHYSICIANS, LAWYERS, AND JAILERS, SHORT OF EMPLOYMENT.—While the Maine Liquor Law has proved a very great blessing to some, and a benefit to all in our community, a few are prevented in part, or in whole, obtaining the income of their former employment, viz., physicians and lawyers, who have less to do; and a jail-keeper in an adjoining county declares he is out of business in his line, for the jail is without a tenant. One year ago it had about fifty.

RELIEVING DISTRESS.—So far as I can learn, the law works well here, and is doing wonders in relieving distress in many poor families.

THE PRODIGAL RETURNED.—There is in my congregation a young man of a respectable family, kind, pleasant, and agreeable, who earned good wages as a mechanic—the only support of a widowed mother and an only sister—had got into dissipated habits, and for four or five years past would have gone on a drunken spree for weeks together, and was, consequently, a great source of affliction to his friends. Reasoning and remonstrance were in vain. But the law came to his aid. The temptation was removed, and he has since done well. He has recently purchased a small house for his mother and sister, and furnished it comfortably. He is a regular attender at church, and expresses very feelingly his gratification at the enforcement of the law.

YALE COLLEGE.—*Consumption of Wine in the College.*—Professor Silliman says:—" My impression is that the law has worked very favorably. I am not now in the college, and can not say so much from actual experience there, but I have heard several of the students speak of the law as having produced a very decidedly good effect upon the students generally. Not a quart of wine or liquor is drunk now, where before gallons were used. I am decidedly of opinion that it has produced a very marked change in the college."—*Customs of Society.*—" It has also produced a great change in the general customs of society. My wife has been in the habit of visiting among the poor, and in houses where before she used to find misery and vice, she now finds happiness and comfort."

Effect of the Maine Liquor Law on Students.—Professor Thacher says:—" I am convinced that the law has made a very great difference among our students. Formerly some of them used to drink so as to be affected by it. They got the liquors at the medical halls, nicely labeled as cordials, and kept it in their own rooms. Such a thing is now entirely unknown. We have had no case of intemperance in the college since the law passed, that I know of. It was whispered about that the chief of police had escorted two young gentlemen to their lodgings recently, who, but for his kindness, might have been arrested. It is believed that he has frequently made himself serviceable in this way. But we have no outward indications now among the students that drink is used. There is none of that noise and uproar among them that used to be. The only objection we can have to the law is, that it does not stretch far enough. Persons can send to New York for a basket of champagne, and get it delivered at their houses without any difficulty. It has been reported that some of the students have done this, but I have seen no instance of it myself."

College Government More Easy.—Mr. Dwight, Resident Tutor, says:—" The results of the law have been much more favorable on the institution than I had any idea they possibly could be. The law has made a very decided difference in the college. I have no doubt there is some drinking still, but it must be greatly diminished, for its outside developments are entirely done away. I live in the college, and have an opportunity of seeing what goes on, and I am satisfied that college government is now much more easy than it was before the operations of the Maine Law.

Classes Free from Liquors.—Mr. Mathieson, Freshman, says: —" All our classes are free from the use of liquors. I think if they were inclined to intemperance I should have heard of it. There are no places about college that I know of where liquor of any sort can be got."

TESTIMONY OF METHODIST EPISCOPAL PREACHERS.—The New London District Preachers' Meeting of the M. E. Church, at its recent session, unanimously

Resolved, That having come together from all parts of the eastern portion of the State, we most cheerfully unite our testimony in favor of the efficiency of our new Prohibitory Liquor Law, and unanimously declare that its success has been hitherto marked and triumphant.

PRISON CELLS TO BE LET.—At a convention on the 27th instant, New London reported: " Prison Cells to be Let."

OUT OF BUSINESS.—The jailer of New London County. The county prison is empty. The Maine Liquor Law is justly held responsible for this result. Last year, before the law went into operation, from the 1st of August to the 1st of January inclusive, there were upwards of fifty prisoners in the county jail; since the 1st of August last the number has been gradually diminishing, till on New Year's day there was but one poor fellow in durance, who, " solitary and alone," was awaiting trial for the violation of the Liquor Law.

Dens of Iniquity Closed.—Three dens of iniquity have been closed, their inmates, numbering forty or fifty souls, scattered, and some of these persons are now honestly employed.

MAINE.

Statements of the Governor.—His Excellency Governor Morrill, in his recent Annual Message, makes the following valuable statements:—

Sustaining the Maine Liquor Law.—The law for the suppression of drinking houses and tippling shops has been very fully discussed by the people of this State, and become a question of prominence and deep interest in our elections. The result proves conclusively that the people are by a very large majority in favor of sustaining that law—a happy verdict for the cause of humanity throughout the land. Had Maine declared against the law, her decision would have been felt most disastrously by other communities, where strong efforts are being made to obtain similar legislation.

Control of the Traffic.—That any law which human wisdom can devise will at once rid the public of an evil so vast and deep-rooted as intemperance, should not be expected; but that the traffic which produces it can be circumscribed and controlled by penal enactments, as surely and as legitimately as other crimes, there can be no reasonable doubt. And it is equally clear that the people are determined to pursue the effort faithfully, and give the law a fair trial. They see and feel the terrible ravages the traffic in intoxicating drinks has made on society and its best interests. They feel deeply the loss of many valued citizens who are constantly being hurried to the inebriate's grave. They fully realize that the sale and use of alcoholic liquors as a beverage, are in direct conflict with the health, morals, industry, peace, and happiness of society, and that this fact is so apparent, that those individuals who insist on selling in violation of law should be made to feel its consequences.

The Traffic a Crime.—It is too late to plead that making men inebriates, or giving them the facilities to become such, is no crime; none but the more depraved or reckless will support a doctrine so pernicious and absurd; and it is believed that few are now engaged in the traffic in this State except those persons who are alike indifferent to public sentiment, the demands of humanity, and their own best interests.

Enforcement of the Maine Liquor Law.—Persuasive efforts having been exhausted on this class of men, the law should be enforced in protection to society and in mercy to the offender. This important statute has not had a fair trial. Executive officers have been culpably negligent in seeing it enforced. Too often has the officer, whose duty it was to honor and execute it as the law of the Commonwealth, been found more willing to exculpate the offender than to bring him to justice. Such official dereliction of duty emboldened violators of the law to repeated offences, which they would not have committed, with the full assurance that the law was to be faithfully administered. This error must be corrected, the law must be faithfully enforced. The people demand that grog-shops be closed, whether found in spacious saloons and popular hotels, where the temptation is presented in the most alluring form, or in the filthy cellar or den, where poor, degraded humanity is made loathsome to the last degree.

Imprisonment for First Offence.—No man sells ardent spirits in violation of this law through the promptings of patriotism or humanity; he has no higher motive than a reckless or sordid love of gain; he should be held strictly accountable for the mischief his traffic produces. Let this be done, and none will continue in the business except such as are madly bent on suicide. I would suggest the importance of so amending the law as to impose imprisonment for the first offence. The penalty for the first conviction is trifling, and the schemes devised to avoid detection are so numerous, that many sellers, undoubtedly, realize large amounts from the business before a conviction is had. Let the prison be opened for their reception and reformation, as it is for offenders of less magnitude, even the unhappy victims of their traffic, and be assured its prospective chastening influences will be felt more restrainingly than merely taking by fine, from the pockets of the delinquents, a trifling part of the money the business had given them.

Prohibition of Rum Carrying.—The willingness of rumsellers in other States to supply those in the same business, and the facilities afforded by steamboats and other common carriers to bring liquors into this State for unlawful purposes, call for such improvement in the law as shall meet this prolific source of evil and cut off a great artery which is pouring the poisonous liquid into this State.

Evasion of the Maine Liquor Law.—Other amendments may be desirable to give efficiency to the law and meet the modes of evasion which the ingenuity and cupidity of determined violators have invented.

STATEMENTS OF HON. NEAL DOW.—*Consumption of Liquor in the State Diminished.*—The amount of liquors consumed in the State I think is not one quarter so great as it was seven months ago, and it will become less very rapidly, as the people in the country towns are now enforcing the law more extensively and vigorously every day. From many towns in the State the illegal traffic is entirely banished.

Support of Temperance Men.—The law calls out new and increased interest (even enthusiasm) from temperance men, and has brought over the timid and wavering.

Implements of the Warfare.—The law is easily enforced in every town, if you have three temperance men who are not afraid, one good justice of the peace, and one good constable.

GENERAL RESULTS OF THE MAINE LIQUOR LAW.—I can state that, under the operations of this law, I have seen drunkards made sober; families, sunk to the depths of poverty and wretchedness, raised to competency and respectability; rumsellers abandon their business and engage in honourable callings; villages and cities morally transformed, and Sabbath-riots giving way to the sanctity which becomes the day. I have seen men who fought the law at first as the worst law in the world, now supporting it as one of the best.

ECONOMY OF THE MAINE LIQUOR LAW.—A tract, issued by the Maine State Temperance Society, makes the following remarks on this subject :—

" Before the enactment of the Maine Liquor Law there were expended by the people of this State annually for strong drinks, at the lowest estimate, more than two million of dollars, and this expenditure involved a loss to the people in time, diminished industry, in unthrifty habits and other sources of loss, to an amount of at least two millions more; so that we had an expenditure for these drinks, directly and indirectly, of at least four million of dollars per year. Now what is the result to the State of this great expenditure for strong drinks? Have the people been the happier for it—better fed, better clad, better sheltered, better educated? No; but just the contrary. This enormous amount of four million of dollars has been a dead loss to the people year by year; and even worse than that, for they have not only had no valuable equivalent for it, but have received that which undermines their morals, and tends directly to their impoverishment and degradation; while no persons are benefited by the rum traffic, except a few men who have grown rich in furnishing the means of ruin to their countrymen. What a vast amount of good may be accomplished by four million of dollars properly expended! That sum would construct a railroad every year as costly as the Atlantic and St. Lawrence; would furnish every city and town in the State with churches, academies, school-houses, and libraries, and support comfortably all the pastors and teachers necessary for them; would construct elegant hospitals for the gratuitous accommodation of all our sick; asylums for the reception of the superannuated poor, and all the orphans in the State who have none to care properly for them; and would endow all these institutions with ample funds; would create a fund whereby all our State and municipal taxes might be paid, so that the people of Maine would be entirely exempt from taxes for the support of government. In one word, the entire suppression of the traffic in intoxicating drinks within our borders would render the people of Maine in a few years, in proportion to their numbers, the richest people in the world; they would be the most virtuous and the happiest people; better fed, clad, sheltered, and educated, and more industrious and prosperous, than any other people. Intemperance would be entirely unknown among them, except as yellow fever is known to us by a few imported cases; our jails and prisons would be tenantless, or nearly so; of paupers we should have none, or if any, so few that alms-houses would not be necessary; and vice and crime would be so far reduced in amount as to be scarcely known to exist among us. Such will be the effect of the Maine Law, if it remain upon our statute-books and be steadily enforced. Men of Maine! is all this desirable, or not? Do you prefer that rumselling, with its long train of fearful evils, shall exist among us, or that it shall be suppressed, that we may enjoy the wonderful benefits of the change? For many generations all the governments of Europe and America have felt the rum traffic to be a great evil, and have endeavored to protect their people from its effects as far as possible. All these governments have often enacted laws to regulate and restrain this traffic; they did not think it could be destroyed; but Maine has undertaken to expel this traffic entirely from her borders, and with wonderful success. The civilized world is now looking with admiration upon this great experiment; if it succeed, the people of Maine will be happy and prosperous, and all the nations of the earth will follow her example; if it do not succeed, it will be through the indifference or timidity of professedly good men, who fear to resist bad men in their efforts to overthrow this law, which restrains their appetites and passions and affects their interests. In the year during which this law has been in existence, its effects have been more decisive and salutary than its warmest friends had anticipated. The wholesale traffic in strong drinks has been entirely annihilated throughout the State; the grog-shops are very few, and are kept in dark and secret places, so that temptation is entirely removed from the way of the young and inexperienced. The quantity of spirits now sold in the State can not be more than one tenth part so great as it was before the enactment of the Maine Law, so that the saving to the people is already at least one million eight hundred thousand dollars per year. The result of this can be seen in the improved habits and circumstances of our people. Many men, formerly miserable drunkards, are now perfectly sober, because temptation is removed out of their way; many families, before miserable and dependent upon the public or upon charity for support, are now comfortably fed, clad, and lodged. Our alms-houses are not crowded as they were; their inmates are greatly diminished in number, and some of them are nearly empty. Our jails are almost tenantless, some of them entirely so; our houses of correction are now almost without occupants, and all this because few men become paupers or commit crimes except under the influence of strong drinks."

STATEMENTS OF HON. NEAL DOW.—Commitments to the county jail:

From June 1, 1850, to March 20, 1851, nine months previous to the enactment of the Maine Liquor Law,	279
Corresponding period 1851 and 1852, after the enactment of the Maine Liquor Law, ... 135	
Deduct Liquor-Sellers committed under the Law, ... 72	
Deduct 63	63
Difference in favor of Maine Liquor Law	216

There were in the jail:

On March 20, 1851, before the enactment of the Maine Liquor Law,		25
Same period 1852, after the enactment of the Maine Liquor Law,	7	
Deduct Liquor-Sellers under Maine Liquor Law,	3	
	4	4
Difference in favor of Maine Liquor Law,		21

Showing a falling off of eighty-three per cent. in the short period of nine months! We understand that the jailer of that year made the remark, that the Maine Law had damaged him (reduced his receipts) more than five hundred dollars in that year. The commitments to the jail for all crimes and offences, as near as can be ascertained, during the succeeding years—1852, '53, '54—have been as follows, viz.: 140, 131, 144.

LIQUOR AS MEDICINE.—So far as my medical practice goes, I think liquor can be dispensed with even as a medicine. I have always been of opinion that it does more harm than good, even as a medicine. I do not say that it is never useful, but I do say that the balances are against its use as a medicine. If a strictly prohibitory law were introduced into the House, restricting its use as a medicine, I would most certainly vote for it.

THE EFFECT OF TEMPTATION.—One man who had been reclaimed from intemperance by the operation of the Maine Liquor Law, having been tempted during his visit to a rum-drinking State, died of intemperance soon after his return home, leaving a young wife and two or three children.

EDUCATION.—Better school-houses are now built, more school-money raised, and children are better educated.

The Police have Little to Do.—I am assured by the members of the police and watch that they now have little to do, while before the enactment of the law against tippling shops their number was insufficient to preserve entirely the quiet and peace of the city from the numerous persons to be found in our streets at all times of the night more or less excited by strong drink.

Religious Meetings Undisturbed.—I am also informed on sufficient authority that religious meetings, held in the evening, formerly suffered serious disturbance and interruption from persons who would come there from oyster-shops and drinking saloons, strongly excited by intoxicating drinks, but at present no trouble is experienced from this cause.

Testimony of City Missionary.—Mr. Mitchell has been city missionary for many years. He has had under his supervision from six hundred and fifty to seven hundred families, and he adds that not one twentieth of intemperate drinking can now be found of what existed when the Maine Liquor Law went into effect. In his constant walks about the city, he does not meet one intoxicated person a day; and he does not recollect more than five or six cases for the last six months of complaints of wives that their husbands drink too much. In many inveterate cases which he knows, where both husband and wife drank to excess, they are entirely reformed through the effect of the law, and live happily together.

New Churches Erected.—Since the passing of the law five new churches have been erected in this city. I remember at the time these churches were commenced, objections were raised by some that it would draw off the people from the old congregations; but such has not been the case. Every old congregation has increased, and our new churches are well filled. The fact is, we require one or two more churches.

Sabbath Schools.—With regard to Sabbath schools, I know of many children now attending Sabbath school, who, before the passing of the law, were children of intemperate parents, and were never to be seen at a Sunday school.

Camp Meetings.—In camp meetings and religious assemblages we find a great benefit from the Maine Liquor Law. The intemperate used to be a great obstacle in our way, but now this curse is out of the way. This is true of all assemblies of the people, and with few exceptions; once it was otherwise.

Bibles in the Place of Dissipation.—I was at Booth Bay a year ago last summer. At certain periods of the year there are immense fleets of mackerel-fishers, come with their boats, sometimes from 300 to 400 at a time. One Sunday morning I was passing by the head of the pier, where about 300 of the mackerel fishermen were seated. Everything was perfectly quiet as I passed by. Some had out their Bibles, and were reading. As I passed one group, I said, "Had you not better go to church, shipmates?" Some remarks were made, and simultaneously they all rose and accompanied me to the church where I intended to preach that morning. The scene was so very gratifying that I could not help saying to the landlord of the hotel that he must have a curious class of fishermen in that quarter. "Ah!" said he, "if you had been here before the Maine Law passed, you would, on such a day as this, have seen these rocks all along covered with blood. No female dared venture out of the house at such a time." That Sunday, I assure you, was as orderly as any Sunday could be, and there was not a bottle to be seen in the whole company when they left in the evening, but one bottle of vinegar.

A Better Trade than the Liquor Traffic.—The tavern-keeper, above quoted, continued: "I opposed the law with all my might because I thought it was going to injure my trade; but now I make much more money when these men are on shore than I did by supplying them with liquor. When they go away they take with them whole canoe-loads of eggs and hams, and other necessaries."

Maine Liquor Law among the Lumbermen.—The firm to which I belong employed 700 men in the lumbering business last winter. We supplied no liquor to the camp, nor was any used by the men, and both employers and employed were delighted with the workings of the law. The men worked better without it, and the winter passes away much more pleasantly and cheerfully. Last winter there were on the Aroostook River a large number of men waiting to be engaged for the season, and the quiet way in which they conducted themselves was a general subject of remark. It was, indeed, gratifying to see scores of our hardy lumbermen, who formerly were in the habit of drinking very freely, spending their leisure days—which with all that class are days of temptation —soberly and orderly.

How is it Now?—The law of 1858, which went into effect on the 15th of July, is a stringent prohibitory law. It will enable magistrates to shut up drinking houses, that are practical nuisances, and may perhaps allow summary proceedings in case the public authorities are in any way remiss in their duty. Public opinion has clearly settled the rights, duties, and proprieties of the whole question, and while it justly regards the selling of liquor, for the purpose of making drunkards, as a heinous crime, it does not call for any extreme measures to punish or prosecute the proper use of liquor. All Hotels and Eating Houses are entirely safe from any interference, unless they shall prostitute their business to the making of drunkards. If they do this, shut them up, and use the strong arm of the law.

On We Go!—The usual difficulties attend the prosecution of liquor dealers. Since the passage of the new Maine Law by the people, they have been carrying up their cases from the Municipal Court and from the Supreme Court to that of the full bench, on exceptions and demurrer. Chief Justice Taney recently announced the decision of the court, which was, that *the exceptions are overruled, and all the cases are remanded to the other court for judgment!!* The civic authorities are doing what they can to enforce the law.

MASSACHUSETTS.

The Law best Enforced where there has been most Energy among Temperance Men.—It would seem that the public officers of every town would feel bound to enforce every statute of the Commonwealth, or else to resign their places to others; but with a law which enlists against it the basest passions of man, this may not be always the case. Public officers, we regret to say, are not always regenerated by being put into office. Even if disposed to act, they often look to the courage and energy of a few persons outside to sustain them in their duty. It is one of the merits of this law that a few resolute men, sustained by the moral sentiment of the better part of the community, can in most places insure its execution. If those men happen to be in office (as at Lowell and elsewhere), it is so much the better. But experience has already proved that where this is not the case, it costs less trouble for energetic men to do the work themselves than to urge an unwilling or timid board of officers to do it. A town government, especially, is not apt by its nature to be a strong government. We caution the friends of good order, therefore, against relying exclusively upon such an one. If they can secure a body of selectmen or policemen who will act as a vigilance committee, very well; if not, let them form themselves into a vigilance committee to sustain the public authorities, if desired; or if not, to do the work in their own way, provided they can find a single reliable justice and constable. We are acquainted with one town in Worcester County where a committee of twelve citizens has held weekly meetings ever since the law took effect. They have made, or caused to be made, five seizures, of which four have been successful, and the fifth is still pending; and the trade in intoxicating drinks may, for the first time, be considered as suppressed in that town. We commend that example to the friends of temperance generally, believing that the law will be best enforced where private energy is greatest, and that it will be most popular where it is best enforced. It will of course be understood that every effort must, nevertheless, be made in all cases, to induce the public authorities to do the duty which plainly devolves upon them. The law must be recognized as standing in precisely the same position with all other laws, and to be enforced by the same methods.

IN SPITE OF ALL DRAWBACKS, THE LAW HAS SUPPRESSED THE OPEN SALE OF LIQUOR THROUGH A LARGE PORTION OF THE STATE.—The accounts which have reached us from all portions of the Commonwealth go to indicate this fact,—an immense diminution in the *open* liquor traffic. They believe this form of traffic to have ceased in nine tenths of the towns in the State. The unlawful trade has been in some cases—in many cases—annihilated; in many cases it has been only driven into secret retreats. But what a blessing is even this! How many does it save from the beginnings of vice, which is most attractive only when it becomes reputable. No law can annihilate sin, but only diminish it by making it disgraceful. Law has not suppressed licentiousness or gambling; it has not even suppressed theft and murder; it has only diminished them by making them more difficult and disgraceful; yet what legislator would repeal such laws as these? The friends of the Temperance Law only claim that it is doing its work as rapidly and thoroughly as can reasonably be demanded of any law which has a moral purpose in view; and it is only more important than these other laws because it lies at the foundation of them all. Its results are not more numerous; they are only *as* numerous, and *far more valuable.*

THE RETAIL TRADE.—Excepting the cities of Worcester and Boston, the retail trade is pretty effectually broken up. There is no such trade carried on *openly.*

IMPROVEMENT AMONG FISHERMEN.—A large portion of the class of persons engaged in the fishing business had no other permanent employment. Their supply of rum was from three to six barrels for a crew of eight to twelve or fourteen hands, and almost everybody drank as freely when at home. I hardly need say that we believe now there is not a vessel from our ports provided with stores of liquor more than for medical purposes.

SUPPORT OF THE GOSPEL, ETC.—I suppose at this time we have advanced five hundred per cent. in the support of the Gospel, schools, and public improvements, since our prohibition commenced.

DUKE'S COUNTY, on the island of Martha's Vineyard, is one of the favored spots of the earth, or, rather, of the ocean. Situated at a distance from the continent, it has made a declaration of freedom from intoxicating liquors for more than eighteen years. The results of prohibition, continued for this long period, are such as every temperance advocate would naturally expect. The enormous reduction of crime, and the peacefulness of the neighborhood on the island since prohibition has been enforced, are some of the happy consequences of this great reformation. — Population, 4540.

CRIME BEFORE PROHIBITION COMMENCED.—While the traffic continued, the courts were in session for about two weeks each term.

CRIME SINCE PROHIBITION TRIUMPHED.—What has been the result? Crime has not only diminished, but it seems to have entirely left the Vineyard. We are informed that no case of crime has come before the courts for something like sixteen years. Civil cases have been greatly diminished, and there are now very few that come in for trial. The judges go down in one boat and back in the next.

A BLESSING TO THE COMMUNITY.—Within two years past there were open grog-shops in very many of the towns in the county of Franklin. At this moment I do not think there are ten in the whole county. The decrease is owing entirely to the enforcement of the law. - It has been a blessing beyond anything we have ever had, and I am satisfied that wherever it is enforced it will prove a blessing to the community. Its effects in lessening rowdyism are very marked. Before the law passed, our streets were noisy and riotous, and it was unsafe for any female to venture out in the evening unprotected; but now it is not so.

EFFECTS ON YOUNG MEN.—Its effects are very marked upon our young men. Since the fashionable saloons were shut up, they have formed a Young Men's Literary Association, where they meet regularly to read essays, and for general mutual improvement. Our Lyceum lectures were never half so well attended as they have been this winter. In addition to our usual lectures two or three evenings a week, we have recently had two courses, of six lectures each, on geology, by Dr. Boynton, and they were thronged every evening. The first course was so crowded, that he was prevailed upon to give a second, that those who had not heard him might have an opportunity of doing so; and our hall, capable of containing one thousand people, was crowded all the evenings. You saw there precisely the same class of people that in Montreal you will see at the theatre. Our young men now feel that a ticket to the Lyceum lectures is an absolute necessary of life. This feeling has increased so much that we have no building large enough to contain the applicants. I believe that three thousand tickets could have been sold as easily as one thousand. To meet, so far, the demand, an extra course is intended to be given on a different evening for those who could not get tickets for the regular course.

MICHIGAN.

THE OTSEGO WOMEN VINDICATED.—This evening I attended a meeting in Allegan in vindication of the course taken by the women of our adjoining town, Otsego. A president, secretary, and committee of three were appointed to present resolutions. The Hon. Judge Booth said the women of Otsego had adopted a declaration of rights, in which they stated that they will continue to work for the cause of temperance till the traffic in liquor is suppressed.

THE INFLUENCE OF WOMEN AT ELECTIONS.—There are many true women in Michigan; they are active in some places, and have the cause at heart. Two young ladies of Pinckney (and, by-the-by, they are *handsome* and the *first* in the village) went to the polls on election day and handed over *temperance tickets* to every one that could be induced to deposit them. They even went after a rumseller, one *lady* taking hold of one arm, and the other guarding him on the other side; in this manner they walked him to the *ballot-box*, and he, as a matter of course, deposited his vote for no rum.

PERIOD OF ENFORCEMENT.—The act of 1853 was in operation about two months.

A MARKED CHANGE.—A marked change for the better was apparent in all directions, and among the lovers of rum in particular. They did not return home from our village near as *smart*, nor stay as long, as when under the old law of free trade in alcohol.

CRIME.—Crime was evidently on the decline during the observance of the law.

PUBLIC OPINION.—It can be said in truth that nearly all respectable persons of the different religious professions, and of the political parties, are of one mind and of one sentiment as to the law. Let it go into operation, be sustained, and work out its legitimate result, which will be to *prevent* crime of nearly every grade, and extreme pauperism in the country need hardly be known.

PERSONAL EXPERIENCE.—I have had charge of pretty extensive farming operations for thirty three years. I have never found it necessary to procure a drop of ardent spirits to be used as a beverage.

RHODE ISLAND.

Soon after the passage of the Prohibitory Law in Rhode Island, H. A. C. Barstow was elected mayor of Providence, and he referred to the law as follows:—

Penalties of the Old Laws too Light.—At the last session of our Legislature a law was passed for the suppression of drinking houses and tippling shops, which is to go into operation on the third Monday of July next (1852). Our present laws prohibit the sale of spirituous liquors as a beverage, except when the freemen of the towns, by vote, allow their town council to license the traffic; but the penalty for their violation is so light as to render them entirely worthless in this city or in the densely populated towns. The law which is soon to go into operation, contains a variety of features more stringent than were ever embodied in any former legislation upon this subject. Heretofore we have sought to regulate this traffic by law, now we seek to suppress it. It is believed that a wise and firm enforcement of this law will soon suppress the traffic in these liquors to a great extent, and thus rid our city of much of the alarming amount of evil resulting therefrom.

Prevention Better than Cure.—As it is better, and in the experience of a sister State (where a similar law is in operation) cheaper, to prevent the evils resulting from this traffic than to punish the crimes and alleviate the poverty and distress occasioned by it, I shall deem it my duty to see that this, as well as every other law, is justly and impartially enforced. I trust that those who have been engaged in this traffic will deem it a matter of policy and duty to yield a quiet submission to the law, and thus save the magistrate the necessity of performing a disagreeable duty. The law must be honored, either in its observance or in the infliction of its penal sanctions. Every interest of society demands it; every sentiment of my heart approves it. I deem it my duty, thus early, to make the announcement, that all may have timely warning.

The Greatest Good to the Greatest Number.—The execution of this law may seem hard and oppressive to a few who are engaged in this traffic, but they must bear in mind that the want of such a law has been esteemed a greater hardship by a multitude who either directly or indirectly have suffered by it. Under our happy government, law is the will of the people constitutionally expressed. All government necessarily abridges individual liberty. Living in a state of nature, a man' rights may be measured by his might;

but in voluntarily entering a state of society, he agrees to unite with others in fixing rules for the government of the whole. If any of these rules in their operation bear with undue severity upon himself, he has a legal remedy; or if in their just execution they limit or restrain his liberty too far, to suit his taste, or supposed interests, he may choose another society more congenial to his feelings. If, however, he continues in the society, he is bound, as a good citizen, to respect its rules, and bow with proper submission to its decrees. Private interest must yield when the public requires it; and the individual who resists the law in any other than a constitutional way, on the ground of private right, commits treason against the State, shows himself unworthy of the society which has hitherto sheltered and protected him, and as a transgressor of one law, cuts himself off from all claim for protection under any other.

These were the opinions of the mayor prior to the enforcement of the law. After it had been in operation three months, he published the following statistics, showing that the law in that short time had made a reduction of nearly 60 per cent. in monthly committals:—

The Watch-House.—Committals to the Watch-House for Drunkenness, and small Assaults growing out of drunkenness:

From July 19 to October 19, 1851,........................... 282
For corresponding months of 1852,........................... 177

Difference in favor of the Law, ... 105

Butler's Hospital.—The number of insane persons in this hospital has been reduced about one fifth.

VERMONT.

INFLUENCE OF THE LAW.—That the law has exerted an immense influence, and accomplished great good, is as plain to him whose eyes are not resolutely closed to the light of truth, as is the light of the sun to him who opens, at mid-day, eyes that have not been deadened and darkened by paralysis or vailed by cataract.

POWER REQUIRED TO ENFORCE THE LAW.—Five energetic men can enforce the law in any locality in our State.

NO REACTION.—I may say there is no place in this State where a reaction has taken place against the law, and there is no danger of a reaction against the law, for its friends are gradually increasing, and its beneficial effects are becoming generally felt. These will secure its enforcement.

TESTIMONY OF THE GRAND JURY.—The Grand Jury, not composed of friends of the law, but a body appointed to note offences against the laws generally, in their last report say: "We would also say that we feel highly gratified to find the jail destitute of inmates, a circumstance attributable, in a very great measure, we believe, to the suppression of the sale of intoxicating liquors."

TESTIMONY OF THE OVERSEER.—A year ago, when the law was much less enforced, the overseer of the poor told me it had reduced the poor-tax at least $500. It will be more this year, although provisions are very high this winter.

VIGILANCE COMMITTEE.—About a year ago we had a public meeting, and appointed a vigilance committee to go round and raise money for the enforcement of the law, to pay counsel and all other necessary expenses; and you may judge of the feeling in favor of the law, when, in a short time, we had 1000 names on the subscription list.

EFFECTS OF THE LAW ON THE BURLINGTON UNIVERSITY, VERMONT.—With respect to its effects upon our own institution, I can safely say there is a very great diminution in the use of liquors by the students. Some five or six years ago we were much troubled with cases of intemperance among our students. Since the law passed there has been a great improvement. Though we have no doubt it is still used in a secret manner by some of the students, from the effects which sometimes manifest themselves yet there is none of it used openly. We find the results of the law in that respect highly beneficial. We have not had for a year past any of that kind of rowdyism which is sometimes manifested among students in such an institution as this. These noises grow mostly out of intemperance, for if students drink, they will be noisy in some shape or other.

BRAGGADOCIO OF THE ENEMY.—A great many offered resistance; a man who kept a public house in Rutland prior to the passing of the law, swore that they should never search his house; but it was all braggadocio; he was brought up and fined, and made no resistance whatever; now he has left the tavern and *cleared out.*

Montpelier, Vermont, 13th Oct., 1859.

GOVERNOR'S MESSAGE.

Intoxicating Drinks.

"Our laws prohibiting the traffic in intoxicating liquors have become the settled and approved policy of the State. If any additional legislative provisions to increase their efficiency should be found necessary, I shall be very ready to concur in them."

CHAPTER IV.

CANADIAN ACTION.

Petition for Prohibitory Liquor Law, 1859—Memorials to Councils—Petition for Prohibitory Liquor Law, 1860—Form of Act submitted therewith.

PROHIBITORY LIQUOR LAW FOR CANADA—PETITION SENT IN TO PROVINCIAL PARLIAMENT, 1859.

This circular is signed by the Grand Scribe, E. Stacey, on behalf of the Sons; and Grand Worthy Secretary W. A. Ferguson, for the Good Templars.

In connection with this subject, we give the following form of petition which has also been adopted by the same committee, and which we hope will be signed by the entire temperance community, whether they belong to these orders or not. We are more and more convinced that we must have a Maine Law in all its stringency and power before we can expect to grapple effectually with the evils of intemperance.

"*To the Honorable the Members of the Legislative Assembly, in Parliament Assembled,* THE PETITION *of the undersigned Inhabitants of the——————of——————,*

"*Humbly Sheweth:*

"That your Petitioners reiterate the conviction expressed in numerous petitions to your honourable body, that the traffic in intoxicating liquors, as drink for man, is the immediate cause of most of the crime and pauperism, and much of the disease and insanity, that afflict our fair and fertile Province; that everywhere, and in proportion to its prevalence, it deteriorates the moral character of the people, and is the chief outward obstruction to the progress of religion; that your petitioners regard intemperance, (the legitimate fruit of the liquor traffic,) as a great moral and social evil, destructive of health, virtue, and happiness, and producing disease, lunacy, and crime; entailing heavy burdens on society, and erecting a fatal barrier in the path of individual and national greatness; that observation and experience prove that all measures of regulation and restriction, however good, so far as they go, are inadequate to the prevention and removal of these pressing evils, and therefore pray for the abolition of the traffic in intoxicating liquors, by legal enactment.

"And your Petitioners earnestly pray that your honorable body will, without delay, enact a stringent Prohibitory Liquor Law; and, as in duty bound, will ever pray.

"———————————— 1859."

The petitions presented had 150,000 names appended—but the measure did not carry!

Memorial to Councils of Corporations of the Different Townships throughout Canada West.

"That the matter of petitioning the Legislature of the Province of Canada, for the enactment of a Prohibitory Liquor Law, has engaged the attention of your Memorialists, and they would respectfully submit that the Township, County, and City Municipal Corporations, more properly represent the feelings and desires of the People of Canada than any other in the land, and that Intemperance, being peculiarly a social evil, consequently comes within their province.

"That the partial recognition of the principle of legal prohibition contained in the recent Municipal enactments of the Legislature, your Memorialists hail as the precursor of future good.

"That your Memorialists are of the opinion that the present License Laws have failed in accomplishing the objects for which they were enacted, that Intemperance is still fearfully prevalent, and that the only way effectually to suppress it will be by enacting a Law entirely prohibiting the traffic in intoxicating liquors as a beverage, and that such a law is desired by a majority of the inhabitants of Upper Canada.

"That the baneful effects of the traffic in intoxicating drinks are the same everywhere. The latest Report of a Parliamentary Committee on Public Houses, published by authority of the Imperial Parliament, distinctly admits '*that the licensing system has totally failed*, and that something much more stringent must be adopted to cure the evils of this trade in strong drink": and Special Committees' Reports of our Provincial Legislature have presented equally startling facts—that the traffic in intoxicating drinks has proved to be the great source of our pauperism, disease, lunacy, immorality, and crime.

"From a Return of Convictions, ending December, 1858, from a comparatively new and sparsely settled county in Canada West, there have been during 270 days, 500 criminal cases of petty and major crimes and misdemeanors, chiefly induced by 200 places where intoxicating liquors can be procured. The statistics of crime in our Cities, Towns, and Villages, are also proved to be just in proportion to the prevalence of the liquor traffic. Of the crimes charged against 3089 male, and 1098 female, prisoners in the City of Toronto for the past year, there were directly charged with the crime of drunkenness 1073 males and 704 females; and directly and indirectly induced by the same cause, there were arrested for assaults, fighting, keeping disorderly houses, riot, selling liquor without license, and larceny, 1171 males and 277 females, being upwards of three-fourths of the whole of the arrests —chiefly imputable to the shameful enticement of dram-shops and the facilities for procuring intoxicating drinks.

"That the burden of taxation arises from the expenses of pauperism, the administration of police and criminal justice; and your Memorialists are of the opinion that no Government can be justified in deriving its revenue from any system, the tendency of which is to degrade and demoralize the mass of the people; that the suppression of the liquor traffic would be a great blessing to this rapidly growing country, would advance the social and moral condition of the people, lessen crime and lawlessness, and lighten taxation.

"That the liquor traffic presents an insuperable barrier in the path of individual and national progress, whether religious, moral, educational, commercial, or economical.

"That at this crisis in the history of our beloved and highly-favored country, when the prospect is brightening, to show us that at no distant day Canada will be a great and glorious empire, whose just and beneficent sway may extend over that vast tract—those fertile vales of the Assiniboine and Saskatchewan—capable of sustaining millions of people (an area of country equal in extent to France and Austria), it is the imperative duty of the people of Canada, in whose hands is the destiny of posterity, to place the laws of our country upon so just, healthy, and solid a foundation, as to assure the greatest amount of happiness, peace, and prosperity, to the future intelligent, virtuous, and loyal millions who may people this noble Province.

"Your Memorialists therefore respectfully and earnestly pray that your Worshipful Body will, without delay, petition the Legislature of Canada to enact a stringent Prohibitory Liquor Law for this Province."

PETITION NOW (FEB. 1860) IN COURSE OF SIGNATURE.

A Meeting of the Joint Committee of the Grand Division Sons of Temperance of Canada West, and the Grand Temple Independant Order of Good Templars, appointed to consider the best means of petitioning Parliament during its approaching Session, for the passage of a Prohibitory Liquor Law, was held in the Rooms of Hamilton Division S. of T., in this city, at two o'clock p.m. this day.

Present on behalf of the Grand Division, Brothers W. Wheaton of London, Edward Lafferty of West Flamboro, and C. H. Vannorman of Hamilton; on behalf of the Grand Temple, Brothers D. Able of Simcoe, R. D. Wadsworth of Hamilton, J. G. Curtis of Markham, and Sister Mechell of Claremont.

On motion, R. D. Wadsworth was appointed Chairman, and C. H. Vannorman Secretary, after which the following Resolutions were severally proposed and unanimously adopted.

Resolved 1*st*,—That, for the present, the mode of petitioning recommended by the Grand Division at its late Session be adopted, namely, that instead of circulating petitions, as heretofore, for individual signatures, the Grand Division and Grand Temple, together with the Subordinate Divisions and Temples under their jurisdiction, do each petition in the name of the Division or Temple, as the case may be, each petition to specify the number of members represented by the body petitioning, and be signed under official seal by the Presiding Officer and Secretary.

Resolved 2*nd*,—That the following Form of Petition be adopted:

"*To the Honorable the Legislative Assembly of the Province of Canada, in Parliament Assembled,* THE PETITION *of ———————————, located in ———————, representing ——— Members,*

"*Humbly Sheweth:*

"That your Petitioners regard Intemperance as a great moral and social evil, destroying health, virtue, and happiness; producing disease, lunacy, and crime; entailing heavy burdens on society, and erecting a fatal barrier in the path of individual and national progress. That your Petitioners regard Total Abstinence from the use of intoxicating liquors, as the only effectual means of prevention or cure of this great evil, and they deem it the duty of a wise and patriotic government to protect the community from the immense pecuniary sacrifices, the mental and physical maladies, the outrages on life and property, and the moral contamination, consequent on the use of alcoholic beverages. Therefore, your Petitioners would reiterate the prayer expressed in numerous petitions heretofore presented to your Honorable House, and humbly pray that you will pass a legislative enactment prohibiting the manufacture and sale of intoxicating liquors except for medicinal or mechanical purposes. And your Petitioners, as in duty bound, will ever pray."

Resolved 3rd,—That the Chairman and Secretary of this Committee be authorized to get a sufficient number of the foregoing Form of Petition printed to serve the purpose intended, and that they be forwarded to the Grand Scribe and Grand Secretary for distribution. The expense of printing to be borne equally by the Grand Division and Grand Temple.

Resolved 4th,—That the Secretary of this Committee be instructed to forward a copy of the Form of Petition adopted, to each of the other Temperance Organizations in the Province, in the hope that the same may be adopted by them, and signed in similar manner by their proper officers respectively.

FORM OF ACT SUBMITTED WITH THE ABOVE PETITION.

BILL.

AN ACT FOR THE SUPPRESSION OF INTEMPERANCE.

Whereas the common traffic in Intoxicating Liquors, and their use as a beverage, is a fruitful source of crime and demoralization; and whereas it is the first duty of Government to prevent those evils, as far as possible, and to protect the people against them; therefore Her Majesty, by and with the advice and consent of the Legislative Council and Assembly of Canada, enacts as follows:—

§ 1. From and after the passing of this Act, it shall be unlawful for any person or persons to import into this Province, manufacture, buy, receive, barter, sell, or dispose of in any way, or for any purpose wherever, except as hereinafter provided, any Intoxicating Liquors; and for the purposes of this Act, any liquor known as being alcoholic or intoxicating shall be deemed and taken to be Intoxicating Liquor, as well as any other liquor which does or may produce intoxication. All liquor kept in violation of any provision or provisions of this Act, shall be deemed, and are hereby declared to be, a public nuisance.

§ 2. The Council of each Municipality in Canada shall appoint a suitable person or persons, as the agent or agents of said Municipality, for the purchase and sale of Intoxicating Liquor for medicinal, chemical, and mechanical, and wine for sacramental purposes only, and said agents shall receive such compensation for their services as the Council appointing them may allow, and in the purchase and sale of Intoxicating Liquor such agents shall conform to this Act, and to such rules and regulations as the Council may from time to time prescribe for their guidance, not contrary to the provisions of this Act; provided that there shall be no more than two such agents at the same time in any township or village municipality, or in any ward of a town or city. No such agency shall be kept in, or connected with, any tavern, store, grocery, druggist or apothecary shop, boarding or victualing house, saloon, oyster shop, or any place for dancing or gambling, or for using Intoxicating Liquors for chemical or mechanical purposes, nor in or connected with any house or place of permanent or casual entertainment, amusement, or recreation, nor shall the owner or keeper of any such house or place be eligible to hold the office of such agent.

§ 3. Before entering upon his duties every such agent shall receive a license from the Council appointing him, authorizing him, for not more than twelve months from the date of such license, to sell Intoxicating Liquors, at the place specified in such license, for the purpose authorized by this Act only; but such license shall not be given to such agent until he shall have executed and delivered to the Council appointing him, a bond in favor of the municipality, with two good and sufficient sureties, to be approved by the Council, in the sum of not less than one thousand dollars each, conditioned as follows:—

" Know all men by these presents that A B (the principal) and C D and E F (the sureties) are jointly and severally held and firmly bound unto the municipality of   in the penal sum of   dollars; for payment whereof we bind our-

selves, and each of us binds himself, our and each of our heirs, executors, and administrators, firmly by these presents. Sealed with our seals and dated this   day of
A. D.

" Whereas the above bondman, A B, has been appointed agent for the said municipality, to sell at (*here name the particular place*) Intoxicating Liquors for medical, chemical, and mechanical, and wine for sacramental purposes only, from the
day of   to the   day of   ,
unless sooner removed from such agency.

" Now the condition of this bond is such that if the said A B shall in all respects conform to the provisions of an Act passed in the 23rd year of the reign of Her Majesty Queen Victoria, and entitled, ' An Act for the Suppression of Intemperance,' and to such rules and regulations as now are, and from time to time shall be established, by the said municipality, touching the sale of Intoxicating Liquors, the same not being contrary to the provisions of this Act, then this obligation to be void, otherwise to be, and remain in full force and effect."

And such agent may purchase Intoxicating Liquors from any licensed manufacturer, or import the same from abroad. In the purchase and sale of said Liquors each such agent shall observe and be governed by the following rules, to wit:—

1st. He shall not purchase any intoxicating liquor in this Province, from any person except a licensed manufacturer, or another duly authorized agent for the sale of such Liquor.

2nd. When making application for such liquor he shall exhibit his license if required.

3rd. No liquor shall be removed from a manufactory, nor imported into the Province, for him, unless the vessel containing the same be plainly marked upon some conspicuous part thereof, or upon a card or label attached thereto, with the name of the liquor, the name of the vendor, the place where purchased, the name of the agent, and the place where consigned; somewhat after the following form, but varying to suit the occasion:—

BRANDY.

From
    Craig & Co.,
                of Toronto,

To
    John Green,
                Agent, Oshawa.

4th. He shall give a written or printed receipt for all purchases of such liquors, and receive and file all bills of purchase.

5th. He shall not sell to any minor or apprentice, knowing him to be such, without the written order of his parent, guardian, or master, nor to any Indian, soldier, or seaman.

6th. He shall not sell to any person known to be of intemperate habits, nor to any person whatever, after having received a written notice from a Councillor of the municipality, a minister of the Gospel, or a Justice of the Peace, that the use which such person makes of Intoxicating Liquor renders it improper to sell him such liquors on any account whatever.

7th. He shall not sell for medicinal purposes more than one quart at one time, except to a practising physician, and in no case shall he dispose of any liquor having reason to suppose an improper use will be made of the same, and he shall only sell or dispose of such liquor for cash.

8th. He shall not permit any intoxicating liquor to be consumed upon or about his premises.

9th. He shall enter in a book a correct account of all purchases and receipts of liquors made by him or for him, with the price paid therefor, the cost of transportation, and all expenses connected therewith, and the date and place of purchase, and name of vender.

10th. He shall also enter in a book all sales made under his directions, in manner or to the effect following:—

Date of Purchase.	Name of Purchaser.	Residence of Purchaser.	Kind and Quality of Liquor.	Purpose for which Purchased.	Price per Gallon.	Total Cost.

11th. Such book shall be opened at all reasonable times to the inspection of all the electors of the municipality.

12th. He shall file with the clerk of the municipality in which he sells, between the 1st and 10th days of each month, a copy of all sales and purchases made as entered in his books, with an affidavit that said copy contains a true account of all the purchases and sales and manner of disposing of liquor, by him, or for him, during the previous month.

13th. He shall attach to each vessel in which liquor shall be conveyed from his premises, a card, or label, upon which shall be legibly written, or printed, a statement of the date of sale, the kind and quantity of liquor therein, the purpose for which purchased, as stated by the purchaser, and his own name; in form or to the effect following:—

Toronto, April 1st, 1860.

Sold James Brown One Quart Brandy for Chemical Purposes.

MOSES CROWN,
Agent.

§ 4. Every such agent shall properly account to the municipality for all monies coming into his hands by virtue of such agency, paying the same to the council when required; and when directed shall deliver to the council said books and accounts, with all funds and property in his hands belonging to the municipality, and if any such agent shall violate any provision of this Act, he shall forfeit his license and be deemed an offender against this Act, after which he shall be ineligible to act as such agent; and the imposition of any fine shall not discharge him from any other penalty or liability.

§ 5. The council of any county or city may license one or more persons, being freeholders and residents of such county or city, to manufacture intoxicating liquors at such place, within the municipality, as may be designated in such license, and to sell the same to licensed agents only; but no such license shall be valid for more than twelve months from the date thereof, nor be granted until a bond be delivered to the municipality, with two good and sufficient sureties, to be approved by the council, in a sum not less than two thousand dollars, conditioning that such manufacturer will not, during the continuation of his license, violate any provision of this Act or of the council not contrary to this Act; but no person engaged in the manufacture of intoxicating liquors at the passing of this Act shall be refused such license, if he apply therefor. Every person so licensed may manufacture and sell intoxicating liquor, and shall enter in a book each sale of liquor made by him, or for him, during the continuation of his license, inserting the date of sale, the name and place of residence of the purchaser, the quantity and kind of liquor sold, and the price paid therefor, which book shall at all reasonable hours be open to the inspection of any Justice of the Peace or Councillor of the municipality,— and at the end of every quarter he shall file a true copy of such book with the clerk of the municipality which granted his license, with an affidavit that the same is a correct copy of said book, and contains a true account of the manner in which all intoxicating liquors were disposed of at his manufactory during the preceding quarter. Said manufacturer shall not permit any intoxicating liquor to be consumed upon or about his premises, and shall be deemed an offender against this Act for every sale or disposal of intoxicating liquors at his establishment to any person or persons other than agents for the sale of such liquors, and shall also forfeit his license and be rendered ineligible to engage in such manufacturing for twelve months thereafter. The imposition of any fine for a breach of this Act shall not relieve him from any other penalty or liability. He shall also attach a written or printed card, or label, to each vessel in which liquor shall be taken from his premises, in manner or to the effect following:—

Toronto, March 1st, 1860.

Sold 40 Gallons Whisky to John Coon, Agent of Municipality.

TIMOTHY CAREY,
Manufacturer.

§ 6. No defect in bond, or writing, or recognizance, with security required by this Act, shall, in any manner, invalidate the same, but the person executing it shall be bound to the full extent of the law requiring the bond, writing, or recognizance.

§ 7. The clerks of the peace of the several counties shall keep a record of the names, residences, and certificates in full of all persons authorized by said municipalities, respectively to manufacture and sell, as hereinbefore provided in sections third and fifth, which record shall be open to public inspection at all reasonable times; and they shall furnish a list of said names, with their residences, to all persons authorized by boards respectively to manufacture and sell spirituous or intoxicating liquors, and to all agents of towns and cities, whose names have been furnished them as aforesaid, within their respective counties.

§ 8. If any person shall adulterate, for the purpose of sale, any beer, or other malt liquor, or any wine, or any distilled liquor, or any spirituous or intoxicating liquor, intended for drinking, with coculus indicus, vitriol, grains of paradise, opium, alum, capsicum, copperas, laurel water, logwood, Brazil wood, cochineal, sugar of lead, or any other substance which is poisonous or injurious to health, or if any person shall sell any such liquor, intended for drinking, adulterated as aforesaid with any substance above named, or any other substance which is poisonous or injurious to health, knowing the same to be so adulterated, he shall be punished by imprisonment in the county jail not more than three years.

§ 9. All intoxicating liquor found in this Province, except in the possession or under the control of an officer of the law, having seized the same under this Act, or an agent for the sale of such liquor, or a person duly authorized to manufacture the same, without having attached to the vessel containing such liquor, a written or printed card, label, or mark, as herein before provided, and all liquor kept, used, or held for use, in violation of this Act, and the vessels, or casks, containing the same, are hereby declared to be forfeited to the municipality in which the same are found, such card, label, or mark, being attached to the liquor, shall not be taken as proof that the same is not held, or intended, for unlawful sale or use.

§ 10. Any mayor, alderman, councillor, sheriff, deputy sheriff, chief of police, or deputy chief of police, city clerk, deputy or assistant clerk, police officer, constable, or watchman, in his city, village, or township, may, without a warrant, arrest any person or persons whom they may find in the act of illegally selling, transporting, or distributing intoxicating liquors, and seize the liquors, vessels, and implements of sale, in the possession of said person or persons, and detain them in some place for safe keeping until warrants can be procured, on complaint made, for the trial of said person or persons, and for the seizure of said liquor, vessels, and implements, under the provisions of this Act; and it shall be the duty of the several officers aforesaid to enforce the penalties provided in this Act, or cause them to be enforced, against every person who shall be guilty of any violation thereof of which they can obtain reasonable proof. And if any sheriff, deputy sheriff, chief of police, or deputy chief of police, constable, or police officer, shall be furnished with a written notice of any violation of this Act, and the names of witnesses thereof, and shall for two weeks neglect to commence an action thereon, or prosecute any complaint thereafter, shall be liable for all fines imposed and collected for said violation of this Act.

§ 11. If any expressman, common carrier, or other person, shall, for the purpose of conveying to any other person, receive any spirituous or intoxicating liquor which has been sold, or is intended for sale, in violation of this Act, he having reasonable cause to believe that the same has been so sold, or is so intended to be sold, such expressman, common carrier, or other person, shall, on conviction thereof, pay twenty dollars and the costs of prosecution, and shall stand committed until the same be paid; the same to be recovered on complaint before any justice of the peace, or police court having criminal jurisdiction, either in the place where said liquor may be received, or in any place through which it may be carried, or in the place at which it may be delivered to the purchaser or any person for him.

§ 12. It shall not be lawful for any corporation, person, or company, knowingly, to receive, transport, or carry, any intoxicating liquor, from one place to another, within this Province, nor bring such liquor from abroad into the Province, excepting in bond, unless each vessel, or cask, containing the same, be plainly marked or labelled as aforesaid.

§ 13. No person shall procure intoxicating liquor from an authorized agent or manufacturer, professedly for purposes permitted by this Act, and make an unlawful use of the same, nor procure such liquor by forging, or improperly obtaining, any card, mark, or label, referred to in this Act.

§ 14. If any three municipal electors shall make oath, or affirmation, before any Justice of the Peace, that they have reason to believe, and do believe, that intoxicating liquor, intended for sale or barter, or to be used in contravention of this Act, is kept or deposited in any house or place, in such municipality, or on any adjoining water, the said Justice of the Peace shall issue his warrant to any Sheriff, police officer, bailiff, or constable, requiring him, forthwith, to search for, and seize such liquor, if found, and the vessels or casks containing the same, and to arrest the owner or keeper thereof, and to convey the liquor, and vessels or casks, so seized, to some proper place of security, there to be kept until final action thereon, and the owner or keeper, so arrested, shall be brought before said Justice, or some other Justice of the Peace, and if it be proved that the said liquor was kept, or intended, for sale or use, contrary to the provisions of this Act, it shall be, together with the vessels or casks containing the same, declared forfeited, and the owner or keeper of such liquor shall be deemed an offender against this Act.

§ 15. In any proceeding for a violation of the provisions of this Act, it shall not be necessary to specify or prove the precise kind of liquor which is the subject of the charge, but to allege it as "intoxicating liquor" only, and proof of the unlawful charge in relation to any such liquor, shall be deemed sufficient, although the particular kind may not be able to be shown. All clerks, agents, and servants, shall be proceeded against as principals, and incur the same penalties for a violation of any section of this Act.

§ 16. It shall be the duty of the county attorney to prosecute all suits, under this Act, which may be brought before the mayor, or other presiding officer appointed by law, of any city, if so requested, and it shall be the duty of the county attorney, by himself, or by deputy, to prosecute all suits under this Act, which may be brought before a justice of the peace, or before the court of common pleas of the county or district, and to prosecute all appeals of suits under this Act, in the circuit courts and courts of common pleas of his county or district; and where there is no city attorney, he shall prosecute all suits under this Act, before the mayor of any city, &c., &c.

§ 17. If the owner or possessor of liquor seized under this Act, shall be unknown to the officer making such seizure, the liquor shall not be forfeited until the fact of such seizure shall have been advertised, with the number and description of the casks or packages, as near as may be, by posting up a written or printed notice thereof in at least three public places in said municipality, and publishing the same in a paper, if one be published in the municipality, and if it shall be proved to the satisfaction of said Justice, within two weeks from the time of said seizure, that said liquor was, at the time of the seizure, the property of any person authorized under this Act to hold the same, it shall be delivered to the owner claiming it, who shall give his receipt therefor, which shall be filed with the other papers relating to the case.

§ 18. If any person claiming any interest in any spirituous or intoxicating liquor seized as a nuisance, and having knowledge or notice, as required by this Act, of the seizure, shall not assert his claim upon the trial, he shall be deemed to have waived his claim, and shall not afterward assert any right thereto whatever, or any claim for damages. Judgment of forfeiture against any spirituous or intoxicating liquor, under the provisions of this Act, shall operate as a judgment, *in rem*, and the validity of such judgment shall not be contested, or questioned in any action, in any court, by any person, except by appeal of the cause in which the judgment of forfeiture is declared; and no court shall take jurisdiction of any action of replevin, or any other action, to try the validity of the proceedings in which the forfeiture is declared, except as herein provided.

§ 19. Any peace officer, policeman, or constable, receiving satisfactory information that any intoxicating liquor is kept for sale, or use, or is sold, or used, contrary to this Act, in any tent, shanty, hut, or place, not being a dwelling house, or at any public fair, or on, or near, the ground of any cattle show, exhibition, militia or military muster, or on any public occasion of any kind, is hereby required to make diligent search of such place or places, and if such officer shall find therein or thereat, any intoxicating liquor, he shall seize the same, with the vessels containing it, and arrest the keeper of such place, or the owner or keeper of the liquor found as aforesaid, without warrant, and forthwith take him before any Justice of the Peace, having jurisdiction, with the liquor and vessels so seized, and upon proof that the said intoxicating liquor was found in the possession, or under the control, of the accused, in any tent or shanty, or other place, as aforesaid, and was there kept to be sold, or in any way furnished, to the persons there assembled, he shall be deemed an offender against this Act; and the liquor and vessels, so seized, shall be declared forfeited by the order of said Justice, who shall award such costs as he shall deem just;—provided, that should such prosecution fail, no officer making such seizure shall be condemned in costs unless it be proved that he was moved to make such seizure by malice.

§ 20. Whenever a judgment for damages has been or may be recovered against any justice of the peace, justice of any police court, sheriff, deputy sheriff, constable, or other magistrate or officer, in any action brought against him on account of anything heretofore done by him in good faith in his official capacity under and by virtue of the Act entitled

he shall receive the amount of damages and costs, so recovered against him, of the treasurer of the municipality; *provided* the judge or justice before whom the case may be tried shall certify, under his hand, that the said judgment was recovered against such magistrate or officer on account of some act done by him in good faith in his official capacity under the statute aforesaid; and the treasurer of the municipality shall also pay to any such magistrate or officer, against whom judgment may be recovered as aforesaid, such further sum as the judge or justice who may try the case shall, in his said certificate, certify has been fairly and reasonably expended, by said magistrate or officer, in carrying on the defence of any such suit.

§ 21. All cases under this Act which shall come by appeal, writ of error, or in any other manner, before any higher court than a justice's court, shall in such higher court be conducted by the county attorney or Queen's counsel in behalf of the prosecution, and shall take precedence in such court of all other criminal business, except those criminal cases in which the parties accused are actually under arrest awaiting trial; and the prosecuting officers shall not have authority to enter a *nolle prosequi*, except by consent of the court, and where the purposes of justice manifestly require it; nor shall the court grant a continuance in any case arising under this Act, except where the purposes of justice manifestly require it.

§ 22. Any person feeling aggrieved by any judgment of the mayor of a city, or justice of the peace, may appeal, within thirty days, to the court of common pleas, or circuit court of the county, but the appellant shall, before the appeal is granted, enter into a recognizance before the justice or mayor, with approved security in the penal sum of twice the amount of the judgment and costs, conditioned that the appellant will personally appear in the appellate court, and pay the judgment and costs that may be rendered against him, and abide the order of the court, and not depart without leave.

§ 23. When any appeal is taken, the magistrate shall forthwith make out a fair transcript of the proceedings, and file it with all the papers in the cause, and the appellate court shall try the cause with or without a jury, and render a judgment, and enforce it according to the provisions of this Act.

§ 24. Whenever any spirituous or intoxicating liquor is seized as a nuisance under any provision of this Act, the officer seizing it shall keep the same safely in some secure place until final judgment; and if judgment of forfeiture be given against such liquor, or any part of it, he shall deposit such liquor with the county agent, duly appointed to sell intoxicating liquor, for safe keeping, and take his receipt therefor for safe keeping; and if no appeal is taken within thirty days, the officer shall return the receipt for safe keeping, and take and destroy the liquor under the order of the court trying the cause. But if any appeal is taken, the officer shall return his order to the proper court, indorsed that he had delivered the liquor so seized to the county agent for safe keeping, and the county agent shall keep such liquor subject to the order of the appellate court. Whenever judgment is given against the complainant upon the seizure of such liquor as a nuisance, the attorney prosecuting the action, or the district attorney, may cause the action to be taken to the appellate court upon appeal, at any time within three days, without any bond being filed on the part of the complainant. And the officer seizing the liquor shall not return it to the place of seizure until the expiration of three days; and upon an appeal being taken on the part of the defendant, he shall deposit the liquor seized with the county agent for safe keeping, and make his return accordingly. Whenever final judgment is given against the complainant in such cause, that the liquor so seized is not a nuisance, and not subject to forfeiture, the county shall pay the costs of the seizure, carriage, safe keeping, and return of the liquors, and the fees of officers, jurors, and witnesses in such cause; but the county shall be liable for no other costs in any case except the keeping of persons under arrest and imprisonment for a violation of this Act, as in other cases.

§ 25. Every contrivance or device made use of to sell, or deal out to, or provide for, any person, intoxicating liquor, contrary to the tenor of this Act, and at the same time to conceal or disguise the vender of such liquor, is hereby declared to be a public nuisance—and both the keeper and owner of the premises where such device exists, shall be deemed offenders against this Act, unless it appear, upon the examination, that such device was unknown to said owner, which shall free him from such offence.

§ 26. No spirituous or intoxicating liquors shall be given away, or be kept with intent to be given away, in any tavern, boarding-house, public eating house, grocery, oyster shop, store, bar-room, confectionery, or other place of public entertainment; or in any theatre, museum, or other place of public resort; or on any steam-

L*

boat, or other craft; carrying passengers; and for any violation of this section, the person so offending shall be fined to the same extent as for selling such liquor contrary to this Act.

§ 27. If any person shall knowingly let any building or tenement owned by him, or under his control, for the illegal sale or keeping of intoxicating drinks, or shall knowingly permit any such building or tenement, or part thereof, to be so used while under his control, or shall, after due notice of any such use of said building or tenement, omit to take all reasonable measures to eject the said person from said premises as soon as the same may lawfully be done, he shall be deemed and taken to be guilty of aiding in the maintenance of such nuisance, and be punished by a fine of not less than one hundred, nor more than one thousand dollars, or by imprisonment in the county jail not less than thirty days, nor more than six months.

§ 28. That for all fines and costs assessed against any person or persons, for any violation of this Act, the real estate and personal property of such person or persons, of every kind, without exemption, shall be liable for the payment thereof; and all such fines and costs shall be a lien upon such real estate until paid. And in case any person or persons shall rent or lease any building or premises, and knowingly suffer the same to be used and occupied for the sale of intoxicating liquors, contrary to this Act, such building and premises so leased and occupied shall be held liable for, and may be sold to pay, all fines and costs assessed against the person occupying such building or premises, for any violation of this Act; and in case such building or premises belong to any minor, insane person, or idiot, the guardian or guardians of such minor or minors, or insane person, or idiot, who has control of such building or premises, shall be liable for, and account to such ward or wards, insane person, or idiot, for all damages, in consequence of the use and occupation of such building and premises, and liabilities for such fines and costs, as aforesaid.

§ 29. Intoxication shall be deemed an offence against this Act, and if any person shall be found intoxicated in any public house, or place, or on any street or highway, or, being intoxicated, shall be found any where committing a breach of the peace, or disturbing other persons, by making an unusual noise, any peace officer shall, without warrant, arrest such person, and take him before a Justice of the Peace, and if such person, so arrested, shall fully disclose the name of the person from whom, and the place, time, and manner, in which he procured the liquor which produced his intoxication, he shall be retained as a witness against the vender of such liquor, if furnished in contravention of this Act, and then discharged;—but if such intoxicated person refuse to give said evidence, he shall be deemed an offender against the Act.

§ 30. If any person in a state of intoxication shall commit any offence against the person or property of any one, the person who furnished such offender the liquor, or any part thereof, which occasioned his intoxication, if the same was furnished in violation of this Act, shall be subject to the same action, on behalf of the party aggrieved, as might be brought against the person intoxicated, and the aggrieved party, or his representative, may bring either a joint action against the person intoxicated and committing such offence, and the person who furnished the liquor, or a separate action against each.

§ 31. Any person may maintain an action, in any court in this Province, against any other person who shall, unlawfully, sell or deliver any liquor to the husband, wife, parent, child, guardian, ward, apprentice, or servant, of the plaintiff, or to any Indian of kin or otherwise, and it shall not be necessary in any such action to aver or prove any specific damage to the plaintiff by such sale or delivery, but upon such proof the court or jury shall assess the damage at not less than twenty-five cents and the costs of suit, and if any special damage be shown, then at such higher sum as may be just, and judgment shall be given accordingly. Any married woman may prosecute and maintain such action in her own name, with or without the consent of her husband, and upon the trial of any action under this section, the defendant, plaintiff, wife, or husband of the plaintiff, may be examined as a witness, any law or rule of court to the contrary notwithstanding. All damages recovered by a married woman shall go to her separate use. In case of the death of any party to or against whom action is given by this section, it shall survive to or against his or her executors or administrators.

§ 32. Upon the trial of any complaint or information, under any provision of this Act, proof of the keeping, delivery, or sale or barter, of intoxicating liquor, by the defendant, shall be sufficient to sustain an allegation that the same was unlawful, and unless he prove the contrary, judgment shall be rendered against him.

§ 33. Any person violating any of the provisions of this Act, shall be liable to a fine of not less than twenty-five dollars, nor more than one hundred dollars, and the costs of prosecution, in the discretion of the convicting justice, which fine shall belong, one half to the prosecutor, and the other to the municipality where the offence is committed; unless the prosecution be brought in the name of the municipality, which in such case shall receive the whole amount of fine; and in default of payment of any such fine, and all costs, the offender shall be imprisoned at hard labor until the same be paid, such imprisonment, however, not to be less than ten days, nor more than two calendar months, as the convicting justice may direct.

§ 34. No person proved to have been engaged in the unlawful sale of intoxicating liquor, within one year of the time of any trial under this Act, shall be competent to sit as a juryman thereon; and if his disqualification be known, he shall be challenged when called as such juror. Neither shall such person be eligible to hold any public office in the municipality for one year thereafter.

§ 35. Liquors seized under this Act, and the vessels containing them, shall not be taken from the custody of the officer in charge by writ of *replevin*, or any other process, while the proceedings herein provided for are pending, and final judgment thereon shall, in all cases, be a bar to all suits for the recovery of liquor or casks seized, or the value of the same, or alleged damages by reason of such seizure and detention.

§ 36. Either the complainant, or other person prosecuting on his own behalf or that of a municipality, or the defendant, in any action arising under this Act, may appeal from the decision of a justice of the peace, and the laws regulating appeals from decisions of justices shall apply in all cases under this Act.

§ 37. It shall specially be the duty of all peace officers, municipal officers, justices of the peace, and collectors of customs, to enforce the provisions of this Act, and every person legally required to enforce, or to assist in enforcing, its provisions, refusing or neglecting so to do, shall be deemed an offender this Act.

§ 38. Nothing in this Act shall be construed to prevent the making of cider from apples, or wine from grapes, currants, or other fruit, grown and gathered in this province by the manufacturer, or the sale thereof by him, in quantities not less than three gallons at any one time, no part of which shall be drunk upon or about the premises, nor shall this Act be construed to prevent the manufacture and sale of burning fluids of any kind, perfumery essences, drugs, varnishes, nor any other article of trade or commerce, composed in part of alcohol or other spirituous liquor, if not capable of being used as a beverage, nor intended for use as a beverage, or in evasion or contravention of against this Act.

§ 39. Nothing contained in this Act shall be construed to prevent any chemist, artist, or manufacturer, in whose art or trade they may be necessary, from keeping at his place of business such spirituous liquors as he may have occasion to use in his art or trade, but not for sale.

§ 40. That it shall be right and proper to appraise intoxicating liquor (the personal property of individuals) for legal purposes, and it shall not be deemed any violation of this Act for the public auctioneer to dispose of the same at vendue; but such sale shall be only to one or more licensed agents, and to no other person or persons.

§ 41. In any case where, under the provisions of this Act, intoxicating liquor, and the vessels containing the same, are declared forfeited, the officer having the same in charge shall deliver said liquor, and the vessels, over to an agent for the sale of liquor in the municipality or ward where the offence was committed, and file a receipt for the same with the convicting justice, and if in the opinion of such agent the liquor is unfit for sale, he shall destroy it, otherwise sell the same for the municipality.

§ 42. All payments or compensation for money, labor, or personal or real property, made by sale or delivery of intoxicating intoxicating liquor, contrary to this Act, are hereby declared to be void, and in any action touching such money, labor, personal or real estate, the purchaser and seller of such liquor may be examined as witnesses, and all contracts, notes, bills, bonds, and agreements, made in whole, or in part consideration of intoxicating liquor, illegally sold, shall be void, except in the hands of innocent holders.

§ 43. Any person offending against or violating any of the provisions of this Act, may be prosecuted before any one or more justices of the peace having jurisdiction where the offence was committed; and for the purpose of enforcing the provisions of this Act, such justice or justices shall have, and may exercise, all the power and authority vested in him, or them, by the 14th Vic., cap. 178, entitled, "An Act to facilitate the performance of duties of Justices of the Peace out of sessions in Upper Canada, with respect to summary convictions and orders," and any false oath or affirmation under this Act shall be perjury.

§ 44. No action or other proceeding under this Act, or which may be necessary to carry out its provisions, shall be held to be void, or allowed to fail for any defect of form, and no particular form of words shall be requisite in any information, prosecution, or action, instituted or made for enforcing any of the provisions of this Act, and any such information, prosecution, or action, may be laid and prosecuted to judgment and execution before any one justice of the peace. No specific forms are necessary, but the following are recommended :—

Form of Indictment in case of Common Seller or Manufacturer.

County of   , ss. At the   Court, begun and holden at   , within and for the County of   , on the   Tuesday of   , in the year of our Lord One Thousand Eight Hundred and Sixty

The Jurors for said   , upon their oath present, that A. B., of   , in said County, yeoman, at   , in said County of   , on the   day of   , in the year of our Lord One Thousand Eight Hundred and   , and on divers other days and times between said   day of   aforesaid, and the day of the finding of this indictment, without any lawful authority, license, or permission, was a common seller of intoxicating liquors, against the peace of said   , and contrary to the form of the Statute in such case made and provided. (In case of a former conviction add) and the Jurors aforesaid, upon their oath aforesaid, do further present, that the said   has been   before convicted as a common seller under the Act   in said County of

A true bill:

, County Attorney.

, Foreman.

Form of Complaint and Warrant in case of Seizure.

County of   .   , ss. To A. B., Esquire, one of the Justices of the Peace within and for the County of   .

A. B., C. D., and E. F., of   , residents in said County, and competent to be witnesses in civil suits, on the   day of   , in the year Eighteen Hundred and   , in behalf of said   , on oath complain, that they have reason to believe, that on the   day of   in said year, at said   , intoxicating liquors were, and still are, kept and deposited by   , of   , in said County, in   [Here describe with precision the place to be searched] said   , not being authorized by law to sell said liquors within said   ; and that said liquors are intended for sale within said   in violation of law, whereby said liquors, and the vessels in which the same are contained, have become forfeited to be destroyed; and said   , by reason of the premises, has incurred and become liable to pay a fine of twenty dollars to said   , and costs of prosecution, and to be imprisoned   , and also to be imprisoned thirty days additional in default of payment of said fine and costs.

They therefore pray that due process be issued to search said   , and any yard or building, other than a dwelling-house, adjoining the premises herein before mentioned, if occupied by the same person herein described, where said liquors are believed to be deposited; and if there found, that the said liquors and vessels be seized and safely kept until final action and decision be had thereon, and that said   be forthwith apprehended and held to answer to said complaint, and to do and receive such sentence as may be awarded against him, and that said liquors and vessels be declared forfeited and ordered to be destroyed.

A. B.
C. D.
E. F.

         , ss. On the   day of   aforesaid, the said A. B., C. D., and E. F.,   made oath that the above complaint by them signed is true.

Before me,   , Justice of the Peace.

CANADIAN ACTION. 181

County of   , ss. To the Sheriff of our said
   County of   , or either of his deputies, or the
   Constables of the Town of   , or either of the
towns within said county.

Whereas, A. B., C. D., and E. F., of   , resident
in said County, and competent to be witnesses in civil suits, on
the   day of   , in the year Eighteen Hundred
and   , in behalf of said   , on oath complained
to the subscriber, one of the Justices of the Peace within and for
the said County, that they have reason to believe, and did believe,
that on the   day of   in said year, at said
         , intoxicating liquors were and still are deposited
and kept by   , of   , in said County, in
 [Here follows a precise description of the place to be searched],
said   not being authorized by law to sell said liquors
within said   , by reason of the premises, incurred and
became liable to pay a fine of   to said   , and
costs of prosecution, and to be imprisoned   days, and
also to be imprisoned thirty days in default of the payment of said
fine and costs, and prayed that due process be issued to search
said   and any yard or building, or other than a
dwelling-house, adjoining the premises herein before mentioned, if
occupied by the same person herein described, where said liquors
are believed to be deposited, and if there found, that the said
liquors and vessels be seized and safely kept until final action and
decision be had thereon, and that said   be apprehended
and held to answer to said complaint, and to do and receive such
sentence as may be awarded against him, and that said liquors and
vessels be declared forfeited and ordered to be destroyed.

You are therefore required, in the name of the   , to enter
the   before named, and therein search for said liquors,
and if there found, to seize and safely keep the same, with the
vessels in which they are contained, until final action and decision
be had on said complaint; and to apprehend the said

forthwith, if he may be found in your precincts, and bring him before me, the subscriber, or some other Justice within and for said County, to answer to said complaint; and to do and receive such sentence as may be awarded against him.

Witness,   , Esquire, at   aforesaid, this   day of   , in the year Eighteen Hundred and   .

          , Justice of the Peace.

Form of Complaint for Single Sale.

County of   ss.

To   , Esquire, one of the Justices of the Peace within and for the County of   .

A. B., of   , in said County, yeoman, on the   day of   , in the year of our Lord One Thousand Eight Hundred and   , in behalf of said   , on oath, complains that   , of   , in said County, laborer, on the   day of   aforesaid, at said   , not being appointed by the proper authorities of said   as the agent of said   to sell therein intoxicating liquors, did sell a quantity of intoxicating liquors therein, to wit: 'one   of intoxicating liquor to one   (or if the individual be unknown, to some person to said complainant unknown), against the peace of said   , and contrary to the form of the statute in such cases made and provided.

A. B.

On the   day of   aforesaid, the said   makes oath that the above complaint, by   subscribed, is true.

Before me,   , Justice of the Peace.

Form of Warrant upon the Same.

County of   , ss.

To the Sheriff of our said County of   , or either of his Deputies, or either of the Constables of the town of   , or either of the towns within said county—Greeting.

Whereas A. B., of   , on the   day of   ,
A. D., 186 , in behalf of said   , on oath complained to me,
the subscriber, one of the Justices of the Peace within and for the
county of   , that   , of   , in said
county, on the   day of   , at said   , not being
appointed by the proper authorities of said   as the agent of
said   to sell therein intoxicating liquors, did sell a quantity of
intoxicating liquors, to wit: one   of intoxicating liquor to
one   , against the peace of said   , and contrary
to the form of the statute in such case made and provided.

Therefore, in the name of the   of   , you are commanded forthwith to apprehend the said   , if he may
be found in your precincts, and bring   before me, the
subscriber, or some other Justice of the Peace within and for said
county, to answer to said   upon the complaint aforesaid.

Witness my hand and seal at   aforesaid, this
day of   A. D., 186 .

          , Justice of the Peace.

Form of a Recognizance in case of a Single Sale.

Be it remembered, that at a Justice Court held by me, the subscriber, one of the Justices of Peace within and for the county of
          , at my office in   , in said county, on
the   day of   , in the year of our Lord One
Thousand Eight Hundred and   , personally appeared
          and   , and severally acknowledged themselves
to be indebted to the   of   in the respective sums
following, to wit:

The said   as principal, in the sum of
dollars, and the said   and   as sureties,
in the sum of   dollars each, to be levied of their respective
goods, chattels, lands or tenements, and in want thereof, of their
bodies to the use of the State, if default be made in the condition
following.

The condition of this recognizance is such, that whereas the said   has been brought before said court, by virtue of a warrant duly issued upon the complaint on oath of   , charging him, the said   , with having sold at   , said   , one   of intoxicating liquors to one   , the said   not being appointed by the proper authorities of said   as the agent of said   to sell intoxicating liquors therein, against the peace of said   , and contrary to the form of the statute in such case made and provided. And said   having pleaded not guilty to said complaint, but having been by said court found guilty of the same, and been sentenced to   ; and the said   having appealed from said sentence to the next   Court next to be holden at   , within and for said county of   , on the   Tuesday of   :

Now, therefore, if the said   shall appear at the court aforesaid and prosecute his said appeal with effect, and abide the order and judgment of said court, and not depart without license, then this recognizance shall be void; otherwise remain in full force and virtue.

Witness, &c.   Justice of the Peace.

Form of Recognizance in case of Seizure.

Be it remembered, that at a Justice Court held by me, the subscriber, one of the Justices of the Peace within and for the county of   , at my house in said   , on the   day of   , in the year of our Lord One Thousand Eight Hundred and Sixty   , personally appeared A. B., C. D., and E. F., and severally acknowledged themselves to be indebted to the   of   in the respective sums following, to wit:

The said   as principal, in the sum of   dollars, and the said   and   as sureties, in the sum of   dollars each, to be levied of their respective goods, chattels, lands or tenements, and in want thereof, of their bodies to the use of the   , if default be made in the condition following.

The condition of this recognizance is such, that whereas the said   has been brought before said court by virtue of a warrant duly issued upon the complaint, on oath, of G. H., I. J., and K. L., of said   , all competent witnesses in civil suits, and resident within said county, charging him, the said   , with having at   , on the   day of   , kept and deposited certain intoxicating liquors in   [here describe the place where the same are deposited], with the intent to sell the same in said   , in violation of law; said   not being authorized or appointed to sell the same in said   , and a search warrant having been duly issued upon said complaint, and said liquors above described having been seized thereon, and the said   . duly arrested thereon, and said   having pleaded not guilty to said complaint, but having been by said court found guilty of the same, and been sentenced to   ; and the said having appealed from said sentence to the next Supreme Judicial Court, next to be holden at   , within and for said County of   , on the   Tuesday of   .

Now, therefore, if the said   shall appear at the Court aforesaid, and prosecute his said appeal with effect, and abide the order and judgment of said Court, and not depart without license, then his recognizance shall be void; otherwise, remain in full force and virtue.

Witness, &c.   , Justice of the Peace.

Form of Mittimus.

Province of Canada.   County of   , ss.

To the Sheriff of the County of   , or his deputies, or the Constables of the Town (or City) of   , and to the keeper of the jail in   in our said County— Greeting.

Whereas, E. F., of   , in our County of   , now stands convicted before me, A. B., one of the Justices of the Peace in and for the County of   , on the complaint of   , who, on his (or their) oath, complains that
[Here insert the substance of the complaint.]
against the peace of the   , and contrary to the form of the statute in such case made and provided, for which offence, he, the said E. F., is sentenced to pay a fine, for the use of the   , of twenty dollars and costs of prosecution, taxed at   , (and to stand committed until the sentence be performed, all which sentence the said E. F., now before me, the said Justice, fails and refuses to comply with and perform).

These are, therefore, in the name of the   of   , to command you, the said Sheriff, Deputies, and Constables, and each of you, forthwith to convey the said E. F. to the common jail in   , in the County aforesaid, and to deliver him to the keeper thereof, together with this precept: And you, the keeper of the said jail in   aforesaid, are hereby in like manner commanded, in the name of the   of   , to receive the said E. F. into your custody, in said jail, and him there safely to keep until he shall comply with said sentence, or be otherwise discharged by due course of law.

Given under my hand and seal this   day of   , A. D.

A. B., Justice of the Peace.

When the sentence shall be, in addition to the fine, thirty, sixty, or ninety days' imprisonment, the substance of the complaint being duly set forth, insert in the mittimus instead of the words included in the foregoing form, in brackets, as follows: (and   days of imprisonment in the common jail, all which sentence, the said E. F. now being before me, remains to be performed). If the fine and costs are paid, insert (which sentence to   days' imprisonment, the said E. F. now being before me, remains to be complied with and performed,) and in like manner in all cases, the substance of the complaint being set forth, and the recital of the sentence conformed to the fact, the same form in substance may be used, and shall be sufficient in law.

§ 45. In the construction of this Act, words importing the singular number only, may be applied to the plural of person or things; and words importing the masculine gender only, may be extended to females also.

§ 46. In all cases under this Act, reasonable costs, fees, and expenses, shall be allowed by the Justice or Court, in the same manner as are now allowed in criminal cases, and as near as possible corresponding thereto.

§ 47. All persons convicted of having violated any of the provisions of this Act, shall enter into recognizance for good behaviour for the term of one year after judgment rendered in the case, with two sufficient sureties, for an amount not less than $100.00, nor more than $5000.00:—the first violation, thereafter, of this Act, in any of its provisions, will forfeit the recognizance, and the party so offending shall enter into new recognizances. Where proper sureties cannot be found, the offending party shall be imprisoned for not less than one month, nor more than six months.

§ 48. It shall be the duty of the presiding judge of every court of oyer and terminer, and of every court of sessions, specially to charge every grand jury to inquire into all violations of, or offences under, this Act.

§ 49. Nothing in this Act shall be construed to affect the right of any person now having license to sell intoxicating liquor, as a tavern-keeper, or under the provisions of the Act entitled, "An Act regulating the sale of intoxicating liquors," during the period for which his license was granted, with respect to such license, but such person shall have and exercise the rights and privileges which he now enjoys, until the expiration of such time, subject to all the provisions of law now in force regulating his conduct under such license, which provisions are for this purpose, and with respect to such persons respectively exempted from the operation of section until the expiration of their respective licenses.

§ 50. All Acts and parts of Acts of this Province, contrary to the provisions of this Act, are hereby repealed, but such repeal shall not affect any suit or proceedings commenced previous to the passing of this Act, nor have the effect of reviving any Act or part of Act formerly repealed.

§ 51. This Act shall come into force and take effect upon the   day of   1860.

J. J. E. Linton's Form of Bill.

[This Form was rejected by the Joint Committee of the Sons of Temperance and I. O. Good Templars, because of two things—first, it referred only to the Retail Traffic; and, secondly, it applied only to Western Canada.]

An Act to Prohibit the Sale by Retail of Spirituous and Fermented Liquors, within that part of the Province called Upper Canada.

Whereas it is provided by Section 245, Sub-section 6, of the Act passed in the twenty-second year of Her Majesty's reign, chapter ninety-nine, intituled *An Act respecting the Municipal Institutions of Upper Canada,* that the sale by retail of spirituous and fermented liquors in any inn or other house of public entertainment, and in shops and places other than houses of public entertainment, in every township, city, town, and incorporated village, in Upper Canada, may, by a by-law, be prohibited, provided, before the final passing of such by-law, the same has been duly approved by the electors of the municipality; and whereas it has been found inconvenient and of doubtful accomplishment, for universal purposes, the passing of such by-laws,—Therefore, Her Majesty, by and with the advice and consent of the Legislative Council and Assembly of Canada, enacts as follows:—

1. That within the limits of each municipality of every township, incorporated village, town, and city, in Upper Canada, there shall not be (excepting as in this Act excepted) from and after the passing of this Act, any sale by retail of any spirituous or fermented liquors, in any inn or other house of public entertainment, or in any shop or place, other than houses of public enterment; *Provided* hereby, that any sale by retail of said liquors, not herein in this Act excepted and provided for, shall be illegal, and shall be punishable, as hereinafter enacted:—

2. That there shall be saved and excepted from the operation of the preceding section, the rights and privileges by the licenses which are or may be issued on behalf of each of the said municipalities, until the expiry of the period for which these licenses respectively were issued,—and also there shall be saved and excepted as said is, the sale of said liquors, as herein in the next section of this Act provided for, for medicinal, chemical, and mechanical, or wine for sacramental, purposes,—and for such purposes the order, certificate, or requisition, signed by a licensed medical practitioner, or signed by the mayor, or a justice of the peace of any city or town, or by a justice of the peace of the county wherein either of the aforesaid municipalities shall be, or by a reeve, or deputy reeve, in such county, or by any three ratepayers of either of said municipalities wherein the vendor after mentioned shall be licensed, or in the case of sacramental purposes, an order, certificate, or requisition, signed by the clergyman of the church, meeting house, or place of worship, where the same may be required, shall be required to be produced and delivered by the vendee, or his agent, to the licensed vendor or his agent.

3. That for the purpose of providing for the sale by retail of said liquors for the aforesaid purposes, each of the municipalities by the respective councils thereof, shall have the power, and they are hereby authorized to grant a license or licenses available within the limits of each of their said municipalities, to any person or persons, he or they being freeholders in the county where

such license is granted, (who may be known as the licensed vender or venders,) for the sale by retail of said liquors for the aforesaid purposes; provided hereby that there shall only be one such license, and one place for the sale by retail of said liquors, for any number of inhabitants in any municipality, not exceeding two thousand, and for every two thousand inhabitants, or part of two thousand inhabitants, over and above the first two thousand, one license and one such place; each such license to be for one year, said year to end on the last day of February in each and every year; and for each of such licenses the said municipality shall be entitled to demand, and to receive, and to apply for corporation purposes as by law provided, any sum not less than twenty-five dollars, nor more than eight hundred dollars, the same to be inclusive of the duty payable under the imperial statute referred to in the Act cited in the preamble hereof, but exclusive of the sum payable to the Province, in conformity with the present laws thereof; and provided also that each of said municipalities shall have power by by-law to fix the amount payable for each such license in conformity with the provisions in this Act contained, and also to decide on the person or persons, he or they being freeholders in the county where such license is granted, to whom said license shall be given, and also shall have power by said by-law to make restrictions or rules as to the character and standing of the said person or persons; but no act by either of said municipalities to be done, shall be contrary to, and if so done contrary, shall not affect or annul the enactments and provisions of this Act.

4. That it shall be lawful, for the said medicinal and sacramental purposes, to sell as said is the said liquors on any day; provided hereby, that said liquors, or any of them, allowed to be sold by this Act, shall not be used for drinking purposes as a beverage, nor shall they, or any of them, be consumed or drunk, on the place or premises of the vender, or his agent, where sold; and also provided, that such place or premises shall not be in, or attached to, any store or shop, saloon, eating-house, house of en-

tertainment, inn, hotel, tavern, or place, where by law the said liquors now are, or hitherto have been allowed to be, manufactured or sold.

5. That the said licensed vender or his agent shall keep a book, and shall therein enter and record each sale made, and shall for each such sale enter and record the same by entering and recording in said book, the name of the vendee or his agent, the name or names signed to, and the date of, said order, certificate, or requisition, the date of sale, the quantity sold, the kind or quality and name of said liquors so sold, the purpose for which the same is so sold, and the price or sum so paid by the vendee or his agent therefor, according as nearly as may be to the form set forth in schedule A to this Act subjoined; and shall also keep and retain the said order, certificate, or requisition, for at least one month after the date of said entry; and any rate-payer of the municipality wherein said vender or his agent shall so sell, shall be entitled, and have the right and privilege, on any lawful day, during the hours of the ordinary business of said vender or his agent, to inspect said book, and also the said order, certificate, or requisition, and to make therefrom any extracts, on paying to said vender or his agent, for said inspection and making said extracts, the sum of ten cents; and each one of the said licensed venders, or his agent, shall, on the first Monday of the month after he commences to sell, deposit a copy, duly certified as "a true copy," of the entries in said book up to the date of said first Monday, and shall thereafter deposit on each succeeding first Monday of each succeeding month, for the time while said license continues, a copy, duly certified as "a true copy," of the entries in said book, from the time when so previously made, up to the date of said last mentioned first Monday, with the clerk of the municipality which granted said vender the license; and all sales made by said vender or his agent shall be for cash and not on credit.

6. That any person or persons, or body, who shall be found by himself, or herself, or themselves, or itself, or his, her, or their, or its, servants, agents, or tenants, to have contravened or vio-

lated, at any time or place, the first enactment, and the provisions in the fourth enactment, in this Act contained, or any part thereof, the same shall be considered as an offence against this Act, and shall pay for said offence a fine of not less than fifty dollars, with costs, in case of conviction, and the said fine and costs, when not paid, shall be recoverable from, and leviable against, the goods and chattels of the person or persons convicted; and upon a certificate on oath by the constable, or other legal officer, that there is no sufficient distress to be found and to be levied upon, belonging to the person or persons so convicted, the said person or persons so convicted shall be imprisoned in the common gaol of the county wherein the said offence may have been made, for the space of one month, with hard labor, unless the said fine and costs, and costs of imprisonment, be sooner paid, —and in the case of refusal or non-compliance, by the vender or his agent, to keep said book, or to enter and record the said sales therein, or to deposit the copy or copies of the entries, or to allow the inspection or the extracts to be made, all as provided for in the fifth section of this Act, the person or persons so refusing or non-complying shall be considered as offending against this Act, and shall for each case of refusal or non-compliance be liable to pay a fine of not less than twenty dollars, to be prosecuted for, and to be recoverable, and imprisonment therefor for one month to be made in the same way and manner as is provided for in this section as to other offences and fines; and it is hereby enacted that convictions, when made, shall not relieve the person or persons convicted, of the liability to be prosecuted for a misdemeanor under this Act, if amenable to be so prosecuted; and that convictions for several said offences against this Act may be made under this Act, although such several offences may have been committed in the same day.

7. Any person or persons may be the informant or informants, complainant or complainants, in prosecuting under this Act,—all proceedings shall be begun within twenty days from the date of the offence, all informations, complaints, or other necessary pro-

ceedings may be brought and heard before any one or more justices of the peace of the county, mayor, or police magistrate, or justice of the peace of a town or city, reeve, or deputy reeve, where the offence or offences were committed or done, and the mode of procedure in, and the forms appended to, the Act sixteenth Victoria, chapter one hundred and seventy-eight, for summary proceedings, may be followed as regards the cases and proceedings under this Act.

8. The said fines, or any portion of them, which may be recovered, shall be paid to the convicting justice, mayor, police magistrate, reeve or deputy reeve, or other acting justice in the case, and by him paid equally, one half to the informant or complainant, and the other half to the treasurer of the municipality where the said offence or offences were committed or done.

9. The word "Liquors," in this Act mentioned, shall be understood to comprehend and mean all malt liquors, and all liquors, and combinations of liquors, or drinks, used as drinking beverages, which are intoxicating.

10. That any knowingly false pretence, or false statements or representation, done or made, and whether knowingly done or made in writing or verbally, by the vender or his agent, vendee or his agent, or by any person or persons, or body, or his, her, or their, or its, servants, agents, or tenants, in and as respects the selling and buying, obtaining or procuring, the liquors specified in this Act, and as allowed to be vended and sold as in this Act provided, shall be considered as a misdemeanor, and shall be dealt with according to law.

11. All provisions in any Acts relative to the sale by retail of said liquors in that part of the Province called Upper Canada, inconsistent with the provisions of this Act, are hereby repealed.

12. This Act shall apply to Upper Canada only.

CHAPTER V.

GREAT BRITAIN.

Maine Law Movement in Great Britain—United Kingdom Alliance Permissive Bill—Prohibition in Great Britain—Lord Brougham on Prohibition.

MAINE LAW MOVEMENT IN GREAT BRITAIN.

P. P. Carpenter, Esq., in a lecture on this subject, gave an account of the formation and progress of the "United Kingdom Alliance for the Suppression of the Liquor Traffic." It had only been organized about six years, and yet had advanced far beyond the expectations of its most sanguine friends. It had gained more members, raised larger funds, and made itself more felt through the community, than even the mighty Anti-Corn-Law League during the same period of time. Not only the friends of temperance, but the drunkards, were rising to demand protection against the liquor traffic. An active canvass was now being carried on in various parts of Great Britain, to ascertain how the voting class would exercise their franchise if the right to make and sell were left to their decision. The lecturer produced the results of the canvass up to the moment of his leaving England. Warrington, a town of some 25,000 inhabitants, famous for its strong ale and hard drinking, has been thoroughly canvassed, and gave results as follows:—[F would vote in favor of prohibition; A would vote against; N, no opinion on this important subject]—

	F	N	A
Streets of Shopkeepers and Gentry,...	68	90	18
,, Irish Operatives,............	175	17	19
,, English do.	325	52	37
Total of Ratepayers,.................	2,248	722	312
,, Non-voting Adult Males,...	2,154	—	183

Analyzing the votes according to political status, it appears that of those who have an opinion, there are 12 in favor of prohibition to 1 against in the non-voting class, 7 to 1 in the rate-paying, $5\frac{1}{2}$ to 1 in the municipal, and $2\frac{1}{2}$ to 1 in the parliamentary franchise; shewing that the working classes, who are generally considered the most addicted to liquor, are the most anxious to be protected from its temptations. The general results, up to the present time, were as follows, of adult males canvassed:—

	F	N	A
English Agricultural Districts,	622	221	45
Part of Manchester,	3,194	862	480
English Boroughs,	8,120	1,707	989
Part of Glasgow,	1,169	126	139
Galashiels,	1,811	299	186
Greenock,	14,352	1,858	349
Scotch Towns and Villages,	24,157	3,527	1,195

Of the total number canvassed, viz., 40,623, nearly 33,000 decided for prohibition, or 15 to 1. England decided by 8 to 1, and Scotland 20 to 1. And even if the whole mass of nobodies were turned over to the opposite party, there would still be a grand total of 3 to 1 in favor of prohibition.

UNITED KINGDOM ALLIANCE PERMISSIVE BILL.

In the November 20th number of the *Weekly News*, we find a formidable list of appointments for one month, one hundred and fifty-four, in over one hundred different places, embracing the principal cities and towns in the two kingdoms, and all these appointments seem well supplied with speakers; there would seem to be twelve or fourteen paid agents, besides special deputations to some of the principal cities, and quite a number of others associated with these in adding interest and importance to each meeting. And it should be observed, that these men are not content with holding a public meeting, letting off a little steam, and then settling down into a state of indifference as to the results, but have committees in all these towns thoroughly canvassing the electors, not only to ascertain, but also to correct their opinions of the measure about to be laid before Parliament.

This is the kind and degree of effort that at once test the sincerity of the men at the head of this movement, and the best calculated to ensure success; as is evident from the fact, that in almost all, if not all, the places where a vote of the people has been taken, or where their opinion has been ascertained, they have in large majorities given for the Permissive Bill.

As this measure may not be well understood by our readers, we give the following short history of it and some of its principal provisions, taken from the Leeds *Mercury* of the 16th Nov., 1859. The writer does not seem to be a member of the Alliance, but is evidently well qualified to give an opinion, and does so with candor.

PERMISSIVE BILL TO SUPPRESS THE SALE OF INTOXICATING LIQUORS.

" It is known that the adoption and comparative success of the Maine Liquor Law in the Free States of America, combined with the numberless evils and miseries produced by drunkenness in this country, led many good men some years since to propose that a similar law should be recommended to the legislature of the United Kingdom. For this object an association was formed, called 'The United Kingdom Alliance,' to which many of the advocates of total abstinence gave in their adhesion. Others, however, withheld their concurrence,—first, because they could not approve of the principle of a compulsory law, although they saw immense benefit from the voluntary renunciation of intoxicating liquors; and, secondly, because it seemed to them perfectly hopeless to attempt to obtain such a law in England, or to maintain it if it were passed, whilst there was danger that it might provoke a reaction of popular feeling against the cause of temperance.

" It deserves to be known, more generally than we believe it is, that the advocates of a Maine Law in England, influenced by the objections which were made to their proposition, introduced an essential change in the measure. They no longer proposed a law to suppress the liquor traffic throughout the kingdom, but they asked that Parliament would pass a '*Permissive* Bill,' empowering 'cities, boroughs, parishes, and townships,' to decide, each for itself, by the free and popular vote of the ratepayers, whether they would allow or forbid 'the common sale' of intoxicating liquors within their own locality; and as the measure would still, if adopted, be compulsory in the locality, they proposed that 'a majority of at least *two-thirds* of the votes taken' should be required in favor of the bill, before it was put in operation. They also proposed that in every case an agent should be appointed by the justices, who might sell liquors ' for purposes declared legal by the Act '—we presume where they were testified by medical certificate to be needful. Of course there would be no interference with private brewing.

"It is evident that the Permissive Bill would be a very different thing from the Maine Law, and would have a much better chance of adoption by Parliament. The arguments in its favor are something like the following:—Intoxicating liquors are not necessary for health, but, on the contrary, are generally injurious (where it is otherwise, they might be obtained under the Permissive Bill):—they are confessedly the cause of that prevalent and even national vice of intemperance, which does more than all other causes to demoralize, degrade, sensualize, impoverish, and render miserable the people of this country:—it is therefore right and necessary, in the interests of public morality and the general happiness and welfare, to give the inhabitants of each district the power of deciding whether they will or will not allow of the public sale of the liquors, in places which notoriously allure the young and unwary into dangerous indulgence and ruinous habits:—no direct legislative prohibition is asked, but only the authority of the legislature to the people of each district to act for themselves, as they do in municipal self-government:—in order to prevent any large minority from being oppressed, it is admitted that the consent of two-thirds of the rate-payers who vote should be made indispensable to the introduction of the law:—if the people should change their minds, they may re-open the liquor traffic."

Prohibition in Great Britain.

In Great Britain, amid much of evil from internal contention, great advance has been made by the efforts of moral suasionists and the advocates of prohibitory law. In England alone, amid 18 millions of people, are 120,000 public-houses, beer shops, and gin palaces, which, in the year, have sent 75,000 persons to the lock-up for drunkenness, and 76,000 to the penitentiaries for assaults through drunkenness; and now the cry is, as it never was before, "Down with the traffic—shut up the beer shops and the gin palaces." On the Permissive Bill, or the question of leaving the people to do it in their own respective places, 11 to 1 have expressed themselves favorable in large districts in England; 17 to 1 in Scotland; 44 to 1 in Ireland. 55,441 have expressed themselves favorable in districts where only 9794 were neutral, and 4921 were opposed.

Immense and enthusiastic temperance meetings have been held throughout the kingdom, at which distinguished gentlemen have presided and able speeches been made. Most liberal subscriptions have been made to carry on the cause.

In answer to the petitions from liquor dealers and victuallers of Scotland, for a repeal of the Forbes M'Kenzie Act, which closes all drinking houses on the Sabbath, the British Parliament have requested the Queen to send a royal commission to Scotland, to examine and report on the results of the Act, and Her Majesty has complied with the request.

Temperance Meeting in the English Parliament.— That the great British Parliament should ever be converted into a Temperance Meeting, who would have thought it? Yet so it is. So it was, we know, in the days of Buckingham, when he brought in his great Parliamentary Report on drunkenness. So it has been now on the subject of the Royal Commission. For several hours genuine temperance speeches were made on the floor, and much important information was communicated to minds unenlightened before. Such a discussion is half the battle. It is, in fact, worth everything to the cause. The question was on having a committee in London, or a Royal Commission to visit Scotland and see what were the results of closing the Sunday liquor traffic. In favor of the first were the liquor-dealers. Lord Melgund and Sir George Grey spoke for them. On the other side were Mr. Bruce (Lord Advocate), Mr. Hardy (Under Home Secretary), Sir Andrew Agnew, Mr. Dunlop, Mr. Baxter, Mr. Kinnaird.

PROHIBITORY LANDOWNERS.—A suggestion has been thrown out, says the *Alliance Weekly News*, by a much respected friend of the Alliance, which we trust will, when carried out, supply us with another good document in favor of prohibition. Meanwhile, we must request our friends to kindly forward to us, as soon as possible, the names and addresses of all proprietors of estates, known to them, by whom the liquor traffic has been entirely prohibited on the whole, or at least some one, of their estates. On looking over our fyles, we find that many such cases have been mentioned in the *Alliance Weekly News;* and from that and other sources we have prepared a list of such noblemen, gentlemen, or ladies, as have been reported to us as endeavouring to secure their tenantry from the perils of the drink, by discouraging the existence of the liquor trade on their estates. Additional names, we hope, will be forwarded by our readers in time for our next number.

- The Duke of Argyle.
- The Duke of Grafton.
- The Duke of Buccleugh.
- The Marquis of Breadalbane.
- The Marquis of Cholmondeley.
- The Marquis of Westminster, at Shaftesbury, Dorsetshire.
- The Earl of Beverley.
- The Earl of Ducie, at Tortworth Court, Gloucestershire.
- The Earl of Harrington.
- The Earl of Minto, at Minto and Ashkirk.
- The Earl of Zetland, Upleatham, Cleveland.
- Lord Walsingham, Weston Hall, Norfolk.
- Lord Delamere, Cheshire.
- Lord Boyne, Brancepeth Castle, Durham.
- Lord Tredegar, South Wales.

Lord Llanover, South Wales.
Lord Strathmore, and other Proprietors of the Parish of Inverarity, Forfar.
Lord Belper, at Kingston, Notts.
Lady Byron, near Leamington.
General Sir Arthur Clifton, at Barton, Notts.
Sir Walter C. Trevelyan, Bart.
Sir Wilfred Lawson, Bart.
Sir Geo. Strickland, Bart.
Sir John Lowther, Wilton, Cleveland.
Sir Horace St. Paul, Northumberland.
C. R. Mansell Talbot, Esq., M.P.
H. H. Vivian, Esq., M.P.
Captain Byron, Thrumpton, Notts.
— Nevill, Esq., Llanelly.
Joseph Pease, Esq., J. P., Darlington.
Timothy Hutton, Esq., Clifton Castle, Yorkshire.
John Michell, Esq., Forcett.
W. W. Congreve, Esq., Burton Parish, near Neston, Cheshire.
John Richardson, Esq., Great Ayton.
R. E. Stanley, Esq., Paddington, Cheshire.
Rev. Peregrine Arthur Ilbert, Rector of Thurlestone, near Kingsbridge.
Wm. Hulton, Esq., Hulton Park, Bolton-le-Moors.
Rev. Frank Hopwood, Rector of Winwick, brother-in-law of the Earl of Derby.
Rev. Mr. Witham, Lartington, near Barnard Castle.
Rev. H. W. Sitwell, Leamington Hastings, near Rugby.
Rev. Bavazon Lowther, J. P., Shrigley Hall, Cheshire.
Mrs. Newcomen, Kirkleatham Hall, Yearby, Cleveland.
Stockton and Darlington Railway Company.
John Fullerton, Esq., Thrybergh Park, near Rotherham.
Thomas Bosvill Bosvill, Esq., Ravenfield Park, near Rotherham.
Randle Wilbraham, Esq., Rode Hall, Cheshire.
Titus Salt, Esq., M.P. for Bradford, at Saltaire.
Robert Howard, Esq., at Ashmore, near Ludwell, Dorsetshire.
The Proprietors of Horton Parish, Gloucestershire.
Neath Abbey Coal and Iron Company, South Wales.
The Proprietors of Scorton Parish, near Lancaster.
George Vivian, Esq., Moyallen House, Down.
Wm. Hollins & Co., Pleasley Vale, near Mansfield.
R. D. Alexander, Esq., LL.D., Ipswich.

Among them we see the names of the Duke of Buccleugh and the Marquis of Westminster, two peers who possess the largest yearly revenues both in England and Scotland, and the territories of others of them are very large indeed; nearly all Argyleshire belongs to the Duke of Argyle; and the estates of some of them are not reckoned by acres, but by miles, and nearly comprise whole counties. These landed proprietors, seeing the evil effects of intemperance, have discouraged it so far as they can, by refusing to lease houses for the sale of spirits, and bringing their influence to bear against it. The moral effect of this will be great, and will strengthen the hands of the friends of sobriety and progress. As those who comprise the list are all Justices of the Peace, and have the decision of applications for license, the effect of this action on their part is enlarged incalculably. Besides, the very fact of such a list of influential persons shews that the opinion is pervading all classes that intemperance is a moral nuisance, and that the dens where it is engendered ought to be abolished, and that the fate of the liquor traffic will gradually but surely be sealed.

Lord Brougham on Prohibition.

Intemperance is the common enemy; it attacks even persons of cultivated minds; spreads havoc widely among the multitudes of our inferior orders; and fills our workhouses and our jails. To lessen its force and contract its sphere, no means must be spared, if we really mean to stay the progress of destitution and of crime. The philanthropist has no more sacred duty than to mitigate, if he cannot remove, this enormous evil. The lawgiver is imperatively bound to lend his aid, when it appears manifest that no palliatives can avail. Certainly we have the example of the United States to prove that repression is practicable, and their experience to guide us toward it. That no legislative interference can be contemplated until the public mind is prepared, we must admit. Such was the course in America, and our palliative measures tend to afford the required preparation. The evil of drunkenness had reached such a height that in the State of Maine, thirty-five years ago, associations to promote temperance were formed; they spread through the country; they influenced by degrees the whole community; they induced the magistrates to refuse licenses; and finally they obtained a law of rigorous prohibition. Six other States, having a population of seven and a half millions, have made considerable progress towards the same end, more or less rigorously discouraging the sale of intoxicating liquors; and the greatest benefits have resulted to these portions of the Union. But the most important fact is the attempt to repeal the law in Maine, and its signal failure. Like all subjects in a country which, from the nature of the government, and the changes in the holders of all offices, is under the influence of perpetual canvass, this of temperance became a party question; and governors were chosen and removed upon it. Four years ago its supporters were defeated, and a stringent licensing system was substituted in its place. For two years and upwards this plan was tried, with every disposition of the authorities to favor its success. Pauperism and crime, which under the prohibitory law had been reduced to an incredibly small amount, soon renewed their devastations; the public voice was raised loudly and with rare concert against the license plan; a resolution was passed at the State Convention that the liquor law should no more be treated as a party question, and the repealing act was, without opposition, itself repealed. Another effort was made to restore the repeal; but the resolution of the State Convention was referred to, which stood unrescinded; and all attempts to get rid of the liquor law were abandoned henceforth as hopeless. The happy result has been a continuance of the same diminution both of pauperism and of crimes, which had followed upon the original enactment of the law. Upon this very remarkable passage in the history of social science it may be observed that at least it affords proof of the experiment having been made, and successfully made, of dealing rigorously with the evil; and if the same preparation of the public mind which led to that experiment being tried, and secured its success, takes place in other countries, the great example may then be followed safely and successfully. Then the philanthropist would no longer complain, with the Recorder of Birmingham, that into whatever path of benevolence we may strike, the drink demon starts up before him and blocks his way; or, comparing what is cheerfully squandered upon the fuel of intemperance with what is grudgingly bestowed upon the means of mental improvement, lament to find tenfold the price of food to the mind paid for poison to the body; but would delight to hear our poor, reclaimed from the worst excesses, free from the yoke of the cruel, though perfidious tyrant, declare, as they did to the American missionary, that the law must have come from heaven, for it was too good to be the work of man.

CHAPTER VI.

APPEAL.

Temperance Appeal to the People of Canada.

A crisis, pregnant with importance to you and your children, has come! The question is to be settled by you, whether this land, overshadowed with the wings of the Almighty, shall belong to drunkards, and be under the dominion of that most heartless of all tyrants, the *drunkard maker*.

The press, the pulpit, and the rostrum, have all been put in requisition to awaken you to the evils of intemperance—the beauties and excellencies of total abstinence have been fully illustrated by precept and example—the various plans of organized effort, to accomplish the work of reform, have each had their advocates, and need not here be discussed. Our object in this address, is simply to call your attention to some of the evils of the traffic in intoxicating beverages, your connections with it, and point out what we conceive to be the only remedy.

Evils of the Traffic.

The traffic in intoxicating drinks depraves those who are engaged in it, wastes their property, ruins their morals, and unfits them for honest industry. It burdens the community, by compelling it to furnish liquor-sellers and their families with the necessaries and luxuries of life without returning any equivalent therefor. It multiplies paupers, maniacs, and criminals. It increases taxation, and endangers the security of life and property. It furnishes a place of resort for idle and vicious persons, perils the peace and quiet of neighborhoods, and furnishes schools of vice for the young. It fosters habits of indolence and extravagance both on the part of the vendor and his victim. It leads men into temptation, and thus destroys many who would otherwise be sober and virtuous citizens. In short, there is no vice that it does not foster, and no crime that it does not promote.

Dishonesty of the Traffic.

Again, the traffic is necessarily dishonest. It takes money and property without returning any equivalent, furnishes what is absolutely worthless, nay more, what is positively hurtful and poisonous.

It is unjust; for no person can sell liquor without being a burden to the community. It brings overwhelming and numberless calamities upon a community, without a single countervailing benefit.

Your Connection with the Traffic.

You are in partnership in the business. It is not enough that the venders of the poison should be ruined in property, morals, and life—it is not enough, that schools of vice, idleness, and crime, should be located in every city, village, and hamlet—it is not enough, that dishonesty and injustice should go unrebuked—it is not enough, that almshouses and prisons should be crowded with citizens, victimized by the unhallowed traffic—it is not enough, that the physical, intellectual, and moral powers of men, should be destroyed—that disease, poverty, misery, and death, in their most terrific forms, should be spread through our land—but the agents of all this mischief require and receive at your hands your license and protection. They pay a pittance into your treasury, of their ill-gotten gold, and thus the partnership is complete. In all our public and private walks, you have stationed your sentinels, to watch for victims. "He sitteth in the lurking-places of our villages; in the secret places doth he murder the innocent; his eyes are privily set against the poor. He lieth in wait, secretly as a lion in his den; he lieth in wait to catch the poor." And you, people of Canada, (hear the unwelcome truth,) Judas-like, stand by and say to these your minions, "What will ye give, and we will betray the innocent into your hands?"

Were you living under the dominion of a despot, whose word was law, you would not be responsible for this alliance of government with the grog-shops; but your legislators and judges are your own servants, and for their actions you are accountable. If a family is beggared, robbed, or murdered, by the traffic in strong drink, the bonus given for the privilege is in your treasury. Every farthing thus received by you is the price of blood! Every tear wrung from wretched wives and helpless children—every dying groan of the wild and infuriate drunkard—every family altar desolated—every stain of this moral leprosy, which has marked society with spots, redder, more indelible, and infectious, than ever polluted the house of Israel—all these, and all other untold and indescribable evils of the traffic, are authorized and sanctioned by your laws!

The Remedy to be Applied.

Repeal every law that licenses, or sanctions, or protects, the vender of intoxicating beverages. The despotism that originated this abominable system of indulgence, and every government, free or despotic, that has adopted it, have assumed a prerogative that no power in heaven, earth, or hell, can claim to exercise. Society may be impotent to punish, but it never can license a wrong. Is the sale of intoxicating beverages a wicked business? Does it corrupt our youth? Does it waste property? Does it impair health? Does it destroy reputation? Does it endanger life? If so—what government can license or protect the traffic, without downright injustice, without absolute oppression? Every subject has a right to demand protection for his property, health, reputation, and life. Experience proves that all are in fearful peril in a land of grogshops.

Dissolve your Partnership with the Traffic.

If our children, our property, our friends—if all that we hold dear—must be sacrificed to fires more cruel, more deadly, than were ever kindled at the funeral pile of Pagans, in the name of humanity and humanity's God, let the *partnership* between you and the workers of this iniquity be dissolved.

The Traffic must be Branded as Criminal.

Another thing which we think imperatively demanded, is, to declare the traffic in intoxicating beverages a crime, and punish it as such. If all the evils to which we have referred result from this business, what crime recognized by our statute compares with it for turpitude: We are aware that universal custom has sanctioned the practice, but this furnishes no reason why it should not be stripped of its legal robes, and branded as we brand other vices, with the seal of infamy. The African slave trade was once not only recognized as a lawful trade, but the guilty thieves who stole negroes from the coast of Africa were many of them church members; now they are hung up as pirates. The long standing of any business, or the respectability of the actors, can never sanctify a crime. You have laws to punish the thief, the highwayman, and the murderer—you have even provided a punishment for the petty gambler, the profane swearer, and the Sabbath breaker—yet for the crime of liquor selling, which necessarily and universally results in profanity, Sabbath breaking, and gambling—which directly incites to most of our murders, arsons, robberies, and thefts,—you have fixed no penalty, but have even licensed "*good moral men*" to perpetrate it with impunity. Either repeal your laws making murder and robbery a crime, or punish the creature who nerves the robber's arm, and whets the murderer's knife.

The Rumseller must be Punished as a Criminal.

People of Canada! would you throw a protection around the sanctuary of home—would you have your sons and your daughters shielded from the desolating scourge—transform society: empty your lazar houses, and open the " prison doors to those who are bound?" If this be your desire, you must seal up the fountain whence flows the blighting and desolating flood. You must declare that the vile panderer to degrading passion shall be cut off from all fellowship with reputable society. You must consign the incorrigible rumsellers to the prisons now occupied by their ruined victims.

It is our firm conviction that the dark flood of evils growing out of intemperance will never be averted until liquor vending be declared a misdemeanor, and those who bid defiance to moral appliances be punished as other culprits who rob the community of property and life. In the progress of the temperance reform, the power of moral suasion has been ineffectual upon those who are engaged in the murderous traffic.

Moral Appliances alone Cannot Arrest the Traffic.

The miserable drunkard, the heart-broken wife, the ragged and starving child, have all made their touching and eloquent appeals. Alms-houses and prisons, crowded with wretched inmates, have sent forth their piteous tales. A countless company of liquor sellers, ruined in body, estate, and reputation, have lifted their voice of warning; and, that the whole earth might know the wickedness and the blighting and damning nature of their business, God has uttered his voice, and pronounced a woe upon him who dares to put the bottle to his neighbor's lips. The voice of the majority has in some places been heard through the ballot-box, but with like results. A large and powerful *Guerilla band*, " armed and equipped as the law directs," still make war upon us, without pity—visiting their death-blows, without mercy, upon every age, sex, and condition.

Our Position is Right and should be Maintained.

We know that we are taking an advanced and high position; but if it be true, why not occupy it?—why not assume a battle ground from which you cannot be driven, while God's moral government endures? Here you may deal blows upon your enemy that must sooner or later overthrow him.

Petition the Legislature.

Petition the Legislature, again and again, to abolish all laws regulating the sale of liquor, and to incorporate the traffic among its kindred crimes of theft, arson, robbery, and murder. Let there be harmony of sentiment and unity of action among the friends of temperance, and the day of deliverance shall be hastened. Be calm, but resolute—patient, but untiring—kind, but comprehensive—zealous, faithful, and constant—and soon, by the terrors of the law, you will persuade those men who cannot be reached by moral means, to abandon the inhuman and bloody traffic. Amen!

PART THIRD.
THE TEETOTALER'S HAND-BOOK.

POETRY, SONGS, AND HYMNS.

CONVIVIAL BANQUETS.
By Mrs. BALFOUR.

Oh! subtle Falsehood, what a wide dark realm,
   Amid this rash and erring world, is thine;
What dreary mists too oft the mind o'erwhelm,
   What idols desecrate fair reason's shrine:
Oh, for a glorious ray of truth divine
   To dissipate the gloom that frowns around!
A light in wisdom's crystal lamp to shine,
   To show the pitfalls in life's treacherous ground,
   And scare the wanderer from sin's gulf profound.

Alas! Temptation, with its meteor glare,
   Bred of foul vapours, lures the thoughtless tread;
False Pleasure, smiling, weaves her flowery snare,
   Her choicest wreaths are round the wine-cup spread;
While erring Genius, each pure impulse fled,
   Lures folly with its sweet pernicious song,
The mazy labyrinth of guilt to tread,
   And strives the vain delusion to prolong,
   Telling of joys that to such course belong.

"Oh, son of earth!" exclaims the tempter's voice,
   "Come quaff the draught that soothes the brow of care;
Drink of the sparkling wine-cup, and rejoice!
   Let cautious grove'ling dullards cry,—'beware!'
Life is a burthen none can gaily bear
   But those who oft partake the generous flow
That streams redundant o'er the banquet fair;
   Then, then, the spirits mount in radiant glow,
   And kindred hearts convivial pleasures know."

Oh, list not to " the charmer's" syren song,
  It is not "wisely" that she charms thine ear;
Joy, virtue, peace, to temperance belong—
  Read history's page, with scrutiny severe,
And, self-abased, impartial truth revere:—
  Then say, what strife, and cruelty abhorr'd,
What foul impiety, what deeds of guilt and fear,
  What lying arts, with fiend-like malice stor'd,
  Men have devised when o'er the festive board!

Belshazzar's impious feast from heaven drew down
  The written doom, the stern emblazon'd sign,
Dark o'er the banquet lowered the avenging frown,
  The awful sentence of the Power Divine!
And was it not o'er flowing bowls of wine,
  When (as some say) the kindly feelings spread,
That vile Herodias planned her foul design,
  And justice, reason, policy, all fled,
  Asked and obtained the Baptist's sacred head?

The Macedonian hero gained a world,
  Wide-spreading conquest on his arms attend—
Where'er his dreaded "phalanx" vengeance hurled,
  The stricken foe beneath his yoke must bend.
Yet, though he gained a world, he could not keep a friend;
  But, mad and murderous o'er his genial wine,
Behold earth's mighty conqueror descend
  To filthy brawls, and grovelling sink supine,
  Imbruted by the draught some call divine.

"*In vino veritas!*" Oh, specious lie;
  Think of the poisoned bowl, the goblet dread,
Where subtle drugs in wine lurked covertly,
  How oft has foul deceit the banquet spread,
And lured the victim to his last low bed.
  Truth dwell in wine? Faith in the drunkard's ban?
Answer, old Time, from records of the dead,—
  " Truth is the soul of nature's faultless plan,
  Wine is the frail, false, erring work of man!"

INTEMPERANCE.

I ask not for a poet's name,
Or laurels from the wreath of fame;
I soar to reach no fabled height,
To tell of things which ne'er had light;
I come not with a lofty theme,
A gaudy tale, or fancy's dream;
My only muse is studious thought,
I speak but what experience taught;
And all I crave is power to show
What sorrows from the goblet flow;
What pain and grief, disease and shame,
Are hidden in its liquid flame;
What pallid cheeks, and blood-shot eyes,
And orphans' tears, and widows' sighs;
What broken hearts, what want and fear,
Have found a lineal birth-place here;

Within that cup there lurks a foe,
A fiend who fills our land with woe,
A traitor to the human race,
Who only shows a rosy face,
But hides beneath that treacherous guise
The source where floods of sorrow rise;
And men, for sake of paltry gain,
Have listed in this demon's train,
And lie like spiders in their den,
With web, to trap their fellow-men.

Yes, they who have the drunkard made,
And still pursue the baneful trade,
Who still the liquid fires display,
And freely sell, in open day,
With each device they weave a charm,
Persuade the cup contains no harm:
'Tis but a julap, punch, or sling,
A very pleasant, harmless thing;
But ye who lift the cup, beware,
An adder's sting is hidden there,
They surely know, and know it well,

'Tis liquid poison that they sell;
'Tis man's bane, 'tis misery's worm,
Why call it by a milder term?

A rose is said to smell the same
If called by any other name;
By this same rule, a poison will,
Whatever called, be poison still.
Oh, is it not enough to bear
The ills to which the flesh is heir,
Without the aid of poison's breath
To strew our land with crime and death;
Is there not power in human laws
That punish crime to stop this cause?
Is there no power can stop this flood,
Now reeking with its victims' blood?
Is there no help; can nought be done?
Or must it still roll recking on,
While thousands, trembling on its brink,
And thousands, yet unborn, must sink,
Sink deep beneath perdition's wave,
Where none can help, where none can save.

ODE TO RUM.
By C. Brown, of Chelsea, Massachusetts, 1828.

"O, thou invisible spirit of wine! if thou hast no name to be known by, let us call thee—Devil."—Shakspeare.

Let thy devotee extol thee,
   And thy wondrous virtues sum;
But the worst of names I'll call thee,
   O, thou hydra-monster—Rum.

Pimple-maker, visage-bloater,
   Health-corrupter, idler's mate;
Mischief-breeder, vice-promoter,
   Credit-spoiler, devil's bait.

Almshouse-builder, pauper-maker,
   Trust-betrayer, sorrow's source;
Pocket-emptier, Sabbath-breaker,
   Conscience-stifler, guilt's resource.

Nerve-enfeebler, system-shatterer,
    Thirst-increaser, vagrant thief;
Cough-producer, treacherous flatterer,
    Mud-bedauber, mock relief.

Business-hinderer, spleen-instiller,
    Woe-begetter, friendship's bane;
Anger-heater, Bridewell-filler,
    Debt-involver, toper's chain.

Memory-drowner, honor-wrecker,
    Judgment-warper, blue-face quack;
Feud-beginner, rags-bedecker,
    Strife-enkindler, fortune's wreck.

Summer's cooler, winter's warmer,
    Blood-polluter, specious snare;
Mob-collector, man-transformer,
    Bond-undoer, gambler's fare.

Speech-bewrangler, headlong-bringer,
    Vitals-burner, deadly fire;
Riot-mover, fire-brand flinger,
    Discord-kindler, misery's sire.

Sinews-robber, worth-depriver,
    Strength-subduer, hideous foe;
Reason-thwarter, fraud-contriver,
    Money-waster, nation's woe!

Vile seducer, joy-dispeller,
    Peace-disturber, blackguard guest;
Sloth-implanter, liver-sweller,
    Brain-distracter, hateful pest.

Utterance-boggler, stench-emitter,
    Strong-man sprawler, fatal drop;
Tumult-raiser, venom-spitter,
    Wrath-inspirer, coward's prop.

Pain-inflicter, eyes-inflamer,
    Heart-corrupter, folly's nurse;
Secret-babbler, body-maimer,
    Thrift-defeater, loathsome curse.

Wit-destroyer, joy-impairer,
  Scandal-dealer, foul-mouthed scourge;
Senses-blunter, youth-ensnarer,
  Crime-inventor, ruin's verge.

Virtue-blaster, base deceiver,
  Spite-displayer, sot's delight;
Noise-exciter, stomach-heaver,
  Falsehood-spreader, scorpion's bite.

Quarrel-plotter, rage-discharger,
  Giant conqueror, wasteful sway,
Chin-carbuncler, tongue-enlarger,
  Malice-venter, death's broad way.

Tempest-scatterer, windows-smasher,
  Death-forerunner, hell's dire brink;
Ravenous murderer, windpipe-slasher,—
  Drunkard's lodging, meat, and drink!

TEMPERANCE.

The glad sound of Temp'rance is echoed afar,
  The breezes have borne the glad tidings abroad;
The light that is beaming from virtue's bright star
  Is chasing the darkness from sorrow's abode.
The wastes of the desert in verdure appear,
  With rich blooming fragrance perfuming the air;
The mountains are sinking, the valleys arise,
And earth is becoming the joy of the skies.

The glad sound of Temp'rance is echoed afar,
  And converts out-number the drops of the morn;
Loud songs of rejoicing are borne through the air,
  From regions long wasted, despised, and forlorn.
Now millions awakening receive the glad word,
  And outcasts reforming, return to the Lord;
The earth and the sea shall be cleansed from the stain,
And Temp'rance triumphant for ever shall reign.

CONFESSION AND APPEAL OF A REFORMED DRUNKARD.

Too often, alas! had I taken the bowl
Whose draughts bring destruction to body and soul;
My blood was on fire, and scorched was my brain,
Yet I still went on tasting, and tasting again,
Till, day after day, I had warning, poor slave,
That this frail shattered frame must soon sink to the grave,
Unless I abandoned that dark, dismal path
Which leads on to ruin the children of wrath.
Then the Lord, in his mercy, gave strength to my heart,
And I cried to the fire-fiend, "Destroyer, depart!"
And I dashed down the goblet that once was so sweet,
And the idol lay, shivered and spurned, at my feet.
No longer the victim of shame and despair,
I breathe as a freeman in Heaven's pure air,
And partake of the blessings which God has bestowed
With a bounteous hand on our earthly abode.
The Vulture which preyed on Prometheus' heart
Could never an agony keener impart,
Than the harpy of drunkenness, when it destroys,
With fierce hellish talons, our hopes and our joys.
Arise! lie not prostrate—arise! and be brave—
Shake off, as the snow-flake, the chain of the slave—
Stand forth in your manhood, and let the world know
You have come out heroic and conquered the foe.

TEMPERATE DRINKING.

"'Tis but a drop," the father said,
   And gave it to his son;
But little did he think a work
   Of death was then begun.
The "drop" that lured him when the babe
   Scarce lisped his father's name,
Planted a fatal appetite
   Deep in his infant frame.

"'Tis but a drop," the comrades cried,
  In truant school-boy tone;
"It did not hurt us in our robes,
  It will not now we're grown."
And so they drank the mixture up,
  That reeling, youthful band;
For each had learned to love the taste,
  From his own father's hand.

"'Tis but a drop," the husband said,
  While his poor wife stood by,
In famine, grief, and loneliness,
  And raised th' imploring cry.
"'Tis but a drop,—I'll drink it still—
  'Twill never injure me;
I always drank—so, madam, hush!
  We never can agree."

"'Tis but a drop,—I need it now,"
  The staggering drunkard said;
"It was my food in infancy—
  My meat, and drink, and bread.
A drop—a drop—O, let me have,
  'Twill so refresh my soul!"
He took it—trembled—drank—and died,
  Grasping the fatal bowl.

INTEMPERANCE.
By Miss SIGOURNEY.

Parent!—who, with speechless feeling,
  O'er thy cradled treasure bent,
Every year new claims revealing,
  Yet thy wealth of love unspent,—
Hast thou seen that blossom blighted
  By a keen untimely frost?
All thy labour unrequited?
  Every glorious promise lost?

Wife!—with agony unspoken,
  Shrinking from affliction's rod,
Is thy prop, thine idol broken,—
  Fondly trusted,—next to God?
Husband!—o'er thy hope a mourner,
  Of thy chosen friend ashamed,
Hast thou to her burial borne her,
  Unrepented,—unreclaimed?

Child!—in tender weakness turning
  To thy heaven-appointed guide,
Doth a lava-poison burning,
  Tinge with gall affection's tide?
Till that orphan burden bearing,
  Darker than the grave can show,
Dost thou bow thee down despairing,
  To a hermitage of woe?

Country!—on thy sons depending,
  Stroug in manhood, bright in bloom,
Hast thou seen thy pride descending
  Shrouded,—to th' unhonored tomb?
Rise!—on eagle-pinion soaring,—
  Rise!—like one of God-like birth,
And, Jehovah's aid imploring,
  Sweep the spoiler from the earth!

TRY, JOHN.

Try, John; try, John: from temptation fly, John;
Drunken Joe and idle Ned—pass such comrades by, John.
  Shun the tempting tavern door,
    Set not foot within, John;
  Each old chum avoid, though dear,
    That would lure to sin, John.
  Every thing and every place
    That tends to lead astray, John,
  Give them up, renounce them all,
    From this very day, John.

Try, John; try, John: I will tell you why, John,—
He who fights 'gainst what is bad, will conquer by-and-bye, John.
    If with all your powers you strive
      With your habits wrong, John,
    While they daily weaker grow,
      You will grow more strong, John.
    What if shopmates jest and scoff
      Because you hate the sin, John,
    Surely, if they laugh that lose,
      They may smile that win, John.

Try, John; try, John: wherefore do you sigh, John?
"I'm afraid I shan't succeed"—is this what you reply, John?
    Nonsense, man—such coward fear
      Never won a fight, John;
    Let's have faith and courage too,
      In what is true and right, John.
    Like the little barking curs
      That love to snarl and scold, John,
    Evil habits soon will fly
      When we're stern and bold, John.

Try, John; try, John: think, in days gone by, John,
Habits have been conquered vile as those o'er which you sigh, John.
    How this idle loon became
      An energetic man, John;
    How that hoary, hopeless sot
      Loathed the pipe and pot, John—
    Mark their upward histories well,
      Histories stern and true, John,
    Teaching you what you may be,
      How you may dare and do, John.

Try, John; try, John: look with faith on High, John:
You've a Father and a Friend, mighty, loving, nigh, John.
    Go and tell him you repent
      Of your evil ways, John;
    Pray for help and strength to live
      Happier, holier days, John.
    Prayer and effort—this, combined,
      All success ensures, John;
    And, with joy and peace of mind,
      Victory shall be yours, John.

POETRY, SONGS, AND HYMNS.

THE DRUNKARD'S HOME.

The Drunkard's home! what words can show
    The scenes of misery there?
What mind conceive, what heart can know,
    Save those compelled to share?
Th' abode of wickedness complete,
    Whence every comfort's fled—
Where want, disease, and ruin meet,
    And every hope is dead!

The Drunkard's home! more cheerless far
    Than ever convict's cell,
With granite walls and iron bars,
    For guilty ones to dwell.
* * * * * * * *

The Drunkard's home! that barren waste,
    That desert of the soul!
Without one green oasis graced,
    Where streams of comfort roll;
Stricken as by the simoon's blast,
    All bliss is prostrate laid;
And Pity, weeping, stands aghast
    To see the ruin made.

The Drunkard's home! the rock-girt strand
    Where Honour, shipwrecked, lies;
The den where Murder dyes his hand,
    Where Virtue, poisoned, dies!
Where Vice spreads round its filthy slime,
    Where Falsehood forms her lair,
The haunt of Infamy and Crime,
    Of Madness and Despair!

The Drunkard's home! Ye generous youth,
    Yet from Intemperance free,
Attend the warning voice of truth,
    And from the poison *flee!*
Touch not the cup of liquid fire,
    Beware of habit's chain;
Quench the first spark of wild desire,
    And spurn the damning bane!

THE DRUNKARD'S WIFE.

Cold, bitter cold! no rosy gleam to light the dreary room,
No sparkling blaze, with cheerful ray, to smile away the gloom;
And through the broken pane the wind comes fiercely shrieking in,
It blows upon my baby's face, so very pale and thin.

Sleep on, sleep on, my pretty child, upon thy mother's breast,
She loves to feel thy pallid cheek above her bosom pressed:
But on thy little upturn'd face her tears fall fast and wild,
Ah! baby, 'tis a fearful thing to be a drunkard's child.

All drearily the midnight hours are slowly gliding by,
The snow is falling thick and fast, the wind is bleak and high;
I sit and listen for his step; but oh! 'tis all in vain,
I only hear the angry storm that beats upon the pane.

My lonely heart, my aching heart, no joy, no comfort now,
A weary weight of care and woe hath fallen on my brow;
That brow, a few short years ago, so lit with hopeful light,
Not dreaming that so soon the day must darken into night.

The past comes sliding back: I stand by his brave loving side,
He takes my trembling hand in his, and proudly calls me "bride";
I meet his dark and glorious eye, I hear his thrilling tone,
And oh! the joy, the bliss to know his heart is all my own.

Sad, sad that o'er so bright a sky the dreary clouds must come,
That shadows dark should softly glide, and gather round our home:
That loves so strong, so true, should change, even for our pretty child;
But oh! the tempter lured him on, the wine-cup drove him wild.

I hear his step: he comes; he comes; he enters at the door:
Be still my heart! what tho' the years of joy and hope are o'er,
Oh, try to greet him with a smile, as in the days of yore,
Thy love for him, still, still thou hast, though his may be no more.

No more! no more! his love doth live, I know it could not die,
'Tis true it is not like the love of blissful days gone by;
But oh! the fearful maddening cup, 'tis that hath hid the flame
In that poor heart, so fallen now, so darkened o'er with shame!

But oh! the yearning, strong and wild, for but one loving word,
A single tone of other days. 'tis vain, no fount is stirred
In that drear heart where I have poured my hope, my love, my life;
Oh! who can tell the fearful gloom that shrouds the drunkard's wife!

WHEN IS THE TIME TO SIGN?

I asked a blooming sportive boy, Will you come now and sign,
Health beams within thy glist'ning eye, this is the golden time;
But no, he cried, and shook his head, now is the time for play;
I cannot, will not yet, he said, then bounded on his way.

I asked him when a youth; but then he stopped me with alarm;
Nay, leave the pledge for grave old men, a drop can do no harm;
Youth is the time for mirth and joy, I'll live thus while I can;
Your sober scheme perchance I'll try when I am quite a man.

I asked a man of middle age, how gleamed his fiery eye?
Such fearful signs his frame betrayed, they gave a full reply;
For many years had firmly fixed the tyrant's iron chain;
His all for drink he'd madly risk, to ask him now were vain.

I questioned next an aged man, a miserable form,
His course of life had nearly run, each short-lived pleasure gone;
Alas, he cried, in accents wild, with anguish on his brow,
Would I had signed it when a child: I cannot do it now.

COME, YOUNG ABSTAINERS.
Tune—"Gentle Zetella."

Come, young abstainers, we on you do call,
For while we are able there's work for us all:
Let this be our motto, and by it stand true,
"While we live let us try what good we can do."

    Then come, young abstainers, &c.

Intemp'rance the plague of our country has been,
Its victims in city and village are seen:
Who then can stand idle, such misery view,
And never once think there is something to do.

    Then come, young abstainers, &c.

United, and boldly together, we'll stand,
And soon shall intemp'rance be banished our land:
Then peaceful and happy our homes they shall be,
And sweetly we'll sing the songs of the free.

    Then come, young abstainers, &c.

WE TEMPERANCE CHIELS.
Tune—"For a' that an a' that."

We temperance chiels are true and leal,
   Yet ne'er get fou for a' that;
We sip nae draps, frae tippling caps,
   O' beer, an' wine, an' a' that
      An' a' that, an' a' that,
         The mountain dew, an' a' that;
      We'll sen' them far frae Scotia's shore,
         Nor let them back for a' that.

It lang was said, without their aid,
   We're stupid, sad, an' a' that;
But now I see, we blythe can be,
   And never taste for a' that,
      For a' that, an a' that,
         Can laugh an' sing, an' a' that;
      Can crack an' joke like sober folk,
         Nor feel remorse, for a' that.

Ye hardy sons of Caledon,
   Assert your rights for a' that;
From vice refrain, from drink abstain,
   An' freemen be, for a' that.
      For a' that, an' a' that,
         Plead virtue's cause, an' a' that;
      The pledge come sign, an' wi' us join,
         We'll do you good, for a' that.

TO THE LASSES.
Air—"Here's a Health."

Take our thanks, teetotal lasses,
Take them cheerily; *peace surpasses*
   All the drunkard's noise profane.
May you live a life of gladness,
Without sorrow, without sadness;
   Every bosom loves your reign.

O TEMPERANCE IS A NOBLE PLAN.

Tune—"This is no my ain lassie."

O temp'rance is a noble plan,
   It makes us blythe and happy O,
We shun the cares, and a' the snares,
   O' them that taste the drappie, O.

O come, our voices let us raise
   Against our country's greatest foe,
And let us advocate our cause,
   And by example we shall show
        That temp'rance, &c.

We'll try the drunkard to reclaim,
   And make him stand erect and free,
For if from strong drink he'll abstain,
   We know that he will happy be;
        For temp'rance, &c.

There's many drunkards in our land
   Who might be free from care and woe,
Had they but known in early life
   The blessings that our cause bestow; &c.

Then parents, come, adopt our plan,
   And teach your children to abstain;
For what you sow in early life,
   In after years you're sure to gain; &c.

Come, children, sign the temp'rance pledge,
   And firmly set it in your mind;
And when you reach maturer years,
   You'll prove a blessing to mankind; &c.

A SLAVE TO THE BOTTLE.

Tune—"Contented wi' little."

Contented I live in my auld minny's cot,
And peace is a flower that I nurse near the spot;
Of fond true love offers I've had twa or three—
But a Slave to the Bottle will never wed me.

He may say he adores me, wae's me and alas!
What love can he gi'e, when its a' in the glass,
For house, wife, or wee anes, he'll care na' a flee—
O, a Slave to the Bottle will never get me.

O, he thinks it nae sin to sit drinking a' night,
To come staggering hame in the face o' daylight;
A' tattered and battered, no worth a bawbee—
O, a Slave to the Bottle will never get me.

What a contrast he is to the douce sober man,
Wha lives in accordance wi' nature's first plan!
Wi' health on his cheek, and true love in his e'e—
O, a Slave to the Bottle will never wed me.

Now ilk lassie wha langs to be ca'd a guidwife,
Let a douce sober chiel be your partner through life;
E'en take my advice, tis the best I can gi'e—
For a Slave to the Bottle will never wed me.

THE MIGHT WITH THE RIGHT.

May ev'ry year but draw more near
   The time when the strife shall cease,
And truth and love all hearts shall move
   To live in joy and peace.
Now sorrow reigns, and earth complains,
   For folly still her power maintains:
But the day shall yet appear
   When the might with the right and the truth shall be;
And, come what there may to stand in the way,
   That day the world shall see.

Let good men ne'er of truth despair,
   Though humble efforts fail;
O! give not o'er until once more
   The righteous cause prevail.
In vain, and long, enduring wrong,
   The weak may strive against the strong:
But the day, &c.

Though interest pleads that noble deeds
    The world will not regard,
To noble minds, that duty binds,
    No sacrifice is hard.
The brave and true may seem but few,
But hope has better things in view—
And the day, &c.

THE TEMPERANCE TRUMPET.

Tune—"Mercy's free."

Hark! hark! the temperance trumpet's sounding:
    Come and sign; come and sign;
Our glorious cause is still abounding;
    Come and sign; come and sign.
Thousands have heard the joyful sound:
    They've signed the pledge, and since have found
Abstinence is the surest ground;
    Come and sign; come and sign.

We call on all professing Christians,
    Come and sign; come and sign;
We'll put to flight the great Philistines,
    If you'll sign; if you'll sign.
The victory's ours, if you will fight;
    The landlords all we'll put to flight,
And gaze upon the glorious sight,
    If you'll sign; if you'll sign.

We call on every little-drop man,
    Come and sign; come and sign;
We cry to every drunkard, stop man,
    Come and sign; come and sign.
Give, give your names, at once abstain;
    Teetotalism will clear the brain,
'Twill free you from contempt and shame,
    If you'll sign; if you'll sign.

TEMPERANCE CHAMPION.

Air—"With a helmet on his brow."

Wake! Temperance warriors wake!
   Attend th' inebriates cry;
Your country calls, your honor stake,
   Up! on to victory!
Intemperance, your foe,
   Exults in misery!
Will you not stay the spreading woe?
   Then "On to victory!"

Chorus—Let the Temperance trumpet sound,
   And Abstinence reply,
Teetotalers must with honor live,
   And then with honor die!

Yes! we will now combine
   To crush the giant pow'r;
Kind Providence will on us shine
   When fierce temptations lower.
Ours is a noble cause,
   Heav'n is our chief ally;
Angels will crown us with applause,
   Come "On to victory!"

Chorus—Let the Temperance, &c.

DESERT THE SPARKLING WINE.

Air—"The gay Guitar."

O leave the Bacchanalian scene,
   The poison'd flowing bowl;
And come with me where joys serene
   Compose the "flow of soul!"
Come where fair Temperance sheds her ray,
   Where hope's mild lustre shines;
I'll shew thee on this festive day
   How we *abstain* from wines!

I'll tell thee of the happy hours
  Which light life's deepest gloom,
I'll lead thee to the beauteous bowers
  Where health and honor bloom!
I'll shew thee the illustrious way
  Where nature's glories shine;
I'll bid thee, on this happy day,
  Desert the sparkling wine!

AULD LANG SYNE.

Can abstinence be now forgot,
And never brought to mind?
Can abstinence be now forgot,
And mercy to mankind?
With all that's true and kind, my dear,
With freemen true and kind,
We'll join the ranks of abstinence,
And blessings on mankind.

So here's a hand, my smiling friend,
And gie's a hand of thine,
We'll pledge ourselves to abstinence,
And mercy to mankind;
And mercy to mankind, my friend,
And freedom from the chain
Of Drunkenness; and Abstinence
Shall have an endless reign.

Let abstinence be ne'er forgot,
But ever brought to mind,
Till ev'ry wretched drunken sot
Our safety boat does find.
And then we'll pull our safety boat
With long oars to the shore,
And, firm on rock of abstinence,
We'll sail on drink no more.

COME AND SIGN.

Air—"Bright Canaan."

Come, my lads, the pledge to sign,
Let us all together join
  To drink the grog no more,
    O that will be joyful,
    Joyful, joyful, joyful,
    O that will be joyful,
  When we drink the grog no more.

Moderate drinkers too should come,
Now give up the wine and rum,
  And brandy all their store.

Working men, you need not fear,
Give up all your ale and beer,
  Your comforts will be more.

Drunkards too, we all invite,
To come and sign the pledge to-night,
  And not get drunk once more.

ALL'S WELL.

Deserted by my dearest friends,
Strong drink despair and sorrow sends;
O'er children, wife, and lowly cot,
There hangs a sad and threatening lot.
Hark, hark, some footsteps hither stray,
But joys can't soothe the drunkard's day.
Is there hope? stranger quickly tell:
Abstain, repent, believe—All's well.

Now listed in the temp'rance band,
With drunken sots on every hand,
Our watchful guard explores the lanes
To snatch the slave from Satan's chains,
And oft he hears the cheering voice
From homes reformed, where all rejoice.
What cheer? neighbours quickly tell:
Abstain'd, believ'd, Christ died—All's well.

THERE'S NAE LUCK ABOUT THE HOUSE.

And are ye sure the news is true,
   And are ye sure he's signed?
I can't believe the joyful tale,
   And leave my fears behind.

If John has signed and drinks no more,
   The happiest wife am I
That ever swept a cottage hearth
   Or sung a lullaby.

     For there's nae luck about the house,
       There's been nae luck at a',
     And gane's the comfort o' the house,
       Since he to drink did fa'.

Whose eye so kind, whose hand so strong,
   Whose love so true will shine,
If he have bent his heart and hand
   The total pledge to sign.

But what puts breaking in my head?
   I trust he'll taste no more;
Be still, be still, my beating heart,
   Hark! hark! he's at the door.

     For there's nae luck, &c.

And blessings on the helping hands
   That send him back to me,
Haste, haste, ye little ones, and run
   Your father's face to see.

And are you *sure*, my John, you've signed?
   And are you *sure 'tis past;*
Then mine's the happiest, brightest home
   On England's shores at last!

     There's been nae luck about the house,
       But now 'tis comfort a'!
     And heaven preserve my ain gudeman
       That he may never fa'!

SOBRIETY'S PRAISE.
Air—"The Canadian Boat Song."

Lovely as beams the cheerful ray
Which gilds the distant ocean spray,
Our social company appears,
Stript of the *cause* of sorrow's tears!
Then brothers come! the song upraise;
And carol with joy fair Sobriety's praise.

Hark! how the gently pealing chime,
With our united songs keeps time!
To heav'n our blending tones shall tend,
For drunkards now have found a friend!
Then brothers come! the song upraise;
And carol with joy fair Sobriety's praise!

No more need the inebriate sigh
Because no friendly hand is nigh;
Here we defy the syren's wiles,
For abstinence disarms her smiles!
Then pledg'd ones all, the song upraise,
And carol with joy fair Sobriety's praise!

ABSTINENCE ROCK.
Air—"In my Cottage near a Wood."

Rock of abstinence rear'd for me,
Let me rest myself on thee,
Till this scene of sin is o'er,
Till vile habits are no more,
Till the soul-seducing spell,
Scar'd from earth, retreats to hell.
    Rock of abstinence rear'd for me,
    Let me rest myself on thee.

Mount of temperance, let me rest
'Neath the shadow of thy crest:
Lest I still unwary, yield
To my enemy the field;
Lest, whilst trembling in despair,
Sin beguiles me in its snare.
    Rock of abstinence, &c.

O the misery that appears,
Where sad sorrow sheds her tears;
Where the vinous draught inspires
Millions of unhallowed fires;
Where in furious rage they blend
To secure a fiend-like end.
  Rock of abstinence, &c.

Sons of virtue now combine,
In a sacred phalanx join;
Crush by a determined blow,
Intemperance, your mighty foe:
Let the world your banner see,
'Tis the flag of victory.
  Rock of abstinence, &c.

TEMPERANCE ANTHEM.
Air—"God save the Queen."

Since time its course began,
 Mortals ne'er found a plan
  Like temperance.
Tee-total, now we'll raise,
Worthy of highest praise,
Protect us all our days,
  Blest temperance.

No brandy will we take,
We'll rum and gin forsake,
  Whiskey despise.
No more fermented wine,
Nor home-brew'd ale so fine,
Or jerry fit for swine,
  Shall dim our eyes.

Drinkers! tee-total try,
Lay jugs and glasses by,
  Reform begin.
Your wives will bless the day,
Your children for you pray,
When at your home you stay,
  Sober and clean.

Join the abstaining band,
With them walk hand in hand,
    At liberty.
Intemperance soon shall die,
Distress before you fly,
Oppression prostrate lie,
    And all be free.

"I LOVE A LITTLE SUP."

The temperance cause, I wish it well,
  It cries, " to help come up";
Help, you that choose, but for myself,
  I love a little sup.

The noble effort I approve,
  And ever cry it up;
But I'll not sign the pledge, because
  I love a little sup.

The doctor says, " It hastens death,
  And why not quit the cup?"
And so I would, but—I know why:
  I love a little sup.

The preacher urges next, " 'Tis sin,
  And shames the church"; give up!
My secret plea is stronger yet:
  I love a little sup.

All argument I can out-brave
  That bids " the pledge take up";
This one is proof against their force,
  I love a little sup.

Tho' groans, and blood, and death, and hell,
  All cry, " Forsake the cup!"
I know 'twere best, but then—but then—
  I love a little sup.

I'M NOT TO BLAME.

Oh, pity me, lady, I'm hungry and cold;
Should I all my sorrows to you unfold,
I'm sure your kind breast with compassion would flame:
My father's a drunkard; *but I'm not to blame.*

My mother's consumptive, and soon will depart:
Her sorrows and trials have broken her heart;
My poor little sisters are starving! oh shame!
Our father's a drunkard; *but we're not to blame.*

Time was we were happy, with plenty and peace,
And every day saw our pleasures increase;
Oh, then with what kindness we'd lisp forth his name;
But now he's a drunkard; *yet we're not to blame.*

Time was when each morning around the fireside,
Our sire in the midst like a saint would preside,
And kneel, and for blessings would call on God's name;
But now he's a drunkard; *but we're not to blame.*

Our father then loved us, and all was delight
Until he partook of this withering blight,
And sunk his poor family in misery and shame:
Oh yes, he's a drunkard; *but we're not to blame.*

My poor dying mother, must she feel the scorn?
Must she be forsaken to perish forlorn?
Oh grief when we call on that affectionate name;
I might well ask the world, *Can that saint be to blame?*

My sisters, poor orphans! Oh, what have they done?
Why should you neglect them, or why will you shun?
Let not foul disgrace be attached to their name:
Though their father's a drunkard, *they are not to blame.*

THE SOCIAL GLASS.

I once was fond of a social glass,
    So was I, So was I,
My days and nights so merrily pass,
But O next morning's misery.

My head would ache, my hand would shake,
My spirits quake, I then would take,
A julep to make my fever break,
O what a horrid bad mistake.
But now I shun my social glass,
    So do I, So do I,
Our days and nights so merrily pass,
Without the drunkard's misery.
I oft caught cold by steaming up,
    So did I, So did I.
To cure this cold, the red wine-cup
I then would quaff unceasingly.
And then the wine, it went so fine
When out to dine, no cost of mine.
So I take glasses to No. 9,
The quantity I thought was fine.
But now I shun my social glass,
    So do I, So do I,
Our days and nights so merrily pass, &c.
I always drank at others' cost,
    So did I, So did I,
For I had plenty of friends to boast,
So I was often very dry.
One night on a spree I happened to be,
When a chap told me of a society,
Which reformed the worthless debauchee,
Such people as we use to be.
But now I shun my social glass,
    So do I, So do I,
Our days and nights so merrily pass, &c.
We signed and became as you see us here,
Temp'rance men, temp'rance men,
We drink no brandy, rum, or beer,
But a glass of water now and then.
We never get blue, you know 'tis true,
All over the town the news it flew,
And all we can do to help you through,
Shall soon be done I promise you.
So now my friends come one and all,
And leave your rum before you fall.
So now my friends come one and all, &c.

POETRY, SONGS, AND HYMNS.

SPARKLING AND BRIGHT.

Sparkling and bright in its liquid light
   Is the water in our glasses;
'Twill give you health, 'twill give you wealth,
   Ye lads and rosy lasses.

Chorus—O then resign your ruby wine,
     Each smiling son and daughter;
     There's nothing so good for the youthful blood,
     Or sweet as the sparkling water.

Better than gold is the water cold,
   From the crystal fountain flowing;
A calm delight, both day and night,
   To happy homes bestowing.

Sorrow has fled from the heart that bled,
   Of the weeping wife and mother;
They've given up the poisoned cup,
   Son, husband, daughter, brother.

THE MAINE LAW.

Hark, hear the people's voices ring,
The Maine law is the very thing
To put the cruel tyrant down,
And temperance, truth, and virtue crown.

Chorus—Then shout, shout, your voices ring,
     The Maine law is the very thing
     To put the cruel tyrant down,
     And temperance, truth, and virtue crown.

The Maine law is the very thing
To make the drunkard's wife to sing,
Restore her husband to her heart,
And bid the cloud of gloom depart.

The Maine law is the very thing
To make the inebriate's children cling
Around their father's noble form,
Cheerful, happy, free from harm.

The Maine law is the very thing
To rob the serpent of his sting,
And bid the anguish'd heart be glad,
While venders sigh, for they are sad.

The Maine law is the very thing
To give the Death-bird speedy wing,
To fly and dwell where demons reign,
And never visit earth again.

THE TEMPERANCE FIREMAN.

When in the night,
The skies grow bright,
With the flames of the poor man's dwelling,
The fireman springs,
As the hall bell rings,
The burning district telling,—
Hark! the cry, Fire! Fire!
As the flames rise higher,
The gallant firemen fly,
At the sleep-dispelling cry,
Fire! Fire! Fire! Fire!
And we'll dash the water on till the flames expire.

See—the last gleam
Of the burning beam
Dies, and the danger is over;
The fireman goes
To his sweet repose,
From his toil and fatigue to recover,
Till the cry, Fire! Fire!
Shall again require
The fireman to fly
At the sleep-dispelling cry,
Fire! Fire! Fire! Fire!
And we'll dash the water on till the flames expire.

Thus in the height
Of his drunken plight,
If the tippler falls in the gutter,
The fireman kind,
Who the pledge has signed,
Plies him with good cold water;
He puts out rum's fire,
Drags him out of the mire,
Nor leaves him there to die
'Neath the cold and stormy sky—
On rum's dread fire,
He pours cold water down till the flames expire.

OUR FLAG.

Fling abroad its folds to the cooling breeze,
  Let it float at the mast-head high,
And gather around, all hearts resolve
  To sustain it there or die.
An emblem of peace and hope to the world,
  Unstain'd let it ever be,
And say to the world where'er it waves,
  Our flag is the flag of the free.

That banner proclaims to the listening earth,
  That the reign of the tyrant is o'er;
The galling chain of the monster Rum,
  Shall enslave mankind no more.
An emblem of hope to the poor and lost,
  O place it where all may see,
And shout with glad voice as you raise it high,
  Our flag is the flag of the free.

Then on high, on high let that banner wave,
  And lead us the foe to meet;
Let it float in triumph o'er our heads,
  Or be our winding sheet.
And never, O never, be it furled
  Till it wave o'er earth and sea,
And all mankind shall swell the shout,
  Our flag is the flag of the free.

WE'RE A BAND OF FREEMEN.

The teetotalers are coming,
The teetotalers are coming,
The teetotalers are coming,
   With the Cold Water Pledge!
   We're a band of freemen,
   We're a band of freemen,
   We're a band of freemen,
   And we'll sound it o'er the world.

Hurrah for reformation,
By all in every station,
Throughout this wide creation;
   Take the Cold Water Pledge.
   We're a band, &c.

We will save our sisters, brothers—
And our fathers, sons, and mothers—
With our neighbours and all others—
   By the Cold Water Pledge.
   We're a band, &c.

May no evil e'er betide us,
To sever or divide us;
But the God of Mercy guide us,
   With the Cold Water Pledge!
   We're a band, &c.

YE SONS OF TEMPERANCE.
Tune—"Marseilles Hymn."

Ye Sons of Temp'rance, wake to glory,
   Hark! hark! what myriads bid you rise,
Your children, wives, and grandsires hoary,
   Behold their tears and hear their cries.
Shall alcohol, foul mischief breeding,
   With hireling host, a ruffian band,
Spread tears and mis'ry o'er the land,
   While peace and liberty lie bleeding,

To arms! to arms! and hurl
The monster from his throne,
March on, march on, all hearts resolved,
On victory alone,
March on, march on, all hearts resolved,
On victory alone,
March on, march on, and strike the blow,
For victory alone.

Oh temperance, can man resign thee,
Once having signed the glorious deed?
Not myriad hosts shall e'er confine thee,
From pole to farthest pole thou'lt spread,
Too long our country wept bewailing,
Her noble sons and daughters slain,
But now is burst the tyrant's chain,
And all his arts are unavailing,
To arms! &c.

DRINKER, TURN AND LEAVE YOUR BOWL.

Music—"Make me no gaudy Chaplet."

Drinker! turn and leave your bowl;
Turn and save your deathless soul:
From your lip the poison fling;
Dash away th' accursed thing.

Husband! turn—nor let your feet
Enter that accurs'd retreat;
Look, your partner's tearful eye
Eloquently asks you why.

Brother! leave the place of glee,
Quick, ah! quickly turn and flee!
See your sister's swelling breast,
Deep, with anxious fear, distrest.

Father! turn—your prattler's voice
Bids you seek your fireside joys:
Leave the revel, homeward haste,
And those purer pleasures taste.

COME, ALL YE CHILDREN.

Tune—"Partant pour la Syrie."

Come, all ye children sing a song,
    Join with us heart and hand,
Come make our little party strong,
    A happy temperance band.
We cannot sing of many things,
    For we are young, you know,
But we have signed the Temp'rance pledge,
    A little while ago.

The Band of Hope shall be our name,
    The temp'rance star our guide,
We will not know the drunkard's shame,
    We will his drink avoid.
Cold water cannot do us harm,
    Strong drink may bring us woe—
So we have signed the Temperance pledge,
    A little while ago.

How many children do we meet
    Who have no clothes to wear!
They scarcely know a mother's love,
    Or feel a father's care;
Their poor and wretched life is spent
    In misery and in woe;
Their parents would not take the pledge
    A little while ago.

We'll try to cheer these helpless ones,
    And take them by the hand,
We'll dance around our temperance flag,
    A happy, happy band.
We will not touch the drunkard's drink,
    We never will, O no;
For we have signed the Temperance pledge
    A good long while ago.

And thus we'll spend our happy days,
   Till we get up to men;
Just like a full-grown English oak,
   We'll be the firmer then.
And if degraded drunkards should
   Invite with them to go,
We'll say we signed the Temperance pledge
   A long, long time ago.

JOYFUL DAY.

A glorious light hath burst around us:
   Joyful day, joyful day!
We see the chain that would have bound us:
   Joyful day, joyful day!
The sparkling wine we ne'er will crave;
To touch, to taste, is to enslave;
We drink the fountain's crystal wave:
   Joyful day, joyful day!

We'll sing to God a holy chorus:
   Joyful day, joyful day!
Truth shines in radiant brightness o'er us:
   Joyful day, joyful day!
A firm and dauntless host we stand,
Ye millions join our Abstinence band,
And plenty then shall bless our land:
   Joyful day, joyful day!

The young and old come forth to hear us:
   Joyful day, joyful day!
Truth shines in radiant brightness o'er us:
   Joyful day, joyful day!
We'll spread the truth where man is found,
Bear it to earth's remotest bound,
Till every wind will catch the sound:
   Joyful day, joyful day!

REJOICE! REJOICE!

Rejoice! Rejoice! the temp'rance cause advances;
Rejoice! Rejoice! its advocates are here,
  Our cause is good, and object pure,
  Our ranks increasing more and more;
  We soon shall banish from our land,
  The tyrant and his deadly band;
Rejoice! Rejoice! the temp'rance cause advances;
Rejoice! Rejoice! its advocates are here;

Rejoice! Rejoice! our number fast enlarges;
Rejoice! Rejoice! the vict'ry shall be ours;
  Let us our efforts still increase,
  And never in our labours cease—
  The vict'ry we shall surely gain,
  And see the many in our train;
Rejoice! Rejoice! our number fast enlarges;
Rejoice! Rejoice! the vict'ry is ours.

Rejoice! Rejoice! the temp'rance banner's waving;
Rejoice! Rejoice! the boys and girls have come—
  They've joined the band of liberty,
  And joyful shout, "We're free! we're free!"
  Who next will in our ranks enlist,
  And thus the monster firm resist?
Rejoice! Rejoice! the temp'rance banner's waving;
Rejoice! Rejoice! 'tis spreading o'er the world.

TEMPERANCE BAND.

Temperance, here in praise of thee:
  Join our Band, join our Band;
Songs we sing so glad and free;
  Join our Temperance Band.
Joyfully the pledge we take:
  Join our Band, join our Band;
Temperance ways we'll ne'er forsake;
  Join our Temperance Band.

Chorus—Firm and true be our Band;
　　True be our Band;
　Firm and true be our Band,
　　Temperance Band of Hope.

Young are we and feeble too:
　Join our Band, join our Band;
Yet there's work that we can do;
　Join our Temperance Band.
In the Holy Book we read:
　Join our Band, join our Band;
Little hands may lions lead;
　Join our Temperance Band.

In our Saviour's name we go:
　Join our Band, join our Band;
He will needful aid bestow;
　Join our Temperance Band.
Haste we on, a rescued host:
　Join our Band, join our Band;
To reclaim the thousands lost,
　Join our Temperance Band.

THE GOOD TIME COMING.

There's a good time coming, boys,
　A good time coming;
The signs around us show it near—
We breathe the very atmosphere
　Of the good time coming.
Intemperance has felt our blow,
　It struggles more and stronger;
Dying throes they are, we know—
　Wait a little longer.

　There's a good time coming, boys,
　　A good time coming;
　There's a good time coming, boys,
　　Wait a little longer.

There's a good time coming, boys,
    A good time coming;
The churches have been waked at last,
Temperance facts are telling fast
    Of the good time coming.
Human rights dare be discussed,
    Faith in man grows stronger;
And though prejudice yet lives,
    Wait a little longer.
      There's a good time coming, boys, &c.

There's a good time coming, boys,
    A good time is coming;
The days of progress now are here,
The seeds are sown—the harvest near—
    Of the good time coming.
Slavery—war—intemperance—
    Cannot now grow stronger;
Love and justice shall prevail—
    Wait a little longer.
      There's a good time coming, boys, &c.

WILL YOU COME TO THE BOWER?

TUNE—"The Spider and the Fly."

Will you walk into the parlour?
    Said a Spider to a Fly;
'Tis the prettiest little parlour
    That ever you did spy;
You've only got to pop your head
    Just inside of the door;
You'll see so many curious things
    You never saw before.
      Will you, will you, will you, will you
        Walk in, Mr. Fly?
      Will you, will you, will you, will you
        Walk in, Mr. Fly?

My house is always open,
    Said the Spider to the Fly;
I'm glad to have the company
    Of all I see go by.
They go in, but don't come out again—
    I've heard of you before!
O yes they do; I always let them
    Out by the back door.
      Will you, will you, &c.

For the last time I will ask you,
    Will you walk in, pretty Fly?
No; if I do, I'd be a fool,
    I'm off, so now good bye!
Then up he springs, but both his wings,
    Are in the web caught fast;
The Spider laugh'd—Ha, ha, my boy,
    I have you safe at last.
      Will you, will you, &c.

Now ye juvenile Abstainers,
    I pray you to attend
Unto the moral of my song,
    Which I've brought to an end;
The Publican's the Spider, so,
    Beware as you pass by,
Lest you get entangled in his net,
    Like the foolish little Fly.
      Remember, O remember
      The foolish little Fly, &c.

WILL YOU COME SIGN THE PLEDGE?
Tune—"Will you come to the Bower?"

Will you come sign the pledge we now offer to you,
To drink only water, as pure as the dew?
Wine may sparkle and glisten as brightly it flows,
But brighter the dew-drop that shines on the rose.
    Will you, will you, will you, will you,
      Come sign the pledge.

See the fall from mountains, as joyous it gleams,
Like jewels that shine in the bright sunny beams;
'Tis no wonder it dances with joy on its way,
'Twill surely find welcome where'er it may stray.
    Will you, will you, &c.

O then, who would drink wine when kind nature has given
A beverage that comes from the bounty of Heaven?
Like the lily and rose from the fountains drink free,
Away with your wine, and bright water for me.
    Will you, &c.

O! awake from delusions, poor drunkard, awake,
Draw near to the fountain, and with us partake
Of its pleasures inviting, so sweet, so divine;
O! drink from the fountains, and peace shall be thine,
    Will you, &c.

WE WILL BE FREE.

Tune—"Auld Lang Syne."

On to the conflict, freemen on!
  The conquest shall be ours;
The victory will yet be won,
  Though now the battle lowers.

The monster Rum, must now be slain:
  His mighty host shall fly;
No longer will we wear his chain;
  We'll conquer or we'll die.

We've served his purpose far too long,
  We've long enough been slaves;
What though his fetters may be strong,
  They shall not be our graves.

We'll rally round our Maine Law flag,
  And swear, "We will be free;"
The monster from his throne we'll drag,
  And make his minions flee.

We will not sell ourselves for gold,
  Much less will we for drink;
The half of slavery is untold,
  If still the slave can think.

Then, to the conflict, Freemen, on
  Our foes—behold! they flee!
The victory will soon be won;
  We shall, we shall be free!

LOOK NOT UPON THE WINE.

Oh, Woman, beautiful and fair,
With thy soft radiant eye,
Look not upon the wine-cup red,
Pass it untasted by.
Oh seal it not with those pure lips,
Whence words of Love should flow,
Give not thy sanction, word or sign,
To guilt, despair, and woe!

Art thou a Mother! look around
Upon thy household pearls;
On the fair brows of noble boys,
And gentle-hearted girls.
Think what their fate, if one, perchance,
With winning grace like thine,
Should press to their unsullied lips,
The poison-draught of wine.

Art thou a Wife! oh, jealous guard
The high and lofty truth,
Of him thy fondly chosen one,
The husband of thy youth;
Place not the bright temptation near,
If Peace thou would'st retain:
The household hearth by wine defiled,
Hope's torch lights not again!

Art thou a Maiden! gentle, young,
With soft, beseeching eye;
Entreat thy heart's elected one
" To pass the wine-cup by."
With firm and steady outstretched hand,
Debar the sparkling bowl;
Keep Reason's impress on his brow,
Its light within his soul.

Oh, Mother, Daughter, Sister, Wife,
Oh, Woman, list the call!
Unused to Life's stern battle strife,
Here let your influence fall.
In pity for the broken heart,
For Reason's shattered shrine,
Lift up your gentle, pleading voice,
" Beware the flowing wine!"

THE THREE TOPERS.

Three topers went sailing out into the night—
  Out into the night, when the day was done;
Each made for the place where he loved to get tight,
  And the news-boys stood chaffing them, out of their fun,
    For men must drink, though women should weep,
    For men get thirsty, and drink is cheap
    Where the lager beer is foaming.

Three Charlies sat up on a door-step snug;
  And they lighted their pipes as the moon went down,
And they looked at the bottle, and looked at the jug,
  As the topers came reeling up, ragged and brown,
    For men will drink, when beer is cheap,
    And Charlies the topers till morning must keep,
  Where no lager beer is foaming.

Three topers lay out on the station floor,
  In the morning gleam, when the van came round
And the Charlies were grinning, at hearing the snore
  Of those who would soon in the Mayor's dock be found,
    For men must drink when lager beer is cheap,
    And the harder the spree, the sounder the sleep,
  And good-by to the beer and its foaming.

THE BOWL.

Oh! shun the bowl!—the draught beware
  Whose smile but mocks the lips of men;
When foaming high with waters rare;
  Oh! never touch the goblet then.
With friends we love, though sweet to sip
  The nectared juice at close of day,
Yet trust ye not the syren lip
  That wins to cheat, and lures to slay.

Oh! shun the bowl, and thou shalt know
  A deeper spell than swims in wine:
Though bright its hours of sunset glow,
  Their crimson clouds as briefly shine.
A few short days in madness past,
  And thou wilt sink unknown to years,
Without a hope beyond the blast,

Oh! leave the bowl—if thou art wise
  To shun the path of guilty fame:
The burning road where anguish lies,
  And perjured honor weeps for shame.
In after years some cheering ray
  From virtue's smile will o'er thee spread,
And thou wilt bless the better way
  Thy erring steps were loath to tread.

Oh! shun the bowl—as thou would'st leave
  The poisoned spot where reptiles tread;
Lest widowed hearts for thee should grieve;
  For thee, untimely tears be shed.
Yea! thine may be the fearful lot
  To prove, ere Time hath dimmed thy brow,
A sire—and yet the witness not
  Of them who weep his broken vow.

Art thou a bride whose every sigh
  But trembles with the joy it gives?
Art thou a child whose deep, mild eye,
  Beams in the light its father lives?
Then shun the bowl! the draught beware
  Whose smile but mocks the lips of men;
When foaming high with waters rare;
  O never touch the goblet then!

THE DRUNKARD'S BOY.

Ye who have felt the joy
  Of childhood's guiltless life,
Pity the drunkard's boy,
  And the drunkard's wretched wife.

For through the winter day
  He leaves them cold and ill;
The night comes on its way,
  But he returns not still.

The fire is getting low,
  And o'er the dreary plain
That barefoot boy must go,
  To seek for wood again.

He weeps when he is told
  That he again must go;
It makes his feet so cold
  To tread upon the snow.

But where's the father, where?
  Go to the groggery's cell,
And ask the question there:—
  The rum-seller could tell.

THE OLD, DIRTY BOTTLE.

There is an old Bottle, a strange Bottle too,
For wonderful feats this Bottle can do;
Wise men he makes foolish—makes cowards feel brave,
Changes rich into poor—makes the honest a knave.
    Then take the old Bottle, and plug up its throttle,
    The world shall grow wiser, and cast it away;
    The Temperance banner is Justice and Honor,
    Then let us unfurl it—hurrah boys!—hurrah!

And oh, this old Bottle, a sly Bottle is,
He'll tempt you by saying: "Well just take a glass;"
And when you take one—oh, of course you'll take more,
Till he'll finish by laying you flat on the floor, &c.

But oh this old Bottle is crafty and deep,
For he'll empty your purse as he puts you to sleep,
And when you awake without money, and dry,
Oh does not the Bottle look distant and shy? &c.

But worse, the old Bottle will enter by stealth,
And rob men of honor, of shame, and of health;
This chain-gang of slaves will he drive to the death,
And kick them at last to the regions beneath! &c.

The wicked old Bottle looks jovial and bright,
But the serpent you know always lurks out of sight;
Let the young and the free of his seeming beware,
If you play with the bottle, you're caught in a snare, &c.

Come storm the old Bottle fair daughters of Eve,
'Twas his father at first did our mother deceive;
On serpents and thorns must you constantly tread,
Till the world of these monstrous wretches is rid, &c.

Oh, the dirty old Bottle—how hardened is he,
He rides o'er our ruin and chuckles with glee;
Come, brothers, take hand—we will hunt this old bore,
Till ashamed he shall leave us to visit no more, &c.

THE DRUNKARD'S SONG.

We come, we come in sad array,
And in procession long,
To join the army of the lost,
Three hundred thousand strong.

Our banners, beckoning on to death,
 Abroad we have unrolled,
And famine, care, and wan despair,
 Are seen upon its folds.

Ye heard what music cheers us on!
 The mother's cry that rang
So wildly, and the babe that wailed
 Above the trumpet's clang.

We've taken spoil; and blighted joys
 And ruined homes are here;
We've trampled on the blighted heart,
 And flouted sorrow's tear.

We come! we come! we've search'd the land,
 The rich and poor are ours,
Enlisted from the shrine of God,
 From hovels and from towers.

But who or what shall balk the brave,
 That swear to drink and die?
What boots to us man's muttered curse,
 Or His that spans the sky?

Onward! though ever on our march
 Hangs sorrow's endless train—
Onward to hell! from rank to rank
 Pass we the cup again.

We come! of the world's scourges, who
 Like us have overthrown?
What woe, had ever earth like woe
 To our stern prowess known.

We come, we come to fill our graves,
 On which shall shine no star,
To glut the worm that never dies—
 Hurrah! hurrah! hurrah!

THE SHIP OF THE SONS.

Our noble Temperance ship well manned,
 With a sweet and pleasant gale,
Resolved on leaving Tipsey land,
 She spreads her swelling sail.
Our noble Pilot takes the helm,
 And steers from dangers free;
Whilst away and away our good ship goes,
 Leaves Tipplers on the lee.

High in the air our colors bright
  Are boldly brought to view;
The Temperance crew hail with delight
  The red, the white, the blue.
With hearts so bold, they scorn for gold
  To sell integrity;
So away and away our good ship goes,
  Leaves treachery on the lee.

The cargo that we have on board
  Was purchased from above;
Benevolence and sweet concord,
  Fidelity and love,
With Temperance for its broadest base,
  And fairest purity;
Thus away and away our good ship goes,
  Leaves intemperance on the lee.

The ladies fair, both far and near,
  They wish our ship success;
And cherub infants' voices low,
  Our noble crew they bless,
While angels bright, with fond delight,
  Watch o'er our destiny;
As away and away our good ship goes,
  Leaves dull care on the lee.

May our noble ship and gallant crew
  Prevail o'er wind and tide;
Until the white, the red, the blue,
  Float o'er the world so wide,
And from the thrall of alcohol
  The mortal race be free;
Then away and away our good ship goes,
  Leaves misery on the lee.

TEETOTAL FOR EVER!
Tune.—"Hearts of Oak."

Hurrah! all the tents have their banners unfurl'd,
And teetotal rings o'er the whole Scottish world;
But the lips of the drunkard are scornfully curl'd,
And his brain in the vortex of whisky is whirl'd.
  Teetotal he sings not, by night or by day;
    But steady, brain, steady—and always be ready
    To sound o'er a bumper, "Hurrah and hurrah."

Through the eyes of the toper a spirit looks out,—
'Tis a snake in the brain, which it coils now about;
There it swims upon oceans of flame, do not doubt,
Which roll through the skull on their desolate route.
 Teetotal he sings not, his griefs to allay;
  But steady, brain, steady, be quiet and ready;
 A mutchkin's at hand; now hurrah and hurrah.

The sweep toddles on 'neath his burden of soot,
And his tongue keeps the time to his musical foot;
Now he turns up his nose at a whiskyfied brute,
And teetotal sounds through his red rusty flute.
 Teetotal he sings as he measures his way;
  'Tis steady, swab, steady, to help you I'm ready;
 Teetotal's the password, hurrah and hurrah.

The babe blithely sits on its grandmother's knee,
With a smile on its lip, and the turn in its e'e,
And it looks in the face of its father with glee,
And thinks what a bliss teetotal must be.
 Teetotal it lisps through the long summer's day;
  Be steady, Pa, steady; and ever be ready
 Teetotal to sing; then hurrah and hurrah.

The youth claps his hands as he sprightly goes by,
And whistles teetotal aloud through the sky;
His heart is all joyous, and bright is his eye,
And he cares not a fig though his bottle is dry.
 Teetotal he pipes as he wends on his way;
  'Tis steady, boys, steady, be active and ready,
 Teetotal's the song; now hurrah, boys, hurrah.

The husband, set free from his wonted alarms,
His partner enfolds with delight in his arms;
He clasps now a cluster of brightening charms,
And his bosom is peace, for affection it warms.
 Teetotal he sings, or by night or by day;
  'Tis steady, wife, steady; be jocund and merry,
 Teetotal for ever; hurrah and hurrah.

HAPPY HOME.
Tune—"Sweet Home."

"'Mid scenes of confusion," from morning till eve,
With no heart to pity, no hand to relieve,
The drunkard abandoned was once left to roam,
His fam'ly neglected, deserted his home.
 Home, home, sweet, sweet home,
 Oh, what drunkard's dwelling was ever a home?

Oh sad was the heart of his grief-stricken wife,
Whom he vow'd at the altar to cherish through life;
His children, once fondled, 'neath heaven's wide dome,
Roamed hungry and naked, unknowing a home.
 Home, home—sweet, sweet home, &c.

For drear was their dwelling, unsheltered from cold,
There Boreas unchcck'd, nightly revels did hold;
The hearts of its inmates were sadden'd and lone,
When hope came once more to brighten their home.
 Home, home—sweet, sweet home—
Even hope, fondly cherished, can sweeten our home.

A band of true freemen did proudly arise,
And scales of delusion quick tore from their eyes;
Now sober'd, to them soon fair Plenty did come,
And Virtue and Peace again sweet made their home.
 Home, home—sweet, sweet home—
Peace, plenty, and joy, can make any place, home.

No secret, deep hidden, is theirs to reveal,
"Sign the pledge," Washingtonians cry, in their zeal,
"Ye drinkers, from vice and from misery come,
And renew the delights of your once happy home.
 Home, home—sweet, sweet home—
Oh, renew the delights of your once happy home!"

Come, arouse, Washingtonians! with confidence say,
The haunts of inebriates shall vanish away;
The day is fast dawning, and surely will come,
When their hearts shall delight in wife, children, and home.
 Home, home—sweet, sweet home, &c.

THE DRUNKARD'S WARNING.
THE SPIRIT VOICES OF TEMPERANCE AND INEBRIATION.

TEMPERANCE.

I come from the bowers of paradise—
Where angelic anthems and songs arise,
Commingled with saintly symphonies—
On an errand of love to man.

INEBRIATION.

I come from the place where lost spirits weep,
Immured in their dungeons dark and deep,
Amid taunting fiends, where there is no sleep,
    And mercy no more will dawn.

TEMPERANCE.

I come with my beautiful sisters three—
Meekness, and Hope, and Charity—
No sin ever mars the harmony
    Of my radiant and joyous train.

INEBRIATION.

I come with my dread attendants by—
Murder, and death, and misery.
And I join in the laugh right merrily,
    'Midst the orgies of souls insane.

TEMPERANCE.

I come with my band at eventide
To the saint's bright dwelling, and we preside
O'er his blessed devotions, while, side by side,
    His children kneel down in prayer.

INEBRIATION.

To the drunkard's hearth, when 'tis night, I hie,
Unmoved by the broken-hearted sigh
Of his dying wife, while her infant's cry
    Is drowned with a father's care.

TEMPERANCE.

'Tis the good man's couch I keep vigil by,
When, with brow serene and irradiate eye,
He welcomes pale death triumphantly,
    And enters celestial bliss!

INEBRIATION.

With my poison the drunkard's soul I ply
Through his short-lived years of infamy,
Till death awakens that frenzied cry—
    "Lost, lost in the lowest abyss!"

SEARCHING QUESTIONS.

Father, the temp'rance lecturer said,
    Not only *liquor-takers,*
But those who in the *traffic were,*
    Were likewise, " Drunkard makers."
And nearly all our lunatics,
    And criminals in court,
Could now be traced to drinking hard,
    If we'd a true report!

And when the sin he followed out,
    And such a picture drew,
It made me quail; for, dear papa,
    I only thought of you!
Nonsense, my son! don't bother me,
    Who cares for what they say?
They truly are our " lunatics,"
    Fanatics of the day.

You'd better run your lesson o'er,
    The tender father said;
Enough about these crazy folks,
    I long ago have read.
But father, such a dreadful tale,
    Keeps running in my mind,
I should not think the wicked trade,
    Could such supporters find.

You used to say that " *Retailers,*"
    Were all these people meant;
But I am sure *Importers* too,
    As much *their aid* have lent.
They talk about the " smaller shops;"
    I wish they all were shut,
But father, is'nt it as bad,
    To sell it by the butt?

They gave us a long catalogue,
    About this heinous sin;
And all the while 'twas in my mind,
    That *you imported Gin.*

And now papa, if you are rich,
   And made all by this trade,
When the great day of reck'ning comes,
   O, won't you be afraid?

For if there is a fearful doom,
   Awaits the drunkards gone,
Won't it be worse for *such as you,*
   Who helped the traffic on ?
Whist! stop your questionings at once,
   You're very saucy, Ned;
Pick up your books, 'tis getting late,
   And find your way to bed.

OH PLEDGE ME NOT WITH WINE.

Oh, pledge me not with wine, dear love!
   I shrink from its ruddy glow:
And white and cold a deathly fear
   Drops into my heart like snow.

Oh, pledge me not with wine, dear love!
   Through its mist of rosy foam
I count the beats of a broken heart—
   I see a desolate home.

Oh, pledge me not with wine, dear love!
   I shiver with icy dread;
Each drop to me is a tear of blood
   That sorrowful eyes have shed.

I have a picture laid away
   Under the dust of years,
Come look on it, and your heart will break,
   Like a summer cloud in tears.

Night, and a storm of autumn sleet—
   A hearth without fire or light—
A woman—an angry man—a door
   That opens into the night.

THE TEETOTALER'S HAND-BOOK.

Hot hands that cling to the crazy latch,
   Lips rigid and white with pain—
A curse—a blow—and a wailing babe
   Borne out in the wind and rain—

A woman dead, with her long loose hair
   Soaked wet in the weeping storm,
And her pallid arms half fallen back
   From a baby's waxen form.

A woman dead in the pitiless rain;
   And, sparkling on the sand,
Dear God!—a golden marriage ring
   Dropped loose from her wasted hand.

A white moon striving through broken clouds,
   A horrified man at prayer—
The cry of a passionate heart's remorse,
   And a passionate heart's despair.

This is the picture laid away
   Under the dust of years,
For thus does the red wine look to me,
   The flowing of bloody tears.

Oh, pledge me not, though the wine is bright
   As the rarest light that flows
Through the sunset's cloudy gates of fire,
   Or the morning's vein of rose.

Put down the cup! it is brimmed with blood,
   Crushed throbbing, from hearts like mine!
For hope, for peace, and for love's dear sake,
   Oh, pledge me not with wine!

WE'LL NEVER DRINK AGAIN.

1. 'Tis good, dear friends, to sign the Pledge,
   That sets the drunkard free—
Come join the happy, happy band,
   Whoever you may be.

CHORUS.

We're marching to the field of strife,
To give the dying drunkard life:
Let temp'rance then triumphant reign,
And never let us drink again.
One Voice—What, never drink again?
　All—No, never drink again—
One Voice—What, never drink again?
　All—No, never drink again—
Let temp'rance, then, triumphant reign,
And never let us drink again!

2. Weep not, dear children, weep no more,
　Weep not, thou loving wife;
　The father and the husband lost,
　Is now restored to life.
　　　　　We're marching, &c.

3. Behold the bright array of men,
　United in the cause,
　That millions of the human race
　Around its standard draws.
　　　　　We're marching, &c.

4. The temperance banner and the Pledge
　By us shall be unfurl'd;
　And it shall be our joyful aim
　To wave it o'er the world!
　　　　　We're marching, &c.

AWAY THE BOWL.

1. Our youthful hearts with Temp'rance burn;
　　Away, away the bowl;
　From dram-shops all, our steps we turn;
　　Away, away the bowl;
　Farewell to rum and all its harms,
　Farewell the wine-cup's boasted charms;
　Away the bowl! away the bowl!
　　Away, away the bowl.

2. See how the staggering drunkard reels,
       Away, &c.
    Alas the misery he reveals,
       Away, &c.
   His children grieve, his wife in tears,
   How sad his once bright home appears.
       Away, &c.
   Boys—We drink no more, nor buy, nor sell.
       Away, &c.
   Girls—The drunkard's offers we repel.
       Away, &c.
   All—United in a Temp'rance band,
   We're joined in heart, we're joined in hand.
       Away, &c.

THE GOOD SAMARITAN'S APPEAL.

O drunkard, haste and leave your rum,
 Dark horrors in it lie;
'Twill sure destruction bring on you—
 For ever from it fly.
Yes, come, it is on you we call,
 O listen to us then—
Fear not, but sign the sacred pledge
 To never drink again.

O who would be a slave to rum,
 When purer joys there be?
Many a heart's now beating high,
 Because from rum they're free.
Then hearken ye unto the call,
 And be it not in vain—
Fear not, but sign the sacred pledge
 To never drink again.

O now reflect, ye tipplers too,
 On what may be your fate;
If you continue at your wine
 Dire mis'ries on you wait;
O leave it then, we say to you,
 Before by it you're slain;
Fear not, but sign the sacred pledge
 To never drink again.

THE VOICE OF SINGING.

'Tis the sweet voice of singing,
  That falls on the ear;
All earth is rejoicing
  That temp'rance is near;
For long-parted kindred
  United once more,
Their tale of deliv'rance
  Recount o'er and o'er.

The soul of the mother
  Is glad in her son,
The long absent father
  Returns to his home.
The hearts that were wither'd
  By sorrow and woe,
Rejoice in the downfall
  Of life's direst foe.

Then come now each sad one,
  With grief sore oppress'd,
The pledge will enliven
  The poor and distress'd.
We kindly invite you
  Our pleasures to share,
O come, and refuse not
  Enjoyment so rare.

COLD WATER FOR ME.

Cold water from the flowing fountain,
  Is the drink that I love best;
As purling, rippling from the mountain,
  It ne'er with evil can molest;
In evening late and morning free,
Cold water is the drink for me,
Cold water, cold water is the drink for me!

Sore grief it gives to all true hearted,
 To see you love and quaff the wine;
Turn from your cups and be converted,
 Nor stay in misery's path to pine.
Drink water from the hill-brooks free;
Cold water is the drink for me—
Cold water, cold water is the drink for me!

Then who 'gainst us cold water freemen
 His bitter words with envy shews,
We cannot hold him as a Christian,
 Since he God's blessing doth refuse.
I'd give him, though for life cried he,
No drink but ice-cold water free—
Cold water, cold water is the drink for me!

THE DRINK OF PARADISE.

Let others praise the ruby bright,
 In the red wine's sparkling glow,
But dearer to me is the diamond light
 Of the fountain's clearer flow!
The feet of earthly men have trod
 The juice from the bleeding vine,
But the stream comes pure from the hand of God,
 To fill this cup of mine.
Chorus—Then give me the cup of cold water!
 The clear sweet cup of cold water;
  For his arm is strong, though his toil be long,
 Who drinks but the clear cold water,
 Who drinks but the clear cold water.

The dew drop lies in the flow'ret's cup,
 How rich is its perfume now,
And the fainting earth with joy looks up
 When Heav'n sheds rain on her brow.
The brook goes forth with a pleasant voice,
 To gladden the vale along,
And the bending trees on her banks rejoice
 To hear her quiet song.

The lark soars up with a lighter strain
   When the wave has washed her wing,
And the steed flings back his thund'ring mane
   In sight of the crystal spring.
This was the drink of Paradise,
   Ere blight on her beauty fell,
And the buried streams of her gladness rise
   In ev'ry moss-grown well.

LADIES' SONG.

Let others raise their giddy songs,
   And mirthful notes employ,
To us a nobler theme belongs,
   A higher source of joy.

Beneath a banner fair we stand,
   And all our influence throw,
To banish from our native land,
   Its foulest, deadliest foe.

Ye maidens fair who stand aloof,
   Come join your strength with ours,
And give the moderate drinkers proof,
   They are no friends of yours.

And Oh! perhaps your influence sweet,
   May fathers, brothers, save!
Restrain it may, their wandering feet,
   From the foul drunkard's grave.

No tippling husbands will we have,
   But keep our smiles for those
Who nobly bear our banner brave
   Against our deadly foes.

Fast by our colours will we stand,
   Till they in victory dance
Gaily o'er every sea and land
   'Neath Heaven's blue expanse.

SING, SISTERS, SING.

Sweetly each tuneful voice we raise,
And joyfully sing our temp'rance lays,
And joyfully sing our temp'rance lays,
Unto the cause our aid we give,
Then brothers, though small, the gift receive.
 Sing! sisters, sing, the cause speeds fast,
 Intemp'rance is falling, all danger's past,
 Intemp'rance is falling, all danger's past,

Why should not woman's aid be given,
To forward a cause that is blessed by Heaven,
To forward a cause that is blessed by Heaven;
Angels to aid it well might sing,
Then cheerfully we our songs will bring,
       Sing, &c.

Come ye who have not joined our band,
Away from our side why fearful stand,
Away from our side why fearful stand?
Come join to aid the cause we love,
And sound forth its praise to realms above,
       Sing, &c.

THERE IS A HAPPY TIME.
Tune—"The Happy Land."

There is a happy time, not far away,
When temp'rance truth shall shine, bright, bright as day:
Oh, then, we'll sweetly sing, make the hills and valleys ring;
Earth shall her tribute bring. Not far away.

Bright in our happy band, beams every eye:
Pledged with our heart and hand, love cannot die;
On, then, to Temperance run, be both health and virtue won;
Bright as the noonday sun shines in the sky.

Come join the temp'rance band, come, come away;
Why will ye doubting stand? Why still delay?
Oh, we shall happy be, when we're from Intemp'rance free,
Haste! from the danger flee! Haste, haste away.

Would you like drunkards reel? Hark, hear one rave!
Would you their miseries feel, with none to save?
Rouse, then, for their relief; soothe their sorrow, calm their grief;
Send none, by unbelief, down to the grave.

Pledge to this glorious cause, pledge, pledge to-day!
Bow no more to fashion's laws, break, break away!
Conquer habit while you can, be an independent man.;
Sign the Teetotal Plan, sign, sign, to-day.

Haste then the happy time, not far away;
When Temperance truth shall shine, bright, bright as day:
Oh, then we'll sweetly sing, make the hills and valleys ring:
Earth shall her tribute bring, not far away.

COME, BROTHERS, COME.

Come, brothers come, join our noble band,
Drive intemp'rance from the land;
Long under bondage you have lain,
Burst asunder now the chain,
Then haste, come and sign while of hope there's a ray,
Remember there's danger each moment you stay;
Then sign, and when all danger's gone,
How sweet will be your welcome home.

   Home, home, home,
   How sweet your welcome home;
   Sweet, oh sweet will be your welcome home.
   Welcome home, welcome home, welcome home.

See how your old companions die,
Soon with them you too may lie;
Friendship and love now loudly call,
Burst from alcohol's dread thrall;
Then sign, and when all danger's gone,
How sweet will be your welcome home, &c.

NO QUARTER TO ALCOHOL.
Tune—" Auld Lang Syne."

A noble band, we fill the land,
   A noble cause we plead;
The fair and true, the wide world through,
   Are wishing us good speed.

Chorus—The plea goes on, the day's our own,
    The good cause must succeed;
  A noble band, with heart and hand,
    Are aiding it to speed.

The potion foul, the drunkard's bowl,
   We pledge to mix no more;
The drunkard's name, the drunkard's shame,
   We'd banish from our shore.

The cause of youth, the cause of truth,
   The cause of man we plead;
The cause that dries the mother's eyes,
   And gives the children bread.

From Labrador, to Erie's shore,
   The cause goes cheer'ly on;
The shouts that rise 'neath eastern skies,
   We echo from Huron.

On ev'ry sea our navies be,
   On ev'ry shore an host;
There ne'er was plan devised by man,
   A league so large might boast.

With such array, who dreads the fray,
   Press onward to the goal;
By night or day, by deed or say,
   No truce with Alcohol!

THE STAR OF TEMPERANCE.
Tune—"Bonny Doon."

Once by intemp'rance I was bound,
  In sorrow pass'd each mournful day;
No friends or kindred gathered round
  To cheer my lonely hapless way—
When on my path there gleam'd a star
  That woke me from my horrid trance;
And scattered all my gloom afar:
  It was the star of Temperance.

That star, the brightest in the sky,
  Has shed its beams of joy and light,
And bid despair and darkness fly,
  And changed to day the gloom of night.
My friends rejoice that I am free,
  Hope beams in ev'ry countenance;
I'll sound its praise o'er earth and sea,
  The star, the star of Temperance.

GO, GO, THOU THAT ENSLAV'ST ME.

Go, go, thou that enslav'st me,
  Now, now, thy power is o'er;
Long, long, have I obeyed thee,
  Now I'll not drink any more.
No, no, no, no,
  Now I'll not drink any more.

Thou, thou, bringest me ever
  Deep, deep, sorrow and pain;
Then, then, from thee I'll sever,
  Now I'll not serve thee again.
No, no, no, no,
  Now I'll not serve thee again.

Rum, rum, thou hast bereft me,
  Home, friends, pleasures so sweet,
Now, now, for ever I've left thee,
  Thou and I never shall meet.
No, no, no, no,
  Thou and I never shall meet.

Joys, joys, bright as the morning,
  Now, now, on me will pour;
Hope, hope, sweetly is dawning,
  Now I'll not drink any more.
No, no, no, no,
  Now I'll not drink any more.

THE MISCHIEFS OF DRINKING.
Tune—"Greenville."

When we think of chill starvation,
  When we think of sighs and tears,
When we think of pale privation,
  When we think of doubts and fears;

When we think of raging madness,
  When we think of reckless beings,
When we think of death-like sadness,
  Nature's most distressing scenes;

When we think of horrid murder,
  Female virtue lost in crime,
When we think of black self-slaughter,
  Let us ever bear in mind,

That the cursed love of drinking
  Hath produced the greater part,
And that thousands now are sinking,
  Pierc'd by dissipation's dart.

THE BUCKET WHICH HUNG ON THE WELL.

How dear to my heart are the days of my childhood,
   When fond recollection presents to my view
The orchard, the meadow, the deep tangled wild-wood,
   And ev'ry lov'd spot which my infancy knew;
The wide-spreading pond, and the mill which stood near it;
   The bridge and the rock where the cataract fell;
The cot of my father, the dairy-house nigh it,
   And e'en the rude bucket that hung on the well—
        The old oaken bucket,
        The iron-bound bucket,
   The moss-covered bucket that hung on the well.

That moss-covered bucket I hail as a treasure;
   For often at noon, when return'd from the field,
I found it the source of an exquisite pleasure,
   The purest and sweetest that nature could yield.
How ardent I seized, with hands that were glowing,
   And quick to the white pebbled bottom it fell;
Then soon, with the emblem of truth overflowing,
   And dripping with coolness, it rose from the well—
        The old oaken bucket,
        The iron-bound bucket,
   The moss-covered bucket arose from the well.

How sweet from the green mossy rim to receive it,
   As pois'd on the curb it inclined to my lips;
Not a full flowing goblet could tempt me to leave it,
   Tho' fill'd with the nectar that Jupiter sips.
And now, far removed from that situation,
   The tear of regret will intrusively swell,
As fancy reverts to my father's plantation,
   And sighs for the bucket which hung on the well—
        The old oaken bucket,
        The iron-bound bucket,
   The moss-covered bucket that hung on the well.
P*

I'VE THROWN THE BOWL ASIDE.

I've thrown the bowl aside;
  For me no more shall flow
Its ruddy stream or sparkling tide,
  How bright soe'er it glow;
I've seen extending wide
  Its devastating sway,
Seen reason yield its power to guide:
  I've cast the bowl away!

My days of revelry
  O gladly I give up;
They're but the masks of misery
  Which still lurk in the cup;
While indolence and want
  And poverty display
Themselves in every drunkard's haunt,
  I've cast the bowl away!

A drunkard's gloomy grave
  Shall ne'er be made for me;
O rather let the rushing wave
  Engulf me in the sea!
And may it be my lot
  To die 'neath reason's ray;
Remember'd by my friends or not,
  I've cast the bowl away!

My path henceforth is plain—
  In honesty to live,
To shun intemperance and its train,
  By industry to thrive;
No duty to forget,
  And live to bless the day
When I was led, without regret,
  To cast the bowl away!

REFORMER'S SONG.

Raise your banner high in air,
Write *Cold Water*—write it there,
   Let its folds be wide unfurl'd,
   Let it float o'er all the world—
Temperance banner—raise it high,
Let it wave against the sky!

March, Reformers, march ye on,
Soon the battle will be won;
   Soon the last poor staggering soul,
   Will have turned—or found his goal;
Press, Reformers, press ye on—
Cease not, till the battle's won!
See, yon star is rising high;
Hope is bending from the sky;
   See, yon rainbow bending o'er
   Ireland's lately deluged shore;
See, her star is rising high—
Hope is bending from the sky!

Raise your banner, raise it high;
Let it float against the sky;
   Let the world adoring see,
     Temperance—Truth—and Liberty—
Temperance banner—raise it high,
Let it float against the sky!

PURE WATER FOR ME!

No love for your old hock—pure water for me,
'Tis the best drink on land, 'tis the best drink at sea;
If the pale lily droopeth, will wine brace its stem,
Or add but a tint to the withering gem?

Less love for your brandy—pure water for me;
It is quaff'd by the wild flowers on mountain and lea;
Does old hock or brandy from mountain streams run,
To freshen their flower-banks when scorched by the sun?

Contempt for your whisky—pure water for me;
It is sipp'd by the violet and strong forest tree.
What is nature's drink? ask in mountain or glen,
The answer is " Water."   What is it 'mong men?

Pure water has beauty and brightness for me,
As it sparkles, and dances, and runs to the sea;
Regrets of to-morrow, *drink* causes to come,
Ne'er cloudeth the brow of the hater of rum.

J. B. GOUGH'S LAMENT.

Where are the friends that to me were so dear,
   Long, long ago; long, long ago.
Where are the hopes that my heart used to cheer,
   Long, long ago; long ago.
Friends, that I loved, in the grave are laid low—
Hopes, that I cherished, are fled from me now—
I am degraded, for *Rum* was my foe,
   Long, long ago; long ago.

Sadly my wife bowed her beautiful head,
   Long, &c.
Oh how I wept when I knew she was dead—
   Long, &c.
She was my angel, my guardian, and guide;
Vainly to save me from ruin she tried—
Poor broken heart—it was well that she died,
   Long, &c.

I can look back at the days of my youth,
   Long, &c.
I was no stranger to virtue and truth,
   Long, &c.
Oh, for the hours that I squander'd away—
Oh, for the love that was pure as the day—
Oh, for the hopes that were *purer* than they,
   Long, long ago; long ago.

POETRY, SONGS, AND HYMNS.

WATER!—OH! WATER FOR ME.

Oh! water for me—bright water for me!
And wine for the tremulous debauchee!
It cooleth the brow, it cooleth the brain,
It maketh the faint one strong again;
It comes o'er the sense like a breeze from the sea,
All freshness, like infant purity.
Oh water, bright water, for me, for me!
Give wine, give wine to the debauchee!

Fill to the brim! fill, fill to the brim!
Let the flowing crystal kiss the rim;
For my hand is steady, my eye is true,
For I, like the flowers, drink naught but dew.
Oh! water, bright water's a mine of wealth,
And the ores it yieldeth are vigour and health.
So water, pure water for me, for me!
And wine for the tremulous debauchee!

Fill again to the brim—again to the brim!
For water strengthens life and limb;
To the days of the aged it addeth length,
To the might of the strong it addeth strength;
It freshens the heart, it brightens the sight—
'Tis like quaffing a goblet of morning light.
So water, I'll drink naught but thee,
Thou parent of health and energy!

When o'er the hills, like a gladsome bride,
Morning walks forth in her beauty's pride,
And leading a band of laughing hours,
Brushes the dew from the nodding flowers,
Oh! cheerily then my voice is heard,
Mingling with that of the soaring bird,
Who flingeth abroad his matins loud,
As he freshens his wing in the cold grey cloud.

But when evening has quitted her sheltering yew,
Drowsily flying, and weaving anew
Her dusky meshes o'er land and sea,
How gently, oh! Sleep, fall thy poppies on me!
For I drink water, pure, cold, and bright,
And my dreams are of heaven the live-long night.
So, hurrah for thee, water, hurrah! hurrah!
Thou art silver and gold, thou art ribbon and star,
Hurrah for bright water! hurrah! hurrah!

THE WATER-KING.

We're soldiers of the Water-King,
  His laws we will obey;
Virtue and health are his reward—
  We want no better pay.

Chorus—Then, let us sing the Water-King,
    Good soldiers, one and all—
    Our banners to the breeze we'll fling,
    And *down* with *alcohol*.

We boast no sword or glittering spear;
  Ours is a bloodless crown—
A purer, brighter, fairer thing
  Than conquerors ever won. &c.

Our strength is in the living spring—
  And long as waters run,
Or grass grows green, we're pledged to keep
  Our temperance armour on. &c.

What though the Fire King mocks our hosts,
  As great Goliath did,
We've temperance Davids in our ranks,
  Who'll bring away his head. &c.

THE COLD WATER ARMY.

With banner and with badge we come,
    An ARMY true and strong,
To fight against the hosts of Rum,
    And this shall be our song:
We love the clear Cold Water Springs,
    Supplied by gentle showers;
We feel the strength cold water brings,—
    "The Victory is Ours."

"Cold Water Army" is our name,
    O may we faithful be,
And so in truth and justice claim,
    The blessings of *the free.* &c.

Though others love their rum and wine,
    And drink till they are mad,
To water we will still incline,
    To make us strong and glad. &c.

I pledge to thee this hand of mine,
    In faith and friendship strong;
And fellow-soldiers we will join
    The chorus of our song:
We love the clear Cold Water Springs,
    Supplied by gentle showers;
We feel the strength cold water brings,—
    "The Victory is Ours."

COLD WATER ARMY.

United in a peaceful band
To drive *intemp'rance* from our land,
We're joined in heart, and joined in hand—
    The cold water army.

We'll raise our happy voices high
In loudest accents to the sky;
While heaven and earth shall then reply—
    The cold water army.

We'll make the woods and valleys ring
With loudest echoes while we sing,
While all around re-echoes bring,
              The cold water army.

O Lord, let now a copious shower
Of grace descending on us pour,
Nor let one blighting prospect lower
              The cold water army.

O may we meet around thy throne,
To praise Thee there, in strains unknown,
And flowers of love and peace be strewn,
              The cold water army.

WATER THE DRINK FOR ME.

The drink that's in the drunkard's bowl
  Is not the drink for me,
It kills his body and his soul,
  How sad a sight is he.
But there's a drink which God hath given,
  Distilling in the showers of heaven,
In measures large and free,
    O, that's the drink for me.

      O, that's the drink for me,
      O, that's the drink for me.

The stream that many prize so high,
  Is not the stream for me;
For he who drinks it still is dry,
  For ever dry he'll be.
But there's a stream, so cool and clear,
  The thirsty traveller lingers near,
Refreshed and glad is he:
    O, that's the stream for me.

      O, that's the stream for me,
      O, that's the stream for me.

The wine-cup that so many prize,
   Is not the cup for me,
The aching head, the bloated face,
   In its sad train I see.
But there's a cup of water pure,
   And he who drinks it may be sure
Of health and length of days,
   O, that's the cup for me.
     O, that's the cup for me,
     O, that's the cup for me.

NEVER FORGET.

Can we forget the gloomy time,
   When Bacchus rul'd the day,
When dissipation, sloth, and crime,
   Bore undisputed sway?
     The time—the time—the gloomy time—
       The time has passed away,
     When dissipation, sloth, and crime,
       Bore undisputed sway.

Can we forget the tender wives,
   Who found an early tomb,
For, ah! the partners of their lives
   Had met the drunkard's doom?
     The wives—the wives—the tender wives,
       May bid adieu to gloom,
     For now the partners of their lives
       Abhor the drunkard's doom.

We'll ne'er forget that noble band
   Who fear'd no creature's frown,
And boldly pledg'd both heart and hand,
   To put intemperance down.

The band—the band—the noble band—
  The band of blest renown—
Who boldly pledg'd both heart and hand
  To put intemp'rance down.

Nor shall the *Pledge* be e'er forgot,
  That so much bliss creates—
"WE'LL TOUCH NOT—TASTE NOT—HANDLE NOT,
WHATE'ER INTOXICATES."

  The Pledge—the Pledge is not forgot—
    The Pledge that Satan hates—
  " *We'll touch not—taste not—handle not,
    Whate'er intoxicates.*"

THE CUP OF DEATH.

Fear to tread, 'tis slipp'ry ground,
Where narcotic streams abound;
Bacchus fills the deadly cup,
Foolish mortals drink it up!

Music, with her harpylæs,
Immoral plays among the trees;
And bewitching spells impart
Poison alike to mind and heart.

Wanton Beauty, Virtue gone,
Draws her veil to lure you on,
And by Music, Wine, and Lust,
Lays your honour in the dust.

There the blushing moonbeams play
On the victims as they lay;
Others dance around the shrine,
"Cursing God!" and praising wine!

THE SOLDIER'S APPEAL.

Yonder floats the temp'rance standard ;
Soldiers plant your footsteps sure ;
Victory's certain if you're steadfast,
If you to the end endure.
    Storm the breaches,
And your general's praise secure.

Tear the monster from his stronghold :
Long, too long, you've been his slaves ;
Raze his palace, let your war-cry
Rouse the drunkards, whom he craves.
    Do your duty ;
Yonder, see, the banner waves !

Thousands, then, shall call you blessed :
Thousands hail you as their friend ;
Through the world your fame shall travel,
And we soon shall gain our end.
    Then be steadfast,
And the temperance cause defend.

Why should soldiers be behind-hand
In this good and glorious cause ;
Buckle on your armour quickly ;
Make the foe, intemperance, pause.
    Shake his kingdom,
For he hosts to ruin draws.

Come then, comrades, one and all, come,
Do not any longer stay ;
Show the world you are in earnest,
Sign the pledge without delay :
    And our country
They will bless us day by day.

THE TEETOTALER'S HAND-BOOK.

SYMPATHY FOR THE DRUNKARD.

Poor drunkard! believe me, thy passions deceive thee,
   Thy false education has led thee astray;
I will not upbraid thee, I wish to persuade thee
   To shun the bright goblet, and I'll lead the way.

I heed not its sparkles, I know therein darkles
   A spirit of evil that blights ev'ry charm;
Take my safe example—its first temptings trample;
   My heart yearns to serve thee and guard thee from harm.

I join not the jeering, or cold-hearted sneering,
   Of those who reproach the poor sot in his fall;
Ah no! I would rather reclaim some lost father;
   One hearth-stone made happy repays me for all.

Thy fortune is flying, thy honour is dying,
   The home of thy musings of comfort is scant:
The wife thou selected, and should have protected,
   And babes of thy bosom, will suffer from want.

I do not despise thee, I labour to raise thee,
   And not make thy follies the theme of my sport;
The world has degraded, and though thus unaided,
   My hand, heart, and favour, shall give thee support.

Dear friend! take this warning, the wine cup hence spurning,
   Oh! wipe the hot tears from thy darling wife's eyes;
And angels above thee, and good men shall love thee,
   And joy to behold thee resolve to be wise.

CLOSING ODE.

   Good night, good night to every one,
     Be each heart free from care,
   May every one now seek their home,
     And find contentment there:
   May joy beam with to-morrow's sun,
     And every prospect shine—
   While wife and friends laugh merrily,
     Without the aid of wine.

ONLY THIS ONCE.

"Only this once;"—the wine-cup glowed,
  All sparkling with its ruby ray;
The bacchanalian welcome flowed,
  And folly made the revel gay.

Then he, so long, so deeply warned,
  The sway of conscience rashly spurned;
His promise of repentance scorned,
  And, coward-like, to vice returned.

"ONLY THIS ONCE;"—the tale is told:
  He wildly quaff'd the pois'nous tide:
With more than Esau's madness, sold
  The birthright of his soul, and died.

I do not say that breath forsook
  The clay, and left its pulses dead;
But reason in her empire shook,
  And all the LIFE OF LIFE was fled.

Yes! angel hearts with pity wept,
  When he whom virtue fain would save,
His vow to her so falsely kept,
  And madly sought a drunkard's grave.

"ONLY THIS ONCE;"—beware, beware!
  Gaze not upon the blushing wine;
Oh! fly temptation's syren snare,
  And, prayerful, seek for strength divine.

THE SAILOR'S SONG.

Speed, speed the Temperance ship!
  Ye winds, fill ev'ry sail;
Behold her sailing on the deep,
  Outriding ev'ry gale;
The tempest's fury she outbraves,
And hosts of deathless drunkards saves.

Speed, speed the Temperance ship!
  Who joins us in the cry?
Mothers and children, cease to weep,
  Our ship is passing by;
We wish to take you all on board—
A freight of mercy to the Lord.

Speed, speed the Temperance ship!
  For her we'll ever pray:
'Tis Israel's God alone can keep,
  In safety, night and day;
On Him we'll evermore depend,
Who is the contrite drunkard's friend.

Speed, speed the Temperance ship!
  Ye young and aged, shout,
Behold her sailing o'er the deep!
  With all her streamers out,
Bound for the true teetotal shore,
Where streams of death are drank no more.

TEMPERANCE STAR.
Tune—"Greenville."

Watchman! tell us of the night,
  What its signs of promise are?
Cloth'd in panoply of light,
  See, that glorious Temp'rance Star.

Watchman! does its beauteous ray
  Aught of hope or joy foretell;
Trav'ller! yes; it brings the day
  Which shall burst the drunkard's spell.

Watchman! tell us of the night,
  Higher yet that Star ascends;
Trav'ller! hail its blessed light,
  Peace and truth its course portends.

Watchman! will its beams alone
  Gild the spot that gave them birth!
Trav'ller! no; all time its own,
  And its heritage the earth.

YOUTH OF CANADA!

TUNE—"National Anthem."

Canadian youth, arise!
Join with the temp'rance cause
   To bless mankind:
Lift up your voices high,
To him who hears your cry,
Who does your wants supply,
   Times without end.

Christians, haste to the field,
Gird on your sword and shield,
   To conquer go;
God will your efforts bless,
Crown you with great success,
And banish drunkenness
   From all below.

Can you the call refuse?
Will you his cause abuse,
   And idle stand?
With folded arms abreast,
In Zion taking rest,
Drunkenness not represt
   From this our land?

Come, then, and join our cause,
Let men or fiends oppose,
   You may be free;
Break off your hellish chains;
Wash off your guilty stains,
While time and health remains,
   Now let it be.

Then victory is sure,
Drunkards will find a cure,
   Without alloy;
Mothers would dry their tears,
Banish their needless fears—
God having crown'd their years
   With mighty joy.

O God! let Temp'rance shine,
Upheld by power divine,
  Till time shall cease;
Let sin and misery
From earth be made to flee,
That all may look to thee,
  The Prince of Peace.

O'er this once happy land,
Let love and Temp'rance stand,
  We look to thee;
No more the orphans' cries
Shall pierce the vaulted skies,
Nor widows' sighs arise,
  O'er land and sea.

Children no more shall roam,
Naked, without a home,
  But be well fed;
Fathers will fathers be;
Mothers rejoice to see
Love, home, and liberty;
  Life from the dead.

BIBLE TEETOTALERS.

Doth Scripture speak of temp'rance men?
  If we've such friends as they,
We shall not be discouraged then,
  Whatever men may say.

The sons of Jonadab were true
  Unto their temperance vow;
God bless'd them, and their children do
  Enjoy the blessing now.

So Daniel and his friends decline
  The king's rich gifts to share;
On water and on pulse they dine,
  Yet flourish strong and fair.

Paul also was a hearty friend
  Unto the temperance vow;
And these inspired examples tend
  To guide and cheer us now.

SELF-PUNISHED!

Self-punish'd here the drunkard is,
    With woes on ev'ry hand;
Guilt, poverty, and dark despair,
    Dance round,—a ghastly band!

Time lost, and all his prospects gone,
    His trembling hands and heart
Declare his constitution worn,
    And he must soon depart.

The wings of hope no plumage bear,
    Faith, wounded, shrinks away;
While charity, disheartened, flies,
    Where shines a brighter ray.

All language fails the curse to tell,
    That drinking doth produce;
Within the soul it makes a hell,
    And turns its legions loose.

Sighs cannot half his guilt express,
    Nor yet the deepest groans,
When death assails his trembling breast,
    When endless vengeance frowns.

TRIUMPH OF SOBRIETY.

Lift up your hearts, and voices too,
To HIM to whom the praise is due;
And let the glorious subject be
The TRIUMPH OF SOBRIETY.

What has been done?—Delightful things,
Beyond our best imaginings!
The Ethiop's white, the lion's tam'd—
And hoary drunkards are reclaim'd!

This is the great deliverance
Achiev'd by God, through Temperance!
And can the Christian ever cease
To pray, and work for its increase!

Christians! this very hour begin
To check our land's peculiar sin;
And seek His pow'r, who can afford
The aid of an almighty Lord!

CAUTION.

While walking, at the close of day,
   Among the silent dead,
Methought I heard a spirit say,
   In accents deep and dread :—

Here lies a youth of tender age,
   Who prematurely fell ;
'Twas tippling rais'd the fever's rage,
   And sunk his soul to hell.

And there lies one whose mould'ring bones
   Were broken by a fall ;
Intemp'rance caus'd his dying groans,—
   That direst curse of all.

But ah! in yonder silent tomb,
   A youth, self-murdered, lies ;
Inflam'd with gin, while in his bloom,
   Were heard his dying sighs.

And then methought the spirit cried,—
   EVIL BEGINNINGS SHUN,
Or you'll into sin's vortex glide,
   And ever be undone.

HARK! O'ER HILL AND DALE.

Hark ! o'er hill and dale is swelling,
   One rejoicing general song,
Triumph of fair Temp'rance telling,
   On the breeze 'tis borne along ;
Happy wives and joyous children,
   Still the cheerful strain prolong.

We would lend our feeble voices,
   On Canada's favor'd shore ;
For our ev'ry heart rejoices,
   And our tongues shall not give o'er ;
What, though few and weak our number,
   If it make our efforts more !

O'er ev'ry land and nation,
  Has her banner wide been flung,
Men of ev'ry clime and station,
  Have the praise of Temp'rance sung :
All have felt her happy influence,
  Poor and wealthy—old and young.

Friends of Temp'rance, be not sleeping,
  Swiftly tread your glorious way!
Famished children—mothers weeping,
  Call on you to haste the day,
When o'er all the wide creation,
  Temp'rance shall her sceptre sway.

Lord, to Thee the praise we render,
  For the good that has been done ;
Thou hast made the conscience tender ;
  Thou hast softened hearts of stone !
Still assist us in our labor,
  For we trust in Thee alone.

HYMN FOR TEMPERANCE ANNIVERSARIES.

Another year its course hath run,
  Since last we thus together met,
To tell of victories we had won,
  Of foes we had to conquer yet,
And means devise by which we might
Still spread abroad true Temp'rance light.

Preserv'd by Providence divine,
  Lord ! in thy name again we meet ;
Now cause thy face on us to shine,
  And make our work in thee complete !
In vain we toil, except thou own
Our work, and with thy blessing crown.

We praise thy name that thou hast wrought
  By instruments so weak as we ;
Abandon'd drunkards have been brought
  To hate their sin, and turn to thee !
To thee in prayer their voices raise !
And blasphemies give place to praise !

Encourag'd by our past success,
  We labour on at thy command;
With warmer zeal we onward press
  To renovate our native land;
Nor will we cease, till o'er the world
The Temp'rance Banner is unfurl'd.

We'll urge our way till Zion wake,
  Put on her strength and garments fair,
Till from the dust herself she shake,
  And captive bands no longer wear—
Till in her courts no more is seen
The thing unholy or unclean!   ISA. c. liiI. v. 1-2.

Then will her moral desert bloom,
  And spread a rich perfume abroad,
Her barren wilderness become
  Like Eden's garden; for the Lord
Will comfort Zion! she shall raise
Her voice in songs of grateful praise!   ISA. c. li. v. 3.

Then will her watchmen join their voice,
  In sweetest strains together sing—
Beholding eye to eye, rejoice
  When God again shall Zion bring,
And to the ends of all the earth
Doth send his great Salvation forth!   ISA. c. llii. v. 8-10.

Arise, O God! thy cause maintain;
  Our efforts bless; our work succeed,
Till every tribe of man abstain,
  And earth from all strong drink is freed:
This curse remove, O God! we pray,
And bring the blest Millenium day.

THE SPARKLING BOWL.

Thou sparkling bowl! thou sparkling bowl!
  Though lips of bards thy brim may press,
And eyes of beauty o'er thee roll,
  And song and dance thy power confess,
I will not touch thee, for there clings
A scorpion to thy side that stings!

Thou crystal glass! like Eden's tree
  Thy melted ruby tempts the eye,
And, as from that, there comes from thee
  The voice, " Thou shalt not surely die."
I dare not lift thy liquid gem,
A snake is twisted round thy stem.

Thou liquid fire! like that which glowed
  On Melita's surf-beaten shore,
Thou'st been upon my guests bestowed,
  But thou shalt warm my house no more,
For wheresoe'er thy radiance falls,
Forth from thy heat a viper crawls.

What though of gold the goblet be,
  Embossed with branches of the vine,
Beneath whose burnished leaves we see
  Such clusters as poured out the wine.
Among those leaves an adder hangs!
I fear him! for I've felt his fangs.

The Hebrew who the desert trod,
  And felt the fiery serpent's bite,
Looked up to that ordained of God,
  And found that life was in the sight;
So the worm-bitten's fiery veins
Cool, when he drinks what God ordains.

Ye gracious clouds! ye deep cool wells!
  Ye gems from mossy rocks that drip!
Springs that from Earth's cool cells
  Gush o'er your granite basin's lip,
To you I look! your largest give,
And I will drink of you, and live.

THE DRUNKARD'S CHILDREN.

Kind lady! as thou hast a heart
  To bid the poor and wretched live,
O! from thy plenty, one small part
  For our sad, starving mother give.

We left her sick, alone, and weak,
  With none to hold her aching head;
Hunger and sickness on her cheek
  Have left their pale hue for the red.

Our father is not what he was,
  In joyous days that have gone by:
Lady! if thou would'st know the cause,
  Ask of yon haughty trader, why?

We begged of him to give us bread—
  He gave a cruel curse and blow:
"Off! off! ye beggar brats," he said,
  "Back to your filthy hovel go."

I knew that we were beggar boys,
  Doomed to a life of want and wo
By the foul poison that destroys
  All peace—but HE HATH MADE US SO.

Lady! 'tis hard to beg our bread,
  As we do now, from door to door;
But give—and blessings on thy head
  May bounteous Heaven in plenty pour.

FEMALES INVITED.
Tune—"Devizes."

Come, gentle daughters of our land!
  A mission waits your care;
Come join the faithful Temp'rance band,
  Their toils and triumphs share.

Come, 'tis a work of faith and love,
  And blessings on it rest;
Oh come! and by example prove,
  That pity warms your breast.

Think of the many wretched wives,
  Steep'd in the bitt'rest woe;
Think of the many valu'd lives,
  Intemperance has laid low.

Think of the infant lips that pine,
  And for deliverance crave;
Think of the grey hairs that decline
  In sorrow to the grave.

Think! when you stand amid the host,
　Before Jehovah's throne,
For souls by your example lost,
　You'll answer with your own!

Then oh! let mercy, faith, and love,
　Constrain you to embrace
That cause, which labours to remove
　Intemp'rance from our race.

TURN, O TURN!

Hallelujah! hallelujah!
To the God who reigns on high,
He hath said to wretched drunkards,
Turn, O turn, ye need not die,
　　　But may with me
Live in bliss above the sky.

Flee, O flee, ye thoughtless sinners,
From the curs'd, the maddening bowl,
Penitently haste to Jesus,
Save thy blood-bought precious soul,
　　　In the fountain
Plunge ye now and be made whole.

While in drunkenness you're living,
　Oh, how wretchedly you dwell,
How sad, how awful your condition,
　You are on the road to hell;
　　　Oh, what folly,
Will you thus your birthright sell?

Now obey your great Creator,
Now for endless glory start,
Haste, repent, believe the gospel,
Seek the new, the contrite heart;
　　　Oh, be sober,
And from ways of death depart.

Then, O then what joy and glory,
Shall your ransom'd soul receive,
Then the drunkard's bitter story,
As your own, no more shall grieve
　　　Your blest spirit,
But in comfort you shall live.

GO NOT BACK.

My brother, go not back—
  The pledge is taken now;
I see it by the healthful smile
  That plays upon thy brow;
I see it in the sparkling eye,
  So dull and dim before;
Then go not back again, my friend,
  To sure destruction's door.

My brother, go not back;
  Press on in virtue's way;
Be steadfast in thy sacred pledge,
  And truth shall be thy stay.
Hope, bright as morning's dawn, shall spring
  Where'er thy feet may tread;
Then go not back again, my friend,
  The path of terror spread.

My brother, go not back
  To sorrow and to vice;
To reap the bitter fruits of sin,
  Where none to glory rise;
Where, stranger to the joys of earth,
  Life will be steeped in woe;
Then go not back again, my friend,
  But upward, heavenward go.

My brother, go not back—
  The fatal whirlpool see,
Where thousands and ten thousands rush
  To hopeless misery.
Behold them perish day by day,
  Determined thus to seek;
Then go not back again, my friend,
  To ruin's fearful brink.

My brother, go not back—
  'Tis wisdom speaketh thus,
And telleth thee the wine-cup is
  Man's greatest, fatal curse.
It well nigh drew thy wary feet
  To a dishonorable grave;
Then go not back again, my friend—
  Each sharp temptation brave.

My brother will not go—
  I read it on his cheek;
I see it in the tears that flow,
  And when I hear him speak.
He has resolved in God's own strength,
  Who will, I know, sustain,
Never, while reason holds her throne,
  To touch the cup again.

ODE.
Tune—"Missionary."

Strike, strike the lyre in gladness,
  Let music fill the air;
Oh give the wing to sadness,
  And heart-corroding care.
For joy, with folded pinion,
  Sits in our presence now,
And 'neath her bright dominion,
  Let heart and spirit bow.

No ruby wine is needed,
  To buoy our spirits up,
For it would flash unheeded,
  Though brimming every cup.
The vows that we have spoken,
  Like Rechab's sons of old,
Shall stand like theirs unbroken,
  While brightness clings to gold.

And God's own lasting blessing,
  Promised to Rechab's band,
Each heart is now confessing
  Is showered o'er our land;
For though no bow is bending
  Its signet from the sky,
Yet thousand hearts are blending
  In covenant reply.

As Jonadab commanded
  His sons in days of yore,
So we in love have banded,
  And made us tents once more—
Raising our signal-banners,
  By Truth's own breezes fanned,
Till thousand of hosannas
  Have echoed through our land.

For many a poor heart, weary
  Of earth's conflicting cares,
And of a lot as dreary
  As desolation wears,
Have sought us in their sadness,
  And like the wearied dove
Have found a home of gladness
  Within our ark of love.

'Tis thus we stem each billow
  Upon life's stormy main,
And " harps hung on the willow"
  Are tuned to joy again.
Then let each chosen brother
  Join in the chorus now—
" We're true unto each other,
  And true unto our vow."

THE FAMILY PLEDGE.

However others choose to act
  Towards the Temperance Cause,
We'll hail its blessings to our home,
  And strictly keep its laws.

We will not TOUCH the drunkard's drink,
  But close our lips to all;
Reject the foe in every form,
  Lest we should TASTE and fall.

We will not GIVE the drunkard's drink
  Our friends to entertain;
But act the more consistent part,
  And teach them to abstain.

POETRY, SONGS, AND HYMNS.

We will not BUY the drunkard's drink,
    Nor KEEP it where we dwell,
'Tis dear—'tis dangerous—and 'tis death—
    It hurries crowds to hell.

O, that our Christian friends would make
    One simultaneous stand,
To execrate the drunkard's drink,
    And drive it from our land.

SUPPLICATION.

Spare, Lord, the thoughtless, guide the blind,
    Till man no more shall deem it just
To live, by forging chains to bind
    His weaker brother in the dust.

Still give us grace, Almighty King!
    Unwavering at our posts to stand,
Till grateful at thy shrine we bring.
    The tribute of a ransomed land.

WE WILL PRAISE THEE!

Parent of the great creation,
    Thou hast open'd wide thine hand;
Thanks we give and adoration,
    Now that we before thee stand.

May all drunkards now enslaved
    Taste those pleasures we enjoy—
They and us through grace be saved,
    And for thee our lives employ.

Safely by thy Spirit guided,
    Till the scenes of life are o'er,
May we taste the bliss provided,
    Hunger then and thirst no more.

Then our sweetest voices raising,
    With the bright angelic host,
Thy great name for ever praising,
    Father, Son, and Holy Ghost.

TEMPERANCE NATIONAL ANTHEM.

Tune—"America," or "God save the Queen."

God save our gracious Queen,
Make her's a happy reign,
    God save the Queen;
May all her subjects be
Blest with sobriety,
Justice and piety,
    God save the Queen.

O Lord our God arise,
Make all poor drunkards wise,
    On thee we call;
May they be brought to hate
Drinks that intoxicate,
And thy word venerate,
    O save them all.

Thy choicest gifts in store,
On all most richly pour
    Who do abstain;
Obeying reason's laws,
Faithful to our great cause,
We'll sing with sober voice,
    God save the Queen.

THANKSGIVING.

Tune—"Woodstock."

Let Temp'rance and her sons rejoice,
  And be their praises loud and long;
Let every heart and every voice
  Conspire to raise a joyful song.

His children's prayer he deigns to grant,
  He stays the progress of the foe;
And temp'rance, like a cherish'd plant,
  Beneath his fost'ring care shall grow.

POETRY, SONGS, AND HYMNS.

I AM A POOR INEBRIATE.
Tune—"Duane Street."

I am a poor inebriate,
  I come to seek relief of you!
O save me from my lost estate,
  I'll sign your pledge, and *keep* it, too.
I've lost my all, I've come to you
  To save me ere it be too late!
Your pity, friends, is all I ask,
  O save me now, for mercy's sake.

My frame is weak—my heart is sick—
  I've suffered more than tongue can tell;
Thoughts run apace; they bring me back
  To home, to friends, where all was well.
I've drain'd the cup, I've revel'd long—
  At Bacchus' shrine no more I'll meet,
My wife is dead, my children gone,
  And now I have no friends to greet.

We never pause, when at our door,
  A wretched, trembling drunkard stands,
To ask the *cause* that made him poor,
  Or why he now should help demand.
Come to the waters flowing wide
  As crystal fountains soft and clear—
Come, take the pledge; nought shall betide;
  You've temp'rance friends—you need not fear.

EXAMPLE.
Tune—"Balerma."

Help us to feel for drunken man,
  In all his sin and woe;
And let our bright example teach
  The way he ought to go.

Let not our conduct harden him;
  But fill our souls with care,
To snatch him from the pit of death,
  And break the fatal snare.

THE DYING DRUNKARD.

Stretch'd on a heap of straw—his bed—
    The dying drunkard lies;
His joyless wife supports his head,
    And to console him, tries:

His weeping children's love would ease
    His spirit, but in vain;
Their ill-paid love destroys his peace,
    He'll never smile again.

His boon companions—where are they?—
    They shar'd his heart and bowl,
Yet come not nigh to charm away
    The horrors from his soul.

What have *such* friends to do with those
    Who press the couch of pain?
Ah! *he* is racked with mortal throes—
    He'll never rise again!

And where is mercy in that hour
    Of dread, and pain, and guilt!
Though Jesus' blood, of matchless power,
    For man's sear'd soul was spilt?

If Justice spurn the fear-urg'd prayer,
    That stream has flow'd in vain;
And, lock'd in thy embrace, Despair!
    He'll never hope again.

PRAYER TO GOD.
Tune—"Hebron."

Hosannas, Lord, to Thee we sing,
    Whose power the giant fiend obeys;
What countless thousands tribute bring,
    For happier homes and brighter days!

Thou wilt not break the bruised reed,
    Nor leave the broken heart unbound;
The wife regains a husband freed!
    The orphan clasps a father found!

POETRY, SONGS, AND HYMNS.

THE DRUNKARD'S WIFE.
Tune—"Ortonville."

Behold her now, the blooming flow'r
  Which once we saw in pride
At morning's dawn, or evening's close
  When fell the vesper tide:
O how her voice rang sweet and wild,
  As winds along a lyre;
And how her eyes expressive shone,
  As sacred Eastern fire.

Behold her now! upon her cheeks
  The print of deep despair,
And in her eye a troubled light
  Speaks want, and woe, and care?
Why is she thus bow'd down in grief?
  Why haggard as from strife?
These awful words will tell the tale—
  She is a drunkard's wife.

ANNIVERSARY.
Tune—"Lennox."

Pledg'd in a noble cause,
  We here each other greet;
And bound by temp'rance laws,
  As friends and brothers meet,
To make a full determin'd stand
Against the foe that rules our land.

'Tis true, the work is great,
  Our army is but small,
The foe is potentate;
  But, if united all
In close array, our little band
  Shall chase Intemp'rance from the land.

ANNUAL MEETING.
Tune—"Ortonville."

On this glad day, O God, we would,
  Through thy beloved Son,
Acknowledge Thee for all the good
  That Temperance has done.

We thank Thee for the thousands sav'd
  From soul-seducing drink,
Who by its power were long enslav'd,
  And cast on ruin's brink.

O let thy Holy Spirit dwell
  Where vice too long has reigned;
For where thy mercy breaks the spell,
  The victory is gained.

BLESSING IMPLORED.
Tune—"Cleft of the Rock."

Father of everlasting love,
  Thou art the source of boundless grace,
Then let us now thy goodness prove,
  While here assembled in this place;
Our work regard, our labours bless,
And crown our efforts with success.

Grant, Lord, to prosper and advance,
  The measures by thy servants used
To spread the cause of Temperance,
  Until throughout the world diffused,
Its happy fruits are fully known,
And all mankind its influence own.

Send forth thy light, thy truth, thy grace,
  Dispel the shadowing gloom of night,
Bring in the reign of righteousness,
  And fill the world with moral light;
Illume the nations by thy word,
And reign the universal Lord.

DRUNKARD'S HOPE.

Tune—"Old Hundred."

"Though sore beset with guilt and fear,
I cannot, dare not, quite despair.
If I must perish, would the Lord
Have taught my heart to love his word?
Would he have given me eyes to see
My danger and my remedy?
Revealed his name, and bid me pray,
Had he resolved to say me nay.

No: though cast down, I am not slain;
I'm fallen, but shall rise again.
The present, Satan, is thy hour,
But Jesus shall control thy power.
His love will plead for my relief;
He hears my groans, he sees my grief;
Nor will he suffer thee to boast
A soul that sought his help was lost.

I'll cast myself before his feet;
I see him on his mercy-seat:
('Tis sprinkled with atoning blood:)
There sinners find access to God.
Ye burdened souls, approach with me,
And make the Saviour's name your plea;
Jesus will pardon all who come,
And strike our fierce accuser dumb."

DISMISSION.

Heavenly Father! give thy blessing,
 While we now this meeting end;
On our minds each truth impressing,
 That may to thy glory tend.
Save from all Intoxication,
 From its fountains may we flee—
When assail'd by strong temptation,
 Put our trust alone in thee.

HELP, LORD.
Tune—"Devizes."

Intemp'rance, like a raging flood,
　　Is sweeping o'er the land;
Its dire effects, in tears and blood,
　　Are trac'd on every hand.

It still flows on, and bears away
　　Ten thousands to their doom:
Who shall the mighty torrent stay,
　　And disappoint the tomb?

Almighty God! no hand but thine
　　Can check this flowing tide;
Stretch out thine arm of power divine,
　　And bid the flood subside.

Dry up the source from whence it flows—
　　Destroy its fountain-head—
That dire Intemp'rance and its woes
　　No more the earth o'erspread.

PRAYER.
Tune—"Helmsley."

Lord of heaven and earth assist us,
　　While the Temp'rance cause we plead,
Though both earth and hell resist us,
　　If thou bless, we shall succeed—
　　　　　　　From intemp'rance
May our country soon be freed.

Let the Temp'rance reformation
　　Still go forward and increase,
Checking vice and dissipation,
　　Filling hearts and homes with peace,
　　　　　　　Till intemp'rance
Shall on earth for ever cease.

POETRY, SONGS, AND HYMNS.

STANDARD.
Tune—"Zion."

Round the Temp'rance Standard rally,
  All the friends of human kind;
Snatch the devotees of folly,
  Wretched, perishing, and blind—
          Loudly tell them
  How they comfort now may find.

Bear the blissful tidings onwards,
  Bear them all the world around;
Let the myriads thronging downwards
  Hear the sweet and blissful sound,
          And obeying,
  In the paths of peace be found.

Plant the Temp'rance Standard firmly,
  Round it live, and round it die;
Young and old, defend it sternly,
  Till we gain the victory,
          And all nations
  Hail the happy Jubilee.

Now unto the Lamb for ever,
  Fountain of all light and love,
Let the glory, now and ever,
  Be ascribed to Him above,
          Whose compassion
  Did the friends of Temp'rance move.

STOP AND THINK.

Stop, ye drinkers, stop and think,
  Before you further go;
Will you sport upon the brink
  Of everlasting woe?
On the verge of ruin stop;
  Now the friendly warning take:
Stay your footsteps—ere you drop
  Into the burning lake.

Ghastly death will quickly come,
   And drag you to his bar;
Then to hear your awful doom
   Will fill you with despair!
All your sins will round you crowd,
   You shall mark their crimson dye,
Each for vengeance crying loud,
   And what can you reply?

Tho' your heart were made of steel,
   Your forehead lined with brass,
God at length will make you feel
   He will not let you pass:
Drunkards then in vain will call,
   Those who now despise his grace,
"Rocks and mountains on us fall,
   And hide us from his face."

TEMPERANCE TRUMPET.
Tune—"Grace."

The Temp'rance Trumpet blow,
   That all may hear the sound,
And shun the drunkard's wretched way
   For paths where bliss is found.

The Temp'rance Trumpet blow,
   And bid the young come near:
Youth is the time to serve the Lord
   With zeal and humble fear.

The Temp'rance Trumpet blow,
   That all with hoary hairs
The cup of death may now renounce,
   And 'scape its countless snares.

The Temp'rance Trumpet blow,
   That all may hear and flee
The drunkard's path of woe and shame,
   And endless misery.

THE WIDOW'S APPEAL.

Stay, stay thy hand—Oh! tempt him not,
  For he is all that's left to me,
The sunshine of my lonely lot,
  The partner of my misery—
    My youngest born,
      His father's pride—
    Oh! tempt him not,
      Take all beside.

Take all beside, but leave my boy,
  Nor tempt him with the accursed bowl;
He is the widow's only joy,
  The solace of her troubled soul.
    Father and friend
      Thy victim fell—
    Oh! spare the boy
      I love so well.

Thrice have I seen the cold grave yawn,
  And swallow, in its darksome gloom,
The forms I've loved from earliest dawn—
  And thou, alas, didst seal their doom.
    The tempting bowl
      Thy hand didst hold,
    And all was done
      For paltry gold.

Those painful scenes I can forget,
  This bruised heart can heal again,
And burning tears shall no more wet
  These pallid cheeks, so sunk with pain.
    All is forgiven,
      If thou'lt but swear,
    By hope of heaven,
      Thou wilt forbear,

And tempt no more my darling boy
  To taste those bitter dregs of woe,
No more the mother's peace destroy;
  But onward let thy footsteps go

To seek the lost
 From virtue's ways,
And joy shall crown
Thy future days.

THE TEMPTER.
Tune—"Devizes."

I hate the Tempter and his charms,
 I hate his flattering breath;
The serpent takes a thousand forms
 To lead our souls to death.

He feeds our hopes with airy dreams,
 Or kills with slavish fear;
And holds us still in wide extremes,
 Presumption or despair.

Now he persuades, How easy 'tis
 To walk the road to heaven;
Anon he swells our sins, and cries,
 They cannot be forgiven.

Almighty God! cut short his power,
 Let him in darkness dwell;
And, that he vex the earth no more,
 Confine him down to hell.

VOICE FROM HEAVEN.
Tune—"Peckham."

I heard a voice from heaven
 Address the thoughtless throng,
Who hasten downward to the tomb
 With revelry and song.

It warned them not to quench
  The holy light within,
And madly dare the fearful doom
  Of unrepented sin.

It warned them of the shame
  That haunts the drunkard's grave,
And of that leprosy of soul
  From which no skill can save.

I looked, and thousands fled
  The tempter's fatal snare;
But some were number'd with the dead—
  Who shall their doom declare?

THE FUNERAL.
Tune—"Balerma."

Mournful and sad upon my ear
  The death-bell echoes stole;
And painful memories opened all
  The feelings of my soul.

The knell—the knell—it told of woe
  That words cannot reveal—
Of desolate and broken hearts,
  Where grief had set his seal.

Again it pealed—and on the air
  It swelled and died along;
And to the dwelling of the dead
  There came a weeping throng.

In tattered weeds, with trembling steps,
  The widow led the train;
And her poor orphans followed on,
  Sad sharers of her pain.

Ashes to ashes, dust to dust,
　Clay to its kindred clay—
They left the dead—and wailed and wept,
　And slowly moved away.

But ah! there hung a heavy cloud
　Upon that husband's name;
And deep disgrace had settled down
　Upon that father's fame.

There was a keenness in their grief—
　A death-shade in their gloom—
As, desolate and fatherless,
　They left the Drunkard's Tomb.

COLD WATER.

By Mrs. Sigourney.

The thirsty flowerets droop; the parching grass
Doth crisp beneath the feet, and the wan trees
Perish for lack of moisture. By the side
Of the dried rills, the herds despairing stand,
With tongues protruded. Summer's fiery heat,
Exhaling, checks the thousand springs of life.

——— Mark ye yon cloud glide forth on angel wing?
Heard ye the herald drops, with gentle force,
Stir the broad leaves? and the protracted rain,
Waking the streams to run their tuneful way?
Saw ye the flocks rejoice, and did ye fail
To thank the God of fountains?

See,—the hart
Pant for the water-brooks. The fervid sun
Of Asia glitters on his leafy lair,
As, fearful of the lion's wrath, he hastes,
With timid footsteps, through the whispering reeds,
Quick leaping to the renovating stream;
The copious draught his bounding veins inspires
With joyous vigor.
            Patient o'er the sand,
The burden-bearer of the desert clime,
The camel toileth. Faint with deadly thirst,
His writhing neck of bitter anguish speaks.
Lo! an oasis, and a tree-girt well!—
And, moved by powerful instinct, on he speeds,
With agonizing haste, to drink, or die.
On his swift courser, o'er the burning wild,
The Arab cometh. From his eager eye
Flashes desire. Seeks he the sparkling wine,
Giving its golden color to the cup?
No! to the gushing stream he flies, and deep
Buries his scorching lip, and laves his brow,
And blesses Allah.
            Christian pilgrim, come!
Thy brother of the Koran's broken creed
Shall teach *thee* wisdom, and, with courteous hand,
Nature, thy mother, holds the crystal cup,
And bids thee pledge her in the clement
Of temperance and health.
            Drink and be whole,
And purge the fever poison from thy veins,
And pass, in purity and peace, to taste
The river flowing from the throne of God.

DASH IT DOWN!

To earth the cup be hurled,
That holds an adder's sting;
And let us pledge the world
With nectar from the spring,
That hence, like Rechab's ancient line,
Though prophets urge, we drink no wine!

THE YOUNG WIFE'S LAST APPEAL.
By J. L. Chester.

"Oh, husband, husband, go not out
   Again, this stormy night;
For snowy clouds have hid the earth
   Within a robe of white.
Hark to the whistling winds, that scream
   Like fiends amid their glee,
And now, subdued, they seem to moan
   A dirge-like melody.

"Oh, husband, husband, do not leave
   Our fire, so bright and warm,
To brave the darkness of the night,
   And danger of the storm.
The fire, it burneth pleasantly
   Upon our tidy hearth—
We may be happy here to-night,
   And join in peaceful mirth.

"Think of the many joyous hours
   We have together spent,
When to my grief your gentle voice
   A charm of music lent.
Think of the holy book we read,
   Ere we in prayer did bow;
And here it is—the same good book—
   Come, read it to me now.

"Look in the cradle, husband, look!
   There sleeps our baby boy;
He wakes—he wakes—to look on thee,
   And curl his lip in joy.
Oh, husband, go not out to-night—
   Thy wife, thy child entreat;
Our eve shall be a pleasant one,
   And our enjoyment sweet!"

He heeded not the fond appeal,
　　But thrust his wife aside—
That gentle being who had been
　　But one short year a bride.
He braved the snow—he faced the storm,
　　And journeyed o'er the plain,
But never to his wife and child
　　The drunkard came again.

THE WIFE'S APPEAL.

By W. C. Bennett.

Winter—A Street outside an Alehouse—A Working Man, his Wife, and Child.

Oh, don't go in to-night, John,—
　　Now, husband, don't go in!
To spend our only shilling, John,
　　Would be a cruel sin.
There's not a loaf at home, John—
　　There's not a coal, you know—
Though with hunger I am faint, John,
　　And cold comes down the snow.
　　　　Then don't go in to-night!

Ah, John, you must remember—
　　And, John, I can't forget,—
When never foot of yours, John,
　　Was in the alehouse set.
Ah, those were happy times, John,
　　No quarrels then we knew,
And none were happier in our lane
　　Than I, dear John, and you.
　　　　Then don't go in to-night!

You will not go!—John, John, I mind
  When we were courting, few
Had arm as strong, or step as firm,
  Or cheek as red as you;
But drink has stolen your strength, John,
  And paled your cheek to white,
Has tottering made your young firm tread,
  And bowed your manly height.
            You'll not go in to-night?

You'll not go in?—Think on the day
  That made me, John, your wife;
What pleasant talk that day we had
  Of all our future life!
Of how your steady earnings, John,
  No wasting should consume,
But weekly some new comfort bring
  To deck our happy room.
            Then don't go in to-night!

To see us, John, as then we dressed,
  So tidy, clean, and neat,
Brought out all eyes to follow us
  As we went down the street.
Ah, little thought our neighbors then,
  And we as little thought,
That ever, John, to rags like these,
  By drink we shou'd be brought.
            You won't go in to-night!

And will you go? If not for me,
  Yet for your baby stay;—
You know, John, not a taste of food
  Has passed my lips to-day;
And tell your father, little one,
  'Tis mine your life hangs on.
You will not spend the shilling, John?
  You'll give it him? Come, John,
            Come home with us to-night!

[*Goes home and reforms.*

PART FOURTH.

THE TEETOTALER'S HAND-BOOK.

FACTS AND ANECDOTES.

ADULTERATION OF BRANDY, GIN, WINE, BEER, ETC., ETC.

There are many reasons why every state and nation should prohibit the manufacture and sale of intoxicating drinks to be used as a beverage; but, waiving every other consideration, the known adulteration of all kinds of liquors that intoxicate should be reason enough for the most stringent laws to prohibit their sale.

Brandy.—This liquor is almost universally a base imposition. The imported article, as a general fact, is adulterated. Unadulterated brandy cannot be sold at less than about two dollars and fifty cents the gallon; the adulterated can be made at about thirty cents per gallon, and so disguised *that no one can tell the difference.* The dealers cannot, nor do they resist the temptation to adulterate, where the gain is so enormous. Chemical compounds are now made and sold to fabricators for making spurious brandy out of common whisky; the whisky itself, often drugged with arsenic.

A dealer in spurious brandy recently imported enough of these compounds to manufacture eight hundred hogsheads of the forged article. He sold it for pure, and at $2 50 the gallon; making a clear profit, as he confessed, of $100,000 on the speculation, the fabricated article costing him only about thirty cents a gallon. The fabricator having used up his compound to his samples, took these to a chemist in Massachusetts for analysis, and for the purpose of having them made in this country, if possible. The chemist made the examination, and found one of the samples a deadly poison: he could not be tempted to have a hand in producing the mixtures. Whether the fabricator found a chemist less honest, or had to wait for a new importation, will not, probably, be made known until the day of judgment, when all such secrets will be made manifest. Who can begin to estimate the results of the use of the contents of these eight hundred casks on those who had the folly to drink them?

Another man, who had either imported or purchased the same kind of compounds, went to California with them; and he boasted to a gentleman, who mentioned it to the writer, that he should make $100,000 out of the operation.

A quantity of French brandy was imported into New-York, and advertised for sale at auction on a given day: it was landed on the wharf. A brandy fabricator purchased the whole lot of the importer, on the condition that the sale should take place as advertised, and *on his account.* During the night it was all removed to his brandy brewery, underwent the process of adulteration, was carted back, and sold next day, *pure as imported.*

A large dealer in Albany declared that when *he* purchased foreign liquors in New-York, on shipboard, he had no confidence in getting the article purchased, unless he watched the casks from the ship to the boat on the river. In former years it was supposed that imported liquors were generally pure; but now this opinion has exploded. The process of adulteration is carried on to a vast extent in Europe, and it is doubtful whether one gallon in one hundred is now landed on our shores in a pure state; and if in a pure state, just so far as it is intoxicating it is worthless and injurious, as a beverage; and none should be drank as such by any human being wishing long life or a healthful body. In a work published by the celebrated chemist, Frederick Accum, London, on adulteration, and dedicated to the Duke of Northumberland, the practices of brandy, gin, beer, and wine fabricators were pretty fully exposed; but as we live in an age of *great progress,* the fabricators of the present day have doubtless entirely eclipsed those of the past. Accum gives the following method of compounding, or *making up*, as it is technically called, *brandy* for retail:—

	Galls.
" To ten puncheons of brandy	1081
Add flavored raisin spirit	118
Tincture of grains of paradise	4
Cherry laurel water	2
Spirit of almond cake	2
	1207

Add also ten handfuls of oak saw-dust, and give it *complexion* with burned sugar."

Gin.—The same author, speaking of this article says: " To prepare and sweeten gin, &c., oil of vitrol, oil of almonds, oil of turpentine, oil of juniper berries, lime water, alum, salt of tartar, and sub-acetate of lead are used. Sulphate of lead is poisonous. I have reason to believe the use of it is frequent, because its action is more rapid, and it imparts to the liquor a fine *complexion;* hence some vestiges of lead may often be detected in malt liquor."

Rum.—As with brandy and gin, so with rum. If whisky will sell for more money under the name of *rum* than under the name of *whisky*, it is as easy to turn whisky into rum as into brandy gin, or wine.

Wine.—Here the fabricators make their greatest profits, exercise their greatest skill and probably do the greatest amount of injury. Unadulterated wine, according to its name and quality, must command a certain price to make it worth dealing in. The fabricator's ingenuity is put to the greatest trial to produce an article resembling the pure, so as to obtain as near as possible, the price of the pure; and as it is impossible to distinguish the pure from impure, and as the impure can be made at one-tenth to one-quarter of the value of the pure, the impure, as a natural consequence, *takes the place* of the pure; the same as the bogus dollar would take the place of the pure silver dollar, provided it was settled by common consent a dollar was a dollar, whether bogus or not.

Says Dr. Nott: "I had a friend who had been once a wine dealer, and having read the startling statements made public in relation to the brewing of wines, and the adulterations of other liquors, generally, I enquired of that friend of the verity of those statements. His reply was, '*God forgive what has passed in* MY OWN *cellar, but the statements made are* TRUE, *and* ALL TRUE, *I assure you.*'"

The process of adulteration is carried on in wine countries, as well as in this country, with regard to Madeira, sherry, claret, and all other kinds of wine.

The Rev. Dr. Baird has stated that "little or no wine is drank in France in a pure state, except it may be at the wine-press. The dealers purchase it at the vineyards in a pure state, but in their hands it is entirely changed, by adding drugs or distilled spirits."

Horatio Greenough, the eminent sculptor, says, "that although wine can be had in Florence at one cent a bottle, the dealers do not hesitate to add drugs and water, to gain a fraction more of profit."

Champagne.—Some cider or whisky, some water, some fixed air, some sugar of lead, &c., form the compound. When this fabricated mixture circulates in the country, it is generally sold as pure, and our young men often quaff it at two dollars the bottle, and an advance on the original cost of only eleven hundred per cent!

A physician in New-York purchased a bottle of what was called genuine champagne of the importers, and had it subjected to chemical tests: it was found to contain a *quarter of an ounce of sugar of lead.* Who would like to drink a mixture of sugar of lead and water?

A gentleman in New-York, who made champagne, purchased some of the regular importer, wishing to give his friends some of the genuine article. At a convivial party he produced his *pure as imported*. When the corks began to fly, one dropped near him; on examining it, he found it was his own fabrication. The supposed importer had purchased it, and, by his French tinsel and French labels, sold it back, as pure, to the original fabricator—*biting* the *biter*. But enough of champagne.

Port.—An Episcopal clergyman, recently returned from the continent of Europe, visited an immense manufactory of all kinds of wine. Logwood came in as a great ingredient; so great that the proprietors kept a vessel in their employ for its importation.

The dyers in Manchester (England) say, "The wine brewers are running away with all the best logwood;" and the London people say, "If you wish to get genuine *Port*, you must go yourself to Oporto, *make your own wine*, and ride outside of the barrel all the way home."

We end our statements as to the brandy, gin, rum, whisky, and wine fabrications, and close with the last, the most filthy, and most disgusting of the whole tribe of intoxicating drinks.

Beer.—The very name of it creates a loathing in the stomach of the writer, a kind of upheaving of disgust, not unlike that of seasickness: the celebrated Beer Trial between John Taylor and Edward C. Delavan sheds some light on the filthy materials used in its manufacture. We give, for the benefit of beer drinkers, some of the testimony:—

Hon. John Savage, late Chief Justice of the State, testified thus: "The water was *always dirty;* never saw it otherwise. *My horse refused to drink it. I have seen dead animals there;* and I believe I have seen dogs, cats, and hogs. The *filth* from the slaughter-house yard was then running and oozing into the creek; the snow was going off; at any rate the slaughter-house was wet, *and I could see filth and water mixed, running into the stream.*"

Thomas Coulson (class-leader in the Methodist Church) testifies: "The water in the pond was *always bad*—in a putrid state in the fall of the year. What was in the water—anything to make it bad? Different kinds of animals floating in the water. In the warmth of the weather *the water was green.* Dogs, and cats, and hogs I've seen. Did you ever try to make glue of that water? *It would not do for that.* Why not? It was what I call *rotten water.*"

WORTHY OF THEIR FOUNDER.—At the Conference of Wesleyan Methodists, recently held at Massachusetts, reports of committees on temperance and tract distribution, were presented and adopted. The report on temperance was short and to the point. It declared that the use of intoxicating liquors as a beverage was an *immorality*, and that it ought to be so regarded by the christian church; that the making and selling of them, to be used as a beverage, was a *crime of the highest order*, and should be so considered by the civil and ecclesiastical law; and that to secure the complete triumph of temperance, its friends should unite their efforts in their social and political capacities, and in no case to consider themselves at liberty to support in business or promote to office, men who are opposed to the temperance enterprise. It concluded with the following:—' Whereas true temperance implies a total abstinence from all things injurious to health, and only a moderate use of those things which tend to promote it, resolved: That while we advocate and practice total abstinence from all intoxicating liquors, we will also, everywhere by *example*, and on all proper occasions by *precept*, discountenance the vulgar use of *tobacco.*'"

OPINIONS OF MEDICAL MEN, MISSIONARIES, AND OTHERS, AS TO THE DESTRUCTION OF LIFE CAUSED BY ALCOHOLIC LIQUORS. —" There are upwards of 600,000 drunkards in Great Britain, 60,000 of whom die every year."—*Parliamentary Report on Drunkenness.*

"The art of preparing liquors is the greatest curse ever inflicted on humanity."—*Dr. Paris.*

" Intoxicating liquors, in all their forms, and however disguised, are the most productive cause of disease with which I am acquainted."—*Dr. Trotter.*

"I repeat it again and again, that alcohol, in all its forms and combinations, whether in the carefully home-brewed, or in the wine that sparkles, is never converted into nourishment."—*A. Courtney, Surgeon, Royal Navy.*

"Under the name of rum, brandy, gin, whisky, wine, cider, beer, and porter, alcohol is become the bane of the Christian world."—*Dr. Darwin.*

"If a man beginning at twenty, were to take one large glassful of spirits regularly every day, he would thereby affect the duration of his life, probably *abridging* it by at least ten years."—*Dr. Cheyne.*

"The use of spirits, even in the greatest moderation, tends to shorten life."—*Professor Hitchcock.*

"Whilst hundreds and thousands have committed suicide by the agency of hemp and steel, tens of thousands have *destroyed* themselves by intoxicating drinks."—*J. Beaumont, Surgeon.*

"The frequent consumption of a small quantity of spirits, gradually increased, is as surely destructive *of life* as more habitual intoxication; and, therefore, the publicans are spreading disease and death to a degree that is frightful."—*Dr. Gordon.*

"Unnatural excitement, by means of strong liquors, occasions a proportionate exhaustion of the vital powers, a diminished capacity for subsequent exertion, a premature old age, a life of suffering, and an early grave."—*Dr. Carrick.*

"Two-thirds of the diseases and *deaths* of Europeans in India are in consequence of their indulging in the use of spirituous liquors, and exposing themselves unnecessarily to the sun during the heat of the day."—*W. Burke, Inspector-General of H. M. Hospitals.*

Dr. Gordon of the London Hospital, in his evidence before the parliamentary committee, stated, from accounts he had kept of the thousands of sick cases coming under his observation during the year, that there were sixty-five out of every hundred clearly arising from strong drink.

In Edinburgh, though we cannot state positively that the sudden deaths, and deaths from apoplexy, in the following list, were caused by drunkenness, yet the general experience of medical men is, that the greatest proportion of such are. The following list of deaths for 1846, is taken from Dr. Stark's tables of mortality:—

Sudden deaths	14
Apoplexy	81
Intemperance	7
Violent deaths and suicides	125
	227

Dr. Tait states that nearly one-half of the accidents, and seventy-three out of every hundred suicides, or attempted suicides, were caused by strong drink. From investigations we have made we are persuaded that instead of seven deaths by intemperance, there is upwards of four hundred deaths from drink in Edinburgh every year.

Read over these facts and opinions of men who have no interest in stating untruths, and add the following testimony of the Rev. J. Williams, Missionary to the South Sea Islands:—" The depopulation of the South Sea Islands has been *most fearful;* but I am not aware that it is traceable to the operation of the cruelty of Europeans. It is traceable, in a great measure, to the demoralizing effects of intercourse with the Europeans—the introduction of ardent spirits and fire arms."

Also from the parliamentary report on aboriginal tribes:—" The copper Indians, through ill-management, *intemperance,* and vice, are said to have decreased, within the last five years, to one-half the number of what they were."

Thus, you see, wherever the natives of our land go, they carry the pestilence along with them; while we who live in the midst of thousands of dying drunkards have become so accustomed to the sight, that it excites no wonder, no effort, to save sixty thousand drunkards from their grave.

STRONG DRINK AND INSANITY.—The healthy operations of the brain are materially hindered by drinking intoxicating liquors.

Inflammation and engorgement are frequent consequences of the use of alcoholic drinks, and may take place at the time of a debauch, or arise some time afterwards, during the stage of debility, from a loss of the healthy balance of action in the system. Inflammation of the organ, when it is acute, is usually attended with furious delirium and other indications of high cerebral excitement. In support of these observations we would direct attention to the following testimonies:—

The use of fermented liquors, and particularly of spirits, is very conducive to the bringing on of insanity; they first act on the stomach, then on the nervous system; they bring on diseased action; disorganization of the brain is the consequence, and all the dreadful results of insanity follow. Out of twenty-eight cases admitted at the Middlesex Lunatic Asylum last year, that were reported to us as having been recent cases, *nineteen* of the twenty-eight were drunkards."—*Dr. Ellis.*

"Among four hundred and ninety-five patients admitted, in four years, into a Lunatic Asylum, at Liverpool, two hundred and fifty-seven were known to have lost their reason by drunkenness."

"Dr. Hallaran ascertained, that at the Cork Lunatic Asylum, out of three hundred and eighty-three male patients, one hundred and three had become deranged through the excessive drinking of whisky."

"In Scotland, where they drink about three times the quantity of spirits that is consumed in England, the number of insane persons is about three to one, as compared with the number in England."—*Parliamentary Report.*

"The intellectual faculties are impaired by alcohol. Every excess is a voluntary insanity, and if often repeated, and carried beyond a certain degree, it often produces the horrible disease called *delirium tremens*, in which, while the animal powers are prostrated, the mind is tortured with the most distressing and fearful imagination."—*Forty Physicians of the State of New York.*

"No man," says an eminent physician, "who has taken only a

single glass, has all his faculties in as perfect a state as the man who takes none."

The Earl of Shaftsbury, after having been a commissioner of Lunacy for twenty years, made the following statement at a meeting held at Manchester:—"I state that having had the whole of the Commission under my personal observation and care, having made enquiries into the matter, and having fortified them by inquiries in America which have confirmed the inquiries made in this country, the result is, that fully six-tenths of all the cases of insanity to be found in these realms and in America, arise from no other cause than the habits of intemperance in which the people have indulged."

LOOK AT THIS, SAILORS!—Captain Ross, in the Arctic regions, induced all his men to discontinue the use of the accustomed grog; the result was they acknowledged themselves better, and more capable of enduring cold, and discharging their duty, than when they indulged the use of it. Dr. Hooker says, "The use of spirits in cold weather is generally prejudicial. It is pleasant and enticing, but does no good. The extremities are not warmed by it; and you are colder and more fatigued a quarter or half-hour after, than you would have been without it." He adds, "Several men on board our ship, and amongst them some of the best, never touched grog during the ant-arctic cruises. They used coffee instead. They were not a whit the worse for their abstinence, but enjoyed perfect health throughout the four years' voyage." "All hands on board the Hawberry brig *Julia*, a south-sea whaler, shipped under the condition that whosoever should be seen intoxicated, whether on board or ashore, should lose his wages. No spirit rations were given out; but, instead, coffee twice, and tea once a day. In cold weather the crew received at night ginger-tea, prepared for every watch twice. The captain remarked that he had never seen a stronger or healthier crew on board any vessel of her size." "The brig *Canada*, Capt. Hardie, ran 63,560 *miles in* 586 *days*, and crossed almost all habitable latitudes. This was more than twice the distance round the world. She had sixteen hands on board, who never, during the whole time, used any intoxicating liquors, and who all returned hence without a day's sickness." "The brig *Globe* has lately returned from a voyage to the Pacific Ocean. She had on board a crew of ten persons, and was absent nearly eighteen months. During the voyage she was in nearly all climates of the world. She had not one sick on board, and brought back all the crew orderly and obedient. All these advantages Captain Moore attributes in a great measure to the absence of spirituous liquors. There was not a drop on board the vessel." "Captain Pearce, of the ship *Cambridge*, of Bristol, stated that he left Hull with a crew of twenty-four men, and that he never used a drop of ardent spirits, nor did he suffer it to be on board. He returned to Liverpool, and his men's health was improved; his pilot said he had never seen a ship in such order." "The Rev. William Scoresby, of Exeter, who was engaged in the Arctic whale fishery twenty-one years, has stated he did not use ardent spirits, and he believes he was better far without them." "Mr. Mimpriss states, when he was purser on board a convict ship, they took out to Botany-Bay nearly three hundred females in one vessel. These convicts were not allowed any other beverage than water, while the crew had their regular allowance of grog. All the convicts were in health during the seven months' voyage. Several of the crew died on the passage; and of the remainder, several were reported sick on landing." "In the year 1619, an English crew of twenty-two men, entered Hudson's Bay without ardent spirits—exposed to the cold—and only two of them died. Other Englishmen have done the same since with spirits, and have not returned to their native land." "Sir John Richardson, the great Arctic traveller, says, "I am quite satisfied that spirituous liquors diminish the power of resisting cold." "Dr. Trotter, late physician to Lord Howe's fleet says, "Human blood and healthful chyle do not acknowledge alcohol to be an ingredient in its composition."

STRANGE BUT TRUE.—King Alcohol's advocates fall when he attempts to support them.

THE PRICE OF BLOOD.—The coin of the dealer in strong drink should be inscribed, "This certifies that the bearer has made a man beat his wife." "This half-crown is a memorial of four nights of wretchedness, which were given to a whole family in exchange for it." "This bag of money certifies, that the possessor has sent two of his neighbors to the jail, and their wives and children to the poor-house." What money for a man to hold in his coffers! It is "the price of *blood!*"

FATHER MATHEW'S CONVERSION TO TEETOTALISM.—For some time previous to the year 1838, William Martin, of Cork, now well known as the "father of Father Mathew," had repeatedly urged Mr. Mathew to give his influence to the temperance society which had been formed in Cork, and of which G. W. Carr, Esq., and others were members. To these solicitations Mr. Mathew listened with his usual candour and politeness; but it was not until April of the year just mentioned that the time appeared to have arrived for the commencement of his glorious career. One Sunday evening, as Mr. Martin was seated with his family in the parlour in Patrick Street, a messenger came from Mr. Mathew, requesting Mr. Martin's company. On the arrival of the latter, Father Mathew said,—" Mr. Martin, I have sent for you to help me in forming a society." " With all my heart," said Mr. Martin; " when shall we begin ?" " To-morrow." The place and time of meeting was at once appointed, and the meeting was held accordingly. Father Mathew presided. After he had explained the object of the meeting, and various addresses had been delivered, he signed the pledge, and about sixty others followed his example. During the meeting an interesting incident occurred, illustrative of the catholic spirit which has ever distinguished the labors of the great Irish reformer. Hearing some whispers at the table, he observed to Mr. Martin, who sat next to him, "What do you think they are saying ?" "They say— 'Here is a Catholic Priest sitting between a Presbyterian minister and a member of the Society of Friends.' " " Well," said Mr. Martin, " is it not pleasant that there is *one* place where we can meet without distinction of creed, and unite in the one object of doing good?" "It is, indeed," rejoined Father Mathew; "and there is *another place*, too, where I hope we shall all unite in like manner." Such was the origin of the "Cork Total Abstinence Society," from which such wonderful results have flowed.

DEATH OF ALEXANDER.—When Alexander was at Babylon, after having spent a whole night in carousing, a second feast was proposed to him. He went accordingly, and there were twenty guests at the table. He drank the health of every person in the company, and then pledged them severally. After this, calling for Hercules' cup, (which held an incredible quantity,) it was filled, when he poured it all down, drinking to a Macedonian of the company, Proteas by name; and afterwards pledged him in the same extravagant bumper. He had no sooner swallowed it than he fell upon the floor. "Here, then," cried Seneca, describing the fatal effects of drunkenness, "the hero unconquered by the toils of prodigious marches, exposed to the dangers of sieges and combats, to the most violent extremes of heat and cold, here he lies, subdued by his intemperance, struck to the earth by the fatal cup of Hercules." In this condition he was seized with a fever, which, in a few days terminated in death. No one, says Plutarch Arria, then suspected that Alexander was poisoned; the true poison which brought him to his end was wine, which has killed many thousands besides Alexander.

THE TENDENCY OF THE TRAFFIC.—A gentleman in Cincinnati is in possession of the names of all the liquor dealers in two streets of that city for the last fifteen years. There were sixty-seven in all, of which number fifty-three are dead—and *forty-six of them died drunk!* One hundred and fifty of the convicts in the Ohio State Prison, and seventy-six in the Connecticut Penitentiary, have occupied the unenviable position of standing behind the bar. The proportion of rumsellers destroyed by their own business is fearfully great, and should warn those who regard their happiness from entering upon so unhallowed an enterprise.

BEER-HOUSES.—At the Romney Agricultural Meeting, under the presidency of Lord Palmerston, the Rev. A. Moore, in returning thanks to the bishop and clergy of the diocese, said he could not help adverting to a movement that was now going on in the parish of Romney. They might laugh at the Temperance movement, but he had known many whose persons and habitations formerly exhibited the greatest degradation, poverty, and misery. Since these persons had joined the Temperance movement he had gone into cottage after cottage, and had found husbands and wives who used to live like dogs and cats, but who now abstained from the habit of drinking, living in domestic happiness, comfort and cheerfulness—(hear.) In Romney, with a population of 5,660 persons, there were 1,235 houses, 52 of which were public houses and beer-houses. There was, therefore, a public house or beer-house to every 112 persons, and one to every 23 houses. He once thought that his parish was one of the worst in the kingdom, but he had seen some reason to modify this opinion. The beer-houses next required attention. Some of his Rev. brethren wished them to be put under the control of the magistrates. For himself he should rejoice to see every beer-house put down. Without a more efficient control over them the labors of the clergy were in vain—(hear.) 1859.

YOUNG MEN RUINED.—The young men of our land are being ruined by thousands. It is astonishing what inroads intemperance is now making into the very best classes of our youth, and how imperceptibly the baneful vice of drinking is creeping into what is called good society. We do not mean that whisky or brandy is drank, but we do mean that the course of beer drinking is rapidly working the ruin of those young men, whom all have so long loved for their intellectual and moral worth.

Never, in the history of the fell destroyer, has there been so much cause to mourn over the fallen youth of our land, as at present. Here, in the streets of Chicago young men, scarcely thirty years of age, wear upon their faces the rum blossom of three score years of olden time; and the carbuncled nose tells a tale that only the toper of fifty could have blazoned forth a few years since. At the same time there are hundreds in our midst who are imbibing the slops of the brewery, who can see no deleterious effects resulting from the use of such mild and fashionable drinks and are scarcely conscious of their ruinous course.

We have no time to waste upon the question as to whether lager beer will intoxicate; for common sense will teach any man that it is impossible to brew it without some per-centage of alcohol. If such a view is not satisfactory, the aspect which the guzzlers present when they are filled, is enough to satisfy any one of the votaries of the beverage just imbibed. The fact is, this lager is not only intoxicating but is so drugged, as to add to its baneful effects, and is the means of under-mining the health of thousands on thousands, implanting the insatiable appetite for stronger drinks, palsying the noblest resolve of noble hearts, and ruining the bodies and souls of the choicest youth of our city and country.

Must we give up these young men? Shall they crowd the road to ruin, as now, uncared for, save by a few whose means are powerless to save? Or will the church arouse, will temperance men awake, will every good citizen bestir himself, and all work for the salvation of our youth? The time has come for thought and for action.—*North-Western Home Journal, March,* 1859.

How to Rise in Life.—About eight years ago, there was a drunken hatter in great disgrace and misery. He signed the Temperance pledge, and then went to work to raise himself in society. Having got employment he toiled hard to save a few pounds, with which he opened a shop in London. His business increased, and he employed a man to help him. More business and more men followed, until he had opened three shops. He has now a prosperous business, a beautiful home, a happy mind, and (to use his own language) "can pay twenty shillings to the pound." He is a clever lecturer on Temperance, and likely to prove a rich, wise, and very useful man.

ASYLUM FOR INEBRIATES.—An exchange remarks:—"The State of New York has set her sister States a good example in the establishment of an Asylum for Inebriates." We hope the good example will be improved until every state, every county, every city and every village where the demon's drink is tolerated, has its asylum for inebriates. Strict justice between man and man, however, seems to require that the rumsellers, who alone have all the benefit of reducing a fellow-creature to poverty and shame, should take care of him afterward. But as they do not choose to do this, and as those who allow the rumsellers to thus destroy members of the social compact are hardly less culpable than the rumsellers themselves, it is clearly their duty to provide a place where the wreck of humanity, when no longer profitable to the rumsellers, shall be taken care of. To-be-sure, a better plan than building asylums for rum-drinkers might be devised as, for example, penitentiaries for rumsellers. And it has been suggested, occasionally, by some "temperance fanatic," who don't know enough even to drink moderately, and then leave off altogether the very moment he finds that he can't govern himself, that if there was no rum trade there would be no need for asylums for drunkards.

But isn't rum property? Haven't millions of dollars been invested in it? If the merchant invests his dollars in rum, is not rum the representative of his dollars? Who is to meddle with the sacred rights of property? Humanity before property? Fudge! As society is now constituted, every man has a right to sell whatever he pleases, especially if it is rum. Suppose there are half a million of drunkards in the United States. It only wants six thousand inebriate asylums to sober them in; and then, when they have got cured, and have become industrious citizens, with a little change in their pockets, the rumsellers will very soon relieve them of their newly acquired cash and character, and send them back to the asylum again. So build asylums, good, benevolent, shortsighted mortals, but don't meddle with the grog-shops.
—*Life Illustrated*.

HISTORY OF A DISTILLERY.—What if the history of a distillery could be written out—so much rum for medicine of real value; so much for the parts of real value. That would be one drop, I suppose, taken out and shaken from the distillery. Then so much rum sold to the Indians, to excite them to scalp one another; so much sent to the Africans to be changed into slaves to rot in Cuba and Brazil; so much sent to the heathens in Asia, and to the Islands of the ocean; and so much used at home. Then if the tale of every drop could be written out—so much pain, so much redness of eyes, so much diminution of productive power in man; so many houses burnt, ships foundered, and railway trains dashed to pieces; so many lives lost; so many widows made, doubly widows because their husbands still live; so many orphans—their fathers yet living, long dying on the earth—what a tale it would be! Imagine that all the persons who had suffered from torments engendered on that plague-spot came together and sat on the ridge-pole and roof, and filled up the large hall of that distillery, and occupied the streets and lanes about it, and told their tales of drunkenness, robbery, unchastity, and murder, written on their faces and foreheads. What a story it would be, the fact stranger than fiction!

LEGAL SUPPRESSION FIFTY-SEVEN YEARS SINCE.—"A few years ago," writes Dr. Trotter in 1803, " the crops of grain were so deficient over this island that the distillery of spirits from malt was prohibited; and thus scarcity, bordering on famine, became a blessing to the human race. But no sooner had fruitful seasons and the bounty of providence-covered the earth with plenty, than the first gift of heaven—abundance of corn—was again, for the sake of taxation, converted into poisonous spirits, by opening the distilleries. Might not other taxes be devised that would be equally productive? *and would it not be a virtuous act of the legislature to abolish the practice forever?*" On page 49 Dr. Trotter states,—" During my residence at Plymouth Dock, towards the conclusion of the late war, I had the satisfaction of getting 200 gin-shops shut up. They were destroying the very vitals of our naval service. In the year 1800 not less than £1,400,000 prize money was paid at that port to the seamen; and every trick was practised to entrap those credulous and unthinking people. An overgrown brewer who had monopolized a number of these houses complained heavily of my representations to the Admiralty, and said that he had lost £5,000 by the business."

FEMALE INTEMPERANCE.—" To those of the other sex who happen to be addicted to the bottle, the hysteric affection is very apt to occur during the paroxysm of inebriety. There are few female drunkards that do not experience this; for as pure spirits are easiest to inflame, so slight irritations that ruffle the temper, and excite anger, are seldom quieted without some degree of hysteric passion. In several cases, the frequent appearance of this affection has first led me to detect the unhappy propensity. That modesty which is innate in the female constitution, preserves them from indulgence in company (in respectable circles) and they are commonly solitary drinkers. This delicacy of feeling sometimes carries them great lengths in concealing their situation, and in making them feign complaints to ward off suspicion. I have known a medical attendant acquire much credit from the administration of his catholican, when a gentle nap had performed the cure of an indisposition of (the cause of) which he formed no conjecture."—*Dr. Trotter.*

A FINE OLD MAN.—There is now living at Tetford (says the *Stamford Mercury*) a man, ninety years old, who worked for many years as a journeyman fellmonger in Mr. Allenby's yard at Horncastle; he can carry twenty stone weight at the present time, can walk four miles in an hour, and he has drank nothing stronger than water for the last forty years. 1853.

LONGEVITY OF QUAKERS.—The *Times* and *Messenger* remarks that it has been ascertained, from authentic statistics that one half of the human race die before reaching the age of twenty-one years; and the bills of mortality published in large cities, show that one half die before attaining the age of five years. With these undisputed facts before us, it will seem strange that the average age of Quakers in Great Britain is fifty-one years, two months and twenty-one days. This is, no doubt, attributed to the restraints and moderation which the principles of that sect impose upon its members—the restraint they are under in mingling in many of the dissipations and pernicious indulgences that hurry thousands to premature graves. What an excellent example for the instruction of the world!

STARTLING TRUTHS.—Lucian Minor says:—Accurate statistics leave hardly a doubt, that in Virginia, the liquor traffic, through its offspring and agent, strong drink occasions—

1. Fifteen hundred deaths in every year!
2. The direct annual expenditure of five million dollars.
3. The loss of as much more by bad bargains, mismanagement, time wasted, and unnumbered nameless forms of ill thrift.
4. More than two thousand declared paupers.
5. The cost of above 100,000 dollars in taxes annually to support these paupers.
6. A countless multitude of impoverished men, women and children, who are not avowed paupers.
7. At least four-fifths of all the murders, thefts, robberies, breaches of the peace, and other crimes and misdemeanors that engage your courts!"

AWFUL FACT!—Dr. Hiram Cox, official Inspector of Liquors in Cincinnati, in a recent report on the adulteration of liquors relates the following:—

"I called at a grocery store one day, where liquor also was kept. A couple of Irishmen came in while I was there and called for some whisky, and the first drank, and the moment he drank the tears flowed freely, while he at the same time caught his breath like one suffocated or strangling. When he could speak, he says to his companion—'Och, Michael, but this is warmin' to the stomach!' Michael drank and went through like contortions, with the remark. 'Would'nt it be foine in a cowld frosthy morning?" After they had drank I asked the landlord to pour me out a little in a tumbler, in which I dipped a slip of litmus paper, which was no sooner wet than it put on a scarlet hue. I went to my office, got my instruments and examined it. I found it had 17 per cent alcoholic spirits by weight, when it should have had 40 per cent to be proof, and the difference in per centage made up by Sulphuric Acid, Red Pepper, Pelitory, Caustic, Potassa and Brucine, one of the salts of Nucis Vomicæ, commonly called Nux Vomica. One pint of such liquor would kill the strongest man.

IMMENSE WASTE.—There are in England 1,093,741 acres of land cultivated for growing barley for malting, besides 56,000 acres growing hops, making a total of 1,149,741 acres, the produce of which, notwithstanding the pressure of the population upon the means of subsistence, produces no bread.

An acre of good land produces about 40 bushels of barley, or, on a moderate calculation, 28 bushels of wheat, equal to three and a half quarters.

How desirable that this large extent of land should be made available for the good of society at large. The produce being $3\frac{1}{2}$ quarters per acre, $4,024,093\frac{1}{2}$ quarters of wheat would be reaped from the land now growing malt and hops.

A quarter of wheat yields about 350 lbs of flour, therefore from 1,149,741 acres, no less than 1,408,432,725 lbs of flour would be obtained; and it is supposed to increase one-third in being made into bread; consequently this land, producing wheat, would supply 1,877,910,300 lbs of bread. According to the census of 1841 we find the population of England and Wales to be 15,911,757, of whom 2,099,152 are under five years old. But allowing this number of young children as well as the adult population one pound of bread each per day, it would more than serve the whole population of England and Wales for 118 days, or nearly one-third of the year.

The total amount levied for poor's rate in England and Wales for the year ending Lady-day, 1841, was £6,351,825. For the sake of elucidating the subject still further, the committee estimate the value of bread at 1½d. per pound, which for 1,877,910,300 lbs, will be £11,736,939 7s 6d, a sum more than sufficient to pay the poor's rate for England and Wales for one year and ten months.

The total amount of money expended annually upon intoxicating liquors in the United Kingdom gives an average of about £2 per head for every man, woman and child; and presuming that the 30,000 inhabitants of York consume a fair portion of those liquors, it will appear that not less than £60,000 are expended every year by them in the purchase of these destructive fluids. And again taking the price of bread at three half-pence per pound, we ascertain that, with the money spent yearly in York, on alcoholic drinks, 9,000,000 lbs. of bread might be purchased; and allowing each man, woman, and child, one pound per day, would serve the whole of the inhabitants 320 days. Nearly as much money expended upon these body and soul-destroying poisons, as would purchase the "staff of life" for the whole population of the city! O shame, where is thy blush! After a serious and careful consideration of the preceding statements, who would cavil at efforts to prevent such a deplorable mis-appropriation of the gifts of providence, or at efforts made to put an end to the prodigal expenditure of a nation's resources?

CONFESSION OF A DRUNKARD.—Has the reader ever read the following authentic statement of his own experience by an English drunkard? Similar has been the experience of many thousands of men who in youth gave promise of a good and useful life:

"Of my condition there is no hope that it should ever change; the waters have gone over me; but out of the black depths could I be heard, I would cry out to all those who have but set a foot in the perilous flood.

"Could the youth to whom the flavor of his first wine is delicious as the opening scenes of life, or the entering upon some newly discovered paradise, look into my desolation and be made to understand what a dreary thing it is when a man shall feel himself going down a precipice with open eyes and a passive will: to see his destruction and have no power to stop it, and yet to feel it all the way emanating from himself; to perceive all goodness emptied out of him, and yet not be able to forget a time when it was otherwise; to bear about the piteous spectacle of his own self-ruin; could he see my fevered eye, feverish with last night's debauch, and feverish for this night's repetition of the folly; could he feel the body of the death out of which I cry hourly, with feebler and feebler cry to be delivered, it were enough to make him dash the sparkling beverage to the earth in all the pride of its mantling temptation."

TEETOTALISM EMINENTLY FAVORABLE TO RELIGION.—1. "It has excited enquiry and concern about religion. What we mean is this—that hundreds of persons who, before they became Teetotalers, never thought about religion—about their souls—about God—eternity—heaven or hell: as soon as they became Teetotalers, they began to think seriously on all these subjects—were greatly humbled on account of their past neglect—sought eagerly for information—and evinced deep concern for the salvation of their souls, and a preparation for the everlasting bliss of heaven.

2. It has led to a diligent use of the means of obtaining religion.
3. It has brought men into the enjoyment of religion.
4. It has assisted to maintain a consistent profession of religion.
5. It has brought many who had gone astray, back into the path of religion.
6. It has greatly enlarged religious congregations and churches.
7. It has promoted revivals of genuine religion.
8. It has augmented the resources of religious institutions."

NOT NECESSARY.—It is a mistaken idea that alcoholic liquors are necessary in order to enable a person to undergo fatigue and exposure. Professor Hitchcock says, "I was called a few years ago to make a geological survey of the State of Massachusetts, which required about five thousand miles travel in an open wagon, at a rate not greater than from twenty to thirty miles a day, and very severe bodily exertion in climbing mountains and in breaking, trimming and transporting more than five thousand specimens of rocks and minerals. I was usually employed from sunrise until ten o'clock at night with little interruption; and I think it was the severest protracted labor that I ever underwent. Yet, during all my wanderings, I drank not one drop of alcohol, nor indeed any kind of stimulating drink, except perhaps from twelve to twenty cups of weak tea, and I found myself more capable of exertion and fatigue than in former years, when I was in the habit of using stimulating drinks."

ABSINTHE.—A French paper thus discourses on this liquor which is so favorite an appetite provoker among Europeans. China has her opium, the East her buchish, England her gin. In France we have a poison that is imbued with the qualities of all these poisons, and a powerful stimulant that galvanizes the nerves and feverishly surcharges the brain: we have *Absinthe*. The effects of the poison are terrible, crushing. A feverish ecstacy, full of delirious dreams, of wild inspirations, is followed by an overwhelming debility, a continual state of somnolency. The eyes become dull, and the hands tremble. No work can be done unless preceded by a dram of absinthe. Beneath these ceaseless attacks reason reels, and a fatal day comes when the drinker finds drunkenness, and never again finds inspiration. Then he is lost beyond the hope of recovery. What was a necessary prelude to his labours becomes a degrading passion, a daily indulgence, which he has not the courage to abandon. The poet is dead within him, and the drunkard alone remains.

WATER.—Smollet thus writes of the French Wines, fifty years ago, the intoxicating strength of which is no more in proportion to the dry wines used in England, than the strength of an infant compared with that of a giant, are but poor and meagre drinks at best. All the peasants who take wine for their ordinary drinks are of diminutive size, in comparison with those who use milk and water; and it is commonly observed that when there is a scarcity of Wine the people are more healthy than in those seasons when it is abundant. The longer I live the more I am convinced that wine and all fermented liquors are *pernicious* to the human constitution; and that for the preservation of health, and proper exhilaration of the spirits, *there is no beverage that can compare with simple water.*"

INCONTROVERTIBLE FACTS.—Dr. Cartwright of New Orleans, communicates the following to the Boston *Medical Journal.* He was one of the three physicians who located in Natchez thirty years ago. They were temperance men, and there was one other who abstained from alcoholic drinks. Within 15 miles of Natchez there were three more. All the others used liquor. Besides these practicing physicians, there were ten others of the same class, who had retired from practice, 17 in all. Of these, five had died; one 75, one 70, two others 60, and one 49. In 1823 the average ages of the 17 was about 24. According to English tables of mortality seven instead of five should have died. Every physician, practicing or retired, in Natchez and vicinity, who was in the habit of using intoxicating drinks, has long been numbered with the dead. Only two of them who were comparatively temperate, lived to be gray. Their average term of life did not exceed 35 years, and those who drank did not live as long. Between the years 1824 and 1835, sixty-two medical men settled there to supply the places of those who have died or had retired from practice. Of these 37 were temperate, and 25 used liquor, although seldom to intoxication. Of the 37 nine have died, and 28 are living. Of the 25 all but three are dead. Here are facts which speak for themselves—they require no comment, and every man capable of reasoning cannot fail of seeing their bearing, and appreciating their importance. And in view of them, who are the friends of their fellow-men, the real philanthropists, those who promote in any way the use of liquor, or those who would use moral and legal means to prevent it?

SAD TESTIMONY.—Young men, read the warning which comes from a poor fellow-mortal just about to atone for the crime of murder upon the gallows. A young man, named Pate, at Esterville Va., sends a letter to the editor of the *Virginian*, which contains words of awful meaning. Beware of the intoxicating bowl, is the import of the warning. Read it one and all. He says: "And now, young men, old men, and middle-aged men, take warning by me, and shun the dungeon's gloom, the clanking chain, and the yet more dreadful execution, by hanging, which I am doomed to experience in a few days. I hope you will think me honest and in good truth when I tell you that the use of liquor was the cause of my taking the life which I could not give back again. 'Twas liquor that influenced my brain to perpetrate those evil deeds with which my past history is marked. Yes, it 'twas liquor!! that inflamed my blood to cause all this cálamity that has befallen me; nor need I say upon me only, but also upon my relations, and the relations of the man whose life I took. My poor old father has heard the fate of his unhappy son, and the sad intelligence was almost too much for him to bear. Little did he think, when I was an infant—when I was a little boy prattling and playing to amuse him—that I would die a death so disgraceful, as that to which I am doomed. 'Tis said he sleeps but little, and eats scarcely anything. Father, should this communication reach your ears, let me say to you, that I am heartily sorry that I have thus caused you pain. Warn all my relations never to use intoxicating liquors—tell them that if it had not been for liquor I should now be free, and no doubt a respectable and useful citizen."

THE SABBATH.—"During the malting season, forty thousand working malsters, and three thousand Excise officers are compelled to attend on the business on the Sabbath as well as on week days." In reference to the above we have the pleasure to quote the following interesting fact from that excellent pamphlet, entitled *Common Sense:*—" We remember, when reading the memoirs of the wife of that good man, the Rev. John Fletcher, that, on going to church one Sabbath morning, Mrs. F. met a man in his smock frock, who told her he could not go to church, having the malt-kiln to attend, and, on Mrs. Fletcher learning that malt could not be made without a desecration of that day, she immediately declared her determination never again to touch the drink, thus *practically* shewing her jealousy for her God, and the honor of His day."

EXPENSIVE.—Three-fourths of the crime, misery, and pauperism of the land, and a large proportion of the expenses of jails, of hulks, of transports, of country rates for police and for prosecutions, of union houses, of poor rates, and of lunatic asylums may be traced to strong drink. Of 495 in an asylum in Liverpool 256 were there from intemperance; in Dublin, Dr. Crawford states of 286 lunatics in one asylum, 115 were there from whisky. A Judge lately stated that he never had a criminal brought before him whose crime might not be traced directly or indirectly to strong drink. Edward Chadwick, secretary to the Poor Law Commissioners, has stated that education and teetotalism will do more to diminish pauperism than all the laws that can be made. It is supposed there are 600,000 drunkards in the United Kingdom—that 60,000 die every year—160 every day—7 every hour! The places of these drunkards are filled up from the ranks of moderate drinkers. It is calculated that 20,000 members of the Christian churches are annually expelled for drunkenness. What says the Scripture of the man who dies a drunkard?

PORTER AND ALE.—Temperance people will find an argument to enforce their doctrines, in the fact that 41,071,636 bushels of grain, paying $25,000,000 duty are annually converted into malt in Great Britain, for ale and porter. From this, some idea may be formed of the vast quantity of the most important staples of life wasted in the production of these beverages there. Franklin was not far from the truth when he ascribed much of the poverty and misery of the people of Great Britain to their habit of drinking their bread instead of eating it.

A Noble Daughter.—The following illustration of how the Maine Law is worked at home, is from the Maine *Temperance Journal*:—

A young lady in Falmouth determined to bring the rumsellers to justice, who were selling her father liquor. She got another young lady, a friend of hers, to accompany her, and they walked into Portland, seven miles, two days in succession, and accompanied her father to the shops visited by him, to ascertain who sold it to him. Having accomplished her purpose, she entered a complaint before the Municipal Court against the offender, who appears to have been one S. McC——.

The case was tried before a jury; only one witness was examined for the defence. The Judge charged the jury, who soon brought in a verdict of guilty, and he was sentenced to pay a fine of $100 and costs, and in default of payment, to be imprisoned three months.

Alcohol a Poison in 1584.—In an address to the Mayor and Corporation of the town of Galway, in 1584, Sir John Perrot, the Lord Deputy of Ireland, "among other articles touching reformation in the commonwealth," advised, "That a more straighter order be taken to bar the making of *aqua vitæ* of corn than hitherto hath been used, for that the same is a consumation of all the provision of corn in the commonwealthie:" and he said, "That the *aqua vitæ* that is sold in the towne out rather to be called *aqua mortis* to poyson the people, than comfort them in any good store, and in officers in reformyng the same have nede to be more vigilant and inquisitive than they be."

A Sunday School Fact.—"I thank God," said a young man lately, "on looking back on my past life, that ever I was led, when attending the Sunday School to join the Temperance Society, and abjure the use of tobacco. By God's mercy, it has been like a tower of strength to me, and I have thereby been saved from many snares. Several of my school-fellows who *laughed at me then*, now fill the *drunkard's grave*."

LONDON CITY MISSION.—The lecturer, J. R. Philips, travelling agent, then dwelt on the fearful extent to which drunkenness and profligacy were carried on in the metropolis, and founded an appeal to the ladies of his audience on the fact of 10,000 of their sex having been taken into custody *in a state of intoxication* in one year. 30,000 children were, until the establishment of ragged schools, sent out to beg or steal every day, though now that number was greatly reduced. 36,000 individuals pass every year through the London gaols."

As to the shops of London, *Chambers' Journal* states that according to the Post Office Directory, London contained in 1848,

  2,500 bakers,
   900 buttermen & cheesemongers,
  1,700 butchers,
  3,000 grocers and tea dealers,
   900 dairy keepers,
   400 fishmongers,
  1,300 green-grocers and fruiterers,

Total, 10,700 and 11,000 public houses.

With respect to the crimes of London, Dr. Forbes Winslow made the following statement to the Medical Society of London, in order to show the depressing, demoralizing, criminal and vicious influences at work in the metropolis. The subjoined estimate, we are told, has been drawn from official documents by persons whose veracity may be relied upon:—

  16,000 children trained to crime,
   5,000 receivers of stolen goods,
  15,000 gamblers by profession,
  25,000 beggars,
  30,000 drunkards,
 180,000 habitual gin drinkers,
 150,000 persons subsisting on profligacy,
  50,000 thieves.

Thus, we have the tremendous total of 471,000 individuals

steeped in crime, demoralization and vice, out of a population of 2,350,000 souls. The result of this appalling calculation is that one out of every five is a worthless member of society! We leave these statements for the consideration of the reader, with this one question,—What must be the understanding, the sympathy, the patriotism, or the religion, of the man who can look at this overwhelming ruin without a single attempt to stem the torrent of intemperance?

THRILLING INCIDENT.—At a temperance meeting in Philadelphia, some years ago, a learned clergyman spoke in favor of wine as a drink, demonstrating it quite to his own satisfaction to be Scriptural, gentlemanly, and heathful. When the clergyman sat down, a plain, elderly man arose, and asked the liberty of saying a few words. Permission being granted, he spoke as follows:

"A young friend of mine," said he, "who had long been intemperate, was prevailed on, to the joy of his friends, to take the pledge of entire abstinence from all that could intoxicate. He kept his pledge faithfully for some time, though the struggle with his habit was fearful, till one evening, in a social party, glasses of wine were handed around. They came to a clergyman present, who took a glass, saying a few words in vindication of the practice. 'Well,' thought the young man, 'if clergymen can take wine and justify it so well, why not I?' So he took a glass. It instantly rekindled his fiery and slumbering appetite, and after a rapid downward course, he died of delirium tremens—a raving madman!" The old man paused for utterance, and was just able to add—"That young man was my only son, and the clergyman was the Reverend Doctor who has just addressed the assembly."

A SAD CASE—THE DEATH OF THE BEAUTIFUL MRS. S——.
—Mrs. S—— was once the most admired of all the ladies in her village. She could sing the sweetest, play the prettiest, talk the most enchantingly, dress the most fashionably of all who moved in the gay circles. Her husband was a man of industry, who doted upon her, was anxious at the least depression of spirits, and allow-

ed her every indulgence. When the temperance reform commenced, he was anxious to sign the pledge; but she said it was "well enough for the vulgar, but for people in genteel life, it would never do; they could neither go into parties, nor give parties. Besides," said she, "how can I ever sing or dance without one or two glasses of wine to give me a spring?" Time rolled on, when the inquiry began to be made, what is the matter with the beautiful Mrs. S———? "She seems to have lost her ballast," said one. On the sidewalk, she was seen to reel to and fro like a ship; and in her parties, she was now as silly as she was once enchanting. At church, especially in the afternoon of a Sunday, no sermons could keep up her eyelids. Her poor husband saw the change. He devised every method to keep liquor from her, but all in vain. He soon died of vexation and a broken heart. She now gave herself up to brandy and opium; and with a handsome property, no resort was too low, no indulgence too disgusting. For the last two years of her life, few saw her, except as she was stealing away, in the twilight of the evening, with a cloak on her head, to the very lowest grog-shop, to fill her bottle. One day her neighbors heard that she was dying. Three respectable women came in to see her, and found her senseless and stupid, just surrendering her lost soul into the hands of her maker. How awful the scene! If there are any young females who read this, let them be admonished to beware of the confectionary and the exhilerating glass. Let them remember that the tissues of their system are peculiarly fine and tender—far more liable to excitement than those of the other sex; and if they once form the drunkard's appetite—though the thought is too horrid to indulge that they may form it—(but they may, the laws of their physical being are fixed,)—there is no redemption. Let every daughter of America put her name to a temperance pledge; and above all, beware of that pronounced most innocent, "sparkling champagne."

MODERATE DRINKING.—The Devil's Railroad, with a steep downward grade, to the Depot of Destruction.

How it Appears to a Dying Man.—A man, long esteemed as an exemplary member both of Christian and civil society, took an active part in the early stages of the Temperance reformation—signed the pledge of total abstinence, and engaged with the friends of the cause in persuading others to the same resolution. Upon subsequent reflection, however, he withdrew his pledge, and retired from the service, convicted of the inconsistency of standing forth as the advocate of the cause of temperance, and being at the same time a wholesale dealer in the article of ardent spirits, for such he was. While yet engaged in this traffic, the state of his health obliged him to retire from active business, leaving it in the hands of partners. A few days before his death, being in great trouble, he sent for a friend and unbosomed the secret—told him he could not die in peace till the traffic was abandoned—sent for his partners, requesting from them an estimate of the annual loss which the house would incur by the proposed measure; this they fixed at $3,000—but great as it was, the sacrifice was made—and then he died full of peace.

Another Dying Man.—A man who had been furnished by his neighbor with the means of destruction, and been brought by it to the verge of the grave, was visited in his last moments, by the author of his ruin, who asked him whether he remembered him. The dying man forgetting his struggle with the king of terrors, said, " Yes, I remember you, and I remember your store, where I formed the habit which has ruined me for this world and the next. And when I am dead and gone, and you come and take from my widow and fatherless children the shattered remains of my property to pay my rum-debts, they too will remember you." And he added, as they were both members of the same church, " Yes, brother, we shall all remember you to all eternity."

Three Good Testimonies.—The Rev. D. Livingston, in a letter from Kurumon, South Africa, dated Nov. 12, 1852, says:—
" I have acted on the principle of total abstinence from all alcoholic liquors during more than twenty years. My individual opinion

is, that the most severe labours or privations may be undergone without alcoholic stimulus, because *those of us who have endured the most, had nothing else than water,* and not always enough of that. The introduction of English drinking customs and English drinks among the natives of this country inevitably proves the destruction of both their bodies and souls."

The Rev. Robert Moffatt, in a letter dated Nov. 15, 1832, says: " For my own part, the severest portions of my missionary labor were performed without anything of the kind. Of one thing, however, there is no doubt; that is, that the introduction of British intoxicating drinks among the natives of this country, would end in the certain destruction of all their temporal as well as their spiritual interests."

Judge McLean says that, "Rum has sunk more seamen than all the tempests that ever blew."

A LONDON BREWER'S PROFITS.—"A Thirsty Soul," in the *Times* referring to Sir Henry Meux's case, says—It might reasonably have been supposed that a career of fifteen years hunting and racing, of French cook, Sevres china, champagne, and double opera-boxes—of *battues*, moors, and deer forests—of Epsom, Newmarket, and Ascot—ending with marriage and a jointure of £15,000 a-year—would have damaged the fortune of even a London brewer. Not a bit of it. Sir Henry Meux appears to have paid his brother-in-law, Mr. Arabin, a few hundreds a year to manage his business for him, and his share in the great monopoly valued in 1841 at £200,000, is now in 1848 estimated at upwards of £600,000.

ORIGIN OF BRANDY.—Brandy began to be distilled in France about the year 1313, but it was prepared only as a medicine, and was considered as possessing such marvellous strengthening and sanitary powers that the physicians named it " the water of life," (eau de vie) a name it retains, though now rendered, by excessive potations, one of life's most powerful and most prevalent destroyers. Raymond Tully, a disciple of Arnold de Villa Nova, considered this admirable essence of wine to be an emanation from the divinity, and that it was intended to reanimate and prolong the life of man. He even thought that this discovery indicated that the time had arrived for the consummation of all things—the end of the world.

BROTHER JONATHAN SAYS:—Men who are cursing a land with taxation, are eloquent over the cost of a liquor suit to the people. Should not the murderer deprecate the expense of the gallows he hangs on?

A living death is the drunkard's existence—no enjoyments, no comfort in the inebriating cup. Home loses every attraction; every endearing tie that once held him close to its circle is broken by the demon that lures him to destruction. Young men! every day you see these things around you. Take warning from the past, and act wisely for the future.

The Temperance Reform is an idea in whose consummation is centered the highest good of the race to-day and for ages to come. And yet there are hosts of minds which cannot comprehend it, and with canting words, talk about one-idea men.

Better one idea, glorious to man and honoring to God, than a legion which never pulse beyond the line of pitiful selfishness. Better to rear one eagle to sweep in the upper sky, than a thousand chickens to scratch in the ground.

It is a blessed thing that there are so called crazy men in the world—that there are those mad with the idea of struggling to beat back the many wrongs which oppress and degrade poor humanity.

The good old cause is marching grandly on in "old England." The sturdy, practical common sense of our fatherland, is moving steadily for the suppression of the rum traffic. We watch the movement there with intense interest. Had we the arm of Coeur de Lion, and could see no work for it in our own land, we should joy to strike with our brethren for the redemption of "Merrie England." May they be prospered in the struggle.

JOHNNY'S PLEDGE.—The following is a very good Temperance Pledge, given in rhyme—which, by the way, does not make it any worse—and we would advise parents to attach it to a strip of letter paper, and give the children an opportunity to declare their hostility " to all that can intoxicate," by signing it before the evil day comes. " Just as the twig is bent, the tree's inclined," is a homely and oft-repeated adage, but a very true one. Here, then, is the

PLEDGE.

This little hand
Do with our hand
The Pledge now sign
To drink no WINE;
Nor BRANDY red,
To turn our head;
Nor WHISKY hot,
That makes the sot;
Nor fiery RUM,
To turn our home
Into a hell,
Where none can dwell—
Whence peace would fly—
Where hope would die,
And love expire,
'Mid such a fire;
So here we pledge perpetual hate
To all that can intoxicate.

ORIGIN OF WINE.—The Persians relate the following anecdote in reference to the invention of wine. It is extracted from Moullah Ackber's manuscript, and is quoted by Sir John Malcolm, in his history of Persia :—" Jem Sheed, the founder of Persepolis, was very fond of grapes, and, with the view to preserve some, placed them in vessels which were lodged in vaults for future use. When the vessels were opened it was found that the grapes (or rather the liquor which had issued from them) had fermented. The juice in this state was so acid that the king believed it to be poisonous. A label, with the word "*poison*," was accordingly placed upon each of the vessels. One of the favourite ladies of the court was afflicted with most distressing attacks of nervous headache in a paroxysm of which she resolved to put an end to her existence. By accident she found one of the vessels with the word ' poison' written on it, and, intent on her purpose, swallowed its contents. Stupefaction, as might be expected, followed this act, and strange to say, unlike similar indulgence in modern times, her headache was gone. Charmed with the remedy, the lady was induced often to repeat the experiment, until the monarch's poison was all drunk. The theft was soon discovered, and the fair culprit confessed the deed. A quantity of wine was again made, and Jem Sheed and all his court partook of the newly discovered beverage. This circumstance gave rise to a name by which inebriating wine is known in Persia in the present day—Zaher-e-Kooshon—"*The delightful poison.*"

HOMER AND POPE.—It may be almost presumed that Homer was a water-drinker, and his great translator too,—from the following passage in the sixth book of the Iliad with the note subjoined.

Hecuba, it will be remembered, offers wine to Hector in the interview with her son which immediately precedes the scene of his parting with Andromache,

"Far hence be Bacchus' gifts (the chief rejoined)—
Inflaming wine, pernicious to mankind,
Unnerves the limbs, and dulls the noble mind."

To which very sober text, Pope has thought proper to append his own opinion as follows:—

"This maxim of Hector's concerning wine, has a great deal of truth in it. It is a vulgar mistake to imagine the use of wine either raises the spirits or increases strength. The best physicians agree with Homer on this point, whatever our modern soldiers may object to this old heroic regimen. One may take notice that Samson, as well as Hector, was a water-drinker, to which Milton alludes in the "Samson Agonistes"—

"Wherever fountain or fresh current flow'd,
I drank. Nor envied them the grape
Whose heads that turbulent liquor fills with fumes"

COMMUNION WINE.—In August, 1858, Mr. R. D. Wadsworth published the following Recipes for making Communion Wine:

Grape Jelly.—The Grapes to be washed and gently pressed. To each pound of fruit add one pound of loaf sugar, which has been clarified previously. The whole to be boiled till it becomes a jelly, which will be ascertained by taking a portion of the juice from time to time and cooling it. To be strained through a muslin bag and put into jars properly coated with paper smeared with white of egg, or patent jars, now easily obtained for preserving fruit. To be diluted with water to suit.

Grape Wine.—The Grapes to be washed and weighed, then gently pressed so as to break the skin. To be tied up in a cotton bag. To every 1½ pound of grapes put three pints of water, and boil down to a pint. Be careful not to squeeze the bag, but let the liquid strain off. Have ready some clarified sugar, and to every pint of juice add a quarter or a half a pint of the sugar, as the same may be required more or less sweet. Bottle and seal carefully with bees wax and rosin. Keep in a cool place, the temperature not to exceed 60° F. When used, to be diluted with water to suit.

The number of Christians who conceive it to be their duty to use unfermented wine in the Holy Eucharist being rapidly on the increase throughout Canada, Mr. Wadsworth is confident the above reliable recipes will be acceptable.

LIQUOR MADE EASY.—There has lately appeared in this city, a neat and compact little manual called " The Bordeau Wine-and-Liquor-Dealer's Guide," published at one and a half dollars—from the preface to which we learn a statistical fact or two, that may be of interest to somebody. (We don't drink ourselves—we "take a pie.") The guide professes to give instructions, clear and simple, for the imitation of all kinds of wines and liquors, from Teneriffe, or Cape, to prime Champagne and pure Cognac. A pleasant book it is for the bibulously inclined, and well calculated to strengthen their faith in—cold water. In justice to the practical author of this " Treatise on the Manufacture and Adulteration of Liquors," we should say that he claims to present *formula* entirely free from all poisonous or deleterious ingredients—always excepting, we presume, the complete compound when duly concocted.

Now for a general fact, first:

" The city of New York alone sells three times as many ' pure imported brandies,' and four times as many 'pure imported wines,' annually, as all the wine-producing countries export." After that statistical "snifter" has been duly imbibed, try the following *formula*, which we give for the benefit of whom it may concern. Of course we have forsworn brandy particularly; so here goes for a Cognac, utterly "impossible to detect by any test, chemical or otherwise":

Formula No. 1.—Cognac Brandy.—" To 40 gallons pure spirits (alcohol), 12 to 18 over proof, add 2 to 3 ounces oil cognac (dissolved in 90 per cent alcohol), 1½ pounds loaf sugar, or its equivalent in white syrup, 2 ounces oenanthic acid, 2 ounces acetic acid, or acetic ether, and 2 ounces tincture of kino. To this body add from 5 to 10 gallons of the brandy to be imitated. Let it stand for eight or ten days. Color as desired."

We shall only add, that we find in the book a *formula* for— hear it, oh Newark!—thy champagne sins are visited upon thee! —a formula for *imitation cider !*

There's always a "lower deep" we are told. We shall, no doubt, soon have an imitation *Lager Beer*.

THE CABLE.—In the September number of the *Journal* of the American Temperance Union, is a very excellent article on that great enterprize of the age the laying of the Atlantic Cable, in which Dr. Marsh undertakes to show how much it is indebted to teetotalism. He says:—

And here let us say, to Temperance is the world not a little indebted for this mighty achievement.

Who brought the lightning from the skies? Franklin, the teetotaller.

Who made it the ready communicator of thought? Morse the teetotaler.

Who sunk it in the ocean deeps, and made one of distant peoples? Field, the teetotaller.

And who stood at the helm of the noble Niagara which bore the cable to our shores? It was Capt. William Hudson, one of our oldest and firmest teetotallers, a Vice President of the American Temperance Union: one who is ever inculcating the great principles of our reform; one who fears God and honors his law.

To WESLEYANS.—"You see the wine when it sparkles in the cup, and are going to drink it. I say there is poison in it! and therefore beg you to throw it away. You answer, 'The wine is harmless in itself.' I reply, perhaps it is so; but still, if it be mixed with what is not harmless, no one in his senses, if he knows it at least, unless he could separate the good from the bad, will once think of drinking it. If you add, 'It is not poison to me, though it be to others,' then I say, Throw it away for thy brother's sake, lest thou embolden him to drink also. Why should thy strength occasion thy weak brother to perish, for whom Christ died?"—*John Wesley.*

"It is expected of all who continue in these Societies that they should continue to evidence their desire for salvation—

"First: by doing no harm, by avoiding evil of every kind, especially that which is most generally practised, such as buying or selling spirituous liquors, or drinking them, unless in cases of extreme necessity."—*Wesleyan Societies' Rules.*

"We verily believe that the single sin of intemperance is destroying more souls than all the ministers in Britain are instrumental in saving. The man who trifles with strong drink may be overcome; whereas he who abstains cannot. It cannot be unwise to throw the guard of abstinence round our moral character and our spiritual interest."—*Wesleyan Magazine* for 1836, p. 905.

Rules of Health.—Mr. Wesley recommends the following:—

"Water is the wholesomest of all drinks; quickens the appetite, and strengthens the digestion most.

"Strong, and more especially spirituous liquors, are a certain, though slow, poison.

"Experience shews there is seldom any danger in leaving them off all at once.

"Strong liquors do not prevent the mischief arising from eating to excess, nor carry it off so safely as water."

Wesley on the Traffic, &c.—"Neither may we gain by hurting our neighbor in his body. Therefore we may not sell anything which tends to impair health. Such is eminently all that liquid fire, commonly called drams, or spirituous liquors. It is true these may have place in medicines; they may be of use in some bodily disorder (although there would rarely be occasion for them were it not for the unskilfulness of the practitioner). Therefore such as prepare and sell them only for this end, may keep their conscience clear. But who are they? Who prepare them only for this end? Do you know ten such distilleries in England? Then excuse these. But all who sell them in the common way, to any that will buy, are poisoners-general. They murder his Majesty's subjects by wholesale, neither do they ever pity or spare. They drive them to hell like sheep; and what is their gain? Is it not the blood of these men? Who, then, would envy their large estates and sumptuous palaces? A curse is in the midst of them; the curse of God cleaves to the stones, the timber, the furniture of them. The curse of God is in their gardens, their walks, their groves—a fire that burns to the nethermost hell. Blood, blood is there: the foundation, the floor, the walls, the roof, are stained with blood! And canst thou hope, O thou man of blood, though thou art "clothed in scarlet and fine linen, and farest sumptuously every day"—canst thou hope to deliver down the fields of blood to the third generation? Not so; for there is a God in heaven, therefore thy name shall be rooted out. Like as those whom thou hast destroyed, body and soul, 'thy memorial shall perish with thee.'" * * * * * * * * *
"This is dear-bought gain. And so is whatever is procured by hurting our neighbour in his soul—by ministering, suppose, either directly or indirectly, to his unchastity or intemperance, which certainly none can do who has any fear of God, or any real desire of pleasing him. It nearly concerns all those to consider this,

who have anything to do with taverns, victualling-houses, opera-houses, play-houses, or any other places of public, fashionable diversion. If these profit the souls of men, you are clear; your employment is good, and your gain innocent. But if they are either sinful in themselves, or natural inlets to sin of various kinds, then it is to be feared you have a sad account to make. O beware, lest God say in that day, 'These have perished in their iniquity, but their blood do I require at thy hands!'"

A CALCULATION.—Here is a calculation made by Judge Capron of New York:—"In New York city there are 15,000 dram shops; 300,000 drinkers, each drinking 2 gills of liquor, being 600,000 gills, or 806 barrels, per day—300,000 barrels a-year. This quantity would fill a reservoir 900 feet long, 50 feet wide, and 63 feet deep, and could float four large ships in full sail. At $30 per barrel, it amounts to $900,000. Out of 6000 cases tried before the Court of Special Sessions during the last year, not more than 94 were sober when arrested. Paupers in the city cost $3,000,000 a-year."

TOBACCO.—The name "tobacco" is curious. It is not, as is generally said in books treating of the origin of things, the indigenous native name. *Petun* in the South American dialects—*kohiha* in the Caribbean language—is the name of the plant. *Tobaco* is the Indian name of the pipe. It follows, therefore, that tobacco was not, as the books say, connected with the island of Tobago, to which it gave, or from which it derived, its designation. On the contrary, the name of the island is modern, and was given by the Spanish discoverer from a fancied resemblance to the Indian pipe or smoking instrument.

DEATH IN THE SNUFF-BOX.—Death was once found in the pot, and now he has been detected in the snuff-box. Long ago, the destroyer was found in the snuff, but he has since been discovered lingering in the box itself. In boxes lined with very thin lead, but especially in cases where the leaden lining is thicker, and which are much used by the Paris retailers, a chemical action takes place, the result of which is to charge the snuff with sub-acetate of lead. The result was suspected by Chevalier, and has been confirmed by Boudet of Paris, and Mayor of Berlin, by long and careful experiments. The latter learned chemist traced several deaths and cases of "*saturnine paralysis*" to the patients having taken snuff from pockets, the inner envelope of which was thin sheet lead, in constant contact with the powdered weed.

WARNING TO SMOKERS.—A singular case of asphyxia is related in one of the French journals. A youth of the name of Lemoine paid a visit to an uncle, who is a farm labourer in the neighbourhood of Havre. This man occupied a small and ill-ventilated apartment. The nephew, at eight o'clock in the evening, went to bed in the room. Soon after, the uncle and some companions entered the room, and all fell to smoking. The youth was asleep. At midnight, the visitors withdrew, and the uncle went to bed. Laying his hand upon his nephew, he found him unnaturally cold, and endeavoured to awake him without effect. Help was called, some faint indications of life appeared, and a physician directed operations for the recovery of the patient. All proved vain; the next day he expired. A *post mortem* examination was made, and the physician pronounced that he died of congestion of the brain, caused by the respiration of tobacco smoke during sleep.

TOBACCO IN FRANCE.—The *Genie Industriel* says, that it is difficult to account for the tremendous increase, during the last few years, of the consumption of tobacco in France: but that it has increased, and that enormously, the following figures will show: In 1830, the value of tobacco consumed was about $13,000,000. In 1840, it had increased to $19,000,000. In 1850, it had increased to $24,000,000, and in 1857 the sum of nearly $35,000,000 was puffed away in smoke.

TOBACCO.—" If teetotalers continue the use of tobacco in any form, they must not expect the full share of health they otherwise would have by abstaining from intoxicating drinks, as affections of the head, chest, and stomach, with low spirits in their train, are continued and aggravated by the use of that narcotic weed. Medical experience has fully proved this fact."—*John Higginbotham, Surgeon.*

WARNING TO STUDENTS.—The Dublin *Medical Press* asserts that the pupils of the Polytechnic School in Paris have recently furnished some curious statistics bearing on tobacco. Dividing the young gentlemen of that college into two groups—the smokers and non-smokers—it shows that the smokers have proved themselves in the various competitive examinations far inferior to the others. Not only in the examinations on entering the schools are the smokers in a lower rank, but in the various ordeals that they have to pass through in a year the average rank of the smokers had constantly fallen, and not inconsiderably, while the men who did not smoke enjoyed a cerebral atmosphere of the clearest kind.

There is another reason for this. One bad habit begets another. It is commonly observed that young men of the description referred to above, fall into idle, lounging ways, and waste many an hour which might have been instructively and usefully employed. Time is a treasure of priceless value. Why should we spend it on trash?

EFFECTS OF TOBACCO UPON THE NERVES.—As it seems to be a matter of question among some as to the effects of Tobacco upon the system, allow me, if you please, to give you a history of that part of my life made miserable by its use. As is generally the case of those that are my age, I was first induced to take Tobacco from seeing others do the same, being unfortunately at the age of sixteen, surrounded by those that used it without regard to quantity or quality. Unlike some who go for years without experiencing any perceptible injury from it, I used it comparatively but a short time, when I was brought to feel its effects in no slight form. I was told by my parents and others, that it was injurious. Still I had a desire to ferret out its mysteries, and, if possible, to know how bad it was. It was not my intention, when I commence-ed, to follow the practice long, for I very naturally supposed that I could stop at any time. In fact, I hardly knew what it was to form a habit, and much less to recede from it when formed. When I first commenced Tobacco, it did not go so well with me, causing, not unfrequently, a sickness of the stomach and dizziness of the head. It took about four weeks for the poison to bring the stomach to that deranged state to allow of the inhalement of its fumes without offering resistance. But by a little preseverance on my part, the weed triumphed; the intestines and brain becoming at the same time perfectly subdued by its powerful and subduing effects. This accomplished, all went smoothly along for about six months, during which time I used it more or less, daily. An instance now occurred in which I had cause for alarm. Being accustomed to spend a part of my leisure hours in gunning, in company with a friend, who, by the way, was a good shot, and a) much taken with the sport as myself, we would when game was scarce, pace the ground and try our dexterity at target shooting, (our target being a knot on a tree or something of the kind. This is an exercise that tries the strength of the nerves, and although at first too much for my comrade in the shooting line, I now began to experience frequent tremblings and unsteadiness of the hand, which was of course accompanied by bad shots. The result was, my friend would not unfrequently come off master of the field. He did not use Tobacco, and therefore I did not hint to him the cause of my late failure. My friend was a good natured fellow, and we passed it by merely as bad luck. I always left him with the hope of being more successful at our next meeting, but alas! my hand grew more and more unsteady, and as often as I brought my piece to bear upon its prize, so often did my nervous system prove treacherous, until at last I was obliged to hang up my rifle and seek amusement elsewhere. As is generally the case with those who are addicted to the habit, I now considered that I could not do without it, in consequence of every thing's going wrong, unless accompanied with the stimulating effects of the article in question. For instance, if I attempted to roll a log over,

I must, in order do it scientifically, roll at the same time a quid over in my mouth. It was impossible for me to keep my mind upon any subject long at a time, unless of the most interesting nature. Such was my case when I left home in the fall of '45, for the city of New York. I used no tea or coffee, and was well aware that Tobacco was destined to "use me up" unless a decided stand was taken. People may rail at my inability to rid myself of the monster, but to such I will only say, that you are not capable of judging of the matter until you yourselves have gone through the task. On arriving at New York I confined myself to one pader of Tobacco per week, but this did not do the work—it was only adding fuel to the flame, and I was obliged to resort to other means; a change of diet, exercise, and keeping the mind at work. This, with the change of life from the dull country to that of a lively city, had the desired effect. Stimulating with the hope of recovering my strength of nerve, I was soon enabled to lay it aside altogether. By keeping something in my mouth as a substitute, I soon had the satisfaction of overcoming the habit, but not wholly the desire for it; for although I have not tasted it for months, my hand will, at times, involuntarily steal into my pocket in search of the filthy weed.

By the aid of a cold bath, mornings, a non-stimulating diet, daily exercise, &c., my hand has regained its wonted steadiness, and as far as my knowledge of physiology goes, it must ever remain so.

If I should chance to meet my friend again I shall not hesitate to challenge him for a shot.—*La More.*

STATISTICS OF TOBACCO.—The present annual production of tobacco has been estimated by an English writer at 4,000,000,000 pounds! This is smoked, chewed, and snuffed. Suppose it all made into cigars, one hundred to the pound, it would produce 400,000,000,000. Four hundred billions of cigars. Allowing this tobacco, unmanufactured, to cost on the average, ten cents a pound, and we have $400,000,000 expended every year, in producing a noxious, deleterious weed. At least one and a half times as much more is required to manufacture it into a marketable form, and dispose of it to the consumer. If this be so, then the human family expend, *every year*, one thousand millions of dollars in the gratification of an acquired habit, or one dollar for every man, woman, and child upon the earth! This sum would build two railroads around the earth, at a cost of twenty thousand dollars per mile, or sixteen railroads from the Atlantic to the Pacific! It would build one hundred thousand churches, costing $10,000 each; or half a million of school-houses, costing $2,000 each; or one million of dwellings, costing $1,000 each! It would employ one million of preachers and one million of teachers, giving each a salary of $500! It would support three and one-third millions of young men at college giving each $300 per annum for expenses! Friendly reader, consider the above basis of this calculation in some measure imaginary, call it conjecture, extravagance, just what you please! Cut these down one half—cut them down to suit your own notions. Even then, if you are a Christian, or a patriot, a friend of God or man, you will not trifle with this stupendous iniquity; but in some manly way, do your part to arrest its destructive power around you.

Boys.—Tobacco has spoiled and utterly ruined thousands of boys, inducing a dangerous precocity, developing the passions, softening and weakening the bones and greatly injuring the spinal marrow, the brain, and the whole nervous fluid. A boy who early and freely smokes, or otherwise uses tobacco, never is known to make a man of much energy of character, and generally lacks physical and muscular as well as mental energy.—1000 *M. D's.*

A Want Stronger than Hunger.—An old man, who had borne an irreproachable character up to the age of seventy-two, was lately brought before one of the tribunals of Paris for stealing a piece of lead worth eight cents. He admitted that he was wholly without means, and for the first time in his life knew not where to find a single sous; but it was not hunger that drove him to

T

steal. After considerable questioning on the part of the judge, as to what could be stronger than hunger, he confessed it was *tobacco for his pipe.* "Tobacco, monsieur judge!" said he, growing violent: "I have the misery to be a hopeless smoker! I smoke at waking; I smoke while eating; I cannot sleep without smoking till the pipe falls from my mouth. Tobacco costs me six cents a day. When I have none I am frantic. I cannot work, nor eat, nor sleep. I go from place to place, raging like a mad dog. The day I stole the lead, I had been without tobacco for twelve hours! I searched the day through for an acquaintance of whom I could beg a pipe full. I could not, and resorted to crime as a less evil than I was enduring. The need was stronger than I!" The eloquence and pathos of the old man's plea mollified the judge, and he condemned him only to eight days' imprisonment.

How Much it Costs.—In this city there are at least 2,400 adult males. Of this number 2,000 use tobacco. For cigars they pay not not less than four cents a day, making for each $15 60 a year, and a total for the 2,000 of $31,200. For tobacco six cents per week, making $3 12 per year. Total for cigars and tobacco, per year, $37,420—for the citizens of Cleveland. The cigars and tobacco cost almost, if not quite, as much as the flour consumed in the city. There are several individuals who pay not less than $100 a year for cigars; at $5 per barrel this would purchase 20 barrels of flour, equal to the supply of four families, or 20 persons with the staple of life. And all of this $37,000 is paid for an article injurious to the human system, and entirely unproductive of any good.

The amount paid in the city of Cleveland for cigars and tobacco is fully equal to the amount of state, county, township and city taxes. And if we include the amount paid for *strong drink* it amounts to more than the state, county, township and city taxes of the whole county, levied on the duplicate for the year 1848. There is no wisdom in these expenditures. There is folly rather. But men will have their own way, and do just as they please, and say that it is nobody's business. Well, agreed! Nevertheless the amount paid for two years in Cleveland for cigars and tobacco and strong drinks, would pay the subscription of the city to the Cleveland and Columbus Railroad, which is only $2,000,000! But who cares, smoke and chew away—if you don't some one else will. Never mind the expense as long as it is paid for. People must live!—*Cleveland True Democrat.*

WAS THE QUAKER RIGHT?—"At a temperance meeting in Western New York, some one alluded to the plea so often urged by the Society of Friends, that it is not well to aid in the reformatory movements of the day, because it leads to 'mixing with the world.' The speaker was followed by Henry Coleman, of agricultural celebrity. In the midst of his remarks he stopped suddenly, pointed out of the window, and looking at a Friend opposite to him, exclaimed in a tone of alarm, 'Dr. Robinson! is that your house that's on fire?' Instantly the whole audience were on their feet. 'Stop, stop!—nobody must go but the Quakers—don't mix with the world!—nobody must go but the Quakers.' The fire was of course, a hoax; but we trust a serious use will be made of its witty application."

BE SURE THE FOX IS DEAD.—The following anecdote, instructive on many other subjects besides that of the Maine Liquor Law, was related by a venerable speaker at the late anniversary meetings of the Free Will Baptists:—"Father Phinney wished to relate an anecdote. While hearing Bro. Peck telling how whist these rumsellers have become, I was reminded of one John Skillins, an old bachelor who lived in Gorham, my native town. Old John was a fox hunter. At one time an old fox came to his trap, eat off the bait and went off. John went to his trap, looked and said, (for he was always talking to himself,) "*What, does that fox think to outwit John Skillins?*" So he fixed the bed and set his trap the other side up, to outwit the fox. But it was one of the cunning old foxes and he managed to get off the bait, spoil the bed, and get off again without being caught. John went to his trap and looked astonished: but was not to be outwitted by a fox; he would show them that he knew more than the whole tribe of foxes. So he borrowed another trap and set two, so that while the fox was in one, he got his hind leg in the other. When John came to his trap he said, "Good morning, Mr. Fox. Did I not tell you that it was no use to attempt to outwit John Skillins?" He then took up a pitch knot and whaled him on the head, till the fox laid down just as Bro. Peck says those rumsellers do (applause). He then turned to fix his traps, and as he happened to look round, he saw the fox's tail just going out of sight among the bushes.—(Roars of applause.)—Now, said Phinney, what I want is, that we should not be deceived, but be sure and kill the fox dead."

TIT FOR TAT.—A reformed character said, "When I was a drunkard, the publican liked my money better than me, and I can see no good reason, now that I have become a sober man, why I should not like my money better than the publican."

TO A PIMPLE ON TOM'S NOSE.

Thrice red that blossom is, alas!
  And thrice red has it been:
Red in the grape—red in the glass—
  Red on thy nose 'tis seen.
Ah, Tom! at that red, red, red blot
  Thy well-wishers bewail;
They say the *redness* of that spot
  'Tis makes thy poor wife pale.
            WM. JERDAN.

A LEVELLING DRINK.—A remarkably acute friend of mine formerly at the bar—the Judges having retired for a few minutes, in the midst of his argument; in which, from their interruptions, and objections, he did not seem likely to be successful—went out of court too, and on his return stated that he had been drinking a pot of porter. Being asked whether he was not afraid that his beverage might not dull his intellect? "That is exactly my object," said he, "to bring me down if, possible, to the level of their lordships."

A WIFE'S VISIT.—A short time since, a poor inebriate who had just been freed from the House of Correction, went into a rum shop in Lowell, to relapse into his old courses. His wife, hearing where he was, put on her bonnet and hastened to the shop and took her seat by the side of her husband, requesting him to go home with her—telling the rumseller at the same time not to sell her husband any more rum.

Said he, "I shall—I get my living in that way—and you look pretty running around in this way."

"I shall make no fuss, Mr. P——," said the wife; "my husband is here, you harbor him, and as long as I behave myself well, I intend to stay here with him, and you may help yourself if you can."

The rumseller finding the wife so resolute, assisted in persuading the poor man to go home with his wife. Thus her perseverance prevailed.

If ever the blush of shame mantle the cheek of any man, it ought one, who would assist in returning to his old courses a man who is trying to save himself from intemperance. Out on such selfishness."

A TEETOTALER.—Jack was the name of a very bright monkey. One day seeing his master and his associates drinking, and very fond of doing what he saw others do, he took up half a glass of whisky and drank it off. He soon began to hop, skip, jump, and tumble as he had never done before. Poor Jack was drunk. The men around thought it was fine fun; but Jack did not, for the next day when they wanted the fun repeated, he lay in one corner of the box, and would not come out. "Come out," cried his master. Afraid to disobey, he came walking on three legs, one paw pressed against his forehead, as if he had a violent headache. After he had got well, his master again brought him to the table. As soon as he saw the glasses, he skulked behind a chair; and on his master ordering him to drink, he bolted out of the window, and was on the housetop in a minute. They called him down, but he would not, not he. Jack did not mean to get into a drunken scrape a second time. His master shook a whip at him. Jack did not care for that. A gun was then pointed at him. Jack was afraid of a gun. With one bound he leaped upon the chimney, and getting down the flue, held on by his fore paws. He would rather be singed than drink. Jack triumphed, and though his master kept him for twelve years, he could never be induced to touch another drop of spirits.

WATER OR BEER.—A devoted minister of the Gospel, whose efforts for the cause of temperance have been much blessed by God, was once dining with a family, when the lady who presided at the table said "Ah! I do not like your doctrine: you go too far in refusing the *good creatures of* GOD."

No notice was taken of the remark by the minister at the time. At length he said, " Pray madam, can you tell me who made *this!*" holding up a glass of water.

The lady replied, "Why, God, I suppose." "Then," said the minister, " I think you do us an injustice, when you accuse us of refusing the good creatures of God."

Silence again reigned. By-and-by, the minister said, " Madam, pray can you tell me who made *that?*" pointing to a glass of *beer* which the lady had at her side.

" Why, no sir, I cannot exactly say: I suppose the brewer and malster."

" Then," replied he, "allow me to say there is some apparent inconsistency in your first remark. You prefer taking a thing that *man* has made, to that which God has so very bountifully provided; and yet you accuse me of rejecting God's good creatures, because I prefer water to beer! Let me leave the matter to your more serious consideration."

TEMPERANCE FABLE.—The rats once assembled in a large cellar, to devise some method of safely getting the bait from a steel trap, which lay near, having seen numbers of their friends and relatives snatched from them by its merciless jaws. After many long speeches, and proposals of many elaborate but fruitless plans, a happy wit standing erect, said:—"It is my opinion that if with *one paw* we keep down the spring, we can safely take the food from the trap with the other." All the rats present, loudly squeaked assent, and snapped their tails in applause. The meeting adjourned, and the rats retired to their homes: but the devastations of the trap being by no means diminished, the rats were forced to call another "convention." The elders had just assembled and had commenced the deliberations, when all were startled by a faint voice, and a poor rat with only three legs, limping into the room stood up to speak. All were instantly silent, when stretching out the bleeding remains of his leg, he said: "My friends, I have tried the method you proposed, and *you see the result!* Now let me suggest a plan to escape the trap,—'*Do not touch it!*'"

Cost of Paint.—Some years ago there lived in Berkshire County, Mass., two Physicians of considerable skill and eminence. One of them used no spirituous liquors—the other drank *freely;* and while the first had acquired considerable property, the other remained poor. Meeting each other one day, when the former was returning from a distant town, with a richly painted and well made carriage, the latter accosted him: "Doctor ——, how do you manage to ride in a carriage painted in so costly a manner? I have been in practice as long and extensively as you, and charge as much; but I can hardly live and drive the old one." "The *paint* on my carriage," he replied, "did'nt cost *half* as much as the *paint on your face.*"

A Lesson in Parsing.—"What case is Mr. Maddle?" said a country school-master, addressing one of his grammar pupils.

"He's a hard case, thir," was the answer.

"Wrong—the next."

"He's an objective case, thir."

"How so?"

"'Cause he objected to sign the pledge."

The 'Teetotal' Apprentice.—Not long ago in a small town in Lincolnshire, a wretched victim of habit thus accosted a lad standing at a shop door: 'I say, boy, can you tell me where there's a dram-shop?' 'No!' replied the youth, 'I never tell anybody where to find such places.' How much more truly noble was this, than the conduct of those fashionable 'abstainers' who, refusing the evil drink themselves, will yet furnish it to others!

Sign of a Tavern.—A little boy, seeing a drunken man prostrate before the door of a groggery, opened the door, and putting in his head, said to the proprietor, "See here, master, your sign has fallen down."

Dreadful Uncomfortable.—The Rev. Mr. Thompson, at a meeting in Faneuil Hall, illustrated the effects of the Washingtonian movement upon the rum sellers, by the following story: An old lady found a frog in her tea-kettle, and politely requested him to come out, which he politely refused to do. "Well," said she, "as you please, I shall not use force to compel you to leave your quarters, but I shall make you *dreadful uncomfortable.*" She then put the kettle over the fire, and the frog was soon glad to hop out.

Do not touch it!—Mr. Van Wagner, the reformed blacksmith, from Poughkeepsie, illustrates the deceptive influence of alcohol by the following fable:—A rattlesnake had got into the fire, so that it was in a fair way of being burnt up. "Please take me out," said the snake to a man who chanced to pass by. "Ah, no," was the reply; "if I take you out you'll bite me." "No I won't," said the snake. The man, after some difficulty, got hold of it and placed it out of danger. "Now look out!" continued the snake, putting itself in a position to spring; "I am going to bite you." "Yes," said the man, in surprise, "but you promised you would'nt." "But don't you know it's my nature to bite?" quoth his snakeship. And so with alcohol. He will make fair promises, but *it is his nature to bite*, and ten to one but all who touch him find it out to their sorrow.

A Distiller's Conscience.—A certain distiller employed a very industrious man to work in his still-house. The man had a small house, a garden, a cow and a pig. At the end of three years, the distiller had a mortgage on the house and had taken the cow, and still the man owed him sixteen dollars. How can this be, thought the distiller to himself, that this man has done no better. At the end of three years, his house, and garden, and cow are all gone and still he owes me sixteen dollars. Is it that he drinks, and this has made him so shiftless and inefficient? Is this the fruit of my employment? He resolved to forgive him the debt, and give him up the cow. But a thorn had found a way into his bosom. He had no rest. Reflection frowned upon his heart and his conscience, till he broke up his distillery and abandoned his business. What condemnation is there on the whole business of making and selling intoxicating drinks, that an enlightened conscience never can stand it?

The Value of a Tract.—Do you see that respectable Fishmonger, said a friend to us not long ago, pointing to a small shop not five miles from St. Paul's. For many years he was a confirmed drunkard, and his family were in wretchedness. About sixteen months ago some one sent him a tract which induced him to sign the temperance pledge. He has sought divine help and has faithfully kept his promise, and he is now a respectable and industrious, thriving man; his family live in comfort, and, to my knowledge, he has saved against "a rainy day," since he became an abstainer, upwards of *one hundred pounds*. Tract distributors! let this fact encourage you.

Puss Breaking her Pledge.—Mr. Gough tells an amusing story of a little boy who had a favorite cat. He one day was carrying her around the house looking for something, "what do you want, Tommy?" said his mother, "I want," said he, "a pen, ink and paper, to make puss sign the pledge." The pen was obtained, and with the help of the boy, the word Puss was put to the pledge. The next day, the boy was seen whipping the cat, "what are you

T*

whipping the cat for?" said his mother, "Because she has broken her pledge. I saw her coming out of Burney's grocery store licking her chops." It is a pretty certain sign said Mr. G. if temperance boys are seen coming out of a tavern or grocery store wiping their mouth, that they have broken their pledge.

WHAT ONE "DRUNK" COSTS.—A man of intemperate habits told his employer, at the close of a day, that he could not work for him the next day, as he was calculating to *have a drunk*. His employer endeavored to dissuade him from his purpose, but without effect. He accordingly on the next day took his wagon, went to the neighboring village of W——, where rum is plenty, got his keg filled, stimulating himself well at the same time;—rode home in high glee; but instead of stopping at his own dwelling, pushed forward to the little village, where he had been at work—was there thrown from his wagon, and injured in the most shocking manner. His drunk therefore cost him,—

1. The price of his rum.
2. The shame and disgrace of getting drunk.
3. A season of the most excruciating agony—for the leg was so badly mangled that the ends of the bones protruded through the integuments.
4. The loss of several months' time.

RIGHT ABOUT FACE.—Mr. Delavan, of Albany, who has devoted money and talent for the promotion of temperance, and who has done as much as any one individual in America, in giving dignity and importance to this noble enterprise, was, in his youth, one of a club of fifty, who were in the habit of meeting at a room in a public house, to enjoy themselves in "the feast of reason and the flow of soul." It was not long however, before Mr. Delavan was led to serious reflection upon the folly and danger of the practice, till on a certain evening, while on his way to the club, he suddenly stopped and exclaimed aloud, "*Right about Face!*" And he did right about face: and, said he, to the gentleman to whom he related the circumstance, "the first block of buildings which I ever erected in Albany, was erected on the corner directly in the front of where I formed the resolution." We have copied the above from the Boston *Temperance Journal;* which also says, in reference to those fifty young men,—"Forty-three of them became drunkards, and most of them found a drunkard's death."

EATING THE FRUIT.—The following anecdote is beautifully illustrative of the beneficial influences of the temperance cause, in restoring confidence and augmenting domestic happiness:—

A blacksmith in one of our villages, had in his possession, but under mortgage, a house and a piece of land. Like many others, he was fond of the social glass. But he joined the temperance society; about three months after, he observed one morning his wife busily employed in planting rose bushes and fruit trees.

"My dear," said he, "I have owned this lot for five years, and yet I have never known you before to manifest any desire to improve and ornament it in this manner."

"Indeed," replied the smiling wife, "I had no heart to do it until you joined the temperance society; I had often thought of it before, but I was persuaded that should I do it, some stranger would pluck the rose and eat the fruit. Now I know that by the blessing of Providence, this lot will be ours; and that we and our children shall enjoy the products. *We* shall pluck the rose and eat the fruit."

A GOOD REPLY.—A gentleman, responding after his health had been drunk, spoke as follows:—"Gentlemen, you have been pleased to drink my health with wine; to the latter you are welcome. Your drinking *me* will do me no harm; your drinking *it* will do you no good. I do not take wine, because I am determined wine shall not take me. You are most daring; but I am most secure. You have courage to tamper with and flatter a dangerous enemy; I have courage to let him alone. We are both brave—but our valour hath opposite qualities. I do not drink your healths. My doing so would be no more than giving change for a sovereign. I would rather drink your disease,—would rather root out from you whatever is prejudicial to your happiness. Suppose, when lifting my bread, or my water, to my lips, I exclaim, "Here's luck to you!" All the luck attending the action would come to me—in the mouthful of meat or drink I should take. But if, in the partial adoption of society's customs, I take opportunity of scattering a few good ideas which may govern your lives hereafter, then there is luck to you and to all of us. In that way I thank you for your cordiality."

A Good Exchange.—I shall never forget, says the Bishop of Norwich, visiting the cottage of a man who had been all his life a drunkard, and which was the abode of misery and wretchedness. He became a teetotaler, and in six months afterwards I found his abode the scene of comfort and domestic happiness. This man, with tears in his eyes, placing his hand on a quarto family bible, said, "This is the first thing I purchased with the money saved by giving up drunkenness; it was an alien to my house before, but it has been my daily comfort and companion ever since."

Anecdote.—A respectable looking woman called recently at a spirit-dealer's shop in Gatashiels, for half a gill of the strongest spirits to sponge a silk gown with. After the quantity requested was drawn from the cask, she was asked for a bottle to hold the same, when she cooly replied, "I haven't far to gang, and I'll just carry it hame in my mouth!"

How to Keep Poor.—Buy two glasses of ale every day, at five cents each, amounting in a year to thirty-six dollars and forty cents; smoke three cigars, one after each meal, counting up in the course of a year to fifty-four dollars and seventy-five cents; keep a big dog which will consume, in a year at least fifteen dollars worth of provisions, a cat five more—altogether, this amounts to the snug little sum of one hundred and ten dollars and twenty-five cents, sufficient to buy several barrels of flour, one hundred bushels of coals, one barrel of sugar, one sack of coffee, a good coat, a respectable dress, besides a frock for the baby, and half a dozen pairs of shoes

A Temperance Fable.—The Nantucket *Islander* says the following story was told by a reformed inebriate, as an apology for much of the folly of drunkards:—"A mouse ranging about a brewery, happening to fall into one of the vats of beer, was in eminent danger of drowning, and appealed to a cat to help him out. The cat replied, "it is a foolish request, for as soon as I get you out I shall eat you." The mouse piteously replied, "that that fate would be better than to be drowned in beer. The cat lifted him out, but the fumes of beer caused puss to sneeze, and mousy took refuge in his hole. The cat called upon the mouse to come out— "You rascal, did you not promise that I should eat you? "Ah," replied the mouse, "but you know *I was in liquor at the time!*"

Colloquy.—We cut the following short but piquant colloquy between an inebriate and a rumseller, from an exchange:

Landlord.—"If you had avoided rum, your early habits of industry and intellectual abilities would have placed you in a situation, and you would now ride in your own carriage."

Inebriate.—" And if you had never sold rum for me to buy, you would have been my driver."

An Epitaph.—Thetford Churchyard rejoices in the following matter-of-fact memorial to departed worth:

" My grandfather was buried here,
My cousin Jane, and two uncles dear;
My father perished with an inflamation in the thighs,
And my sister dropped down dead in the Minories;
But the reason why I'm here interred, according to my thinking.
Is owing to my good living and hard drinking.
If therefore, good christians, you wish to live long,
Don't drink too much wine, brandy, gin, or anything strong.

A Bad Mark.—" I've got a boy for you, sir." "Glad of it; who is he?" asked the master-workman of a large establishment. The man told the boy's name and where he lived. "Don't want him," said the master-workman, "he's got a bad mark." "A bad mark, sir; what?" "I meet him every day with a cigar in his mouth. I don't want 'smokers.'"

THE DRUNKARD NOT THE WORST MAN.—A gentleman stepped into a hotel, and saw a filthy drunkard, once a respectable man, waiting for his liquor. He thus accosted him, "G——, why do you make yourself the vilest of men?" "I ain't the vilest of men," said the drunkard." "Yes, you are," said the gentleman. "See how you look; drink that glass and you will in a very short time be in the gutter." "I deny your poz-zi-tion," stammered the drunkard. "Who is the vi-lest, the tempter or—the tempted? Who—who was the worst, Satan or Eve?" "Why, Satan," said he. "Well—well, behold the tempter," said the drunkard, pointing to the bar. The argument was irresistible. The bar-keeper flew into a passion, and turned the poor fellow out of his house without his dram.

DEATH AND THE WINE BIBBER.—"Bring me wine," said the man to his servants; "bring me wine, that I may drink and be merry." "Here it is," said Death, who answered to the summons, "drink and be merry." As soon as the man saw who brought the wine he turned pale, and trembled exceedingly, and said, "Who art thou, with a grinning and a derisive visage, that bringest wine, and puttest it on my table?" "I am Death!" replied the other; "thou calledst for wine, and here it is; why dost thou not drink?" Death waited, but the man delayed to drink; and after a little consideration, called his servants, and said, "Take away the wine, and never place it upon my table again; for I see it is accompanied by Death!" The grim spectre was then obliged to retire, disappointed of his prey; and the man rejoiced at his escape. Happy are they who have made their escape from the drinking customs of the world, and enroll their names among the friends of temperance; for, by so doing, they have most probably escaped from an early death—death, not only of the body, but of the soul; for the habit of intoxication is calculated to destroy both.

SELF-INFLICTIONS.—Ask any man if he wants a racking head, burning veins, and a diseased stomach, and he will think you mad. And yet hundreds will pay for them.

Who Makes the Drunkards?—"Behold the fruits of drunkenness," said a landlord to an only daughter, whom he almost idolized, as he kicked a poor inebriate into the street.

"Poor fellow! I see," replied the daughter.

"Let me caution you to beware, and not to get a drunken husband!"

"Who makes the drunkards, father?"

The landlord sloped. The last question was a poser.

The Drunkard and the Two Monkeys.—A rich drunkard kept two monkeys for his sport. One day he looked into his dining-room, where he and his guests had left some wine, and the two Jacko's had mounted the table, and were helping themselves generously to the wine—jabbering and gesturing, as they had seen their master and his guests. In a little time they exhibited all the appearances of drunken men. First they were merry and jumped about; but soon they got to fighting on the floor, and tearing out one another's hair. The drunkard stood in amazement. "What!" said he, "is this a picture of myself! Do the brutes rebuke me?" It so affected his mind, that he resolved he would never drink another drop. And from that day he was never known to be any other than a sober and a happy man.

Soap-Suds.—A lady had a daughter about eight years of age, who had never tasted intoxicating drinks. She was asked if she had ever seen any. "Yes," was the reply. "What did it look like?" inquired an elder sister. "Like dirty water with soap-suds at the top," was the reply.

Scripture well Applied.—The *Ohio Organ* gives the following instance of the right application of Scripture in a time of temptation: It is stated that Bishop Doane, of New Jersey, is strongly opposed to temperance, and his sideboard and tables are loaded with wines, brandy, gin, &c. A short time since, the Rev. Mr. Perkins, of the same denomination, and a member of the "Sons," dined with the Bishop, who, pouring out a glass of wine, desired the Rev. gentleman to drink with him, whereupon he replied, "Can't do it, Bishop, 'wine is a mocker.'" "Take a glass of brandy then," said the distinguished ecclesiastic. "Can't do it, Bishop, 'strong drink is raging.'" By this time the Bishop becoming somewhat restive and excited, remarked to Mr. Perkins, "You'll pass the decanter to the gentleman next to you." "No, Bishop, I can't do that, 'woe unto him that putteth the bottle to his neighbor's lips.'" What was the peculiar mental condition or moral state of the Bishop at this stage of the proceedings, our informant did not state.

A True Story.—A village schoolmaster said to one of his pupils, a very small boy, who had just gone ahead of his class for spelling best,—"Well done, my little fellow, you shall have a feather in your cap." The boy burst into tears. "What is the matter?" said the master. "I don't want a feather in my cap," replied the lad. "Why not?" "Because when father has a feather in his cap he always comes home drunk, and scolds mother and whips her."

A Good Reference.—"Do you know Mr. —— ?" asked one friend of another, referring to an old gentleman who was famous for his fondness of the extract of hops.

"Yes, sir, I know him very well."

"What kind of a man is he?"

"Why, in the morning when he gets up he is a beer barrel, and in the evening when he goes to bed he is a barrel of beer!"

Mother's Nonsense.—"Pa, does wine make a beast of a man?"

"Pshaw! child: perhaps once in a while."

"Is that the reason why Mr. Goggins, the tavern keeper, has on his sign, 'entertainment for man and beast?'"

"Nonsense, child, what makes you ask?"

"Because, ma' says that last night you went to Goggin's a man, and came home a beast; and that he entertained you!"

"That's mother's nonsense, dear. Run out and play—papa's head aches!"

TIMING IT.—A minister in the Highlands of Scotland found one of his parishioners intoxicated. The next day he called to reprove him for it.

"It is very wrong to get drunk," said the parson.

"I ken that," said the guilty person; "but then I dinna drink as muckle as you do!"

"What, sir? How is that?"

"Why, gin it please ye, dinna ye take a glass o' whisky and water after dinner?"

"Why, yes, Jemmy, surely I take a little whisky after dinner, merely to aid digestion."

"And dinna you take a glass of whisky toddy every night when you gang to bed?"

"Yes, to be sure, I just take a little toddy at night to help me to sleep."

"Well," continued the parishioner, "that is just fourteen glasses every week, and about sixty every month. I only get paid once a month, and then if I'd take sixty glasses, it would make me dead drunk for a week. Now, you see the only difference is, ye time it better than I do."

THE PESKY KEG.—When the temperance reformation came, the old folks did not so easily fall into it. Their habits were fixed. It was the young people it took, and they carried it forward as young people only can.

There was an old farmer whose boys all joined the teetotal army. He was glad of it, he said; but for *him*, he wasn't so clear. Well enough for young folks.

A keg of rum used to be kept in the cellar. But the boys found out there was no room for it there. It was moved to a storechamber. The flax and the spring wheat left no room for it there. It was put into the bedroom. O, nobody could bear the smell of it there. It got into the corn-house. The corn ousted it forthwith.

"Sir," as the old farmer was called, did not know what to do with his "pesky keg." It wasn't *catching*, as he knew of," he said, "yet people were 'fraid of it as they were of smallpox." Get it out of sight and smell as far as possible he felt he must. One day he called Bob to help him hoist it up into the straw-mow. "Let the boys have their way," he grumbled; "but for *his* part, he wasn't so clear about himself." Bob helped him hoist it up and stow it away. "The pesky thing," muttered the old man. Bob said nothing. Whenever "sir" wanted a glass, he had to go to the barn, mount the ladder, and fumble in the straw for it; the boys could not do it for him, because they had pledged, "touch not, taste not, *handle not;*" and he was sure he would not ask them —no, not one of them—not he.

I do not know how often he made a visit to the mow, for he took the time when nobody was around; but one day, hearing somebody coming, his foot slipped, he fell, and broke his ankle. He never said he fell from the ladder, and the boys were careful not to pry too closely into the case, especially as they were sure the "pesky keg" was not likely to be visited again soon.

For two months the old farmer was laid up in the house, with all the kind attention which his sons could bestow. The first time he hobbled out to the barn, "Well, Bob," he said, "it is clear to my mind now—and my mind is clearer than it's been these forty years—that if I can live two months without my grog, I can live two years—and the rest of my life." The keg was stove up and burned, for the smell could not be rinsed out; it burned blue flames, and the boys sung a temperance song around the bonfire.

Doing right in one thing makes the way for doing right in others. The old farmer began to go to meeting with his boys, and before one year they all joined the church, and became one of the most Christian families in the neighborhood.

AN INNKEEPERS REGRET.—Joseph II., Emperor of Germany, travelling incognito, stopped at an inn in the Netherlands, where, it being "Fair Day," and the houses crowded, he readily slept in an out-house, after a slender repast of bacon and eggs, for which he paid three shillings and six pence. A few hours after some of his majesty's suite coming up, the landlord appeared very uneasy at not having known the rank of his guest. "Pshaw, man," said one of his attendants, "Joseph is accustomed to such adventures, and will think nothing of it." "Very likely," replied mine host, "but I shall; I can never forgive myself for having an Emperor in my house and letting him off for three and six pence."

A BOYISH IDEA.—"George Smith, do you recollect the story of David and Goliah?"

"Yes, sir—David was a tavern keeper, and Goliah was an intemperate man."

"Who told you that?"

"Nobody. I read it; and it said that David fixed a sling for Goliah, and Goliah got slewed with it."

"Wasn't Goliah a giant, a strong man?"

"Yes, he was a giant, but he had a weak head."

"How so?"

"Why he got so easily slewed."

GOOD ADVICE.—Rev. Mr. Pike of Newberry Port, in a pamphlet, published some time since, gives the following advice which should be heeded:—"Mothers, where are your daughters? Whose addresses are they favouring? As you would wish not to plant thorns in your own dying pillow, be entreated to look after this matter; for it is here that your power and influence may have a salutary effect; by frowning on this evil in the bud and checking its first advances, you may, perhaps, protect the pride of your family from the deadly contagion. Teach your daughters the only safe doctrine, namely, Teetotal or no Husband. Let this be their motto, and in nine cases out of ten they will avoid the rock and quicksands on which so many have been destroyed forever. But still in order to make it doubly sure, it might be well to adopt the rule practised by some churches, which is to make the candidate stand six months on trial; you might by this rule discover the mask and avoid destruction.

THE FIVE CRADLES.—A man who had recently became a votary to Bacchus, returned home one night in an intermediate state of booziness. That is to say, he was comfortably drunk, but perfectly conscious of his unfortunate situation. Knowing that his wife was asleep, he decided to attempt gaining his bed without disturbing her, and by sleeping off his inebriation conceal the fact from her altogether. He reached the door of his room without disturbing her, and after ruminating a few moments on the matter, he thought if he could reach the bedpost, and hold on to it while he sliped off his apparel the feat would be easily accomplished. Unfortunately for his scheme, a cradle stood in a direct line with the bedpost, about the middle of the floor. Of course when his shins came in contact with the aforesaid piece of furniture, he pitched over it with a perfect looseness; and upon gaining an erect position, ere an equilibrium was established, he went over it backwards, in an equally summary manner. Again he struggled to his feet, and went foremost over the bower of infant happiness. At length, with the fifth fall, his patience became exhausted, and the obstacle was yet to be overcome.

In desperation he cried out to his sleeping partner, "Wife, wife! how many cradles have you got in the house? I've fallen over five, and here's another before me!"

ANACREON'S PLEA AND THE LADY'S RETORT.—This Bacchanalian poet, in his 19th Ode, makes the following apology for his winebibbing propensities:—

"Sure the black earth drinks, and the trees drink her;
The sea drinks the winds, and the sun drinks her;
And the moon drinks him; so good friends I think,
You shouldn't oppose *me* wishing to drink."

To this ingenious but sophistical sally, a poetess "of our own" has favoured us with a rejoinder, more solid and not less sprightly:

Yes, heathen bard! yet wisdom says
The lesson this has taught her,
Is that the earth, the trees, and sun,
Drink—but 'tis only *water!*

BOTH ONE—"Is a man and his wife both one?" asked the wife of a certain gentleman, in a state of stupefaction, as she was holding his aching head in both hands.

"Yes, I suppose so," was the reply.

"Well, then," said she, "I came home drunk last night, and ought to be ashamed of myself."

This back-handed rebuke from a long-suffering and loving wife effectually cured him of his drinking propensities.

JUDGE SHAW'S DECISION—The papers say that five young women of a company of fourteen, who sacked a groggery in Bristol, Ohio, last June, were tried by three justices for riot, and acquitted, the Court deciding that the groggery was a nuisance, and the girls had a right to abate it.

A HEROIC WOMAN.—A Mrs. Brandon, of Union City, demolished the contents of a groggery some ten days ago, in the constitutional style. Her husband had been reclaimed from drunkenness by the Good Templars, but had repeatedly been induced to drink again, by the heartless murderer who would kill a man for five cents. After enduring the return of her sorrows as long as endurance was a virtue, she went to the groggery, walked into a back room where her husband was playing cards, too drunk to walk. She took him by the arm, and was leading him out through the groggery, supporting him as well as she could, when her eye rested upon the decanters which contained the ruiner of her happiness. She left her husband to take care of himself, and deliberately took the bottles and dashed every one of them upon the floor, even the candy bottle, the craven groggery keeper standing by, and trembling like a leaf in the presence of insulted innocence. Let all such outraged women assert their rights and defend themselves. God and good men are for them, though the Supreme Court and the liquor interest which elected it, are against them.

WHO WOULD?—Who would trust his life in the hands of a drunken physician? Not even the drunkard himself.

A Dashaway.—"Well, Jack, I'm afraid all this will go for grog," said a man about paying one of his ship's crew.

"Never fear, sir, never fear; I'm a *Dashaway* now. Half this goes to my old grandmother, and the other half to get me in good rig for the next voyage."

"A Dashaway! What, you dash away your cups, Jack?"

"Yes, sir. Our brig was boarded by the land sharks at San Francisco, and they took me to their hells, robbed me, and turned me into the street drunk. A man came along. He didn't kick me off the paving. No, sir, he picked me up, and took me to his lodgings, and he kept me there till I was sober. Sir, he was a Dashaway, and he said I must be one. And he said, 'Take the pledge, brother, till you can take something better.' And says I, 'What is better than the pledge?' 'Brother,' says he, 'the pledge dashes away your cups, but it leaves you your appetite. That will gnaw away and gnaw away at you; but the grace of God can dash *that* away.

"Well, sir, I didn't leave him till I took the pledge, total abstinence; and he asked me to go to prayer meeting with him; and blessed be God, it was just like the old meeting at home, and I thought I heard my father pray, and Deacon Eastman. Oh, sir, I thought I'd got among the saints again; and, sir," said the poor sailor, with the tears streaming down his cheeks, "I felt I was *too bad* to be there, and I told 'em so. But said they, 'Jesus Christ is here, the poor sinner's friend,' and *He* says, 'Though your sins be as scarlet, they shall be as white as snow,' and 'him that cometh unto me I will in no wise cast out.' Ah, sir, *I had been* cast out. Well, sir, I knew he was my father and my mother's Saviour, and I felt he'd be mine, and I set a-praying till he came to me, or I got to him, or both, for I believe we met halfway; and, sir, I dashed away my *appetite* then. I don't want grog. I am a Dashaway, sir, blessed be God. You must dash away your bosom sins before the grace of God can get in, and that'll *keep* 'em out.'"

THE RESULT OF A WHIPPING.—" There was one man I heard of who had a daughter, who went home and told her father that she had *signed the pledge*, and her father whipped her severely; but afterwards the father's conscience was pricked at seeing his little daughter's back black and blue, and he went and signed. I think I should not fear being whipped for that act if my father was a " beer seller." Perhaps it may be that he would give up selling the nasty stuff, sign the pledge, as the little girl's father did, and thus be a step towards saving him from the wicked place after death."

NOT QUITE READY.—A young gentleman at a temperance meeting, on being asked to sign the pledge, excused himself by saying, " I am not quite ready." At the close of the meeting he proposed to one of the young ladies present to see her home. " I am not quite ready," was the laconic reply.

"I CAN'T GIVE UP MY BESETTING SIN !"—Another reason which keeps men away from their Saviour, is their love of some besetting sin which they are not prepared to give up.

Doct. Spencer tells us in his "Pastor's Sketches" of a man, between fifty and sixty, belonging to his congregation; serious in spirit, honest and industrious in life, who often manifested much concern for his spiritual state; with whom he often conversed; who seemed very near the kingdom of heaven, and who for months and months remained just there. His pastor could not imagine what kept him from the Saviour. One day he met this parishioner riding towards the village, and as he stopped for a moment's salutation, he noticed a brown jug in his wagon. Although the farmer was a man of irreproachable habits, it flashed upon the pastor's brain that that brown jug had something to do with the peculiar position of mind in which the farmer had so long stood. Upon that hint he spake:

" Mr. ——, where are you going ?"

" To the village store."

" What are going to do with that jug ?"

"The farmer cast his eye down upon it a little confused, but with accustomed honesty replied, "I am going to get some rum in it."

"Do you drink it?"

"Never to do any hurt."

"You never drink any to do you any good?"

"I have thought it did sometimes."

"Do you drink it every day?"

"No—only when I have extra hard work, or when I am not well, or feel badly."

"You take a little when ever you feel troubled?"

"Yes, I feel the need of it then."

"Mr. ——, when you have been troubled by the claims of religion, and have felt depressed in view of your spiritual state, have you not then taken a drink, because you have felt thus troubled?"

"Yes, sir. I believe I have."

The pastor saw at once the solution of the problem that had worried him in reference to the farmer's condition—saw the danger in which he stood. He determined to be faithful, and there by that roadside he proceeded to plead with him to give up that habit at once and forever, as the besetting sin that was ruining his soul. He spoke to him of its inherent folly, of its obvious consequences upon himself—its dangers to his children; accumulating affectionately argument upon argument. The old man answered never a word. He glanced restlessly round, as if he was cornered, and would be glad when the lecture would be over. Then his eye fell upon the brown jug. As the pastor's appeal grew warmer, he watched it more closely. He stooped and touched it. With a very solemn countenance, and still without a word, he lifted the brown jug upon his knee. The pastor kept on beseeching. There was a large rock by the way-side, just where they were. The old man's eyes fell upon the rock. Suddenly rising to his full height, he dashed the jug into a thousand fragments against it, and gathering up the reins, turned his horse and started in a gallop for home.

They never exchanged a word in reference to this unexpected result, but in less than thirty days thereafter, the old farmer's heart was full of the joy of salvation. The besetting sin was shattered—the brown jug no longer stood between him and the Cross, and he found all his difficulties gone.

THE BEGGAR BOY.—" Why don't you come after cold victuals as usual ?" said a lady to a boy who for a long time had been a daily visitor for that species of charity. " Father has joined the Temperance Society, and we have warm victuals now," was the reply. A *whole temperance lecture*, in a few words.

LED ASTRAY.—A good story was recently told at a temperance meeting in New Hampshire. A stranger came up to a Washingtonian, with the enquiry—

" Can you tell me where I can get anything to drink?"

" Oh, yes," said the other, " follow me."

The man followed him through two or three streets, till he began to be discouraged.

" How much farther must I go?" said he.

" Only a few steps farther," said the Washingtonian, " *there is the pump!*"

The man turned about and "moved his boots."

THE TEETOTAL SPOONS.—In the year 1758, Capt. Andrew Ward, of Guilford, commanded a company of provincial soldiers in the service of George II, at the taking of Louisburg, in the Island of Cape Breton. While in the service he drew money in lieu of his rations of spirit, with which he purchased four silver spoons, one for each of his children. The word " Louisburg" was marked on each spoon, that his children might remember how he made use of his rum. These spoons were made by Mr. Ward, father of Col. James Ward of this city. Of all his descendants (and there have been more than one hundred,) but one has been intemperate. George A. Foote, Esq., of Guilford, one of Capt. Ward's descendants, has politely deposited one of these spoons with the Connecticut Historical Society.—*Hartford Courant.*

Song of the Decanter.

There was an old decanter, and its mouth was gaping wide; the rosy wine had ebbed away, and left its crystal side; and the wind went humming, humming, up and down; the wind it blew, and through the reed like hollow neck the wildest notes it blew. I placed it in the window, where the blast was blowing free, and fancied that its pale mouth sang the queerest strains to me. "They tell me, puny conquerors! the Plague has slain his ten, and War his hundred thousands of the very best of men! but I ('twas thus the Bottle spake) but I have conquered more than all your famous conquerors, so feared and famed of yore. Then come, ye youths and maidens all, come drink from out my cup, the beverage that dulls the brain and burns the spirits up, — that puts to shame your conquerors that slay their scores below; for this has deluged millions with the lava tide of woe. Though in the path of battle the darkest streams of blood may roll; yet while I kill the body, I destroy the very soul! The Cholera, the Plague, the sword such ruin never wrought as I, in mirth or malice, on the innocent **HAVE BROUGHT.**"

FACTS AND ANECDOTES.

The Tree of Dissipation.

The sin of Drunkenness expels reason, drowns memory, distempers the body, defaces beauty, diminishes strength, corrupts the blood, inflames the liver, weakens the brain, turns men into walking hospitals;—causes internal, external, and incurable wounds;—is a witch to the senses, a devil to the soul, a thief to the pocket, the beggar's companion, a wife's woe, and children's sorrow;—makes man become a beast and a self-murderer, who drinks to others' good health, and robs himself of his own! Nor is this all; it exposes to the Divine Displeasure here!! and hereafter to Eternal Misery!!! THE Root of all is DRUNKENNESS.

VALUABLE TESTIMONIES.—" Who hath woe? who hath sorrow? who hath contentions? who hath wounds without cause? They that tarry long at the wine; they that go to seek mixed wine. Look not thou upon the wine; at the last it biteth like a serpent, it stingeth like an adder."—Prov. xxiii, 29, 32.

"The works of the flesh are manifest, which are these; uncleanness, murders, *drunkenness*, revellings, and such like; of the which I tell you, that they which do such things shall not inherit the kingdom of God."—Gal. v, 19, 21.

"If ye live after the flesh, ye shall die; but if ye through the Spirit do mortify the deeds of the body, ye shall live."—Rom. viii, 13.

" Let us walk honestly, as in the day; not in rioting and *drunkenness*, not in chambering and wantonness, not in strife and envying. But put ye on the Lord Jesus Christ, and make not provision for the flesh, to fulfil the lusts thereof."—Rom. xiii, 13, 14.

" Be not deceived; God is not mocked; for whatsoever a man soweth, that shall he also reap. For he that soweth to his flesh shall of the flesh reap corruption; but he that soweth to the Spirit shall of the Spirit reap life everlasting."—Gal. vi, 7, 8.

" Woe unto them that rise up early in the morning, that they may follow strong drink; that continue until night, till wine inflame them. Woe unto them that are mighty to drink wine, and men of strength to mingle strong drink."—Isaiah v, 11, 22.

Commodore Joseph Smith states—" So far as my experience goes, I have found the abandonment of the use of spirits by seamen to be beneficial in all respects, lessening both crime and punishment. On my last cruise, the ship in which my flag was worn, the frigate *Cumberland*, with near five hundred persons on board sailed in November, 1843, and returned in November, 1845. The first part of the cruise the men generally drank their grog; by a course of reasoning and discipline they gradually (and voluntarily of course) stopped their liquor, and received the small pittance of *two cents* per day therefor. At the end of the year, all but two had relinquished the spirit part of their ration, and those two requested to be transferred to another ship of the squadron. I gratified them. No person remaining who desired to draw grog, it was pumped off and landed, and the casks filled with good pure water. To the end of the cruise no more spirits were issued. The crew were, so far as I observed, at all times contented and happy. I never heard of a complaint that liquor was in the slightest degree necessary to enable seamen to better endure the hardships and privations of a sailor's life. On the contrary, the men were satisfied they were better off in all respects without it.

The Rev. William Jay, of Bath, says—"I am thankful that all through life I have been a very temperate man, and for more than twenty-five years, generally a teetotaler, but for the last six years I have been one constantly and entirely. To this (now I am past 70) I ascribe, under God, the glow of health, evenness of spirits, freshness of feeling, ease of application, and comparative inexhaustion by public labours, I now enjoy. The subject of teetotalism I have examined physically, morally, and Christianly, and after all my reading, reflection, observation, and experience, I have reached a very firm and powerful conviction. I believe that next to the glorious gospel, God could not bless the human race so much as by the abolition of all intoxicating spirits. As every man has some influence, and as we ought to employ usefully all our talents, and as I have now been for nearly half a century endeavouring to serve my generation in this city, according to the will of God, I have no objection to your using this testimony in any way you please. I am willing that, both as a pledger and a subscriber, you should put down my name."

We, the undersigned Physicians of Canada, are of opinion—

I. That a very large portion of human misery, including poverty, disease, and crime, is induced by the use of alcoholic or fermented liquors, as beverages.

II. That the most perfect health is compatible with Total Abstinence from all such intoxicating beverages, whether in the form of ardent spirits, or as wine, beer, ale, porter, cider, &c, &c.

III. That persons accustomed to such drinks, may, with perfect safety, discontinue them entirely, either at once, or gradually, after a short time.

IV. That *total* and *universal abstinence* from alcoholic liquors and intoxicating beverages of all sorts, would greatly contribute to the health, the prosperity, the morality, and the happiness of the human race.

A. F. Holmes, M. D., L. R. C. S. E.; Wolfred Nelson; P. E. Picault, M. D.; Geo. W. Campbell, M. D.; M. McCulloch, M. D.; Francis Badgley, M. D.; A. Hall, M. D., L. R. C. S. E.; Arthur Fisher, M. D., M. R. C. S. E.; P. A. C. Munro, M. D.; Louis F. Tavernier; A. Rowand, M. D.; John Barber, M. R. C. S. L.; J. B. Lebourdais; John Minshall, M. D.; J. G. Bibaud, M. D.; T. Stearns, M. D.; E. H. Trudell, M. D.; A. G. Regnier; Silas Gregory; J. Emery Coderre; J. L. Leprohon, M. D.; C. H. Keefer; W. Fraser, M. D.; T. Black, M. D.; W. P. Smith; Hy. Mount, M. R. C. S. L.; A. H. David, M. D.; Js. Crawford, M. D.; S. C. Sewell, M. D.; Wm. Sutherland, M. D.; E. Q. Sewell, M. D.; C. A. Regnault, M. D. P.; Samuel Waller, Physician; Duncan McCallum; F. A. Cadwell, M. D.; Louis Boyer, M. D.; O. T. Bruneau, M. D.; P. D. Brousseau; Robert Godfrey, M. D.; Hector Peltier, M. D.; P. H. L. Richelieu.

The foregoing important *medical testimony* has recently been circulated in Great Britain by Mr. Dunlop of Scotland, and received signatures, as follows:—London, 184; Dublin, 14; Edinburgh, 26; Glasgow, 46; Leeds, 53; Liverpool, 184; Manchester, 75; Nottingham, 32; Sheffield, 23; Provincial Towns, 400; in British India, 29—total, 1066. At the request of Mr. Wadsworth, the above named medical gentlemen of Montreal and other places, kindly and promptly gave their names.

THE YOUNG MAN ON FIRE.—He was about twenty-five years of age. I saw him about nine o'clock in the evening; he was then, not drunk, but full of liquor; about eleven o'clock the same evening, I was called to see him. I found him literally roasted from the crown of his head to the soles of his feet: he was found in a blacksmith's shop. The owner discovered a light in his shop, as though the whole building was in one general flame. He ran, and on throwing open the door discovered a man standing erect in the midst of a widely extended silver-colored flame, bearing, as he described it, exactly the appearance of the wick of a burning candle, in the midst of its own flame. He seized him by the shoulder and jerked him to the door, upon which the flame was instantly extinguished. There was no fire in the shop, neither was there any possibility of fire having been communicated to him from any external source. It was purely a case of spontaneous ignition. A general sloughing soon came on, and his flesh was consumed, or removed in the dressing, leaving the bones and a few of the larger blood vessels; the blood nevertheless rallied round the heart, and maintained the vital spark until the thirteenth day, when he died, not only the most loathsome, ill-featured and dreadful picture that was ever presented to human view, but his shrieks, his cries, and his lamentations also, were enough to rend a heart of adamant. He complained of no pain of body; his flesh was gone—he said he was suffering the torments of hell; that he was just upon the threshold, and should soon enter its dismal caverns, and in this frame of mind he gave up the ghost. O how dreadful is the death of a drunkard!

DEFINING A LOW POSITION.—A Minister of high standing and somewhat lofty bearing, happened, while riding into a certain city on a Saturday afternoon, in a public omnibus coach, to express himself somewhat strongly against the signing of the pledge by persons of his character and circumstances. It was well enough for persons in danger of drunkenness, but unnecessary, and indeed improper for him. A poor ragged drunkard in the coach looked up and said, "Parson, where do you preach, I must go and hear you, you are a man after my own heart." The minister saw his position defined for him at once, by an individual whom he perhaps despised as the miserable slave of rum, an outcast from all that is lovely and of good report. Its truth was not to be denied.

An Ancient Pledge.—On the blank leaf of an old English Bible which has been handed down from parent to child through successive generations, and appears at the time to have been the property of Robert Bolton, Bachelor of Divinity, and preacher of God's word, at Broughton, in Northamptonshire, is written the following pledge:—

"From this daye forward to the ende of my life, I will never pledge anye health, nor drink a whole carouse in a glass, cupp, bowle, or other drinking instrument whatever, wheresoever it be, from whomsoever it come, except the necessity of nature doe require it. Not my own gracious kinge, nor anye the greatest monarch or tyrant on earth, not my dearest friende, nor all the gouldein the worlde, shall ever enforce me or allure me. Not an angel from heaven, (who I know will not attempt it,) shall persuade me. Not Satan, with all his old subtleties, not all the powers of hell itselfe, shall ever betraye me. By this very sinne, (for a sinne it is, and not a little one,) I do plainly finde that I have more offended and dishonored my great and glorious Maker, and most merciful Saviour, than by all other sinnes I am subject untoe; and for this very sinne it is, that my God has often been strange unto me, and for that cause, and no other respect, I have thus vowed; and heartily beg my good Father in heaven, of his gracious goodness and infinite mercy in Jesus Christ, to assist me in the same, and to be favourable unto me ffor what is past. Amen. Robert Bolton.—*Broughton, April* 10, 1639."

Cost of Intemperance.—The Hon. E. Everett, minister to Great Britain and President of Harvard College, has computed that the use of alcoholic beverages costs the United States directly, in ten years, 12,000,000 dollars; had burned or otherwise destroyed 5,000,000 dollars more of property; had destroyed 200,000 lives, sent 150,000 persons to our prisons, and 100,000 children to the poor-house; and made 1,000 widows, had caused 1,500 murders and 2,000 suicides, and had bequeathed to the country 1,000,000 orphan children.

In England there are supposed to be 600,000 drunkards!

Amount annually paid for intoxicating liquors,	£50,000,000
Perversion of land to the growth of barley and hops,	20,000,000
Misapplication of labor and capital,	15,000,000
Loss of time and labor by drinking,	40,000,000
Cost of pauperism caused by drunkenness,	3,000,000
Criminal expenses attributable to do.,	2,000,000
	£130,000,000
About equal to	$570,000,000

This large amount of money would in six years wipe away the enormous national debt of England, and so take off *two thirds* of the taxes.

The last census of Great Britain gives the number in connection with the traffic in intoxicating drinks, 90,870; while the number of bakers, corn agents, corn merchants, and millers, is 70,632, or 20,248 less than those engaged in the traffic of intoxicating drinks.

In 1831, Judge Cranch, of Washington, made the following computation of the cost from ardent spirits to the United States:

1st—72,000,000 gallons of ardent spirits at 66⅔ cts,	$48,000,000
2d—100 days' labor, of 375,000 drunkards, lost, at 40 cts,	15,000,000
3d—10 years' labor, of 37,500 men killed by ardent spirits, at $50 per ann. for each man,	18,750,000
4th—¾ of the cost of the crime to the U. States,	6,525,000
5th—¾ of the cost of pauperism to the U. States,	2,850,000
6th—¾ of the amount of private charities,	2,850,000
7th—¾ of one year's labor of 1,200 prisoners lost, at $50,	450,000
Annual loss to the country from ardent spirits,	$94,425,000

The amount annually lost to the United States by the use of

ardent spirits, would be more than sufficient to buy up the houses, lands and slaves once in every twenty years. Judge Cranch did not include the cost of wine, beer and cider, in his estimate.

THE INDIAN AND THE DISTILLER.—An Indian who had a wife and young child, took all their winter food, namely, five bushels of corn and ten bushels of wheat to be ground, at the mill; but he had to pass a distillery. The distiller ran out, as a spider would upon a fly, and asked the Indian to sell his grain. The Indian refused, saying that it was all the provision laid up for his family. The distiller insisted upon getting the corn, saying he would give him *so much whisky* for it, and added that the wheat would be quite enough for his family. The Indian consented: and after he had drank some of the whisky, agreed to sell the wheat too. All that he got for his load, besides what he drank, was a jar containing about a gallon and a half of whisky, and a dollar in silver. With this treasure, the Indian returned home; but, not being very steady, he fell, and fortunately broke a hole in the bottom of his jar. He also lost his dollar; so that when he returned home, a broken jar was all he had to show for his load of grain; and he with his family, were reduced to beggary for the winter. When the distiller was remonstrated with upon the subject, he replied with a grin,—"If I had not got the grain, some other person would." It may be a laughing matter now; but will this man laugh when he stands with his victims before the judgment seat of Him who has said, "As ye would that men should do to you, do ye also to them likewise," and who has required all men to "do justly, and to love mercy?"

THE SCOTCH WASHWOMAN.—A respectable gentleman at Edinburgh related, a few years ago, a most affecting fact:—A religious lady at Edinburgh was sent to visit a woman who was dying, in consequence of disease brought on by habits of intemperance. The woman had formerly been in the habit of washing in this lady's family, and when she came to the dying woman, she remonstrated with her on the folly and wickedness of her conduct, in giving way to so dreadful a sin as that of intemperance. The dying woman said, "you have been the author of my intemperance." "What did you say?" with pious horror exclaimed the lady; "I the author of your intemperance!" "Yes ma'am, I never drank whisky till I came to wash in your family; you gave me some, and said it would do me good. I felt invigorated, and you gave it me again. When I was at other houses not so hospitable as yours, I purchased a little, and by and by I found my way to the spirit shop, and thought it was necessary to carry me through my hard work, and by little and little, I became what you now see me." Conceive what this lady felt.

How to be Safe.—"Doctor," said Squire ———, about five years ago, after reading over the prescription of a distinguished friend of Temperance, whom ill health had obliged him to consult,—"Doctor, do you think that a very little spirits, now and then, would hurt me very much?" "Why, no sir, answered the Doctor, very deliberately; "I do not know that a *little—now and then*—would hurt you *very much;* but, sir, if you don't take *any*, it won't hurt you AT ALL."

A Bad Name.—Mr. Gough tells a story of a tavern keeper by the name of A. S. Camp. The painter in painting the sign, left out the points, so that it read—Tavern kept by A SCAMP. Even the drunkard would not go near him.

Indian Sincerity.—Three Indians in the vicinity of Green Bay, became converts to the temperance cause, although previously given to "putting the enemy into their mouths that stole away their brains." The white men formed the charitable resolution to try their sincerity. Placing a canteen of whisky in their path, they hid themselves in the bushes to observe the different motions of the red men. The first one recognized his old acquaintance with an "Ugh!" and making a high step he passed on. The second laughed, saying "Me know you!" and walked round. The last one drew his tomahawk, and dashing it to pieces, said, "Ugh! you conquer me, now I conquer you."

JACK AND HARRY.—All this, Harry, don't convince me. I do not like the *principle* of total abstinence. I think ardent spirits a *creature* of God; and that we should therefore use it as a blessing.

Harry. I admit Jack that corn and fruit are creatures of God; but gold and silver, too, are creatures of God, and yet you don't think Aaron's calf and the silver shrines that were made to the goddess Diana, were creatures of God, do you, Jack? If not, then you see that the *creature* of God may by man be converted to a bad use. The corn is a blessing while a creature of God, but so soon as it is converted into man's *creature*, whisky, it becomes a curse instead of a blessing. The same may be said of the peach or apple. While it remains the simple fruit, it is truly delightful and pleasant to the taste; but when man murders it by beating, bruising, and boiling, and thus changes its nature, as a *creature* of God, it may then become poisonous, and prove ruinous to the souls and bodies of men.

A NOBLE BOY.—A little fellow, who had become a teetotaler, was sent on one occasion with a note to a friend's house; and while waiting for an answer, was pressed to take a glass of wine, by a young man who was resolved to overcome his scruples; the boy refused, but was the more importunately urged to take it. His rejection became the more decided as the foolish young man more resolutely persevered, until he seized the little fellow by the collar, drew back his head, and forced the wine into his lips. In this emergency, the boy set his teeth so firmly that scarcely a drop of the wine passed them, and the contents of the glass ran down upon a new waistcoat, upon which he set a great value. He said nothing, but buttoned his coat, and returned with the letter. On his return, he told what had passed; showed the stains on his waistcoat, and with an exulting smile said, "The waistcoat is spoiled, but God was not angry with him. God had made his teeth, and no one could get the wine through them."

WATER.—Dr. Cullen says, that "simple water, without any addition, is the proper drink of mankind."

THE MURDERER AND THE LADY.—At a meeting at Delgany, Ireland, a gentleman said he was asked to dine with a lady, and after dinner wine was introduced; he stood up to go; but the lady asked him to remain, and he said to her, "Madam, I am very much obliged to you for your kindness, and would remain, but that I cannot sit in the same room with a murderer." The lady looked frightened, and asked where the murderer was? He said, "was not your husband killed by a fall from a horse, while drunk?" She said "yes." "Then it is that bottle there that killed him, and I am determined never to sit in the room with a murderer." She took away the decanters and never used wine after.

QUOTING SCRIPTURE.—The Rev. Thomas P. Hunt, in his "Wedding Days of Former Times," relates an anecdote of a young couple about to be married. The bride insisted upon having a teetotal wedding. The bridegroom said he should have wine, for he had scripture authority for it as a good thing. David said that God had given wine to cheer the heart of man, and if man should ever be cheerful it should be at his wedding. Very well, she said, and if she could find scripture for anything she was pleased to do, she supposed she might do it. To be sure, said he. The day of the wedding came. The bridegroom was introduced to the chamber of the bride, whom he found in full dress, but her face all besmeared with blubber oil. What! he exclaimed, lifting his hands in surprise—what is this? O nothing, only oil to make the face to shine, which God has given equally with wine to cheer man's heart. O for heaven's sake, said he, wash it off, and we will have no wine.

A BRIGHT GIRL.—"What are you doing there, Jane?" "Why, pa, I'm going to dye my doll's pinafore *red*." "But what have you got to dye it with?" "Beer, pa, beer." "Who on earth told you that beer would dye red?" "Why, ma said yesterday that it was beer that made your nose so red, and I thought——." "Here, Susan, take this child."

Rumseller's Dream.—"Well, wife, this is too horrible! I cannot continue this business any longer."

"Why, dear, what's the matter now?"

"Oh, such a dream! Oh, I connot endure it! Oh, if ever I sell rum again!"

"My dear, are you frightened?"

Yes, indeed, am I; another such a night will I not pass, for worlds."

"My dear, perhaps—"

"Oh! don't talk to me. I am determined to have nothing more to do with rum, any how. Do you think, Tom Wilson came to me with his throat cut from ear to ear, and such a horrid gash, and it was so hard for him to speak, and so much blood, and said he, 'see here, Joe, the result of your rumselling.' My blood chilled at the sight, and just then the house seemed to be turned bottom up, the earth opened and a little imp took me by the hand, saying, 'follow me.' As I went, grim devils held out to me cups of liquid fire, saying, 'drink this.' I dared not refuse. Every draught set me in a rage. Serpents hissed on each side, and from above reached down their heads and whispered, 'rumseller!' On and on, the imp led me through a narrow pass. All at once he paused and said, 'are you dry?' 'Yes,' I replied. Then he struck a trap door with his foot, and down, down we went, and legions of fiery serpents rushed after us, whispering, 'rumseller! rumseller!' At length we stopped again, and the imp asked me as before, '*are you* DRY?' 'Yes,' I replied He then touched a spring—a door flew open. What a sight! There were thousands, aye, millions of old, worn-out rum-drinkers, crying most piteously, '*rum, rum, give me some rum!*' When they saw me, they stopped a moment to see who I was—then the imp cried out, so as to make all shake again, '*rumseller!*' and hurling me in, shut the door. For a moment they fixed their ferocious eyes upon me, and then uttered a united yell, which filled me with such terror, I awoke. There, wife, dream or no dream, I will never sell another drop."

THE GROGSELLER TAKEN IN.—A quick-witted toper went into a bar-room and called for something to drink.

"We don't *sell* liquors," said the law-abiding landlord; "we will *give* you a glass, and then if you want to buy a cracker, we'll sell it to you for three cents."

"Very well," said our Yankee customer, "hand down your decanter."

The "good creature" was handed down, and our hero took a stiff horn, when, turning round to depart, the unsuspecting landlord handed him the dish of crackers, with the remark—

"You'll buy a cracker?"

"Well no, I guess not; you sell 'em so dear; I can get lots on 'em, five or six for a cent, anywhere else."

THE MINISTER AND THE DEMIJOHN.—A clergyman in one of the towns in the State of New York, at the time when the protests against the use of liquors became somewhat earnest from the pulpits—on one Sabbath delivered to his congregation a thorough discourse on the subject. On their way home, some of his hearers inquired of each other, "what does all this mean?" One gentleman who professed some shrewdness at guessing, said, "I will tell you, gentlemen, what is the difficulty; we have none of us sent Mr. —— anything to replenish his decanter lately; and my advice is that we attend to this matter." Accordingly, on Monday a full-sized demijohn of "old spirits," or "cognac," was sent to the Rev. Mr. ——, accompanied with a very polite note, requesting his acceptance of it, from a few friends, as a testimony of their regard.

Our worthy clergyman felt himself at first in somewhat of a dilemma. But wise invention, and a good conscience, are sometimes found in close companionship; and they met in the present instance to help our good minister to "back out" of the difficulty. He took the demijohn to the watering-trough of his stable, and poured some of the liquor in and brought his horse to it. Pony expanded his nostrils, and snorted and blowed at it, as though he thought it rather too hot, and seemed to say "What's this?" Next he drove his cow to the trough, to see if she liked it any better. The cow snuffed at it and shook her horns, and went her way, with no fondness for such a "villanous potation." Mr. ―― then called his pig out of his bedroom, to taste. Piggy grunted and snuffed, dipped his nose in and coughed, and went back again to finish his nap in his straw. Mr. ―― then returned to his study, and penned, in substance the following note to the present-makers, with which he returned the demijohn and its contents:

"Gentlemen,—With due acknowledgments for your present, received this morning, permit me to say, that I have offered some of it to my horse, my cow, and my swine, and neither of them will drink it. That which neither horses, cattle, nor hogs will drink, I cannot think to be either useful or safe for man to drink. I beg you to excuse me therefore for returning the demijohn and its contents; and believe me, gentlemen, your most obedient, &c. ――"

THE TWO PEDLARS.—A pedlar overtook another of his tribe on the road, and thus accosted him: "Halloo, friend, what do you carry?" "Rum and Whisky," was the prompt reply. "Good," said the other, "you may go *ahead*, I carry Gravestones!"

THE MOUTH AND THE GOGGLES.—A landlord, who gave to every customer an example of his moderate drinking, complained of the badness of his eyes, and asked a Quaker what he should do for them, removing his goggles and submitting his swollen, inflamed eyes to the examination of his customer. "My advice, friend," replied the Quaker, "is that thou shouldest put thy brandy on thy eyes, and tie thy goggles over thy mouth!"

THE GROCER'S WIFE.—A man in the town of M――, N. H., who had, while from home, earned about $6, returned one day to his family with the cash. His wife told him that during his absence the family had suffered for food. He replied—"I will go to the store and buy what is wanted, and then we shall have enough." He had refrained from drink for some time; but on arriving at the grocery, it was found that he had money, and he was invited to drink a little beer—then something stronger—till he got drunk and spent all his money for rum, and returned to his half-starved family at two o'clock in the morning, penniless. The poor wife was greatly distressed, and on the next evening ventured to go to the wife of the rumseller, told the story of her suffering family, and the manner in which her husband had been made a pauper, &c.; whereupon the good lady filled a large basket with pork, bread, coffee, sugar, &c., and then called her husband into the entry, and in presence of the drunkard's wife, said—"Last night you took from this poor woman's husband all his money for rum; I have now filled a basket full of articles of food, and so long as you continue to sell liquor, get men drunk, and take from them their money, thereby making their families poor and miserable, I will deal out to them from the house all they want to support them." This was more than the husband could stand; the next morning he went to his store and emptied every cask, decanter and bottle of liquor into the road, saying he would no longer sell liquid fire, but would keep a temperance store.

DRUNKENNESS IN A MENAGERIE.—A drunkard made his way into a menagerie some time since, and the keeper, fearful that he would get hurt, told him to leave the place. An Irishman who was looking on, said to the keeper, "Why don't you let him alone, sure this is the right place for him, don't you see he has been making a *baste* of himself."

A DEATH SCENE.—His abused constitution soon gave way, and the death-scene followed. But, oh, what a death-scene! As if quickened by the presence of the King of Terrors, and the proximity of the world of spirits, his reason suddenly lighted up, and all his suspended faculties returned in their strength. "There," said he, pointing to his bottle and his glass, which he had caused to be placed beside his death-bed, "there is the cause of all my misery: that cup is the cup of wretchedness; and yet—fool that I have been!—I have drank it; drank it voluntarily, even to its dregs. Oh, tell those miserable men, once my companions, who dream of finding in inebriation, oblivion to their miseries, as I have dreamed of this; tell them—but it were vain to tell them—oh! that they were present, that they might see, in me, the dreadful sequel, and witness, in anticipation, the unutterable horrors of a drunkard's death." Here his voice faltered—his eye fell upon the abhorred cup,—and, as his spirit fled, a curse, half articulated, died away upon his quivering lip!

KEEPING TAVERN.—Some twenty years ago, a carpenter, who was tired of making an honest living, came to a friend of mine in Philadelphia, with a petition for a tavern license, which he requested him to sign. My friend looked at him, and asked why he did not stick to his plane and bench? The answer was,

"Tavern keeping is a more lucrative trade—I want to get richer."

"Well, but do you not think you will be affording additional facilities to drunkards to destroy themselves?"

"Perhaps I shall."

"Do you not believe that at least five men every year will die drunkards if you succeed in getting a license?"

"Why, I never thought of that before; but I suppose it would be so."

"Then if the Lord let's you keep tavern ten years, fifty men will have died through your agency—now what becomes of the drunkard? Does he go to heaven?"

"I suppose not."

"I am sure he does not, for no drunkard shall inherit the kingdom of Heaven; what becomes of him then?"

"Why, he must go to hell."

"Well, do you not think it will be just if the Lord, at the end of ten years, sends you down to hell too, to look after those fifty drunkards?"

The man threw down his petition, went back to his honest occupation, and was never tempted to desire a license again.

SEAMEN'S WAGES.—Who puts seamen's wages down? Let me tell you who," said Bob Durant, at the Bethel one Tuesday evening. "It's the chaps who drink rum, not the ones who drink water; no, not by a long shot. It's them who run up a bill for board and sundries; who do as I used to do, drink up, or get charged with drinking (it's all the same, shipmates,) the few shiners they earned the last voyage, and the landlord wants to advance on another immediately, and he goes and gets a ship, and shoves Jack aboard with a skin full and a few duds, not caring whether he receives a fair equivalent for his toil or not. But look at a sailor who, like me, has been a cold water man long enough to get a nest egg in the Seaman's Saving Bank, and has no one to lord it over him and say when he shall go to sea; why, he need not cut the wages down—no, he can stay ashore till the wages are something like fair, and then choose his voyage, ship and officers. Think of that, you that patronize the rum-holes and then growl about low wages.

THE IRISHMAN AND HIS SOUL.—A few days since an Irishman, (one of Father Mathew's people) landed at the wharf in this city, when he was accosted by an old friend. "Arrah, Pat, I am glad to see you in this free country; come up here a bit, and take a drink, for ould acquaintance and ould Ireland's sake."

"No," says Pat : "I've signed Father Mathew's pledge."

"But," says his friend, "this is not Ireland—it's a free country."

"Ah!" replied Pat, "do you think I've brought my body here and left my soul in Ireland?"

THE LIQUOR SELLER'S EXCUSE.—One day a Quaker woman kindly asked a rum-seller some questions about his whisky business, which disturbing his conscience a little, he eased himself with the oft-repeated salvo, that he " sold to sober persons only." " Ah," said she, " and does that better the case? Is it better to make drunkards out of sober men, than to kill the poor old broken down drunkards?" This came upon him like a thunder-bolt; it overset his best excuse, and he stopped the business of making drunkards.

SHINGLING A HOUSE.—James A——, a reformed man, had fallen almost asleep, it being nearly midnight, when he heard the landlord's wife say, "I wish that man would go home, if he's got any one to go to."

"Hush, hush!" says the landlord, "he'll call for something else directly."

"I wish he would make haste about it, then, for its time every *honest* person was in bed," said the wife.

"He's taking the shingles off his house and putting them on ours," said the landlord.

At this time James began to come to his right senses, and commenced rubbing his eyes and stretching himself, as if just awoke, saying, "I believe I'll go."

"Don't be in a hurry, James," said the landlord.

"Oh yes, I must go," says James, "good night," and off he started.

After an absence of some time the landlord met and accosted him.

"Hallo, Jim, why ain't you been down to see us?"

"Why," says James, "*I had begun to take the shingles off my house, and it began to leak!* so I thought it was time to stop the leak, and I have done it."

The tavern keeper was astonished, went home to tell his wife all about it, and James ever since has left rum alone, and attended to his own business. He is now a happy man, and his wife and children happier than ever.

BAD WIVES.—There are no individuals so apt to be afflicted with bad wives, as those men who lead a dissipated life. "I have frequently been," says a reformed inebriate, "with more than a dozen fellow-drunkards, and when we were talking about our wives, it was invariably found that *we all had bad wives.* But since I have become a sober man, I find I have as good a wife as a man can have." Says another,—"I have labored many years to dress that rascally rumseller's wife, but she is nothing but a squaw compared to my wife."

TRUE USE OF THE VINE, BY DR. DUFF.—The Rev. Dr. Duff gives the following excellent observations on the true use of the Vine, while journeying through France to India by way of Alexandria:—" In these countries mantled with vineyards, one cannot help learning the true intent and use of the vine in the scheme of providence. In our land, wine has become so exclusively a mere luxury, or what is worse—by a species of manufacture—an intoxicating beverage, so that we may have wondered how the Bible speaks of wine in conjunction with corn, and other such staple comforts of animal life. Now, in passing through the region of vineyards, in the east of France, we must at once perceive that the vine flourishes on slopes and heights, where the soil is too poor and gravelly to maintain either corn or pasturage for cattle. But what is the providential design in rendering this soil, favoured by a genial atmosphere, so productive of the vine, if its fruit become solely either an article of luxury or an instrument of vice? The answer is, That Providence has no such design. Look at the peasant at his meal in vine-bearing districts: instead of milk, he has before him a basin of the pure unadulterated blood of the grape. In this its native original state, it is a plain, simple, and wholesome liquid, which, at every repast, becomes to the husbandman what milk is to the shepherd—not a luxury, but a necessary—not an intoxicating, but a nutritive beverage. Hence to the vine-dressing peasant of Auxerre, for example, an abundant vintage, as connected with his own immediate sustenance, is as important as an overflowing dairy to the pastoral peasant of Ayrshire; and hence, by such a view of the subject, are the language and sense of Scripture vindicated from the very appearance of favouring what is merely luxurious, or positively noxious, when it constantly manifests a well-replenished wine-press, in a rocky mountainous country like that of Palestine, as one of the richest bounties of a generous Providence."

DISEASES.—Lord Bacon says: "Most diseases have their rise from intemperance."

THE VALUE OF PRAYER.—Rev. J. Hume related the following interesting anecdote, which shows us what prayer can do when employed by a little boy:—"A little boy had a very drunken father, given, like all other drunkards, to swear and lie, and do many other bad things. One day, when his father was drunk and swearing as he was won't to do on such occasions, he felt very much at the thought of his father's wickedness. He remembered that the Lord of heaven had declared that no drunkard should ever inherit His kingdom. When he thought of this, he ran to his aunt and exclaimed, "*Aunt*, if we pray for another person, will God hear us?" "Yes," replied his aunt. Immediately upon knowing this he ran up stairs—went to his own room—shut his door behind him, and prayed to God that he would give his father a new heart—that He would lead him to hate all sin and make him holy—"for without holiness no man can see God and live." Well, what was the result? In a few days his father gave every symptom of being a changed man. He was no longer to be seen coming home drunk. No, verily! he was now enabled, by God's grace, to live "soberly, righteously, and godly," and consequently he was daily becoming more and more meet for glory! Happy boy!—honoured boy!—to be the means of your father's conversion!—to be the means of turning your father from the worship of Bacchus to worship the living God!

HOW TO ADORN A PARSONAGE.—(The following reply has recently been sent by Lord Harrington to a Rev. Gentleman who requested his lordship's aid in adorning his parsonage.)

My Dear Sir,—You ask me to give you trees for the proposed parsonage of St. Paul's, Derby, so that the expense of purchasing them may be saved. Of course you are aware that trees, like corn and cheese, are one of the sources of my income. But to the point. You want my trees to adorn the parsonage of St. Paul's; and I want the advocacy of its incumbent to adorn the sublime profession to which he belongs, by promoting with all his soul and all his strength in the pulpit and on the hustings, the

Maine-law; just as Luther would have done had he lived in our days. The clergy well know that drunkenness is the great source of sickness, pauperism, and crime, and it is their sacred duty to stand boldly forward, as the clergy of all denominations in America have done, to put down this curse of earth. If the incumbent of St. Paul's will act in the true spirit of the Maine-law, the high taste of Mr. Barron and my trees are at your disposal. I remain most truly yours,—HARRINGTON, Elvaston Castle. To the Rev. J. D. Mossingham. March 13, 1856.

EXCITANTS AND TEMPERATURE.—Let those who fancy that they can evert the deadening effects of wet and cold by taking a glass of spirits, read what Dr. Macculloch, of Dumfries, says in a letter he recently addressed to the *Manchester Guardian*. He suggests the following experiments:—

Take a delicate differential thermometer, place the bulb under the tongue, and shut the mouth; the mercury will rise to about 98; take it out, drink one or two glasses of port or sherry, or an equivalent quantity of any other alcoholic drink; or to make the experiment still more obvious, take a glass of spirits neat, or diluted with either cold or hot water; wash out the mouth and throat or not, just as you please; four minutes after, replace the thermometer as before, and you will find that the mercury has fallen and that it continues falling for four consecutive hours! This fact, first ascertained by Davy, has been repeated and stated so often that you surely must have, at least, heard of it. The same fact, namely, the lowering of the temperature of the blood and, of necessity, the temperature of the whole body, for the diffusion of the animal heat through which the blood is the sole medium; I say the same fact is proved by another but more difficult experiment;—measure the amount of carbonic acid expired before taking the liquor, and four minutes afterwards measure it again, and do so for four consecutive hours, you will find that its amount is distinctly and very appreciably diminished; now the amount of carbonic acid expired is an exact guage and equivalent of the cremacausis or combustion which produces the animal heat within the body, and hence beautifully corroborates the thermometric experiment. But you may tell me, that you and others feel yourselves warmed by these drinks. No doubt you feel so, but I need scarcely tell an acute and trained logician like yourself, that that feeling is subjective and deceptive, that the foregoing experiments are positive objective facts, and that all the subjective feelings that ever were, are, or can be, do not weigh a feather in the balance against even one demonstrable objective fact. And what says your sole referee, common experience, on this point? Why, the whole of our Artic voyagers are dead against you, and the proofs adduced in this and other countries are so indisputable, numerous and overwhelming, that I am surprised that you should have advanced this vulgar and long-exploded fallacy. I trust you now begin to see, that common experience, like common fame, is not to be trusted.

APPENDIX.

THE VISIT OF THE PRINCE OF WALES TO BRITISH AMERICA.

Just as the last sheet of this volume was ready for the press, the excitement arising from the visit of Royalty to these Provinces was at its height. Indeed the book was delayed by reason of the bustle and business occasioned by the Prince's sojourn in this city. It was to be expected that foreign visitors and newspaper correspondents would criticize our country and pass judgment respecting our public morals. It would not however be fair to suppose that the people are, under ordinary circumstances, what they appeared to be at the time when each city seemed to vie with the other in decided effort to become the most gay—the most lively, and the most loyal, and when, perhaps few seriously thought how they could appear the most moral. It will, however, we think, be freely admitted that considering the circumstances, there was in every place far less intemperance than could have been expected, and far less than there would have been if our country had not possessed the blessing of a temperance history. We who have been engaged for many years past in endeavouring to suppress the vice of intemperance, have every reason to congratulate ourselves that we have not laboured in vain. We do not see all we could wish for, but we may rejoice that some good has been done.

The correspondent of the London *Times* has thought proper to give his opinion respecting the comparative sobriety of certain places. Writing concerning Montreal he says:—

"On this evening there were firemens' processions all over the town, each man carrying torches and Roman candles, and ringing bells, so that a lively night was the result. I must add, however, that I have seen less symptoms of general inebriety at Montreal than in any of the towns the Prince has yet visited. This can hardly be due to the presence of a large French population, as there are at least as many, if not more French at Quebec than in this city. Yet, on the whole, Quebec managed to maintain as high an average of intoxication as any place of its size I have ever seen, always saving and excepting Charlottetown, the capital of Prince Edward Island. Sailors, as a class, possess a secret of intoxication peculiar to themselves, and somehow manage to get drunk when no one else can get any liquor; so that it has been said, if you locked twenty of them in an empty room, and visited them an hour or so after, you would find them all intoxicated.

The Prince Edward Islanders appear also to enjoy this attribute of mysterious inebriety, for though nearly all their hotels (miserable back-wood shanties) are conducted on temperance principles, and sell neither wine nor spirits, yet, somehow, during the Prince's visit, intoxication seemed to be the normal condition of half the inhabitants."

This is a sad picture of the Islanders of Prince Edward, and we fear there is some truth in it. However it is but fair to say that the statement has been contradicted. The correspondent of the Montreal *Herald* quoting the above has considered it his duty to append the following note in refutation of the report. He says:

" We were not in Quebec during the Prince's visit to that ' Ancient Capital,' and cannot, of course, either confirm or contradict what is above said as to the ' high average of intoxication,' which then prevailed there. We were, however, in Charlottetown while the Prince was there, and we have no hesitation in saying that the 'Special' owes his facts, in reference to the alleged inebriety of the people of Prince Edward's Island, to his imagination, as he does to his memory, regarding the 'mysterious attribute' of sailors and islanders."

We were not in a position to judge between the parties, but we recollect too well the opposition which was given to the prohibitory movement by certain persons in the Legislature of Prince Edward's Island, and we should be surprised if they did not reap the bitter fruit of their shameless course. In Canada the prohibitory movement was not successful, but here at least the agitation was not without good fruit.

We have pleasure in giving a place of permanent record to a document of importance, emanating from the temperance bodies of Upper Canada, and the Temperance Reformation Society of Toronto. It was thought advisable to present an address to His Royal Highness the Prince of Wales. It was graciously received and replied so, and we give both as we find them in the daily papers of this city:—

" At the levee on Saturday, His Royal Highness the Prince of Wales received a deputation from the Temperance Societies, consisting of Hon. Robert Spence, President T. R. S. of Toronto; Hon. Malcolm Cameron, Rev. Dr. Richardson, Rev. Dr. Thornton, Rev. J. H. Robinson, Rev. Wm. Scott, Mr. Nasmith, Mr. Geo. Railton, Mr. N. C. Gowan, Rev. J. Scott, Dr. Vannorman, and Mr. McAlpine, who presented the following **ADDRESS**:

APPENDIX. 407

" *To his Royal Highness Albert Edward, Prince of Wales, &c.*

"May it Please Your Royal Highness,—

"On behalf of the various Temperance organizations of Upper Canada, numbering some tens of thousands of loyal hearts, we desire to welcome Your Royal Highness with feelings of ardent attachment to our Sovereign the Queen, whose condescension in having permitted the Heir Apparent of the British Throne to visit this portion of her vast dominions, we gratefully acknowledge.

"We rejoice that our allegiance is due to a Sovereign whose glorious reign has never been tarnished by the excesses of former Courts, but that the truly Christian example of your Royal Mother has called forth universal commendation.

Emulating the Christian graces of our Queen, many thousands of our youth are banded together to check the current of intemperance; and we look forward to a brilliant future for Canada, because in the youth of the present day the principles and practice of total abstinence are growing with their growth, and strengthening with their strength.

"We sincerely trust that the visit of Your Royal Highness may be in every respect agreeable, and that when you have returned home, your Royal Highness may be enabled to assure Her Majesty that amongst the glorious institutions of the Province, enjoyed by a free and happy people, none seem to be more blessed of Heaven than those established to discourage intemperance.

"As it has pleased the Almighty long to spare the Queen to wear unspotted the brightest crown of modern nations, so may she hereafter wear an everlasting crown of life, and when it shall please the King of Kings to call her hence, may it be the fondest desire of your heart to wear unsullied that crown which has so long adorned the brow of our beloved Queen, whose goodness and whose virtues will form the choicest page of England's history.

"Robert Spence."

" Toronto, Sept. 8, 1860."

In answer, Mr. Spence received the following reply:

"Toronto, September 8, 1860.

"Sir,—I have the honour to convey to you the thanks of His Royal Highness the Prince of Wales, for the address presented to him by you on behalf of the various Temperance organizations of Upper Canada.

"I am, Sir, Your obedient Servant,

Newcastle.

The reply is brief and ordinary, avoiding all reference to the principle of total abstinence, although but few associations have been more useful in the realm of England, than those which are identical with the bodies who thus approached His Royal Highness. The Duke and his Secretary may not be of our opinion, but it is nevertheless true that England is deeply indebted to the Temperance Societies for her present moral status, and would be speedily injured if they were to withdraw their influence. "The excesses of former Courts" are contrasted with the "Christian example" of our beloved Sovereign, and very properly too, but how much of the difference is owing to the reformation of the masses by the means employed in modern times, who can tell? Let us thank God for the change, and cherish the hope, that no evil example will destroy the beneficial effects of the good example of millions beside that of the good Queen of England, upon the mind and habits of him who enjoys the anticipation of sitting upon the throne of England.

We consider it no derogation from the dignity of Royalty to give distinction in this connection to the names of the Hon. Robert Spence and the Hon. Malcolm Cameron, the former as presenting the temperance address to the Prince of Wales, and forever firm to his principles, amidst the temptations and allurements of official and private life. Long may he live to enjoy his well-earned reputation, and propagate his sound temperance opinions. To the latter, all honor is due for his unflinching advocacy of temperance and prohibition at all times and places, but more especially in the Halls of Legislation, often amidst the jeers of the profane, and the mockery of the inebriate. Recently elected without opposition to the Upper House, we are gratified to know that in the Legislative Council, as in the House of Assembly, the Hon. Malcolm Cameron will raise his voice against prevailing intemperance and the traffic in strong drinks. Let him have the hearty co-operation of all the temperance people of Canada, and let us cheerfully persevere in harmonious effort until the pestilential traffic is swept from our land!

W. S.

Toronto, Oct. 4th, 1860.

www.ingramcontent.com/pod-product-compliance
Lightning Source LLC
Chambersburg PA
CBHW051242300426
44114CB00011B/863